The Ultimate Encyclopedia of

EUROPEAN SOCCER

THIS IS A CARLTON/
HODDER & STOUGHTON BOOK

Copyright © Carlton Books Ltd 1997

First published in 1997 by
Hodder & Stoughton, a division of
Hodder Headline PLC

10 9 8 7 6 5 4 3 2 1

A CIP catalogue record for this book is
available from the British Library

ISBN 0 340 708 174

Project Editor: Martin Corteel
Editorial Assistant: Roland Hall
Project Art Direction: Paul Messam
Production: Sarah Schuman
Design: Steve Wilson

Printed and bound in Spain

Hodder and Stoughton Ltd
A division of Hodder Headline PLC
338 Euston Road
London NW1 3BH

DEDICATION
To my father, for introducing me to the beautiful game

PICTURE CREDITS

The publishers would like to thank the following sources for their kind permission to
reproduce the pictures in this book:

AKG, London; Allsport UK Ltd./Shaun Botterill, Howard Boylan, Clive Brunskill,
Simon Bruty, David Cannon, Jonathan Daniel, Stu Forster, John Gichigi, Mike Hewitt,
Ross Kinnaird, Clive Mason, Don Morley, Steve Morton, Stephen Munday, Steve
Powell, Ben Radford, Pascal Rondeau, Billy Stickland, Claudio Villa; Allsport
Historical Collection/Hulton-Getty, MSI; Allsport/Vandystadt/Stephane Kempinaire,
Richard Martin; Associated Press; Colorsport/Andrew Cowie, Matthew Impey,
Olympia, Nobert Rzepka; Empics Sports Photo Agency/Massimo Sestini; Football
Archive/Peter Robinson; Hulton Getty; Juventus Press DI Salvatore Giglio;
Popperfoto/Dave Joyner, SAG; Press Association; Presse Foto Dieter Baumann;
Spaarnestad Fotoarchief; Sporting Pictures (UK) Ltd.; Topham Picturepoint

Every effort has been made to acknowledge correctly and contact the source
and/copyright holder of each picture, and Carlton Books Limited apologises for any
unintentional errors or omissions which will be corrected in future editions of this book.

Overleaf: *HOT STUFF* Brazilian
superstar Ronaldo in Barcelona
strip before his Italian move.

Opposite: *QUE SERA SERA*
Spanish fans at Euro 96.

The Ultimate Encyclopedia of
EUROPEAN SOCCER

The definitive illustrated guide to football in Europe

Keir Radnedge

Editor of *World Soccer* Magazine

CARLTON

Hodder & Stoughton

CONTENTS

GREAT CLUBS *Red Star Belgrade, Yugoslavia*

FAMOUS STADIUMS *Olimpico, Rome, Italy*

LEGENDARY PLAYERS *Matthias Sammer*

INTRODUCTION

The names have rolled so easily off the tongues of fans down the years: Bastin, Meazza, Puskas, Di Stefano, Eusebio, Beckenbauer, Cruyff, Platini, Ronaldo ... and on, and on. That is the ultimate triumph of football. Its popularity rests not alone on fading figures of antiquity but on the historical continuity which links past and present, yesterday and tomorrow. At an organisational level, clubs such as Manchester United and Real Madrid represent football traditions as varied as the English and Spanish cultures which raised them. Their achievements span the gaps of age, generation, class and civic pride. Not merely United and Madrid, of course, but all the other great clubs – whether acclaimed internationally such as Arsenal and Milan or in a more modest domestic context such as Sparta Prague and IFK Gothenburg. Football has captured the soul of the century on the varied levels represented by national teams, by club sides and by individual personalities.

Never mind the European Union or Comecon. International trading blocks have appeared, expanded and faded down the decades. But football ... that's different. Football is the unique force which has unified not merely Europe but the world.

Football is the force which bypasses political barriers and customs posts. For instance, the players of Partizan Belgrade were once allowed into Spain through an airport side door to play Real Madrid in the Franco era when frontier guards were forbidden to allow the bearers of communist passports through the official security gates. How the game has changed down the years. In the summer of 1930 only four European nations attended the World Cup finals in Uruguay because the sea voyage would take players and officials away from homes and jobs for time they could not – literally – afford.

Yet now clubs and countries think nothing of jetting to the Far East and back in midweek for the financial benefit offered by a mere friendly match.

Blame Europe – or thank Europe.

It was in Europe that the modern game was founded. It was European visionaries who dreamed up the World Cup. It was Europeans who set in motion the first prestigious international club events – the Mitropa Cup of the inter-war years and then, in the 1950s, the Champions Cup. Across Europe and the world – and far beyond the simple green grass rectangle – football has triumphed. It has helped spawn multi-billion fortunes through the intertwined businesses of broadcasting, of sportswear and of sponsorship. But it also represents, at the other extreme, the nobility of athletic achievement – the factor once known as sportsmanship and now defined by the game's spin doctors as "fair play."

In the summer of 1997 Spain mourned the death of a former Barcelona player, Pedro Zaballa. He once kicked the ball out of play rather than into the open goal yawning in front of him, because the Real Madrid goalkeeper was lying, unconscious, in the goalmouth. Players, officials and fans, like Zaballa, pass on. But not the true, enchanting, alluring spirit of the sport.

Keir Radnedge
London, July 1997

UPS AND DOWNS Sol Campbell and
Christophe Dugarry battle it out at
Le Tournoi 1997.

THE ORIGINS OF EUROPEAN FOOTBALL

Every society, down the ages, has needed something to kick around, either metaphorically or literally. At one social level, particularly in medieval times, that meant the nobles, metaphorically, kicking the peasants. As social relations grew more refined so everyone joined in together with an inanimate object as the object or victim of such physical exertion.

Perhaps one of the most remarkable developments of the last 150 years has been the way in which this inanimate object – a simple football – has turned the tables. The leathern sphere beloved of the first sports reporters has been transformed. The football is no longer mere subject but ruler. The dreams it evokes govern people's lives. Not merely in Europe but around the world. It has developed its own culture and financial power. Billions of pounds, francs, marks and dollars are expended annually in its service. The football rolls not merely to serve the interests of 22 football players on a rectangular patch of earth in all weathers but a huge industry.

Association Football, as the game came to be called, exists on two levels. It is, for the amateur, the provider of enormous pleasure (as well as addictive frustration) but it is also the most effective medium of show business. Actors and singers are bound by language and culture. Not football. A pensioner in Brighton and a child in Beijing share exactly the same emotions in participating in the ritual – as player or spectator – half a world apart.

Ancient origins

The universal foundations have been traced by the world's scholars, all eager to claim for their own culture the origins of the greatest game of all. The hieroglyphical musings of ancient reporters have been found dating back 2000 years in China and 1600 years in Japan. The Greeks and the Romans found a form of football a restful way of passing the time between their respective cultural and acquisitive empire-building. One of the first records of football in England relates to London in 1175. In the fourteenth century both Edward II and Edward III tried to stamp out a practice which was drawing young men away from either their trades or archery practice.

Not only England was assailed by this sporting revolution. France, too, and Italy. In 1397 the Provost of Paris recommended that football games should be played only on Sundays. Could he have imagined that one day not merely the continent of Europe but the entire known – and then unknown – world would one day make Sundays reverberate to the chants of watching crowds?

In Italy, the renaissance gave birth to a theatrical football-pageant in which two teams of 27 men each threw themselves bodily into propelling a ball up and down the squares of Santa Croce or Santa Maria Novella to provide entertainment for visiting princes. Thus the Medici family established the example of rich patronage which would be emulated in the twentieth century by the Agnelli, Moratti, Berlusconi, Mantovani, Matarrese and Rizzoli families.

**AS IT WAS The original Calcio
re-enacted in Florence for tourists.**

An organized team game

Here football remained for five more centuries, an unregulated street free-for-all with as many unwritten rules and regulations as there were communities indulging in the passion of its pursuit. But then, in the middle of the nineteenth century, sport was transformed from an abomination of the masses into an educational icon. The reasons deserve an encyclopedia

in themselves. For one reason or another, the English education system placed, some would say, inordinate value on the health of both mind and body. For some mystical reason, that meant team sports. And no outdoor sport involves every team member in quite the way of football.

Football would long be considered a working man's game. Yet it was the universities of Oxford and Cambridge who first set about nailing down an agreed code of rules and regulations in the 1840s. It took

precisely seven hours and 55 minutes to create the original Cambridge Rules. The prospect for competition between educational institutions led on to the founding of The Football Association – not "English" please note – in 1863 at the Freemasons Tavern in Great Queen Street, London "with an object of establishing a definite code of rules for the regulation of the game."

A leading light was Lord Kinnaird who played in a record nine FA Cup Finals with Wanderers and the Old

Etonians before being appointed to the FA Committee in 1868 and going on to become treasurer then president.

The rules which Kinnaird helped draft were taken up throughout universities and public schools ... and taken around the world by the mixed bag of soldiers, sailors, civil servants, doctors, engineers and adventurers who built the British Empire. How ironic that arguably the most enduring legacy of their world-encompassing efforts should have been the absorption of association football.

THE GOOD OLD DAYS back in 1897, when Italy's Juventus (above) played in pink.

to miss the afternoon's match. Football widows the world over may testify that nothing has changed in almost a century.

The Italian connection

Athletics education in Italy in the nineteenth century had developed through the gymnastics schools, strongly influenced by the German academies. In 1896 the Italian gymnastics federation organized the first local football tournament between regional representative teams as a side-show to a weekend conference in Treviso. One of the pioneer societies was the Andrea Doria of Genoa, a distant predecessor of what today is the Sampdoria football club.

Contact between these societies and English sailors and merchants soon had the Italians won over to the merits of Association Football. A leading light was Edoardo Bosio, whose business took him from Turin to London and back again. In March 1887 he brought a "proper football" home with him and fascinated his friends with his tales of the "matches" he had seen. In 1891 Bosio founded the Internazionale Football Club of Turin.

More clubs sprang up – created both by Italians and by English residents, including the quaintly named Genoa Cricket and Athletic Club in 1892 and the Milan Cricket and Football Club in 1899. Of course, cricket soon fell by the wayside. But with Genoa and Milan, as with Bilbao in Spain, the historic link of the English names survives proudly to this day.

The first heroic player was Genoa's Dr Spensley who organized the first formal match against Bosio's FC Torinese on January 6, 1898. Genoa won with a goal by Mr Savage. Italy had awoken to modern football though, with an eye to history, it borrowed the ancient Florentine title of "Calcio".

France and Germany join the fold

To the north, France had its own history built around a football game called la soule whose roots are buried in Roman and Celtic folklore. But the game had been banned, on grounds of public order, by the end of the

Bewitching the world

Naturally, the sea-bound nations of Europe were among the first to fall under the football spell. In Portugal British university students played football in Lisbon in 1866. The Lisbon Football Club was founded in 1875 and the locals were forming their own clubs a decade later.

In Spain, the first footballs were imported to the northern Basque provinces by British mining engineers in the 1890s. Today pride in the historical link to football's "mother country" is evidenced still by the mere name of the Athletic Club of Bilbao. (Forced, under Franco, to become "Atletico" the club reverted to their historical title as soon as political shifts permitted. Not that the fans had ever taken any notice.) British military personnel took the game to the great cities of Madrid and Barcelona. It was a Swiss, Hans Gamper, who founded FC Barcelona but Real Madrid proudly recall an Englishman, Arthur Johnson, as their first trainer-manager at the turn of the century. Football was so important to Johnson that he set his wedding in the morning in order not

NOBLE HERITAGE from founding father Lord Kinnaird (left).

eighteenth century. It took British sailors – starting formally with Le Havre Athletic Club in 1872 – to reintroduce the game's modern equivalent.

For many years, well into the twentieth century, rugby proved a more popular import than soccer. Many rugby clubs were thriving before, in 1891, British residents in Paris founded the country's first two clubs devoted exclusively to soccer. These were the all-Scottish White Rovers FC and Gordon FC (later re-named Standard). White Rovers beat their rivals 10–1 in 1892 in the first formal match recorded between French clubs. That same year Stade Francais, the first club founded by Frenchmen, was created.

In Germany, too, association football faced early resistance, in this case from the established gymnastics and athletics societies. In many cases football crept in through the back door, being adopted as just one extra section of existing sports clubs. One of the most famous examples was TSV 1860 Munchen – founded, obviously, in 1860 and proud of the fact. Originally the football section was just one team. Now TSV 1860 Munchen is renowned only for football and it is the basketball, orienteering, water sport, handball, weightlifting, sailing, athletics, skiing, tennis and volleyball sections which have faded into the background – in the general public's perception at least.

Football crossed the border into Germany through the North Sea ports of Hamburg and Bremen in 1870. An Oxford University XI toured Germany in 1875 in what is considered as one of the first formal foreign tours undertaken by an English football club. The first German translation of the rules of the game was undertaken in Hamburg in 1876 and the game rapidly spread south via Berlin and on down to Dresden, Leipzig and Munich.

Leipzig may be considered the birthplace of Germany's football organization because the Deutscher Fussball-Bund was founded there in 1900. The DFB, still the governing body of German football, has proved a remarkably resilient organization down all the years of political turmoil.

Arrival in the Lowlands

The birth of football in Holland came in the form of a kick-about among British workmen at a textiles factory in Enschede in the 1860s. In the 1870s, students at a Jesuit college near Utrecht organized a team. So did British embassy staff in The Hague. But these were isolated developments. It took a Dutchman to popularize association football with his fellow countrymen.

Pim Mulier came upon a cross between football and rugby while attending boarding school in Noordwijk near Leiden in 1870. Few of his fellow students were impressed. But nine years later, in a shop in Amsterdam, he saw a football for sale and all the old enthusiasm was rekindled. Mulier bought the ball, told friends about this strange British pastime and they played throughout the summer on a park in Haarlem. In the September they formally set up what is now the oldest club in Holland: the Haarlemse Football Club.

Parents and teachers were not nearly as enthusiastic. The game was too rough. So Mulier ordered a copy of the "proper" rules from England, cut out the kicking and hacking, and won over many more converts. In 1885 he translated the rules into Dutch and, four years later, Haarlemse FC and nine other clubs formed a Dutch federation – later to become, with royal patronage, the present KNVB.

Early royal enthusiasm was not confined to Holland. In neighbouring Belgium King Leopold II donated a league championship trophy as early as 1897 and the proliferation in Spain of clubs with the "Real" (or "Royal") prefix records the enthusiastic support of the pre-Franco monarchy.

To the north and east of Britain sea and trade spread the soccer gospel. That is why Gothenburg is the traditional heart of Swedish soccer rather than the capital, Stockholm, and why old histories of the Russian game refer to the Charnock family's textile mills at Orekhovo as having given birth to the club which would one day be the foundation for the legendary Moscow Dynamo.

Across the varying regions of Europe, football also developed along distinctly different cultural style lines. In Britain and northern Europe football was a robust outdoor enterprise for the hardy, on the Mediterranean shores it was an exercise in passion while in central Europe it reflected a more languidly artistic temperament.

The influence of Meisl

The late Willy Meisl, in the matchless book "Football Revolution," left a vivid first-hand account of how football sparkled into life simultaneously in Prague, Vienna and Graz in the old Austrian monarchy. Vienna depended on a large and influential British colony which ran many of the most fashionable shops as well as local gasworks which lit the streets. As in Italy and Spain, so in Austria the English origins survive in club names such as First Vienna, which not only included Baron Rothschild's gardeners William Beale and James Black among its founding players but also adopted his blue and yellow racing colours.

Such was the enthusiasm generated by the first matches that when Vienna played the Vienna Cricket and Football Club in 1897 an entrance fee of sixpence was imposed "to reduce the number of spectators."

M.D. Nicholson, who worked for Thomas Cook in Vienna, was the first president of the Austrian federation

DUTCH COURAGE Haarlemse Football Club in 1887–88 with Pim Mulier in the centre of the front row.

ROLL OF HONOUR

FIFA PRESIDENTS
1904–1906
Robert Guerin (France)
1906–1918
Daniel Burley Woolfall (England)
1921–1954
Jules Rimet (France)
1954–1955
Rodolphe Seeldrayers (Belgium)
1956–1961
Arthur Drewry (England)
1961–1974
Sir Stanley Rous (England)
1974–
Joao Havelange (Brazil)

UEFA PRESIDENTS
1954–1962
Ebbe Schwartz (Denmark)
1962–1972
Gustav Wiederkehr (Switzerland)
1973–1983
Artemio Franchi (Italy)
1983–1990
Jacques Georges (France)
1990–
Lennart Johansson (Sweden)

which was built up by the subsequent work of Hugo Meisl, son of a local banker who turned his back on the family business for the sake of football. It was Meisl who arranged touring visits of a string of British clubs and national teams and imported the legendary coach, Jimmy Hogan.

Budapest linked Vienna and Prague in a founding core of central European football and the Hungarian Alfred Schaffer earned an honorary title of the Football King long before the days of Puskas, Kocsis and Co.

International dimension
Before the First World War brought organized football to a halt through Europe – barring Scandinavia – almost every country had its own thriving football association and active national team. Professionalism, in one form or another, was also developing apace. Association football was not merely an aesthetic exercise for the participant, it was rapidly becoming the major spectator entertainment.

To develop into a coherent world-wide force, football needed a governing body with the power and authority to encourage international development through mutual co-operation and competition, as well as through control and refinement of the laws of the game.

Naturally, the English had no interest in such internationalization. A Dutch banker, C.A.W. Hirschman, wrote to the Football Association with his idea in 1902. A similar suggestion was sent by the Union des Societes Francaises de Sports Athletiques in 1903. Sir Frederick Wall, secretary of the FA, replied: "The Council of the (British) Football Associations cannot see the advantages of such a federation but, on all matters upon which joint action was desirable, they would be prepared to confer."

So the English were absent when, on May 21, 1904, delegates from Belgium, Denmark, France, Holland, Spain, Sweden and Switzerland met in Paris to found the Federation Internationale de Football Association. In due course England relented a little and D.B. Woolfall became second president of FIFA. But it was his successor, a Frenchman, Jules Rimet,

president from 1921 to 1954, who brought FIFA and world football through its adolescent years and moved FIFA to the neutral haven of Zurich, Switzerland, in 1932.

Football's presence at the Olympic Games grew increasingly important up until 1928. Then, as amateurism was pushed aside amid virtual sporting civil war in some countries, so Rimet inspired the creation of the all-embracing World Cup which was launched in Uruguay in 1930.

The South Americans were unimpressed when timorous Europe sent only four nations to compete. Mutual suspicion between the old world and the new has never been far from the surface. It emerged in full political colours in 1974 when the incumbent English autocrat, Sir Stanley Rous, was defeated in elections for the FIFA presidency by Brazil's Joao Havelange.

THE BIG DRAW Jules Rimet, FIFA's French president, oversees the draw for the 1938 World Cup finals.

TRUE AMATEURS Germany at the 1912 Olympic Games in Stockholm.

The era of Havelange

Havelange ushered in football's brave new world. He invoked the bankrolling potential of the twin powers of television and sponsorship to turn FIFA not only into the richest sports authority in the world but one of the globe's most powerful business corporations. His long-time aide, general secretary Sepp Blatter, would joke that "new nations find it hard to decide which to join first – the United Nations or FIFA."

But it was no joke. Havelange invested World Cup profits into world-wide development programmes and a wide-ranging competitive structure. In 1974 there was just the World Cup. By the end of 1996, when Havelange announced his intention to retire as FIFA president, FIFA controlled world championships in youth, junior, women's and indoor categories of football.

Also by this time, with the promotion to independent regional status of Oceania, football's pyramid of power comprised FIFA at the apex, then the six regional confederations (Africa, Asia, Europe, North and Central America, Oceania, South America) with a total membership of around 200 national associations.

The power of football's English founders had dwindled. England, Scotland, Wales and Northern Ireland were allowed to retain – as a gesture to history – their independent status. But that was worth only one vote apiece in the bi-annual FIFA Congress, precisely equal to the voting power of, say, the Faroe Islands. Even on the law-making International Board the four British associations now had to share their power with four representatives from FIFA.

European focus

Back in 1904 FIFA and European football represented one and the same force. But by the mid-1950s the game was spreading apace as Europe's imperial shackles were released in Africa, Asia and the Far East. Now Europe wanted to rebuild its power base. Thus, on June 15, 1954, in Basle, on the eve of the World Cup finals, the Union of European Football Associations (UEFA) was founded in Switzerland with Ebbe Schwartz of Denmark as the first president.

Initially UEFA comprised 25 national federations; by 1996, after the fragmentation of the former Soviet Union and original Yugoslavia, its membership had doubled. UEFA was founded to help focus its own members' increasing demand for international competition and co-operation. Within five years of its foundation it had launched a European Championship for national teams as well as taken control of the prestigious European Cup for Champion Clubs (now the UEFA Champions League).

The two central individuals within UEFA are the president and the general secretary. Current president is Lennart Johansson of Sweden, who took up his mandate in 1990 after the retirement through ill health of Jacques Georges of France. He is a former president of the Swedish federation and is a vice-president of the world governing body, FIFA. German Gerhard Aigner has been general secretary since 1988.

In addition to the club competitions, UEFA also supervises a wide range of other events from the senior European Championship for national teams to youth events in various categories from Under-21 down, to a women's championship and a full range of coaching and development programmes.

UEFA's ambition and financial power led, in 1996, to icily polite diplomatic warfare with FIFA over a perceived under-selling of the World Cup television rights and the autocratic manner in which president Joao Havelange wielded control, particularly over selection of members to the most influential committees.

But, also in 1996, and with far greater significance as far as the mass of fans were concerned, UEFA granted England the honour of hosting the finals of the European Championship for the first time.

Some 133 years after that historic meeting at the Freemasons Tavern in Great Queen Street, football came home. Whether Lord Kinnaird would have recognized "his" game is another matter entirely.

INTERNATIONAL COMPETITIONS

Football's two most prestigious international competitions are European in origin. First to be launched was the World Cup. The European Championship, suggested in the 1920s, had to wait for another 30 years and the formal creation of a European federation. Over the next three decades it expanded from a finals tournament of four nations to one involving 16.

THE EUROPEAN CHAMPIONSHIP

In football terms, only the British have ever been seriously Euro-sceptic – and that did not last long. Every other European nation has sought as much competition as possible with the rest of the region, except when political difficulties got in the way, as with Albania and East Germany in the 1950s.

Competition at the highest international level, of course, means the World Cup and the European Championship – now the twin pillars of the national representative game.

The World Cup was launched in 1930 in Uruguay. Yet the dream of a specific European Championship had been raised on 5 February 1927, at a meeting of FIFA in Paris. The originator was Henri Delaunay, general secretary of the French federation.

In those early international days FIFA was the only international body available to consider such initiatives. Hardly surprisingly, in the circumstances, priority was given instead to the creation of the World Cup. Thus Delaunay's dream had to wait until after the creation of the European federation, UEFA, in 1954. Then Delaunay, as general secretary of UEFA, was in an ideal position to help turn his vision into reality.

He died before the launch of the initial event in 1959–60 but it was deemed only fitting that the trophy for which Europe competes every four years should bear his name – the Henri Delaunay Trophy.

(opposite) OVER Jürgen Klinsmann typifies the game's competitive spirit.

(right) FOOTBALL HIGH-FLYER ... French superstar Michel Platini.

FINAL HERO Lev Yashin, gold-medal Soviet goalkeeper in 1960.

1960 FRANCE
Soviet hegemony

The first championship, then known as the European Nations Cup, drew a cautious response. Only 17 federations entered. The absentees included the only two European nations who had won the World Cup, Italy and Germany, as well as England – whose resistance to international competition has been consistent. (England did not enter the World Cup until 1950 and Chelsea were forbidden from competing in the initial European Champions Cup.)

Moscow's Lenin stadium, now simply the Luzhniki after the local

RESULTS 1960

SEMI-FINALS
Yugoslavia 5
(Galic 11, Zanetic 55, Knez 75, Jerkovic 77, 79)

France 4
(Vincent 12, Heutte 43, 62, Wisnieski 52)

Soviet Union 3
(V. Ivanov 35, 58, Ponedelnik 64)

Czechoslovakia 0

THIRD PLACE PLAY-OFF
Czechoslovakia 2
(Bubernik 58, Pavlovic 88)

France 0

FINAL
(10 July, Parc des Princes, Paris)

Soviet Union 2
(Metrevelli 49, Ponedelnik 113)

Yugoslavia 1
(Galic 41)
HT: 0–1. 90 min.: 1–1.
Att.: 17,966.
Ref.: Ellis (Eng)

Soviet Union: Yashin, Chekheli, Maslenkin, Krutikov, Voinov, Netto, Metrevelli, V Ivanov, Ponedelnik, Bubukhin, Meshki.

Yugoslavia: Vidinic, Durkovic, Miladinovic, Jusufi, Zanetic, Perusic, Matus, Jerkovic, Galic, Sekularac, Kostic.

suburb, was the stage for the historic first match. The date was 28 September 1958, and a 100,572 crowd saw the Soviet Union defeat Hungary 3–1. The first goal was scored by Anatoly Ilyin, an outside-left with Spartak Moscow, after four minutes. The Soviet line-up included heroes of the era such as centre-forward Nikita Simonian, though not goalkeeper Lev Yashin, who was temporarily out of favour. Only right-winger Laszlo Budai survived in Hungary's line-up from the great team of a few years earlier.

The qualifying formula was a direct elimination knock-out system with home and away legs, the pattern which was becoming familiar in the European club events. A preliminary round was necessary to reduce the field for the first round proper to 16 teams. The preliminary draw matched the Republic of Ireland against Czechoslovakia. Goals from Liam Tuohy and Noel Cantwell (from a penalty) brought the Irish a 2–0 win at Dalymount Park in Dublin but they lost 4–0 away in Bratislava. The Czechoslovaks won 4–2 on aggregate.

Cold war politics threatened to kill off the event before it barely begun. The Soviet Union were drawn against Spain in the quarter-finals but the Spanish dictator, Francisco Franco, told his federation that the Soviet delegation would be refused entry to Spain. Ultimately UEFA, facing its first political wrangle, decided that Spain should be deemed to have withdrawn. The Soviets thus qualified for the finals.

These were staged in France, appropriately in Delaunay's honour. The format would remain unchanged until the 1980s. Four nations were involved, playing knock-out semi-finals then a third place play-off and Final. (The third place play-off was discontinued after 1980.)

The Soviet Union, with Lev Yashin restored in goal, thrashed Czechoslovakia 3–0 in the Velodrome in Marseille with goals from Valentin Ivanov (two) and centre-forward Viktor Ponedelnik.

The hosts, France, were badly handicapped by the absences of injured spearhead Just Fontaine and argumentative schemer Raymond Kopa, and lost a thriller 5–4 against Yugoslavia in Paris. The French goalkeeper, Georges Lamia from Nice, took most of the blame. He was dropped for the third place play-off but France lost again: this time by 2–0 to Czechoslovakia.

The final was also played in the old Parc des Princes in Paris – just like the first Champion Clubs Cup Final four years earlier. The first goal was almost an own goal, Soviet skipper Igor Netto deflecting a shot from Milan Galic. But right-wing Slava Metrevelli equalized and centre-forward Ponedelnik claimed an extra-time winner.

MAN OF THE TOURNAMENT 1960

LEV YASHIN

Yashin was the Soviet Union's inspirational goalkeeper. Nicknamed the Black Octopus because of his black jersey, Yashin played all his club career with Moscow Dynamo. He helped the Soviets win Olympic gold in Melbourne in 1956 but then faced a challenge from Viktor Belyayev for his place with both club and country. Belyayev played in the early qualifying ties but the Soviets needed experience – and Yashin provided precisely that on his return for the finals.

1964 SPAIN
The hosts reign in Spain

The Soviet holders were favourites to retain the trophy in its second edition in 1964. The finals were something of a political triumph for football. In the 1960 quarter-finals, Spain had refused to play the Soviets. Now, under the shrewd managerial guidance of the under-rated Jose Villalonga, Spain not only provided a host's welcome for the Soviet Union but met them in the final – and beat them.

As far as the overall competition was concerned, progress was still achieved on the two-leg, direct elimination basis. England dipped their toes in the water for the first time and had a nasty shock. France were their first-round rivals. The first leg was played at Hillsborough, Sheffield – the only time that England have ever strayed from Wembley for a major competitive international – and ended 1–1. The second leg was staged nearly

five months later when Alf Ramsey's first competitive experience at national team level ended in a 5–2 defeat. France were inspired from midfield by veteran Raymond Kopa while two-goal right-winger Marian Wisnieski ran England's defence ragged.

In the quarter-finals Spain beat the Irish Republic 7–1 on aggregate while the Soviet Union accounted for Sweden. The Soviets had previously beaten a reviving Italy thanks to a penalty save by goalkeeper Lev Yashin from the young Sandro Mazzola. This was also Italy's first foray into the European Championship under a manager in Edmondo Fabbri who was seen as a breath of fresh air … until the 1966 World Cup disaster against North Korea.

Denmark and Hungary also qualified for the finals in Spain. But the Danes were well beaten 3–0 by the Soviet Union in their Barcelona semi-final. Spain, meanwhile, leaned on two fine products of the football

school of La Coruna, in the north-west, to make progress. The midfield inspiration of Internazionale's Luis Suarez and the right-wing magic of Amancio sparked a 2–1 victory over Hungary in Madrid.

Spain coach Villalonga knew all about European competition since he had managed Real Madrid to their historic initial Champions Cup success in 1956. Yet he included only two Madrid players in his "new"

ALL MINE Victorious Spanish players carry manager Jose Villalonga in triumph in 1964.

Spain – Amancio and lanky wing-half Ignacio Zoco – and mixed in the stars of less fashionable Atletico Madrid, Athletic Bilbao and Zaragoza.

Barcelona's Jesus Pereda shot Spain into an early lead in the final in the Estadio Bernabeu. But the great

MAN OF THE TOURNAMENT 1964

LUIS SUAREZ

Suarez still ranks as the greatest of all modern Spanish footballers. Born in La Coruna he starred with Barcelona but had moved on, at coach Helenio Herrera's insistence, to Italy's Internazionale by the time the 1964 finals came round. Suarez held midfield together and developed an understanding with the speedy right winger, Amancio, which the slow Soviet defence could not withstand in the Final. The pair pulled gaps in the holders' defence which provided Pereda and Marcelino with time and space to win the match.

IN COMMAND Spain's midfield maestro, Luis Suarez.

Basque goalkeeper, Jose Iribar, was then beaten at the other end two minutes later when Khusainov struck back for the Soviet Union. A second-half goal from Zaragoza centre-forward Marcelino was the signal for Spanish celebrations.

Nevertheless, reaching the quarter-finals was as far as Spain got next time. In 1968, for the second tournament in succession, the hosts ended up as champions. But unlike Spain in 1964, Italy struggled and teetered on the brink of disaster before defeating a ruggedly skilful Yugoslavia in a replayed final at the Olympico in Rome.

RESULTS 1964

SEMI-FINALS

Spain 2
(Pereda 35, Amancio 115)

Hungary 1
(Bene 85) after extra time

Soviet Union 3
(Voronin 19, Ponedelnik 40, V. Ivanov 88)

Denmark 0

THIRD PLACE PLAY-OFF

Hungary 3
(Bene 11, Novak 107 pen, 110)

Denmark 1
(Bertelsen 81) after extra time

FINAL

(21 June, Santiago Bernabeu, Madrid)

Spain 2
(Pereda 6, Marcelino 83)

Soviet Union 1
(Khusainov 8)
HT: 1–1.
Att.: 125,000.
Ref.: Holland (Eng)

Spain: Iribar, Rivilla, Olivella, Calleja, Zoco, Fuste, Amancio, Pereda, Marcelino, Suarez, Lapetra.

Soviet Union: Yashin, Shustikov, Shesternev, Mudrik, Voronin, Anichkin, Chislenko, V Ivanov, Ponedelnik, Korneyev, Khusainov.

1968 ITALY
Football paradiso

By now the European Championship was recognized as a major success and an established feature of the international football calendar. Such recognition was reflected in an increased entry and UEFA thus converted the qualifying competition from the direct elimination knock-out system into a mini-league formula.

Italy earned the right to stage the finals not through seeding but thanks to a qualifying campaign in which a team under the managership of Ferruccio Valcareggi overcame Cyprus, Switzerland and Romania in the group round, then Bulgaria in the knock-out quarter-finals.

The other finalists were experienced Yugoslavia and Soviet Union as well as World Cup-holders England – who had beaten holders Spain in the quarter-finals. England won the first leg at Wembley 1–0 with a goal from Bobby Charlton and the second leg 2–1 in Spain with strikes from Martin Peters and Norman Hunter.

Hosts Italy brought to the finals a squad which included great figures such as goalkeeper Dino Zoff, left-back Giacinto Facchetti and attackers Pietro Anastasi and Luigi Riva. Anastasi drew enormous interest because Juventus were just about to pay what was considered the fantastic, world record-breaking sum of £500,000 to buy him. For all that talent, however, the Italians needed the luck of a toss of a coin to earn a place in the final after their semi against the Soviet Union finished goalless following extra time. (The penalty shoot-out had yet to be introduced into top-level competition, though it was already widely used in the popular summer club tournaments in Spain.)

In the other semi-final Yugoslavia beat England 1–0 in Florence. The occasion was doubly disappointing for England boss Ramsey – now Sir Alf. Not only did England lose, but wing-half Alan Mullery suffered the disgrace of becoming the first player sent off while representing his country in a senior international. Left-winger Dragan Dzajic – inevitably nicknamed "Magic Dragan" by the English media – inspired the Slavs and scored the decisive second-half goal.

The comparative performances of the semi-final winners persuaded many observers that Yugoslavia were likely to defeat Italy in the final in Rome's Olympic stadium. Dzajic did provide the Slavs with an early lead but Italy's workhorse right-winger Angelo Domenghini equalized controversially from a free-kick with 10 minutes remaining. Extra-time failed to provide any more goals so the final went to a replay in the Stadio Comunale in Florence. Yugoslavia should have felt at home, having beaten England there. But by now they were too tired to resist a much-changed Italian team. Italy, with five fresh players, were too resourceful in attack, with Riva and Anastasi perpetual dangers. Both scored goals in the first half and Facchetti and Co. at the back shut up shop in the second. Italy were champions of Europe for – remarkably – the first and only time.

FIRST STRIKE Luigi Riva (right) shoots Italy ahead in the 1968 final replay.

MAN OF THE TOURNAMENT 1968

DRAGAN DZAJIC
Dzajic was heir to a great Yugoslav footballing tradition as the latest hero of Red Star Belgrade. As a traditional outside-left he was welcome proof that not everyone subscribed to the "wingless wonders" policy of England's Sir Alf Ramsey. In the semi-final in Florence Dzajic tormented the England defence with his old-fashioned talents but Italy took much greater care of him in the final and the replay. Dzajic played later in France, then returned to Red Star as a director.

RESULTS 1968

SEMI-FINALS

Yugoslavia 1
(Dzajic 85)

England 0

Italy 0

Soviet Union 0
(Italy on toss of a coin) after extra time

THIRD PLACE PLAY-OFF

England 2
(Charlton 39, Hurst 63)

Soviet Union 0

FINAL

(8 June, Olimpico, Rome)
Italy 1
(Domenghini 80)

Yugoslavia 1
(Dzajic 38)
after extra time
HT: 0–1. 90 min.: 1–1.
Att.: 85,000.
Ref.: Dienst (Swz)

Italy: Zoff, Castano, Burgnich, Guarneri, Facchetti, Ferrini, Juliano, Lodetti, Domenghini, Anastasi, Prati.

Yugoslavia: Pantelic, Fazlagic, Holcer, Paunovic, Damjanovic, Acimovic, Trivic, Pavlovic, Petkovic, Musemic, Dzajic.

REPLAY

(June 10, Olimpico, Rome)
Italy 2
(Riva 12, Anastasi 31)

Yugoslavia 0
HT: 2–0.
Att.: 50,000.
Ref.: Ortiz de Mendibil (Spain)

Italy: Zoff, Salvadore, Burgnich, Guarneri, Facchetti, Rosato, De Sisti, Domenghini, Mazzola, Anastasi, Riva.

Yugoslavia: Pantelic, Fazlagic, Paunovic, Holcer, Damjanovic, Acimovic, Trivic, Pavlovic, Hosic, Musemic, Dzajic.

***ALL OURS!** Italian captain Giacinto Facchetti collects the Henri Delaunay trophy.*

1972 BELGIUM
Class performance

In all the history of the European Championship no national team has successfully defended the crown. Italy were no exception. Their defence in 1970–72 was halted in its tracks by Belgium. Italy were held goalless in Milan then beaten 2–1 in Brussels. The

COMMAND PERFORMANCE... skipper and sweeper Franz Beckenbauer.

Belgian goals were scored by Wilfried Van Moer and Paul Van Himst – both of whom would later become national manager. Van Moer was the midfield general and Van Himst the spearhead of a team whose success helped earn their country not only a place in the last four but the right to play hosts to the entire programme of semi-finals, third place play-off and final.

Belgium were not, however, the most outstanding team in the tournament. That honour – very, very clearly – belonged to West Germany.

MAN OF THE TOURNAMENT 1972

FRANZ BECKENBAUER

The 1972 European Championship was the first time Beckenbauer had been used as attacking sweeper by his country. He had developed the role with Bayern Munich since the mid-1960s but German boss Helmut Schön kept him in midfield for fear of the risks involved – until 1971. Then Beckenbauer's inspirational link with Gunter Netzer provided the key to West Germany's triumph. Indeed, this may have been a better West German side than the World Cup-winners of two years later.

RESULTS 1972

SEMI-FINALS

Soviet Union 1
(Konkov 53)

Hungary 0

West Germany 2
(G. Müller 24, 72)

Belgium 1
(Polleunis 83)

THIRD PLACE PLAY-OFF

Belgium 2
(Lambert 24, Van Himst 28)

Hungary 1
(Ku 53 (pen.))

FINAL

(18 June, Heysel, Brussels)

West Germany 3
(G. Müller 27, 57, Wimmer 52)

Soviet Union 0
HT: 1–0.
Att.: 50,000.
Ref.: Marschall (Austria)

West Germany: Maier, Höttges, Beckenbauer, Schwarzenbeck, Breitner, Hoeness, Netzer, Wimmer, Heynckes, G. Müller, E. Kremers.

Soviet Union: Rudakov, Dzodzuashvili, Khurtsilava, Kaplichni, Istomin, Kolotov, Troshkin, Konkov (Dolmatov 46), Baidachni, Banishevski (Kozenkevich 65), Onishenko.

Manager Helmut Schön had cast aside the ageing stars who had taken West Germany to third place at the 1970 World Cup. The retirement of Uwe Seeler had forced Schön to rebuild his attack and, while he was at it, he took the opportunity to rebuild the style and tactical shape of his team.

The top two German clubs of the era, Bayern Munich and Borussia Monchengladbach, provided both the engine room and the inspiration. The telepathic creative understanding which developed between Bayern's revolutionary attacking sweeper, Franz Beckenbauer, and Borussia playmaker Gunter Netzer, lit up the

SWEEPING UP Franz Beckenbauer foils the Soviets again in the 1972 Final.

European game. Helping, supporting and pulling the opposition all over the place were an adventurous young left-back in the frizzy-haired Maoist, Paul Breitner, and hard-working attacking midfielders in Herbert Wimmer and Uli Hoeness. Ahead of them Gerd Müller, one of the greatest opportunists in international football history, provided the cutting edge. These were worthy European champions; possibly even the finest team ever to win the European Championship.

The format was now established. The first round took place on a group basis followed by two-leg, knock-out quarter-finals. It was at this stage that Schön's Germans made history by scoring their first-ever Wembley win. Goals from Hoeness, Netzer and Müller secured a 3–1 victory which

was all the sweeter for Beckenbauer, full-back Horst-Dieter Höttges and striker Sigi Held – Germany's three survivors from the side beaten at Wembley six years earlier in the World Cup Final of 1966.

The return was a 0–0 draw in the Olympic Stadium in West Berlin, then a western political island anchored deep within Communist East Germany. Joining West Germany in the finals were the Soviet Union, Hungary and their Belgian hosts.

The Soviet Union had few problems defeating Hungary in the Heysel stadium in Brussels to gain a place in what was their third European Final in four events. The second semi-final, in Antwerp, saw hosts Belgium fall 2–1 to West Germany. Müller scored both the visitors' goals and the Germans

GUESSING GAME Gunter Netzer (right) dominated midfield in Brussels.

cruised through as favourites into the Final in the Heysel, in the shadow of the Atomium.

Victory was achieved more easily than Schön had believed possible. The Soviets were led by a rock of centre-back in Murtaz Khurtsilava but even he could not cope with the deceptively nimble Müller. Beckenbauer and Netzer controlled the match. Netzer even struck a post before two more typically opportunist goals from Müller and another from Wimmer secured medals for all the squad. That 3–0 margin of success remains the largest of any European Championship Final.

1976 YUGOSLAVIA
Bohemian rhapsody

The 1972 finals had produced an outstanding team in West Germany. The subsequent 1976 event went three better by producing no fewer than four superbly competitive sides. Hosts Yugoslavia finished fourth after losing the third place play-off to Holland – but there could be no embarrassment in that. These stand as the most outstanding finals of the "first" generation of the tournament – with the climactic final between outsiders Czechoslovakia and holders West Germany a dramatic classic.

The pattern remained the same: a first round of mini-leagues was followed by direct elimination quarter-finals and then the four-match finals.

Vaclav Jezek guided the Czechs to a first surprise victory over the favoured Soviet Union by 2–0, 2–2 in the quarter-finals. Holland, World Cup runners-up two years earlier and inspired by Johan Cruyff and Johan Neeskens, defeated Belgium, their old neighbourhood rivals.

Helmut Schön's West Germans, now also the world as well as European champions, overran Spain while Yugoslavia won a bad-tempered tie with Wales – the referee in Cardiff needed a police escort after disallowing two Welsh goals – to earn first a place in the last four and,

MAN OF THE TOURNAMENT 1976

IVO VIKTOR

Great goalkeepers can provide untold inspiration for their teammates. Czechoslovakia approached the 1976 finals as rank outsiders but, once in Yugoslavia, Dukla Prague's Viktor rose to the occasion. He pulled off some sensational saves in the semi-final victory over Holland then defied a thrilling West German revival in the Final. Viktor's ultimate achievement was filling his goal in the penalty shoot-out to provoke the decisive miss by Uli Hoeness.

CHAMPION OF EUROPE
Antonin Panenka hails his decisive penalty past Sepp Maier.

subsequently, in the corridors of power, rights to host the event.

It was the first time a major European tournament had gone to eastern Europe – and, so far, the last.

Czechoslovakia set a high standard of excitement when they defeated Holland 3–1 after extra time in the first semi-final – the Dutch succumbing after referee Clive Thomas sent off Neeskens and Wim Van Hanegem. Then it was West Germany's turn to need extra-time as they hit back from 2–0 down to secure a 4–2 win over hosts Yugoslavia.

A new Müller – Dieter Müller from Köln – led the German attack following the international retirement

RESULTS 1976

SEMI-FINALS

Czechoslovakia 3
(Ondrus 20, Nehoda 115, F. Vesely 118)

Holland 1
(Ondrus o.g. 74)
after extra time

West Germany 4
(Flohe 65, D. Müller 80, 114, 119)

Yugoslavia 2
(Popivoda 20, Dzajic 30)
after extra time

THIRD PLACE PLAY-OFF

Holland 3
(Geels 27, 106, W. van de Kerkhof 39)

Yugoslavia 2
(Katalinski 43, Dzajic 82)
after extra time

FINAL

(20 June, Crvena Zvezda, Belgrade)

Czechoslovakia 2
(Svehlik 8, Dobias 25)

West Germany 2
(D. Müller 28, Holzenbein 89)
HT: 2–1. 90 min.: 2–2.
Att.: 33,000.
Ref.: Gonella (Italy)
(Czechoslovakia 5–3 on penalties) after extra time

Czechoslovakia: Viktor, Pivarnik, Ondrus, Capkovic, Gogh, Dobias, Panenka, Moder, Masny, Svehlik (Jurkemik 79), Nehoda.

West Germany: Maier, Vogts, Beckenbauer, Schwarzenbeck, Dietz, Wimmer (Flohe 46), Bonhof, Beer (Bongartz 79), Hoeness, D. Müller, Holzenbein.

of Gerd. He scored a hat-trick against Yugoslavia and led the German fight-back in the final after they had gone 2–0 down in 25 minutes to Czechoslovakia. One minute remained in normal time when Bernd Holzenbein's equalizer from a corner by Rainer Bonhof sent the game into the extra 30 minutes.

For once, no one scored in extra time, largely due to the splendid goal-keeping of Viktor and Sepp Maier, and Czechoslovakia then proceeded to win the first major event decided on a penalty shoot-out. Midfield general Antonin Panenka sent Maier the wrong way with the decisive kick after Uli Hoeness had failed for Germany. They had to wait 20 years for their revenge. The shoot-out lesson did not go unheeded. German teams quickly became among the most adept and practised at beating the pressure. Subsequent high-level shoot-out victories against France, Mexico and England – twice – would prove the point.

IVO VIKTOR The most appropriately named goalkeeper.

1980 ITALY
West Germany win again

Panenka's decisive penalty in Belgrade marked the end of an era. By 1978–80 such was the popularity of the tournament and the pressure for places that UEFA decided to increase the scope of the finals to take in eight countries – split into two groups of four with the group winners meeting in the final and the runners-up playing off for third and fourth places.

The Italians became the first nation to host the finals twice – this time they did not have to qualify – and were matched in their group with England, Belgium and Spain. The other mini-league at the finals featured old rivals West Germany and Holland, newcomers Greece and defending title-holders Czechoslovakia.

After all the excitement of 1976, the group format proved a major disappointment as the 12 games produced a total of only 22 goals.

CORNER KING Germany's Karl-Heinz Rummenigge pierced Belgium's defence.

RESULTS 1980

GROUP 1

West Germany 1
(Rummenigge 55)
Czechoslovakia 0

Holland 1
(Kist 56 pen)
Greece 0

West Germany 3
(K. Allofs 15, 60, 68)
Holland 2
(Rep 75 (pen.), W. van de Kerkhof 86)

Czechoslovakia 3
(Panenka 5, Vizek 25, Nehoda 63)
Greece 1
(Anastopoulos 11)

Czechoslovakia 1
(Nehoda 13)
Holland 1
(Kist 58)

West Germany 0
Greece 0

	P	W	D	L	F	A	Pts
W. Germany	3	2	1	0	4	2	5
Czech	3	1	1	1	4	3	3
Holland	3	1	1	1	4	4	3
Greece	3	0	1	2	1	4	1

GROUP 2

England 1
(Wilkins 32)
Belgium 1
(Ceulemans 38)

Italy 0
Spain 0

Belgium 2
(Gerets 17, Cools 64)
Spain 1
(Quini 35)

Italy 1
(Tardelli 78)
England 0

England 2
(Brooking 18, Woodcock 62)
Spain 1
(Dani 48 (pen.))

Italy 0
Belgium 0

	P	W	D	L	F	A	Pts
Belgium	3	1	2	0	3	2	4
Italy	3	1	2	0	1	0	4
England	3	1	1	1	3	3	3
Spain	3	0	1	2	2	4	1

THIRD PLACE PLAY-OFF

Czechoslovakia 1
(Jurkemik 48)
Italy 1
(Graziani 74)
(Czechoslovakia 9–8 on penalties) after extra time

FINAL
(22 June, Olimpico, Rome)

West Germany 2
(Hrubesch 10, 88)
Belgium 1
(Vandereycken 71 (pen.))
HT: 1–0.
Att.: 48,000.
Ref.: Rainea (Rom)

West Germany: Schumacher, Kaltz, Stielike, K. Forster, Dietz, Briegel (Cullmann 55), Schüster, H. Müller, Rummenigge, Hrubesch, K. Allofs.

Belgium: Pfaff, Gerets, L. Millecamps, Meeuws, Renquin, Cools, Vandereycken, Van Moer, Mommens, F. van der Elst, Ceulemans.

That, however, certainly did not reduce the passion among the crowds – particularly in Turin where riot police unleashed tear gas to quell unrest among supporters in the tumble-down Stadio Comunale during England's opening draw against Belgium. At one stage play had to be halted for five minutes so that players could be treated as the tear gas drifted down and across the pitch.

Belgium beat Spain 2–1 in their next game but England's dreams of a place in the final in Rome disintegrated as they lost 1–0 to their hosts. Juventus midfielder Marco Tardelli scored the winner 10 minutes from the end. A goalless draw with Italy on the last group matchday was enough to

GERMAN GLADIATORS hail their victory over Belgium in Rome's Olympic stadium.

send Belgium into a senior final for the first time in their history.

The other group ended with favourites West Germany leading the way. They began with a 1–0 revenge victory over Czechoslovakia, followed up with a 3–2 win over Holland in Naples. This was the match in which the TV-watching world "discovered" the inspirational midfielder Bernd Schüster – who was promptly rested for the concluding goalless draw with Greece.

Yet another German hero, now that Gerd Müller and Franz Beckenbauer had moved on, was one of their Munich apprentices – Karl-Heinz Rummenigge. He justified his reputation in the final against Belgium in Rome. Rummenigge it was who contributed the inch-perfect corner from which giant Horst Hrubesch headed a last-minute winning goal. Hrubesch had also scored the first

MAN OF THE TOURNAMENT 1980

KARL-HEINZ RUMMENIGGE

Bayern Munich have provided the backbone for all successful German international teams in the modern era. Beckenbauer had retired from the national team by 1980 but Rummenigge – a raw junior in the Beckenbauer era – took over his mantle as "leader" and captain. In the Final against Belgium it was Rummenigge's craftily flighted corner which provided the last-minute winner for Horst Hrubesch. Sadly, injury prevented Rummenigge from repeating the magic at the subsequent 1982 World Cup.

while the Belgians fought back on terms early in the second half with Rene Vandereycken converting a penalty awarded against German sweeper Uli Stielike.

A 48,000 crowd, well below capacity in Rome, watched events passively. It would have been different if Italy had been playing but they had

finished as runners-up in their group and failed even to get the better of Czechoslovakia in the third place play-off in Naples. A dull goalless draw was followed by a lengthy penalty shoot-out which the Czechoslovaks eventually won 9–8. Europe's football rulers took the hint and scrapped the third place play-off thereafter.

1984 FRANCE
Platini rules the roost

By 1984 it was 16 years since a host team had won "its own" tournament. France became the first home winners since Italy in 1968. But whereas the Italians certainly benefited from playing in their own back yard, it would be fair to say that France would have won "their" tournament anywhere. They were worthy European champions – sweeping all before them in magnificent style to seize the crown for the first time in Paris's new Parc des Princes stadium. Their brilliance stemmed from the midfield trio of hard-working Luis Fernandez and Jean Tigana plus effervescent little Alain Giresse ... all topped off by the all-round attacking genius of Michel Platini, the French

LE ROI MICHEL Platini holds Spain at bay in the 1984 Final.

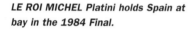

RESULTS 1984

GROUP 1

France 1
(Platini 77)

Denmark 0

Belgium 2
(Vandenbergh 27, Grun 44)

Yugoslavia 0

France 5
(Platini 3, 74, 88, Giresse 32, Fernandez 43)

Belgium 0

Denmark 5
(Ivkovic o.g. 7, Berggren 16, Arnesen 68, Elkjaer 81, Lauridsen 83)

Yugoslavia 0

France 3
(Platini 59, 61, 76)

Yugoslavia 2
(Sestic 31, Stojkovic 80)

Denmark 3
(Arnesen 40, Brylle 60, Elkjaer 83)

Belgium 2
(Ceulemans 25, Vercauteren 38)

	P	W	D	L	F	A	Pts
France	3	3	0	0	9	2	6
Denmark	3	2	0	1	8	3	4
Belgium	3	1	0	2	4	8	2
Yugoslavia	3	0	0	3	2	10	0

GROUP 2

West Germany 0

Portugal 0

Spain 1
(Carrasco 20)

Romania 1
(Boloni 34)

West Germany 2
(Voller 24, 65)

Romania 1
(Coras 46)

Portugal 1
(Sousa 51)

Spain 1
(Santillana 72)

Spain 1
(Maceda 89)

West Germany 0

Portugal 1
(Nene 80)

Romania 0

	P	W	D	L	F	A	Pts
Spain	3	1	2	0	3	2	4
Portugal	3	1	2	0	2	1	4
W. Germany	3	1	1	1	2	2	3
Romania	3	0	1	2	2	4	1

SEMI-FINALS

France 3
(Domergue 24, 114, Platini 119)

Portugal 2
(Jordai 73, 97)
after extra time

Spain 1
(Maceda 66)

Denmark 1
(Lerby 6)
(Spain 5–4 on penalties) after extra time

FINAL

(27 June, Parc des Princes, Paris)

France 2
(Platini 56, Bellone 90)

Spain 0
HT: 0–0.
Att.: 47,368.
Ref.: Christov (Czechoslovakia)

France: Bats, Battiston (Amoros 72), Le Roux*, Bossis, Domergue, Fernandez, Giresse, Tigana, Platini, Lacombe (Genghini 79), Bellone.

Spain: Arconada, Urquiaga, Salva (Roberto 84), Gallego, Senor, Francisco, Victor, Camacho, Julio Alberto (Sarabia 76), Santillana, Carrasco.
*Le Roux sent off, 84 min.

MATCHLESS IN PARIS French players celebrate their country's only major trophy.

captain, Juventus superstar and European Footballer of the Year.

Denmark's arrival in the finals was another gesture towards a new balance of power within Europe, as was the failure of West Germany to reach the reconstituted knock-out semi-finals.

The rapidly improving Danes had reached the finals by winning a qualifying group in magnificent fashion and including a sensational 1–0 win away to England. Former European Footballer of the Year Allan Simonsen converted the crucial penalty at Wembley.

In the finals, however, Denmark's prospects were upset when Simonsen broke a leg during their opening 1–0 defeat by France. Platini was the

match-winner with the first of his nine goals in five games. His haul included hat-tricks against Belgium and Yugoslavia, a last-minute extra-time winner in the semi-final against Portugal – one of the greatest games in the tournament's history – and, in the final against Spain, the first goal from a free-kick.

Spain had reached the Final thanks to a penalty shoot-out victory over Denmark in the semis. But the game plan prepared to deal with France by veteran coach Miguel Munoz was upset by a string of injuries and suspensions. Still, Spain were giving as good as they got when a rare mistake by goalkeeper-captain Luis Arconada – Platini's low drive from a free-kick spun through the keeper's hands – proved decisive after 56 minutes.

Bruno Bellone scored a second for France in the very last minute,

shortly after Yvon Le Roux had been sent off, but then it was academic. The first goal had knocked all the stuffing out of the Spaniards.

France were not the only nation for whom European Championship success had long proved elusive. The same could have been said of Holland until the World Cup-runners-up from

1974 and 1978 finally secured the major prize for which their pre-eminence in the international game had long since earned.

Indeed 1988 was a glorious year for Holland, with club side PSV Eindhoven also putting the Dutch seal of success on the European Champions Cup.

MAN OF THE TOURNAMENT 1984

MICHEL PLATINI

No single player has dominated a European finals in the way Platini commanded "his" home tournament in France in 1984. He had already achieved superstar status with Juventus in Italy, where he was league top scorer. Then he returned home to not only captain the hosts, but shine as their finest player, score two hat-tricks, open the scoring in the Final and then receive the Henri Delaunay trophy itself after France's 2–0 defeat of Spain. Platini would return to the finals in 1992 – this time as national manager.

1988 W. GERMANY
Tangerine dream

European Championship success made a nonsense of fears that the generation which produced Johan Cruyff, Rob Rensenbrink, Johan Neeskens and Co. had been a mere slip in time. Holland's victory over the Soviet Union in the 1988 final in Munich's Olympic stadium was serious evidence in favour of the Dutch approach to youth coaching and to all aspects of general football education.

West Germany played hosts to the first event in three which had not featured a format change. A qualifying section of mini-leagues was climaxed by two groups of four teams each in the finals followed by two knock-out semi-finals and then the final itself in the Olympic stadium in Munich – where Holland had suffered their most famous defeat, in the 1974 World Cup Final.

England arrived in West Germany for the finals with the best record of any of the qualifiers, having won five matches and drawn one, scoring 19 goals and conceding just one. Their form then deserted them. For the only time in any major event they lost all three of their group matches – starting with a 1–0 setback against the Irish Republic newcomers and continuing with a devastating defeat against Holland, for whom Marco Van Basten scored a hat-trick.

The Milan centre-forward had been uncertain of his place with the Dutch at the start of the finals. In fact it even took the words of his friend and mentor Johan Cruyff to persuade him to stay with the squad after the

AT LAST *Captain Ruud Gullit celebrates in Munich – 14 years after Holland's World Cup defeat there.*

RESULTS 1988

GROUP 1

West Germany 1
(Brehme 55)

Italy 1
(Mancini 51)

Spain 3
(Michel 5, Butragueno 52, Gordillo 67)

Denmark 2
(M Laudrup 25, Povlsen 85)

West Germany 2
(Klinsmann 9, Thon 85)

Denmark 0

Italy 1
(Vialli 73)

Spain 0

West Germany 2
(Voller 30, 51)

Spain 0

Italy 2
(Altobelli 65, De Agostini 87)

Denmark 0

	P	W	D	L	F	A	Pts
W. Germany	3	2	1	0	5	1	5
Italy	3	2	1	0	4	1	5
Spain	3	1	0	2	3	5	2
Denmark	3	0	0	3	2	7	0

GROUP 2

Republic of Ireland 1
(Houghton 5)

England 0

Soviet Union 1
(Rats 53)

Holland 0

Holland 3
(Van Basten 23, 71, 75)

England 1
(Robson 53)

Soviet Union 1
(Protasov 75)

Republic of Ireland 1
(Whelan 38)

Soviet Union 3
(Aleinikov 3, Mikhailichenko 28, Pasulko 72)

England 1
(Adams 16)

Holland 1
(Kieft 82)

Republic of Ireland 0

	P	W	D	L	F	A	Pts
Soviet Union	3	2	1	0	5	2	5
Holland	3	2	0	1	4	2	4
Rep. of Ireland	3	1	1	1	2	2	3
England	3	0	0	3	2	7	0

SEMI-FINALS

Holland 2
(R Koeman 73 pen, Van Basten 88)

West Germany 1
(Matthäus 54 (pen.))

Soviet Union 2
(Litovchenko 59, Protasov 62)

Italy 0

FINAL

(June 25, Olympiastadion, Munich)

Holland 2
(Gullit 33, Van Basten 54)

Soviet Union 0

HT: 1–0.
Att.: 72,300.
Ref.: Vautrot (France)

Holland: Van Breukelen, Van Aerle, R. Koeman, Rijkaard, Van Tiggelen, Vanenburg, Wouters, E. Koeman, Muhren, Gullit, Van Basten.

Soviet Union: Dasayev, Khidiatulin, Demianenko, Litovchenko, Aleinikov, Zavarov, Belanov, Mikhailichenko, Gotsmanov (Baltacha 69), Rats, Protasov (Pasulko 71).

MAN OF THE TOURNAMENT 1988

MARCO VAN BASTEN

Holland's centre-forward at the 1988 finals wanted to go home after the opening defeat by the Soviet Union. Old coach, friend and mentor Johan Cruyff persuaded him to think again – and Van Basten proved his commitment to the cause by thrashing a hat-trick past England. Even better, in the Final against the Soviet Union, Van Basten volleyed one of the most spectacular goals ever seen at such a rarefied level. A pity for football as a whole that ankle trouble should later curtail his career.

opening defeat by the Soviet Union in Cologne. When, however, Van Basten was substituted towards the end of the England game, he shook hands with veteran coach Rinus Michels as he left the pitch. That handshake came to symbolize the new-found unity of spirit which carried the

Dutch to their ultimate well-deserved victory.

West Germany topped the other group without appearing convincing but led Holland in their semi-final in Hamburg thanks to a controversial Lothar Matthäus penalty after what was judged to have been a foul on Jürgen Klinsmann. German forward Frank Mill laughed as the teams ran back to restart and told Dutch skipper Ruud Gullit: "If one of you falls over, you'll get one, too." They did just that. Ronald Koeman fired home an equalizing penalty after what seemed a fair tackle, and then Van Basten snatched a late, late winner.

As in the 1974 World Cup Holland reached the Final as favourites. Their

opponents were a Soviet side seriously disrupted by the suspension of stopper Oleg Kuznetsov. Even Kuznetsov, however, would not have been able to control the attacking flair of Van Basten and Gullit. Gullit scored the first goal and Van Basten the second – volleying home one of the greatest individual goals ever seen in any major international event from Arnold Muhren's long, tantalizing left-wing cross. Hans Van Breukelen then conceded a penalty but made amends by saving Igor Belanov's kick, and the last Soviet hope had gone.

ONE DOWN... Two more to go for Holland's hat-trick hero Van Basten against England.

1992 SWEDEN
Scandinavian fairy-tale

The magic that Van Basten and the Dutch conjured up in 1988 was not be repeated four years later in Sweden. Indeed, Van Basten missed a penalty in a semi-final shoot-out against a Danish team surely inspired by the fairy-tale genius of Hans Christian Andersen.

The Danes thus came from nowhere to win the tournament for the first time in their history and overcame the favourites to do so: first Holland in the semi-finals and then Germany in the final itself.

Sweden had been a welcome peaceable venue for the climax of a championship which had been shaken by political upheavals in the Soviet Union, in Germany and in the Balkans.

The Soviet Union, for example, collapsed between their national team qualifying for the finals and the finals themselves. In the last appearance of a pillar of post-war European competitive football the Soviets played under the interim banner of the Commonwealth of Independent States before fragmenting into a plethora of new republics (Russia, Ukraine, Belarus, etc.).

The former East Germany had been consigned to history just as the qualifying tournament began. The GDR federation, as one of its last acts, withdrew from the event just before competition started. Key players such as midfielder Matthias Sammer and forwards Thomas Doll and Andreas Thom thus played for a unified Germany in the finals.

Most complex was the Balkan situation. Yugoslavia had been one of the most outstanding of the qualifiers. But the spring of 1992 saw the onset of the country's violent collapse. UEFA barred them from the finals on security grounds and recalled Denmark – the Slavs' qualifying group runners-up – in their place and at two weeks' notice. Manager Richard Moller Nielsen was just embarking on a summer holiday task of decorating his kitchen when the summons came from UEFA.

THOMAS HÄSSLER

The 1992 finals ended in a shock anti-climax for Germany, as they crashed to rank outsiders Denmark in the Final. Consolation was the superb form of Köln's Hässler in midfield – form which earned him the accolade of the Golden Boot as the tournament's star individual. Not for Hässler the simple square pass – he always sought to surprise opponents with his sleight of foot and surprised his team-mates too with the swerving danger of his free-kicks.

Hosts Sweden, in the finals for the first time, deservedly topped Group A. A wonderful goal by Tomas Brolin brought Sweden a place at the top of the group and a 2–1 victory over a disappointing England. A win, now with three points instead of two, would have put England in the semi-final. Instead they were last, their pain exacerbated by controversy over the substitution of skipper and top scorer Gary Lineker by manager Graham Taylor in the closing stages. Denmark, as runners-up, quietly followed the Swedes into the semi-finals despite the absence of their finest player – Michael Laudrup – who had squabbled with Moller Nielsen.

In Group B Holland and Germany possessed too much firepower and experience for newcomers Scotland and the CIS. Holland then threw it away against Denmark in the semi-final, being held 2–2 and losing 5–4 on penalties. Remarkably the decisive

DANISH DYNAMITE Peter Schmeichel and his team-mates can hardly believe their achievement.

penalty miss was contributed by Marco Van Basten, intimidated for once by the overwhelming presence of goalkeeper Peter Schmeichel.

Brolin scored again for Sweden in their semi-final but this time in vain in a 3–2 defeat by West Germany, for whom Player of the Tournament Thomas Hässler scored a superb goal from a free-kick.

Berti Vogts's men were clear favourites to win the Final in Gothenburg's Ullevi stadium. But Denmark – from manager Moller Nielsen through goalkeeper Schmeichel, skipper Lars Olsen, midfielder Kim Vilfort and forward Brian Laudrup – had not read the script. Goals from John Jensen and Vilfort duly produced the greatest shock in the competition's history.

HIS GREATEST GOAL Denmark midfielder John Jensen.

RESULTS 1992

GROUP A

Sweden 1
(Eriksson 26)
France 1
(Papin 59)

Denmark 0
England 0

France 0
England 0

Sweden 1
(Brolin 58)
Denmark 0

Denmark 2
(Larsen 7, Elstrup 78)
France 1
(Papin 58)

Sweden 2
(Eriksson 51, Brolin 84)
England 1
(Platt 3)

	P	W	D	L	F	A	Pts
Sweden	3	2	1	0	4	2	5
Denmark	3	1	1	2	2	3	3
France	3	0	2	1	2	3	2
England	3	0	2	1	1	2	2

GROUP B

Holland 1
(Bergkamp 7)
Scotland 0

Germany 1
(Hässler 90)
CIS 1
(Dobrovolski 63)

Germany 2
(Riedle 29, Effenberg 47)
Scotland 0

Holland 0
CIS 0

Holland 3
(Rijkaard 3, Rob Witschge 15, Bergkamp 73)
Germany 1
(Klinsmann 53)

Scotland 3
(McStay 6, McClair 17, McAllister 83 pen)
CIS 0

	P	W	D	L	F	A	Pts
Holland	3	2	1	0	4	1	5
Germany	3	1	1	1	4	4	3
Scotland	3	1	0	2	3	3	2
CIS	3	0	2	1	1	4	2

SEMI-FINALS

Germany 3
(Hässler 11, Riedle 59, 88)
Sweden 2
(Brolin 64, Andersson 89)

Denmark 2
(H Larsen 5, 32)
Holland 2
(Bergkamp 23, Rijkaard 85)
(Denmark 5–4 on penalties)
after extra time

FINAL

(26 June, Nya Ullevi, Gothenburg)
Denmark 2
(Jensen 18, Vilfort 78)
Germany 0
HT: 1–0.
Att.: 37,000.
Ref.: Galler (Switzerland)

Denmark: Schmeichel, Sivebaek (Christiansen 66), K. Nielsen, L. Olsen, Piechnik, Christofte, Vilfort, J. Jensen, H Larsen, B. Laudrup, Povlsen.

Germany: Illgner, Reuter, Kohler, Helmer, Brehme, Buchwald, Effenberg (Thom 80), Sammer (Doll 46), Hässler, Klinsmann, Riedle.

1996 ENGLAND
Football comes home

By now the European Championship was well established as the top national team event after the World Cup itself. Pressure to reach the finals was growing more intense all the time. UEFA thus decided to ask potential hosts for 1996 to submit bids based on a tournament for the established eight nations but also for an enlarged 16-team competition.

As far as England were concerned, it was a case of the bigger the better. England's main club stadia had been redeveloped and converted into all-seater venues to comply with the recommendations of the Taylor report following the Hillsborough disaster. Add in the infrastructure, technological know-how and the attraction of "bringing football home" and England were streets ahead of the potential opposition. (In fact, a tacit agreement had already been reached

early on in the process that England would not bid to host the 1998 World Cup in return for French support for Euro 96.)

The Football Association entrusted its foreign affairs expert, Glen Kirton, to organize Euro 96. His vision was that of a peaceful, enjoyable celebration of the game which would do much to transform the image of English football, tarnished by hooliganism for the best – or worst – part of two decades.

From that standpoint, the tournament was a massive success, a major public relations triumph for the game in general and England in particular. The only regret England took from the tournament was that Terry Venables's team did not also win the event for the first time. Instead England were victims of an old jinx – a semi-final penalty shoot-out – and it was their German conquerors who went on to beat the outsiders from the Czech Republic 2–1 in the Final.

Germany thus secured a record

third European Championship success and did so by taking advantage of the controversial golden goal rule. Substitute striker Oliver Bierhoff scored the event-stopping winner five minutes into extra time at Wembley. It was the first time a major senior tournament had been settled by this method.

Not that England had appeared likely even to reach the last four when they struggled for a 1–1 draw against

NEW WEMBLEY WIZARDS Skipper Jürgen Klinsmann and Germany's latest European champions.

Switzerland in Group A in the Opening Match. The Opening Ceremony had featured a tableaux in which St George slew a huge dragon. But England were not able to emulate their patron saint until further down the group matches when they defeated old enemy Scotland 2–0 and then annihilated Holland 4–1 with the controversial Paul Gascoigne in irresistible mood.

Group B opened with a temperamental clash between Bulgaria and Spain at Elland Road, Leeds. Bulgarian defender Petar Hubchev and Spain striker Juan Pizzi were sent off in a 1–1 draw from which Spain snatched a point courtesy of a first-touch goal from newly arrived substitute Alfonso. Bulgaria had finished fourth at the 1994 World Cup yet they fell here in the first round along with eastern European neighbours Romania. Instead, Spain qualified along with a French side who had controversially ignored the claims of English-based forwards Eric Cantona and David Ginola.

In Group C, Croatia barely justified their pre-event billing as dark horses – except in one superb victory which effectively eliminated holders Denmark, whose goalkeeper, Peter Schmeichel, was given a torrid time by the teasing footwork of Croat striker Davor Suker. The Croats still qualified for the quarter-finals, however, along with a Portuguese side whose high-speed movement off the ball deserved a more effective strike force than that provided by shot-shy Ricardo Sa Pinto and Joao Vieira Pinto.

It was not only Portugal who needed such a marksman in their team. Italy were the shock first-round failures precisely because they could not score the goals they needed.

First-time out the Italians might have beaten Russia more easily than 2–1 had Fabrizio Ravanelli converted two easy chances in the closing 10 minutes after he arrived as a substitute. Second-time out Italy should have at least salvaged a draw instead of losing a thrilling match against the Czech Republic. Coach Arrigo Sacchi took the blame for having made half a dozen unnecessary changes.

That shock defeat left Italy needing to beat group leaders Germany at Old Trafford while depending, simultaneously, on the outcome of the Czechs' Anfield clash with homeward-bound Russia. Italy dominated all the match but Gianfranco Zola fluffed an early penalty and Germany held out for a 0–0 draw thanks to their masterful defensive discipline. They qualified for the quarter-finals along with the Czechs, who equalized in the last minute.

RESULTS 1996

GROUP A

England 1 (Shearer 23)
Switzerland 1 (Turkyilmaz 82 (pen.)

Holland 0
Scotland 0

Holland 2 (Jordi 66, Bergkamp 79)
Switzerland 0

England 2 (Shearer 52, Gascoigne 79)
Scotland 0

Scotland 1 (McCoist 36)
Switzerland 0

England 4 (Shearer 23 pen, 57, Sheringham 51, 62)
Holland 1
(Kluivert 78)

	P W D L F A Pts
England	3 2 1 0 7 2 7
Holland	3 1 1 1 3 4 4
Scotland	3 1 1 1 1 2 4
Switzerland	3 0 1 2 1 4 1

GROUP B

Spain 1 (Alfonso 74)
Bulgaria 1 (Stoichkov 65 (pen.))

France 1 (Dugarry 25)
Romania 0

Bulgaria 1 (Stoichkov 3)
Romania 0

France 1 (Djorkaeff 48)
Spain 1 (Caminero 85)

France 3 (Blanc 20, Penev o.g. 62, Loko 90)
Bulgaria 1 (Stoichkov 68)

Spain 2 (Manjarin 11, Amor 84)
Romania 1 (Raducioiu 29)

	P W D L F A Pts
France	3 2 1 0 5 2 7
Spain	3 1 2 0 4 3 5
Bulgaria	3 1 1 1 3 4 4
Romania	3 0 0 3 1 4 0

GROUP C

Germany 2 (Ziege 26, Moller 32)
Czech Republic 0

Italy 2 (Casiraghi 5, 52)
Russia 1 (Tsimbalar 20)

Czech Rep 2 (Nedved 5, Bejbl 36)
Italy 1 (Chiesa 18)

Germany 3 (Sammer 56, Klinsmann 77, 90)
Russia 0

Italy 0
Germany 0

Czech Rep 3 (Suchoparek 7, Kuka 19, Smicer 89)
Russia 3 (Mostovoi 49, Tetradze 54, Beschastnikh 85)

	P W D L F A Pts
Germany	3 2 1 0 5 0 7
Czech Rep.	3 1 1 1 5 6 4
Italy	3 1 1 1 3 3 4
Russia	3 0 1 2 4 8 1

GROUP D

Denmark 1 (B. Laudrup 22)
Portugal 1 (Sa Pinto 53)

Croatia 1 (Vlaovic 85)
Turkey 0

Portugal 1 (Fernando Couto 66)
Turkey 0

Croatia 3 (Suker 53 pen, 89, Boban 80)
Denmark 0

Portugal 3 (Figo 4, Joao Pinto 33, Domingos 83)
Croatia 0

Denmark 3 (B. Laudrup 50, 84, A. Nielsen 69)
Turkey 0

	P W D L F A Pts
Portugal	3 2 1 0 5 1 7
Croatia	3 2 0 1 4 3 6
Denmark	3 1 1 1 4 4 4
Turkey	3 0 0 3 0 5 0

QUARTER-FINALS

England 0
Spain 0
(England 4–2 on penalties) after extra time

France 0
Holland 0
(France 5–4 on penalties) after extra time

Germany 2 (Klinsmann 21 pen, Sammer 59)
Croatia 1 (Suker 51)

Czech Republic 1 (Poborsky 53)
Portugal 0

SEMI-FINALS

Czech Republic 0
France 0
(Czech Republic 6–5 on penalties) after extra time

Germany 1 (Kuntz 16)
England 1 (Shearer 3)
(Germany 6–5 on penalties) after extra time

FINAL

(June 30, Wembley Stadium)
Germany 2 (Bierhoff 73, 94)
Czech Republic 1 (Berger 58 (pen.))
(Germany on Golden Goal)
HT: 0–0. 90 min.: 1–1.
Att.: 76,000.
Ref.: Pairetto (It)

Germany: Köpke, Babbel, Sammer, Helmer, Strunz, Hässler, Eilts (Bode 46), Scholl (Bierhoff 69), Ziege, Klinsmann, Kuntz.

Czech Republic: Kouba, Hornak, Rada, Kadlec, Suchoparek, Poborsky (Smicer 88), Nedved, Bejbl, Berger, Nemec, Kuka.

GOLDEN MOMENT *Stefan Kuntz salutes Oliver Bierhoff's Wembley winner.*

Oddly, the quality of football on view nose-dived once the knock-out stages had been reached. Only one of the quarter-finals provided any serious entertainment and even that – England vs. Spain – had to be settled by one of the six penalty shoot-outs which were ultimately needed.

England were fortunate first when French referee Marc Batta twice refused apparently justified penalty claims against Paul Gascoigne and Tony Adams. More fortune followed with victory in the penalty shoot-out. France defeated a disappointing Holland the same way. The Czech Republic, quite surprisingly, defeated

Portugal 1–0 with the goal of the tournament from Karel Poborsky, while Germany managed to overcome the wilful violence of Croatia by 2–1.

Attacking sweeper Sammer was the German hero: his forward dash led to the handling offence which provided Germany's opening penalty goal by Jürgen Klinsmann, then Sammer scored the second himself. His contribution would ultimately earn him the accolade of European Footballer of the Year.

Both semi-finals went to penalties. The Czechs defeated France after a match which was as depressingly dull as England vs. Germany was dramatic.

England opened the scoring almost immediately through the tournament's five-goal top scorer Alan Shearer; injury-ravaged Germany hit

back within the first quarter-of-an-hour through Stefan Kuntz. It was still 1–1 at full-time. Both sides were within inches of the golden goal in extra time but when it went to penalties Andy Moller held his nerve and scored with the decisive kick after Gareth Southgate had failed.

Playmaker Moller missed the Final through suspension after collecting two yellow cards and his absence threatened to prove significant when Patrik Berger shot the Czechs ahead from a 59th-minute penalty.

Germany had lost to underdogs in the Final four years earlier of course in Sweden and history appeared about to repeat itself ... until coach Berti Vogts brought on substitute centre-forward Bierhoff. Within four minutes Bierhoff had headed the Germans level and

then, in the fourth minute of extra time, he fired home the most golden of goals.

Klinsmann climbed the 39 steps to Wembley's Royal Box to receive, and hold aloft, the Henri Delaunay Trophy. Germany had triumphed on the pitch. But football itself was the greatest winner from Euro 96.

The European Championship looked forward to its first jointly hosted event, in Belgium and Holland in 2000, and England dreamed of bidding to host the World Cup in 2006 on the strength of their success as Euro 96 hosts. As in many other walks of international life, they would find Germany in the way. A decision on who plays host for the second World Cup of the 21st century will be taken by FIFA's executive committee in the year 2000.

GERMANY'S EUROPEAN CHAMPIONSHIP-WINNING COACHES

HELMUT SCHÖN

Schön, born on 15 September 1915, guided Germany to European Championship success in 1972 and to World Cup victory in 1974. He died just four months before the 1996 European finals, aged 80. Schön was a star inside-forward in the 1940s who played his best club football for the old Dresden club and then moved to Berlin after the Second World War. He scored 17 goals in 16 internationals for Germany before retiring to become one of the most successful national team coaches in world football history. Schön managed the Saar national team which was beaten by West Germany in the qualifying competition for the 1954 World Cup and so impressed opposing manager Sepp Herberger that he was later contracted as Germany's No 2. Schön succeeded Herberger in 1964, taking West Germany to World Cup runners-up two years later. Under Schön they were third in 1970 and winners in 1974. In the European Championship, Schön's Germany won in 1972 and were runners-up to Czechoslovakia, only after a penalty shoot-out, four years later. He retired after the 1978 World Cup finals and duly handed over the reins to his assistant, Jupp Derwall.

SCHÖN not only succeeded Sepp Herberger but emulated his achievements.

JUPP DERWALL

Derwall, born on 10 March 1927, was only Germany's fourth national manager (after Otto Nerz, Herberger and Schön) when he was appointed in the summer of 1978 after the loss of the World Cup in Argentina. Derwall had been assistant to Schön. In fact, he had already made a winning debut as manager in a caretaker capacity in spring of 1978, when Germany beat England 2–1 and Schön was absent because of illness. Derwall made his name as a player with Fortuna Dusseldorf in the 1950s when he also played twice at full-back for West Germany. After retiring he followed a similar path to Schön, coaching in the Saarland before joining the DFB staff. As national manager he guided to Germany to victory in the 1980 European Championship and then took them to runners-up spot at the 1982 World Cup. A disappointing exit in the first round of the 1984 European finals led to Derwall's resignation. He later worked briefly in Turkish club football.

DERWALL paid a heavy price for the loss of the European title.

HANS-HUBERT "BERTI" VOGTS

Vogts, born on 30 December 1946, played 96 times for West Germany, mainly as a terrier-like right-back. A qualified toolmaker, he spent 14 years (1965–79) with his only professional club, Borussia Mönchengladbach. Trophies as a player included the World Cup in 1974; the UEFA Cup twice; German league champion five times; and German cup winner once. Vogts was voted Footballer of the Year in 1971 and 1979.

He then joined the DFB coaching staff in 1979 – first as youth, then as under-21 team coach. Vogts became assistant to national manager Franz Beckenbauer and succeeded him after the 1990 World Cup victory in Italy. Vogts guided Germany to runners-up spot in the European Championship in 1992 and to the World Cup quarter-finals in 1994. Victory at Euro 96 was generally considered an overdue reward for his dedication and thorough command of the job. For example, asked whether his players volunteered to take penalties in the semi-final shoot-out against England, Vogts said: "Certainly not. I told the players which ones would take penalties and I told them in which order they would take them. I even told Möller that his penalty would be the winner ... ."

VOGTS As demanding a manager as he had been a player.

THE WORLD CUP

Towards the end of the 1920s, it became clear that, with much of mainstream football having turned professional, the Olympic Games, with its amateur ethic, was no longer credible as a world championship. Professionalism had developed initially in Europe whose officials provided the greatest impetus towards a World Cup, notably FIFA president Jules Rimet.

A slow start

Unfortunately, only four European nations then undertook the long Atlantic crossing to take part in the inaugural finals in Uruguay – Rimet even had to badger his own reluctant French federation to send a team. The rest of the European challenge was made up of Romania, Belgium and Yugoslavia. Continental powers such as Italy, Germany, Hungary and Austria all ignored the event. As for the British home countries, they had already withdrawn from FIFA in what now appears to have been a nonsensical dispute over so-called broken-time payments for amateurs.

A Frenchman, Lucien Laurent, made history by scoring the first goal in World Cup history, 19 minutes into the opening match between France and Mexico.

The tournament, featuring only 13 nations, comprised four first round mini-leagues – one of four teams and the others of three each. Argentina, Yugoslavia, hosts Uruguay and the United States were the four group winners who qualified for the semi-finals. Yugoslavia then crashed 6–1 to Uruguay, while Argentina thrashed the US by the same margin. Uruguay went on to defeat their southern neighbours 4–2 in the Final.

Italy dominate

The 1934 finals were awarded to Italy, whose fascist dictator, Benito Mussolini, saw the event as an ideal vehicle for political propaganda. It was propaganda which was wasted as far as most of South America was concerned since both Uruguay and Argentina stayed away. That left the field clear for manager Vittorio Pozzo to make history by turning Italy into Europe's first World Cup-holders – albeit with the assistance of three Italian-based Argentines in wingers Guaita and Orsi and rugged centre-half Luisito Monti, who had been a World Cup runner-up with Argentina in 1930.

Czechoslovakia, in the Final in Rome, appeared not to have read Mussolini's script and dared take the lead against their Italian hosts, through Antonin Puc, with 19 minutes remaining. Raimundo Orso equalized 10 minutes later, and only in extra-time did veteran Angelo Schiavio – who had run himself to a near standstill and been pushed out to the right wing – strike the winner.

Pozzo rebuilt his Italian team in radical fashion for the Cup defence in France in 1938. The only survivors from 1934 were his star inside-forwards, Giuseppe Meazza and Gino Ferrari. He envisaged one of the biggest dangers being Brazil with their explosive centre-forward Leonidas. But when the teams met in the semi-finals an overconfident Brazil rested Leonidas ... to keep him fresh for the Final! A grateful Italy won 2–1, then defeated Hungary 4–2 in what was to be the second successive all-European Final.

Ottorino Barassi, a senior official of the Italian federation, hid the World Cup trophy under his bed during the

DOUBLE DELIGHT Manager Vittorio Pozzo and his Italian world champions in 1938.

war to save it from being melted down for the war effort. It was thus not seen again in public until the 1950 finals in Brazil.

Post-war expansion

Like the 1930 finals, the 1950s finals were a South American fiesta. Italy, their preparations wrecked by the Superga air disaster a year earlier in which 10 internationals died, never looked like bringing the Cup back to Europe. Nor did England, competing for the first time and crashing out after a notorious 1–0 defeat by the United States. Sweden and Spain did finish third and fourth in the climactic mini-league but hosts Brazil played the most spectacular football before losing the final match – sensationally – by 2–1 to Uruguay.

Hungary, in 1954, were even greater favourites than Brazil had been in 1950. They had been unbeaten over a four-year term which included historic 6–3 and 7–1 victories over England at Wembley and in Budapest, respectively. Inside-forwards Sandor Kocsis and skipper Ferenc Puskas starred within a revolutionary tactical concept which had the centre-forward, confusingly for opponents, dropping back into midfield.

In the semi-finals Hungary justified all the praise heaped upon them by defeating holders Uruguay 4–2 after extra time in what was was hailed as the greatest match of all time. But Puskas had missed the match through injury and Hungary gambled on recalling him for the Final against West Germany. It appeared to pay off when they seized a 2–0 lead inside eight minutes. But Hungary relaxed fatally. Germany hit back and were level long before the interval. Then a late goal from right winger Helmut Rahn manufactured one of the greatest World Cup upsets.

Brazil dominate

Not for 12 years would the old world celebrate another European success in the World Cup as Brazil, in both 1958 and 1962, produced the results which provided an overdue double reward for years of providing the world with technically spectacular football.

Europe could not live with Brazil – and superstars such as Didi, Vava, Garrincha and, above all, Pele – in either 1958 or 1962. In 1958, Brazil became the first nation to win the World Cup in the "away" continent as they swatted hosts Sweden by 5–2 in the Final in Stockholm. Pele, just 17 years old, scored twice.

Four years later, in Chile, Czechoslovakia finished runners-up for a second time as they were rolled over 3–1 in Santiago. Czechoslovakia scored first in the Final through midfield general Josef Masopust, but Brazil – even in the absence of the injured Pele – were on a different plane.

Europe's only consolation was that Moroccan-born Frenchman Just Fontaine, in 1958, set a record which still stands by scoring 13 goals in the finals tournament.

England win at home

The World Cup returned to European

HITTING BACK Max Morlock's stunning revival goal against Hungary in the 1954 Final.

hands in 1966 when England's 4–2 extra-time victory over West Germany earned a knighthood for manager Alf Ramsey and places in legend for skipper Bobby Moore, Bobby Charlton and striker Geoff Hurst – the only man to have scored a World Cup Final hat-trick.

Yet England found goal-scoring tough in the first round, being held goalless in the Opening Match by Uruguay and beating Mexico and France "only" 2–0 apiece. No such problems lay in store for West Germany. A brilliant youngster named Franz Beckenbauer inspired a five-goal show first time out against Switzerland.

Brazil were kicked out of the tournament by stop-at-nothing defenders from Bulgaria and Portugal, while Italy succumbed to a historic 1–0 upset at the hands of the mysterious North Koreans – who very nearly

ENGLAND'S GLORY *after victory over West Germany in extra time.*

MUNICH MASTER *Gerd Müller turns away after scoring the winner against Holland in Munich.*

repeated the medicine against Portugal in the quarter-finals. Portugal went 3–0 down before recovering to win 5–3 and go on to achieve their best-ever third place thanks to the nine-goal power-shooting of Eusebio.

Four years later, in Mexico, the Germans took dramatic revenge over England when they recovered from 2–0 down to beat – and eliminate – the holders 3–2 in the quarter-finals. The semi-finals then saw the Germans feature in an even greater contest which they lost eventually to Italy 4–3. The Italians, mentally and physically drained, were then no match in the Final for Brazil, whose 4–1 win secured the first World Cup hat-trick.

Hosts reign on

Host advantage proved decisive in both succeeding World Cups. West Germany won on home soil in 1974 even though Holland – with their revolutionary total football – were, by general agreement, the finest of the contesting nations. Referee Jack Taylor awarded the first-ever Final

penalty within two minutes of the kick-off in Munich. But West Germany, thanks to a penalty equalizer of their own and a typically opportunist strike from Gerd Müller, won their second World Cup 20 years after the first.

Argentina became, in 1978, the second successive host winners. Like West Germany four years earlier, they beat Holland in the Final – though the Argentines needed extra time and the intimidating support of their fanatical followers.

Italy finished fourth and had the extra consolation of unearthing a new hero in quick-silver centre-forward Paolo Rossi – whose goals shot them to their own World Cup hat-trick in Spain in 1982.

Coach Enzo Bearzot took a huge gamble in including Rossi, who had played only the final three games of the league season after a two-year ban for his alleged involvement in a match-fixing scandal. But he responded with a hat-trick in a marvellous 3–2 second-round defeat of Brazil and then the opening goal in the 3–1 despatch of West Germany in the Final in Madrid.

The Maradona era

World Cup football then entered, for both better and worse, the era of Diego Maradona. The greatest natural talent since Pele, the youthful Maradona had savoured a tempestuous World Cup debut when he was sent off against Brazil in a group match in the 1982 finals. But his genius persuaded first Barcelona and then Napoli to pay world record transfer fees to bring him to Europe.

Every four years, of course, he turned his back on Europe to lead Argentina at the World Cup. In 1986 that meant inspiring his country to victory in Mexico, albeit amid controversy. In Argentina's quarter-final against England, Maradona punched one of the most notorious goals in World Cup history and, a few minutes later, displayed the other side of his talent by scoring one of the finest individual goals in World Cup history. In the Final against West Germany, Maradona was well-policed by Lothar

MAGICAL MARCO *Goal-scorer Tardelli takes possession of the World Cup for Italy.*

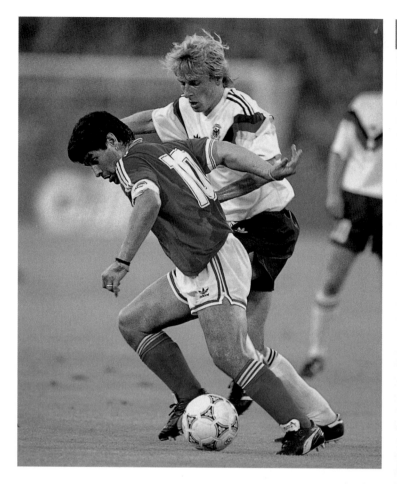

GIANTS OF TWO WORLDS *Maradona against Klinsmann in Rome in 1990.*

Matthäus, but after the Germans had hit back twice in the closing stages to draw level at 2–2, it was Maradona's pass which sent away Jorge Burruchaga for the winner.

Maradona also led Argentina to the Final in Italy four years later. Again they met a German team managed by Franz Beckenbauer with the World Cup at stake. But this was a mean-spirited Argentine side who played with a chip on their shoulder. Cameroon, from Africa, were the surprise force of the finals, and only naivety cost them a 3–2 defeat by England in extra-time in the quarter-finals.

England were also taken to extra time in the semi-final by West Germany. The score was still 1–1 after the 120 minutes when Stuart Pearce and Chris Waddle missed the penalties which justified Paul Gascoigne's tears. Ironically, the Germans then went on to beat Argentina in the Final with a "real" penalty – converted by Andy Brehme after a trip on striker Rudi Voller.

Maradona grabbed the headlines

again, in the United States in 1994. The Americans were controversial but generously enthusiastic hosts. A clamp-down on cynical time-wasting, the feigning of injury and the tackle from behind provided a glorious advertisement for the game. Seven of the eight quarter-finalist nations were European. Only Brazil squeezed in among them on behalf of the rest of the world. Argentina had fallen to Romania in the second round, their spirit and morale punctured after Maradona had failed – for the second time – a dope test.

Europe's other title contenders were Germany, Holland, Sweden, Bulgaria, Spain and Italy – and it was the Italians who faced Brazil in the Final. The goals of Roberto Baggio had brought Italy through but, when the Final ended goal-less after extra-time and was resolved for the first time by shoot-out, it was Baggio who missed the decisive penalty.

South America, courtesy of Brazil, Argentina and Uruguay, have won the World Cup eight times; Europe, through Germany, Italy and England, have won seven. Will France '98 widen the gap ... or narrow it?

URUGUAY 1930
(30 July, Centenario, Montevideo)

Uruguay 4 (Dorado 12, Cea 58, Iriarte 68, Castro 89)

Argentina 2 (Peucelle 20, Stabile 37)
HT: 1–2.
Att.: 93,000.
Ref.: Langenus (Bel)

Uruguay: Ballesteros, Nasazzi, Mascheroni, Andrade, Fernandez, Gestido, Dorado, Scarone, Castro, Cea, Iriarte.
Argentina: Botazzo, Della Torre, Paternoster, J. Evaristo, Monti, Suarez, Peucelle, Varallo, Stabile, Ferreyra, M. Evaristo.
Third place: Not played.
Top scorer: Stabile (Arg) 8 goals.

ITALY 1934
(10 June, Flaminio, Rome)

Italy 2 (Orsi 81, Schiavio 95)

Czechoslovakia 1
(Puc 71)
after extra time
HT: 0–0. 90 min.: 1–1.
Att.: 55,000.
Ref.: Eklind (Swe)

Italy: Combi, Monzeglio, Allemandi, Ferraris, Monti, Bertolini, Guaita, Meazza, Schiavio, Ferrari, Orsi.
Czechoslovakia: Planicka, Zenisek, Ctyrocky, Kostalek, Cambal, Krcil, Junek, Svoboda, Sobotka, Nejedly, Puc.
Third place: Germany 3, Austria 2.
Top scorer: Nejedly (Cz) 5 goals.

FRANCE 1938
(19 June, Stade Colombes, Paris)

Italy 4 (Colaussi 5, 35, Piola 16, 82)

Hungary 2 (Titkos 7, Sarosi 70)
HT: 2–1.
Att.: 55,000.
Ref.: Capdeville (Fr)

Italy: Oliveiri, Foni, Rava, Serantoni, Andreolo, Locatelli, Biavati, Meazza, Piola, Ferrari, Colaussi.
Hungary: Szabo, Polgar, Biro, Szalay, Szucs, Lazar, Sas, Vincze, Sarosi, Zsengeller, Titkos.

Third place & top scorer (continued)
Third place: Brazil 4, Sweden 2.
Top scorer: Leonidas (Brz) 8 goals.

BRAZIL 1950
(16 July, Maracana, Rio de Janeiro)

Uruguay 2 (Schaffino 66, Ghiggia 79)

Brazil 1 (Friaca 48)
HT: 0–0.
Att.: 199,854.
Ref.: Reader (Eng)

Uruguay: Maspoli, M. Gonzalez, Tejera, Gambetta, Varela, Andrade, Ghiggia, Perez, Miguez, Schiaffino, Moran.
Brazil: Barbosa, Augusto, Juvenal, Bauer, Danilo, Bigode, Friaca, Zizinho, Ademir, Jair, Chico.
Third place: Sweden (league format).
Top scorer: Ademir (Brz) 9 goals.

SWITZERLAND 1954
(4 July, Wankdorf, Berne)

West Germany 3 (Morlock 11, Rahn 16, 83)

Hungary 2 (Puskas 6, Czibor 8)
HT: 2–2.
Att.: 60,000.
Ref.: Ling (Eng)

Germany: Turek, Posipal, Kohlmeyer, Eckel, Liebrich, Mai, Rahn, Morlock, O. Walter, F. Walter, Schäfer.
Hungary: Grosics, Buzansky, Lantos, Bozsik, Lorant, Zakarias, Czibor, Kocsis, Hidegkuti, Puskas, M. Toth.
Third place: Austria 3, Uruguay 1.
Top scorer: Kocsis (Hun) 11 goals.

SWEDEN 1958
(29 June, Rasunda, Stockholm)

Brazil 5 (Vava 9, 32, Pele 55, 89, Zagallo 68)

Sweden 2 (Liedholm 4, Simonsson 80)
HT: 2–1.
Att.: 49,737.
Ref.: Guigue (Fr)

Brazil: Gilmar, D. Santos, N. Santos, Zito, Bellini, Orlando,

WORLD CUP FINAL RESULTS

Garrincha, Didi, Vava, Pele, Zagalo.
Sweden: Svensson, Bergmark, Axbom, Borjesson, Gustavsson, Parling, Hamrin, Gren, Simonsson, Liedholm, Skoglund.
Third place: France 6, West Germany 3.
Top scorer: Fontaine (Fr) 13 goals.

CHILE 1962
(17 June, Nacional, Santiago)
Brazil 3 (Amarildo 18, Zito 69, Vava 77)
Czechoslovakia 1
(Masopust 16)
HT: 1–1.
Att.: 68,679.
Ref.: Latishev (SU)

Brazil: Gilmar, D Santos, N Santos, Zito, Mauro, Zozimo, Garrincha, Didi, Vava, Amarildo, Zagalo.
Czechoslovakia: Scroiff, Tichy, Novak, Pluskal, Popluhar, Masopust, Pospichal, Scherer, Kvasnak, Kadraba, Jelinek.
Third place: Chile 1, Yugoslavia 0.
Top scorers: V. Ivanov (SU), L Sanchez (Ch), Garrincha, Vava (Brz), Albert (Hun), Jerkovic (Yug) 4 goals each.

ENGLAND 1966
(30 July, Wembley Stadium)
England 4 (Hurst 19, 100, 119, Peters 77)
West Germany 2 (Haller 13, Weber 89)
after extra time
HT: 1–1. 90 min.: 2–2.
Att.: 96,924.
Ref.: Dienst (Swz)

England: Banks, Cohen, Wilson, Stiles, J. Charlton, Moore, Ball, Hunt, R. Charlton, Hurst, Peters.
West Germany: Tilkowski, Hottges, Schnellinger, Beckenbauer, Schulz, Weber, Haller, Overath, Seeler, Held, Emmerich.
Third place: Portugal 2, Soviet Union 1.
Top scorer: Eusebio (Por) 9 goals.

MEXICO 1970
(21 June, Azteca, Mexico City)
Brazil 4 (Pele 18, Gerson 66, Jairzinho 71, Carlos Alberto 86)
Italy 1 (Boninsegna 37)
HT: 1–1.
Att.: 107,000.
Ref.: Glockner (EG)

Brazil: Felix, Carlos Alberto, Brito, Wilson Piazza, Everaldo, Clodoaldo, Gerson, Rivelino, Jairzinho, Tostao, Pele.
Italy: Albertosi, Burgnich, Cera, Rosato, Facchetti, Bertini (Juliano 75), Domenghini, De Sisti, Mazzola, Boninsegna (Rivera 84), Riva.
Third place: West Germany 1, Uruguay 0.
Top scorer: G. Müller (WG) 10 goals.

W. GERMANY 1974
(7 July, Olympiastadion, Munich)
West Germany 2 (Breitner 25 (pen.), G. Müller 43)
Holland 1 (Neeskens 2 (pen.))
HT: 2–1.
Att.: 77,833.
Ref.: Taylor (Eng)

West Germany: Maier, Vogts, Schwarzenbeck, Beckenbauer, Breitner, Bonhof, U. Hoeness, Overath, Grabowski, G. Müller, Holzenbein.
Holland: Jongbloed, Suurbier, Rijsbergen (De Jong 69), Haan, Krol, Jansen, Van Hanegem, Neeskens, Rep, Cruyff, Rensenbrink (R. Van de Kerkhof 46).
Third place: Poland 1, Brazil 0.
Top scorer: Lato (Pol) 7 goals.

ARGENTINA 1978
(25 June, Monumental, Buenos Aires)
Argentina 3 (Kempes 37, 104, Bertoni 114)
Holland 1
(Nanninga 81)
after extra time
HT: 1–0. 90 min.: 1–1.
Att.: 77,260.
Ref.: Gonella (It)

Argentina: Fillol, Olguin, Galvan, Passarella, Tarantini, Ardiles (Larrosa 66), Gallego, Kempes, Bertoni, Luque, Ortiz (Houseman 75).

Holland: Jongbloed, Jansen (Suurbier 73), Brandts, Krol, Poortvliet, W. Van de Kerkhof, Neeskens, Haan, R. Van de Kerkhof, Rep (Nanninga 59), Rensenbrink.
Third place: Brazil 2, Italy 1.
Top scorer: Kempes (Arg) 6 goals.

SPAIN 1982
(11 July, Estadio Santiago Bernabeu, Madrid)
Italy 3 (Rossi 56, Tardelli 69, Altobelli 80)
West Germany 1 (Breitner 82)
HT: 0–0.
Att.: 90,000.
Ref.: Coelho (Brz)

Italy: Zoff, Bergomi, Collovati, Scirea, Gentile, Cabrini, Tardelli, Oriali, Conti, Rossi, Graziani (Altobelli 8 [Causio 88]).
West Germany: Schumacher, Kaltz, K. Forster, B. Forster, Stielike, Briegel, Dremmler (Hrubesch 63), Breitner, Rummenigge (H. Müller 70), Fischer, Littbarski.
Third place: Poland 3, France 2.
Top scorer: Rossi (It) 6 goals.

MEXICO 1986
(29 June, Azteca, Mexico City)
Argentina 3 (Brown 22, Valdano 56, Burruchaga 84)
West Germany 2 (Rummenigge 73, Voller 82)
HT: 1–0.
Att.: 114,590.
Ref.: Arppi Filho (Brz)

Argentina: Pumpido, Cuciuffo, Brown, Ruggeri, Giusti, Burruchaga (Trobbiani 89), Batista, Enrique, Olarticoechea, Maradona, Valdano.
West Germany: Schumacher, Berthold, Jakobs, K. Forster, Briegel, Brehme, Matthäus, Magath (D. Hoeness 63), Eder, Rummenigge, K. Allofs (Voller 46).
Third place: France 4, Belgium 2.
Top scorer: Lineker (Eng) 6 goals.

ITALY 1990
(8 July, Olimpico, Rome)
West Germany 1 (Brehme 84 (pen.))
Argentina 0
HT: 0–0.
Att.: 73,603.
Ref.: Codesal (Mex)

West Germany: Illgner, Berthold (Reuter 74), Kohler, Augenthaler, Buchwald, Brehme, Hässler, Matthäus, Littbarski, Voller, Klinsmann.
Argentina: Goycochea, Lorenzo, Sensini, Serrizuela, Ruggeri (Monzon 46*), Simon, Jose Horacio Basualdo, Burruchaga (Calderon 53), Maradona, Troglio, Dezotti**.
*Monzon sent off, 65 min.;
**Dezotti sent off, 86 min.
Third place: Italy 2, England 1.
Top scorer: Schillaci (It) 6 goals.

UNITED STATES 1994
(17 July, Rose Bowl, Pasadena)
Brazil 0
Italy 0
(Brazil 3–2 on penalties) after extra time
HT: 0–0. 90 min.: 0–0.
Att.: 94,000.
Ref.: Puhl (Hun).

Brazil: Taffarel, Jorginho (Cafu 21), Marcio Santos, Aldair, Branco, Mazinho, Mauro Silvo, Dunga, Zinho (Viola 106), Bebeto, Romario.
Italy: Pagliuca, Mussi (Apolloni 34), Maldini, Baresi, Benarrivo, Donadoni, Albertini, D. Baggio (Evani 95), Berti, Massaro, R. Baggio.
Third place: Sweden 4, Bulgaria 0.
Top scorers: Salenko (Rus), Stoichkov (Bul) 6 goals each.

THE COUNTRIES

Football's international seesaw is balanced on the power of the national associations. Those in Europe provide the organizational bedrock of FIFA and UEFA and strive to control the ambitions of the clubs and players under their authority. Yet the likes of Albania and the Faroe Islands are just as important as England, Germany and Italy. After all, it's a game of two teams ...

ALBANIA

Federata Shqiptare e Futbollit
Founded: 1930
Joined FIFA: 1932

Albania have never qualified for the finals of either the World Cup or the European Championship. Even the country's recent return to comparatively normal international relations with the rest of Europe, brought no immediate respite for a national team who have ranked consistently among the minnows of European football.

Indeed, the speed with which all Albania's best players headed off into the more lucrative distance, notably to Greece, exacerbated the federation's problems in rebuilding a national image which had become tarnished through years of self-imposed political and sporting isolation.

For instance, the national team once went five years without an international against European rivals because they could not find "politically compatible" opponents; again, when Celtic once had to play a European club tie in Tirana the Albanian authorities authorized only nine visas for players! It took a protest to UEFA and an expulsion threat to get a full team in.

In essence, more than half a century of sporting potential was lost, because football had been organized first at the start of the 1900s. The introductions, of course, were made by foreign residents. A fledgling club named Independencia was launched in Shkoder but the first championship – exclusively organized among the foreigners – collapsed in chaos at the outbreak of World War One.

It took the influence of various occupying forces in the 1920s to reintroduce the game and this time the locals were encouraged to join in. In 1928 King Zog came to the throne and sports activities were, for the first time, recognized as a legitimate area of governmental concern. In 1930 a Sports Ministry was set up and this spawned, two years later, a quasi-autonomous football federation.

A national league was dominated initially by SK Tirana, and Albania even went as far as to join FIFA in 1932. Unfortunately political unrest in the Balkans meant that it was not until 1946 that the national team made their debut, against neighbouring Yugoslavia.

Several outstanding players – Riza Lushta, Loro Borici and Naim Krieziu – played in Italy after Albania's annexation in the early 1940s. But the country's finest all-round players have been Panajot Pano, a star of the 1950s and early 1960s – whose son also became an international – and, most recently, Sulejman Demollari.

The civil unrest which erupted in Albania in late 1996, caused by the sudden collapse of "pyramid" savings schemes, brought chaos to this already backward country, and led to football's suspension for a time – a further blow to the game's development here.

ANDORRA

Federation Football d'Andorre
Founded: 1994
Joined FIFA: 1996

Andorra, a tiny mountainous country best known for skiing and duty-free shopping, became Europe's latest football nation in the summer of 1996 ... with only 300 registered players.

ARMENIA

Football Federation of Armenia
Founded: 1992
Joined FIFA: 1992

Armenia achieved independence after the Soviet Union's collapse. Leading club Ararat Yerevan had featured regularly in the old Soviet top division. Star player was midfielder Khoren Oganesyan, who became first national coach of Armenia.

AUSTRIA

Osterreichischer Fussball-Bund
Founded: 1904
Joined FIFA: 1905

Austria's greatest days remain the inter-war years which were dominated by the legendary Wunderteam – created by one of international football's outstanding early legislators, Hugo Meisl.

Son of a Viennese banking family, Meisl ran the youthful Austrian federation in the early years of the century, brought in the legendary English coach, Jimmy Hogan, and signed the Konrad brothers, from MTK Budapest, on behalf of FK Austria. That turned them into continental Europe's first full-time professionals, inspirations for the man who was to become perhaps the country's greatest-ever player, Matthias Sindelar.

Nicknamed Der Papierene (the Man of Paper) because he was so slim, centre-forward Sindelar was a superstar almost half a century before the term was coined. He led FK Austria to success in the Mitropa Cup and Austria to fourth place at the 1934 World Cup before tragically committing suicide after the German Anschluss of 1938.

After World War Two, Austrian football rebuilt quickly. There were more fine players, among whom Ernst Ocwirk – nicknamed Clockwork – was the last of the attacking centre-halves and Gerhardt Hanappi a great all-rounder.

Austria had been the first continental team to beat Scotland, had given England a real fright at Stamford Bridge in 1929 – England scraped a 4–3 win – had been semi-finalists at the 1934 World Cup and were present again at the finals of 1954 and 1958. But, in the 1960s,

HAPPIER TIMES Austria's Robert Pecl robs Czechoslovakia's Ivo Knoflicek at the 1990 World Cup.

Austrian football hit a slump. Crowds fell and many clubs were forced into mergers to stay alive.

Even FK Austria had to merge with the Wiener Athletik Club and rely on tobacco sponsorship to stay solvent. But they recovered and, in 1978, became the first Austrian club to reach a European final – losing 4–0 to Anderlecht in the Cup-winners Cup Final in Paris.

That same year marked Austria's return to the World Cup finals for the first time in 20 years and they were present again in Spain in 1982 then in Italy in 1990. In the meantime, Rapid Vienna followed FK Austria's example in the Cup-winners Cup, finishing runners-up to Everton in 1985 and to Paris Saint-Germain in 1996.

AZERBAIJAN

Association of Football Federations of Azerbaijian
Founded: 1992
Joined FIFA: 1994

Azerbaijan made their independent international debut in the 1996 European Championship but were forced, because of civil war, to play their home games in Turkey. Not surprisingly, perhaps, they lost nine of their 10 games in the qualifying competition for the 1996 European Championship – drawing the other 0–0 against Poland in their last match. Best-known Azeri club are Nefchi Baku, who played for many years in the top division of the old Soviet Supreme Championship. Top player was Anatoly Banishevski, the attacking leader of the Soviet side who finished fourth at the 1966 World Cup finals in England.

BELARUS

Football Federation of the Republic of Belarus
Founded: 1989
Joined FIFA: 1992

Belarus attained independence after the Soviet Union's collapse. Minsk Dynamo are their most successful club and Petr Kachouro – who joined Sheffield United in 1996 – their most outstanding player of modern times. The country's club structure was badly affected by the reorganization which followed the acquisition of

independence in the early 1990s. For example, the Minsk Dynamo club split into two – known subsequently as Minsk Dynamo and Minsk Dynamo 93. To add to the confusion, both clubs qualified for the early stages of the 1996–97 UEFA Cup.

BELGIUM

Belgische Voetballbond/Union Royale Belge des Societes de Football-Association
Founded: 1895
Joined FIFA: 1904

Belgium are assured of their place at the finals of the 2000 European Championship thanks to their status as joint hosts. But, even though the national team has been in the doldrums for much of the 1990s, Belgium remain dangerous opponents for any nation.

The potential is evidenced by the past. Belgium were runners-up at the 1980 European Championship, then fourth at the 1986 World Cup after developing a generation of players worthy to lace the boots of previous heroes.

In the inter-war years that meant Raymond Braine whose sharp-shooting talents from the wing earned a transfer to the 1930s financial power, Czecho-Slovakia. Then, the late 1950s and early 1960s saw the explosive emergence of Paul Van Himst, who began as a centre-forward and then moved to inside left to exploit his wide range of creative skills in and around the penalty box. Those creative skills were reborn, some 20 years later, in Enzo Scifo, son of Italian immigrant workers.

A strong Anderlecht have, down the years, proved a key to a successful national team.

Belgium were one of the founders of FIFA, the world governing body in 1904. But it took more than 50 years for professionalism to take root and transform the country's football standard and international status. That achievement was emphasized by the international renown achieved by clubs such as Anderlecht and Mechelen (who both won the European Cup-winners Cup) and Standard Liege, Club Brugge and Antwerp (who were all European runners-up).

BELGIAN INSPIRATION Midfield general, Enzo Scifo.

At national team level Belgium were one of only four European nations to attend the first World Cup finals in Uruguay in 1930. They were eliminated in the first round then, in 1934, in 1938 and, again, in 1954.

Braine and Stanley Van den Eynde were among the continent's leading players in the 1930s. In the 1950s they were succeeded by powerful centre-forwards Jef Mermans and Rik Coppens and then – after Van Himst – came the likes of record international Jan Ceulemans, a central figure in the World Cup efforts of the 1980s and 1990.

Sadly, Belgium has also gone down in football history for all the wrong reasons. The Heysel stadium in Brussels – since redeveloped and

renamed the King Baudouin stadium – was the scene of the 1985 tragedy in which 39 Juventus fans died before the Champions Cup Final against Liverpool.

BOSNIA-HERZEGOVINA

Bosnia and Herzegovina Football Federation
Founded: 1991
FIFA: 1992

Bosnia made history, on eventual admittance following independence, as UEFA's 50th member nation. At first UEFA delayed a decision on membership because three different organizations claimed to be the "real" federation. The dispute went to FIFA for resolution.

BULGARIA

Bulgarski Futbolen Soius
Founded: 1923
Joined FIFA: 1924

Bulgaria reached their peak of international achievement by finishing fourth at the 1994 World Cup finals in the United States. Decisive influences were star striker Hristo Stoichkov, midfielders Yordan Lechkov and Krasimir Balakov and goalkeeper Borislav (Boby) Mihailov.

Their 2–1 quarter-final victory over Cup-holders Germany has gone down as Bulgaria's single most outstanding match. It was the high point, to be followed by defeats at the hands of Italy in the semi-finals and Sweden in the Third Place Play-off.

Bulgaria's success owed much to the transfer freedom which had followed the collapse of communist-imposed restrictions. The likes of Stoichkov and Lechkov went abroad to hone their talent and brought the technical, tactical and psychological lessons back to the national team structure with enormous success.

The evidence is clear: before the 1994 World Cup Bulgaria had competed in the World Cup finals on five occasions, playing 16 matches, never winning a game and progressing beyond the first round on only one occasion (in Mexico in 1986). Fourth-place "success" in 1994 duly punctured the image of Bulgaria as a nation of footballers with admirable discipline and physical commitment but a lack of fantasy.

Bulgaria was one of the first of the Balkan states to take to football in the latter years of the nineteenth century. A British university team, engaged on a central European tour, staged the first exhibition of the game in Bulgaria in 1884. Another 25 years passed, however, before the first formal Bulgarian club was set up and another 14 years before the federation was created to run the competitive game. The following year, 1924, saw Bulgaria play their first international. The result was a 6–0 defeat by Austria in Vienna.

PRESSURE POINT *Bulgaria's Hristo Stoichkov (right) chasing down Germany's Jurgen Kohler at the 1994 World Cup.*

GETTING SHIRTY Croatia's Davor Suker upset by Germany's Memmet Scholl.

Bulgaria became a member of FIFA in the same year, and the first league championship was launched in 1925.

International headway had to wait until after World War Two and the communist takeover in 1946. The new regime dismantled all the old sports organizations and created mostly new clubs – notably the army team, CDNA (later CSKA) – on the "state-amateur" basis.

Inside-forward Ivan Kolev, the so-called "Pocket Puskas", was the finest Bulgarian footballer of the 1950s, but death in a car crash cut short the highly promising career of 1960s centre-forward Georgi Asparoukhov. World Cup defenders in the 1960s such as Dimitar Penev and Ivan Voutsov went on to become World Cup coaches in the 1980s and 1990s.

CROATIA

Hrvatski Nogomatni Savez
Founded: 1912
Joined FIFA: 1992

Croatia, quarter-finalists at Euro 96, were not, in fact, total newcomers to international football. The country existed as an independent political – and thus football – entity, albeit under puppet regime conditions, in the 1940s. The Croats organized their own league championship and their own national team. But, under direction from Berlin, they played against only other Axis-aligned nations such as Germany, Italy, Bulgaria and Romania.

Croatia remained a significant source of football strength and talent within the former Yugoslavia after the war. Dinamo Zagreb (now known as FC Croatia) and Hajduk Split built impressive records in European club competitions – which they have

extended since Croatia's independent re-emergence in 1990. The first match of the new era was a 2–1 win over the United States on October 17, 1990.

Outstanding players at Euro 96 included striker Davor Suker of Real Madrid and midfield general Zvonimir Boban of Milan.

CYPRUS

Kipriaki Omospondia Podosferu
Founded: 1934
Joined FIFA: 1948

Cypriot football hit the international headlines for all the wrong reasons in the spring of 1997 when it was revealed that a number of national team players had been allegedly involved in a betting scam on their World Cup qualifying match against Bulgaria in December 1996.

Cyprus lost 3–1 – not a surprise in itself – but the federation was disturbed by reports of huge sums

being gambled on a precise scoreline and a parliamentary inquiry was set up to try to get to the truth.

It all went to prove that, although Cyprus may be considered one of the Europe's minnow nations, the game is followed with enormous passion and intensity. Such passion can be channelled into the wrong areas and this was not the first time that corruption allegations had been raised.

Generally, Cyprus has been considered on a par with the likes of Iceland, Malta, Finland and Luxembourg as European minnows. But the Cypriot national team have rarely been a pushover when playing at home, which says much for the enthusiasm the game engenders on an island split between the Greek and breakaway Turkish communities.

Football control, however, has stayed in the hands of the Greek community and though some of the old Turkish-based clubs remain in domestic league and cup competition they do so only because they moved during the 1974–76 insurrection.

Soccer was played in Cyprus as early as the 1870s by British soldiers and sailors. British troops played the game there during World War One and British residents helped found the Cyprus FA, the league and the cup in 1934.

In 1948, with the island under British control, the Cyprus FA became affiliated to the Football Association in London yet managed to obtain independent membership of FIFA. On July 30, 1949, Cyprus played their first international, losing 3–1 in Tel-Aviv to Israel. The international story since then has been mostly of defeats, with one of the most controversial arising in the 1988 European Championship qualifying competition.

In October 1987, playing Holland in Rotterdam, Cyprus goalkeeper Andreas Haritou was felled by a smoke bomb thrown from the crowd. For half an hour Cyprus refused to play on. When they did so, with a substitute goalkeeper, they lost 8–0. The match had to be replayed but many observers felt Holland were fortunate to stay in a competition ... which they later won with such style in Germany the following year.

By now the bigger clubs could afford to import foreign players and coaches. English managers included Tommy Cassidy, Ian Moores, Peter Cormack, Alan Dicks and Richie Barker. An increasing number of Bulgarian and Yugoslav players arrived on the playing scene.

The most famous home-grown player remains Sotiris Kaiafas who, in 1975–76, scored 39 league goals to collect the Golden Boot as Europe's top marksman.

CZECH REPUBLIC

Ceskomoravsky Fotbalovy Svaz
Founded: 1901/1993
Joined FIFA: 1907

The Czech Republic took part for the first time, formally, in international competition in the 1996 European Championship. They marked the occasion by surprising most observers and reaching the Final, in which they lost famously to Germany by 2–1 and the controversial golden goal rule. They also raised three new international stars in winger Karel Poborsky and

midfielders Patrik Berger and Radek Bejbl.

Previously, of course, the Czechs had played international football as part of the former Czechoslovakia, one of several politically dictated changes to their national identity to take place over the years.

Football began before Czechoslovakia had even been founded in the years before World War One when central Europe was dominated by the Hapsburg empire. The game was launched separately in both what was then Bohemia and in Slovakia.

Sports clubs had already been created on a German-inspired model

NEW GENERATION Czech hero Karel Poborsky outpaces the Portuguese defence at Euro 96.

and it was Slavia of Prague who, in the 1880s, were the first to add football to their curriculum. However it was traditional rivals Sparta who won the first Bohemia championship in 1912. Slavia took revenge a year later. But the competition was abruptly suspended. The region became engulfed in World War One, a conflict which would, ultimately, lead to the creation of a new national identity.

The football federation of the fledgling Czecho-Slovakia (as it was originally styled) was one of the first not merely to accept but welcome professionalism. Thus the Czechs were among Europe's leading football nations throughout the inter-war years. Sparta and Slavia dominated the Mitropa Cup – the forerunner of the present European club tournaments – and the national team finished runners-up to the hosts, Italy, in extra time in the 1934 World Cup Final in Rome. Goalkeeper Frantisek Planicka and forwards Oldrich Nejedly and Antonin Puc were among the great heroes of their day.

Of course, Hitler's greed sliced into Czechoslovakia late in 1938 and though Sparta and Slavia retained their identities in the Nazi Sudetenland football competition, they were made to pay after the war when the communists took over. Both clubs had to change their names and saw their best players enrolled into the armed services so they could play for the new army team, Dukla Prague, later to become feared opponents for any team.

Dukla, with a great left-back in Ladislav Novak and two wonderful, complementary wing-halves in Svatopluk Pluskal and Josef Masopust, provided the foundation for a revived national team which reached the World Cup finals in 1954, in 1958 and in 1962. In 1954 and 1958 they fell in the first round – albeit eliminated in a play-off by Northern Ireland in 1958. But in 1962 they were runners-up in the Final to Brazil – even taking the lead through Masopust before losing 3–1 in Santiago, Chile. Earlier, drawn in the same first-round group, they had held the Brazilians to a 0–0 draw.

Czechosloslovakia never again threatened to repeat that World Cup effort. However they were among the most successful contenders in the

European Championship – winning a thrilling Final in 1976 and finishing third in 1980. Each time they owed their status to penalties – beating West Germany in a shoot-out in the 1976 Final in Belgrade, following a 2–2 draw, and then Italy (by 9–8) after a goalless draw in the Third Place Match in 1980 in Naples.

A quarter-final appearance at the 1990 World Cup in Italy eventually turned out to be the old Czechoslovakia's international swansong. The 1996 European Championship then proved that the Czechs had suffered little from the football split with Slovakia.

DENMARK

Dansk Boldspil Union
Founded: 1889
Joined FIFA: 1904

Denmark's victory in the 1992 European Championship was one of the great international fairytales of modern football times. They should not, for one thing, have been attending the finals in Sweden at all. Manager Richard Moller Nielsen was decorating his kitchen when UEFA decided to send for the Danes only a matter of weeks before the Opening Match.

The Danes gained their wild card

PILE-UP Goal-scorer John Jensen is buried under delighted team-mates in the 1992 European Championship Final.

recall because of the increasingly fragile conditions in the Balkans and fear over security aspects of Yugoslavia's presence in the finals. The Slavs were barred and Denmark, who had finished runners-up in their qualifying group, stepped in.

They were popular competitors from Peter Schmeichel in goal to Kim Vilfort in midfield and Brian Laudrup in attack. Moller Nielsen had refined Sepp Piontek's "Danish Dynamite" team of the 1980s by adding a bomb-proof defence.

Denmark hardly looked like Europe-beaters in the first round but their ultimate victory against the odds – plus Holland in the semi-final and Germany in the Final – proved hugely popular.

Those observers who registered shock over Denmark's success were ignoring the lessons of football history because the Danes had been among the giants of European football in the amateur, pre-First World War days.

Denmark was one of the very first "foreign" lands to be invaded by the football-carrying Brits in the 1860s. British residents carried on playing in Copenhagen and a national team played in an exhibition tournament at the first modern Olympic Games in Athens in 1896. Nils Middleboe – most remarkable son of a famous football family – was English football's first foreign import when he played for Chelsea between 1913 and 1920.

The amateur tradition undoubtedly

held Denmark back at international level as professionalism took over elsewhere during and after the inter-war years. The depth of natural talent available was evident however when Denmark finished runner-ups at the 1960 Olympics in Rome and third at the 1964 European Championship finals. But then, the Danes needed to beat only Malta, Albania and Luxembourg (in a play-off!) along the qualifying path.

Denmark did not reach the finals again until 1984, now under the leadership of former German international full-back Sepp Piontek. This was an exciting new team built unashamedly around exiled professionals such as Michael Laudrup and Preben Elkjaer. They overcame England, Greece, Hungary and Luxembourg (again) in the qualifiers then lost to Spain in the semi-finals only after a penalty shoot-out, having been ahead for more than an hour.

Spain defeated Denmark again in

the second round of the 1986 World Cup. But the foundations for 1992 had been effectively laid.

"Our secret," explained skipper and sweeper Morten Olsen, "is that we are friends. And you run harder and work harder for your friends than you do for workmates."

ENGLAND

The Football Association
Founded: 1863
Joined FIFA: 1905

England regained much of their international prestige at the finals of the 1996 European Championship – otherwise known as Euro 96 thanks to the commercial packaging of the country's biggest sports event since the 1966 World Cup.

On the one hand the England team, under the imaginative guidance of controversial Terry Venables, reached the semi-finals to demonstrate

that they remained competitive in the international arena; elimination was the literal penalty of a shoot-out defeat by Germany. On the other hand, the peaceful exuberance among the fence-free crowds provided a spectacular stage. FIFA observers were so impressed they immediately launched a campaign to try to achieve, long-term, the removal of all football pitch fences worldwide.

England went so close to achieving, also, their first trophy success since 1966. Alan Shearer was the tournament's five-goal top scorer, his success earning him third place in both the FIFA and European player of the year polls and raising his value to a world record £15million when he transferred from Blackburn Rovers to Newcastle United a matter of weeks after the finals.

AHEAD Alan Shearer opens up the scoring for England in the semi-finals of Euro 96.

FOILED Estonia had Scotland's Ally McCoist at bay in the World Cup qualifiers.

The theme of the finals – Football's Coming Home – underlined the moral strength reflecting England's status as the Mother of Football. It was, as we have seen, in England in the mid-1800s that the public schools and universities first codified the modern game.

The Football Association (not, note, the English Football Association) was set up in 1863, the FA Challenge Cup launched in 1871 and the Football League in 1888; in between England played Scotland in the world's first international match in 1872. The basic form of the English game then stood the test of time and set a structural standard for the rest of the world. The league championship is the competitive bulwark of every country's game and the knock-out cup concept dominates the international landscape.

In 1904 England stood aloof from the foundation of FIFA. Later they deigned to join, only to split away in the 1920s in a dispute over broken-time payments for amateurs. That dispute proved critical to the development of the English game. Being outside FIFA, England were excluded from the World Cup, and potentially

vital international competitive experience, until the 1950s. Later that political, technical and tactical isolation could be seen to have cost England a decade of development time.

England rejoined FIFA after World War Two, entered the World Cup for the first time in 1950 in Brazil and wished they had not when they lost devastatingly, by 1–0, to the United States in Belo Horizonte. That result was considered a simple – if embarrassing – freak. Not until 1953, when Hungary won 6–3 at Wembley, was the domestic audience provided with a painful lesson about the lost years.

England produced great players such as Stanley Matthews, Tommy Lawton, Tom Finney and Billy Wright. But it took Manchester United's defiance of domestic authority as the 1950s Busby Babes entered the European Champions Cup – against the advice of the isolationist Football League – to bring English football into day to day contact with the rest of the international game.

Within a decade, lessons were learned. England, in 1966, were not one of the greatest World Cup teams by

Brazilian standards but Bobby Moore, Bobby Charlton, Geoff Hurst and their team-mates could do no more than beat all-comers. Hurst became the only man to score a World Cup Final hat-trick in the 4–2 extra-time victory over West Germany at Wembley.

Simultaneously, Tottenham and Manchester United provided victorious breakthroughs in European club competitions. Liverpool, Aston Villa and Nottingham Forest were other clubs who established a winning pattern in Europe until the hooliganism epidemic – which reached a tragic peak with the Heysel disaster of 1985 – forced a five-year exile from continental competition.

Other crowd tragedies, such as Bradford and Hillsborough, led to a reappraisal of facilities. The Taylor Report enforced all-seater stadia and the higher costs of spectating changed the demography of football crowds. Television, sponsorship, and commercial exploitation provided English football with a fashionably acceptable new face. The big clubs took greater control of their own affairs by creating the Premier League ... and, on the evidence of Euro 96, England regained its status as a football leader.

ESTONIA

Eesti Jalgpalli Liit
Founded: 1921
Joined FIFA: 1923

Estonia, Latvia and Lithuania make up the Baltic states who appeared briefly on the international football map in the 1920s and 1930s, disappeared following the Soviet expansion of the 1940s and then reappeared again at the start of the 1990s following their political independence.

Of the three, Estonia were the busiest in footballing terms in the years between the two wars. They played most of their matches against their Baltic neighbours but also contested nearly 50 matches against nations from further afield and appeared in the World Cup qualifying competitions of 1934 and 1938.

The collapse of the Soviet empire at the start of the 1990s allowed Estonia to reclaim their sporting identity. FIFA bent the World Cup rules to permit their inclusion in the qualifying competition for 1994 which helped raised badly-needed revenue for an impoverished federation.

Flora Tallinn have provided most of Estonia's international players while the first national coach of the modern era was Uno Piir, a local footballing hero in the 1950s with Kalev Tallinn who was later a member of the Soviet coaching staff at the 1966 World Cup finals.

All emergent federations make mistakes, however. Estonia's blunder involved a World Cup qualifying match against Scotland in autumn 1996. Complications over TV coverage, kick-off times and floodlighting, produced the so-called "Match that Never Was." Scotland turned up for the kick-off of their tie in Tallinn while Estonia's squad remained at their training camp 60 miles away.

FIFA, perhaps generously as far as Estonia were concerned, ordered the

match to be replayed in Monte Carlo. Not turning out had put the Estonians in danger of World Cup expulsion which would have been a devastating blow.

FAROE ISLANDS

Fotboltssamband Foroya
Founded: 1979
Joined FIFA: 1988

In the autumn of 1990 the Faroe Islands arrived on the competitive

international scene with a victory which made headlines around the world.

The match was a European Championship qualifying tie against Austria, who had been finalists a few months earlier in the World Cup in Italy. Even though the Faroes had to play hosts in Landskrona, Sweden, they scored a 1–0 success – a football miracle for an islands nation whose federation was then only 11 years old.

The Faroes' domestic championship boasted only 20 clubs, 4,500 registered players and 118 referees. All bar one of the players were amateurs, an image enhanced by the bobble-hat worn, picturesquely, by goalkeeper Jens Knudsen.

The only full-time professional was striker Jan Allan Muller and even he was given a free transfer by the Dutch second division club, Go Ahead Eagles of Deventer, not long after the historic defeat of Austria.

Problems with the weather meant that the Faroes were restricted in the months they could play internationally and lacked any decent natural pitches. One happy consequence, then, of their explosive emergence on to the

international scene was the sponsorship funds to create a "proper" pitch in their 8,000-capacity national stadium at Toftir.

FINLAND

Suomen Palloliitto (Finlands Bollforbund)
Founded: 1907
Joined FIFA: 1908

Football is not the top sport in Finland. That honour belongs, understandably, to the snow-driven winter sports. Thus problems over facilities and the climate means the best players all go abroad to turn professional while the domestic game remains part-time at best, and amateur.

Not, of course, that clubs in Holland, Belgium and Germany have objected. All have benefited by buying Finnish players cheap and, frequently, selling them on at a profit. The most successful export has been forward Jari Litmanen who became, with Ajax Amsterdam in 1995, the first Finnish player to secure a Champions Cup-winners medal.

His most noted predecessors in the emigration stakes were winger Juhani Peltonen and centre back Arto Tolsa in the 1960s. The longest-serving expatriate has been midfielder or central defender Kari Ukkonen who spent more than a decade in Belgium, latterly with Anderlecht.

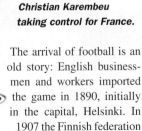

LOOKING GOOD
Christian Karembeu
taking control for France.

The arrival of football is an old story: English businessmen and workers imported the game in 1890, initially in the capital, Helsinki. In 1907 the Finnish federation was set up, to be followed

by a national championship a year later. In 1911 Finland played their first international, losing 5–2 at home to neighbouring Sweden. Finland were also quickly into the international competitive arena at the 1912 Stockholm Olympic Games. But, after defeating Italy 3–2 and Czarist Russia 2–1 they fell 4–0 to Great Britain and were thrashed 9–0 by Holland.

The Finnish national side have never reached the finals of the World Cup or European Championship and none of their clubs has ever progressed beyond the quarter-finals of any of the European competitions.

FRANCE

Federation Français de Football
Founded: 1919
Joined FIFA: 1904

France will stage the 1998 World Cup finals in the sure confidence that they deserved host rights as a reward for their achievements both on the pitch and in the corridors of power.

France competed at the first World Cup finals in 1930; they hosted the first Champions Cup Final in 1956; they were European champions on home soil in 1984; and Just Fontaine holds the 13-goal record as top scorer in the finals of a World Cup (in 1958).

Off the pitch it was Robert Guerinwho was elected first president of FIFA, the international federation, in 1904; Jules Rimet, also FIFA president for more than 20 years, was instrumental in creating the World Cup; Henri Delaunay was the moving spirit behind the European Championship; Jacques Georges was president of UEFA, the European federation, in the turbulent 1980s; and the Paris sports newspaper, *L'Equipe*, set off the chain of events which created the vastly successful European club competitions.

In terms of titles, France were third at the World Cup finals in 1958 and 1986 and fourth in 1982. Apart from winning the European Championship in 1984 they also won the Olympic Games that same year.

At international level, French clubs have played their part in spreading the gospel of a style of football which mixes physical commitment with skill and pace. beyond their own borders, too. Reims reached the European Champions Cup final in 1956 and again in 1959, only to lose to Spain's all-conquering Real Madrid on both occasions. Reims later slid down through the leagues and went bankrupt but Saint-Etienne followed them to the Champions Cup Final in 1976, only to lose 1–0 to West Germany's Bayern Munich at Hampden Park.

A decade further on the controversial self-made millionaire businessman Bernard Tapie arrived on the French football scene. He spent millions bringing Marseille through from the second division to the peak of European football. They were runners-up – after a penalty shoot-out – to Red Star Belgrade in the 1991 Champions Cup Final in Bari, then defeated Milan two years later in Munich. All the gloss and glory which surrounded this first French victory in the Champions Cup swiftly tarnished when it emerged that Marseille had been engaged in a formalized match-rigging exercise both at home and abroad.

It took Paris Saint-Germain's victory in the Cup-Winners Cup in 1996 – they beat Rapid Vienna 1–0 in Brussels – to start glossing over the credibility cracks which the Marseille scandal had created around the French game.

The strength of the French domestic game has rested more on the provincial clubs than in Paris but that has not upset the steady flow of great players. Forward Lucien Laurent scored the first goal in World Cup history, against Mexico in Uruguay in 1930, then Just Fontaine terrorized World Cup keepers in the 1950s thanks to the inspirational promptings of the great Raymond Kopa – who was the first Frenchman to win a European Champions Cup medal after transferring from Reims to Real Madrid in 1956.

The 1960s brought a financial crisis which bankrupted many of the great old clubs but the 1970s brought a renaissance accompanied by a flood of new talent. Manager Michel Hidalgo, a Champions Cup Final loser in 1956, used his international expertise to build a thrilling national team which reached a glorious peak in winning the 1984 European Championship. The foundations were provided by midfielder Alain Giresse, Jean Tigana, Luis Fernandez and defender Max Bossis while skipper Michel Platini established himself as the greatest French footballer of all time.

Platini, who took his talents to Italy with Juventus, was three times European Footballer of the Year before turning to management. He guided the national team to the finals of the 1992 European Championship and then changed career course again as joint president of the French organizing committee for the 1998 World Cup finals.

GEORGIA

Football Federation of Georgia
Founded: 1990
Joined FIFA: 1992

The quality of Georgian football first became seriously evident when Tbilisi Dynamo won the European Cup-Winners' Cup in 1981. Tbilisi played football with a great deal more flair and technical skill than the northern, Moscow clubs from the Russian republic. That's why Georgia was known, in football, as the "Soviet Italy". Tbilisi Dynamo also won the Soviet championship twice thanks to the ability of players such as Alexander Chivadze in defence, David Kipiani in midfield and Ramaz Shengelia in attack.

Around 30 Georgian players won caps for the Soviet Union, the most successful having been central defender Murtaz Khurtsilava, who scored six goals in 67 internationals between 1976 and 1973 and who played in the 1966 World Cup finals. Kakhi Asatiani, a midfielder who scored five goals in 16 internationals for the Soviet Union and played in the 1970 World Cup finals in Mexico, later became Minister of Sport.

At the end of 1989, however, the Georgian federation withdrew from the Soviet federation. This meant that all Georgian clubs dropped out of the Soviet league and were lost to international sight until after the collapse of the rest of the Soviet Union.

On Georgia's re-emergence, Chivadze became national coach but poor results in the 1996 European Championship qualifying event and then in the first matches of the 1998 World Cup led to Chivadze's replacement by Kipiani. Top player was nimble and gifted midfield general Georgi Kinkladze, who turned down a chance to play alongside Diego Maradona at Boca Juniors in favour of a contract, much nearer to home, with England's Manchester City.

GERMANY

Deutscher Fussball-Bund
Founded: 1900
Joined FIFA: 1904

Germany, three times World Cup-winners and current European champions, lay just claim to being the most consistent national team force in Europe. German clubs, oddly, have under-performed by comparison. But at the highest level there can never be any doubting which nation is most dangerous contender for world and European prizes.

The German success rate may be gauged not so much from listing the prizes but the few failures. For example, Germany have been absent from the finals of the World Cup on only two occasions: in 1930 and 1950 and then only because they did not enter. As for the European Championship, Germany did not enter in 1960 and 1964 and failed to qualify

ROMAN HOLIDAY
1990 World Cup-winner Jürgen Kohler.

for the finals in 1968. Since then, however, they have always been there.

In the summer of 1996 they became the first nation to win the European Championship three times when they defeated the Czech Republic 2–1 at Wembley with a golden goal in extra time. The next target was to emulate, at the 1998 World Cup finals, the German team of two decades earlier who held European and World Cup crowns simultaneously.

They were third in their first World Cup attempt in 1934 (as Germany), first-round failures in 1938 (as Greater Germany, having swallowed Austria and its footballers) then winners (as West Germany) for the first time in 1954, when they achieved one of the greatest of international upsets with a 3–2 defeat of the legendary Hungarians. German international prospects were only strengthened when the old part-time regional-league system was scrapped in the early 1960s in favour of full-time professional football and a unified top division. The historical circle was finally closed in the early 1990s with the return to the national fold of the former East Germany – complete with outstanding players such as Matthias Sammer, Ulf Kirsten, Thomas Doll and Andreas Thom.

Their arrival was icing on the cake of success: in 1966, World Cup runners-up; in 1970, third in the World Cup; European champions for the first time – under Franz Beckenbauer's captaincy – in 1972; World Cup-winners on home soil, again starring Beckenbauer, in 1974; European runners-up only after a penalty shoot-out in 1976; World Cup second round finalists in 1978; European champions for a second time in 1980; World Cup runners-up for a third time in 1986; European championship semi-finalists in 1988 then runners-up in 1992; World Cup winners again in 1990; quarter-finalists in 1994; European champions in 1996.

Bayern Munich won the European Champions' Cup three times in a row in the mid-1970s, and also collected the World Club Cup. They had won the Cup-Winners Cup in 1967 and added the UEFA Cup in 1996 – joining Ajax, Barcelona and Juventus as the only clubs to have won all three European trophies. Hamburg have also won the Champions and Cup-Winners Cups.

PUSHING IN Panayotis Tsalouhidis of Greece (left) at the 1994 World Cup.

There have been further European laps of honour for Borussia Dortmund and Werder Bremen in the Cup-Winners Cup and for Borussia Moenchengladbach (twice), Eintracht Frankfurt and Bayer Leverkusen in the UEFA Cup.

A new chapter opened at the start of the 1990s following reunification with the eastern sector of Germany. This had been split away by the Soviet occupying forces after World War Two.

While, in the West, the old German federation, the DFB, carried on as usual an independent East German federation was created (the DFV) with a debut international, a 3–0 defeat in Poland, on September 21, 1952.

In fact, the East Germans achieved little in international football. The GDR systems created – in a suspiciously secretive manner – a host of medal-winning and record-breaking track and field athletes. But there was no potion powerful enough to conquer team sports. Only once did East Germany reach the finals of a major competition and that was the 1974 World Cup. The venue was West Germany, against whom East Germany recorded a unique 1–0 victory before sinking without a trace in the second round of the finals. Jürgen Sparwasser scored the historic

goal turning him into a national hero of East Germany ... until several years later, that is, when he defected.

That was also the year in which East Germany collected their only international club success when Magdeburg surprisingly defeated holders Milan 2–0 in a Cup-winners Cup Final played before a mere 4,000 in Rotterdam.

At home, East German football was dominated by the clubs of the political institutions. First, the army club Vorwärts; then the police team, Dynamo Dresden; finally, the club which operated under the aegis of the secret police, the hated "Stasi", Dynamo Berlin. They won a "fixed" championship for a world record 10 years in a row, but once their communist protectors had gone, the club collapsed into the amateur abyss opened up by football reunification.

GREECE

Eliniki Podosferiki Omospondia
Founded: 1926
Joined FIFA: 1927

The excitement of the moment has long been the key to Greek football. For example, the Greeks were the first nation to introduce three points for a win in league play. That was in the 1950s and was a disciplinary measure.

Teams who won a match were awarded three points, teams who drew a match were awarded two points each and teams who lost but stayed on the pitch to the end of the full 90 minutes (!) were awarded one point. Teams, of course, which lost a match and stormed off in anger before the final whistle got nothing.

Clubs such as Panathinaikos and AEK of Athens and Olympiakos from the nearby port of Piraeus were traditionally considered among the richest in Europe. But the very power of the big clubs worked, for many years, contrary to the interests of the national team. The clubs were reluctant to release their players for internationals and a lack of preparation was reflected in regular failure in the qualifying competitions for both World Cup and European Championship.

The breakthrough came when Greece reached the finals of the European Championship in Italy in 1980 under manager Alketas Panagulias. Greece opened with a 1–0 defeat by powerful Holland, lost 3–1 to defending title-holders Czechoslovakia and finished up with the consolation of a goalless draw against the West German side who would go on to win the title.

Four years later Greece reached the final of the European under-21 championship. Their hero was goalscorer Nikols Nioplias, later one of the stars of the senior national team who qualified – again under Panagulias – for the World Cup finals for the first time in 1994.

At club level, historically, Olympiakos are the greatest club with 25 championships and 19 cup victories. But Panathianaikos, 2–0 losers to Ajax Amsterdam in the 1971 Champions Cup, remain the only Greek side to have reached a European club final.

HOLLAND

Koninklijke Nederlandsche Voetbalbond
Founded: 1889
Joined FIFA: 1904

Holland may be one of the smaller nations in terms of square kilometres. But they are one of the giants of world football – a status which owes everything to the remarkable flowering of talent as bright as the tulips in the country's bulb fields.

Dutch football was strictly amateur for more than half of the century although they qualified for the World Cup finals in 1934 and 1938 – losing each time in the first round.

The 1940s brought war so it was not until the 1950s that conflict of a different sort arose between the amateurs and the impatient would-be professionals. In 1953 a breakaway professional championship was launched. It proved to be the catalyst for reorganization, for progress towards football reality: a vital step down the path which would lead to "total football" and the great days of the 1970s.

Feyenoord – *not* Ajax – were Holland's first international winners. Under the guidance of Austrian coach Ernst Happel they beat Celtic in the 1970 Champions Cup Final, then Estudiantes de La Plata for the World Club Cup. But Feyenoord's achievement was bettered by the sheer spellbinding style with which Ajax – under Rinus Michels and then Stefan Kovacs – conquered Europe for the next three years.

Inspirational superstar Johan Cruyff was sold to Barcelona for a then world record £922,000 but recreated his partnership with Michels to lead the national team to the 1974

World Cup. Holland, beaten 2–1 by hosts West Germany in Munich, finished runners-up. They did so again in 1978, despite Cruyff's decision to abandon the national team six months in advance of the trip to finals. In the Final it was the hosts again, this time Argentina, who beat Holland 3–1 after extra time.

Third in the European championship in 1976, the Dutch began to fade in the 1980 European finals when Rudi Krol, Arie Haan and the rest failed to progress beyond the first round. Then they failed to qualify for the 1982 World Cup finals. "I think," said Krol, by then starring for Napoli in Italy, "that this may be the end. One great generation of players like that cannot be expected to be matched for maybe a century."

Recent history suggests that Krol's understandable logic may have been flawed. Within a very few years, with Michels back in charge, the Dutchmen were flying again.

Michels looked for his team to Ajax who, with Cruyff as coach, had won the Cup-winners Cup in 1987. Marco Van Basten, a young captain, had collected the winning goal against Lokomotive Leipzig in Athens, to revive the memories and inspiration of the glory days. Simultaneously PSV Eindhoven, one of Europe's richest clubs as a result of being owned by Philips, took up the European challenge and won the 1988 Champions Cup in a remarkable summer climaxed by the European Championship triumph.

Holland beat the Soviet Union 2–0 in the Final in Munich. Skipper Ruud Gullit scored the first goal and Van Basten volleyed a wonderful second.

Gullit, Van Basten and Frank Rijkaard went off to turn Italy's Milan into the dominant club force of the 1990s. Meanwhile, another wave of talent burst through in their wake and Ajax duly regained the Champions Cup – at Milan's ironic expense – in 1995.

FEAR OF FLYING has not stopped Dennis Bergkamp becoming an international superstar.

HUNGARY

Magyar Labdarugo Szovetseg
Founded: 1901
Joined FIFA: 1906

Football was taken to Hungary by English students in 1870s. Yet, some eighty years later, the tables were turned and it was the Hungarians who were handing out a football lesson to the English. Ferenc Puskas was the captain and headmaster of the legendary team of the 1950s whose fame and reputation has intimidated, overshadowed and stifled every other Hungarian team to this day.

The foundations were well laid. Even before the turn of the century three of the most powerful domestic clubs had been formed in MTK, Ferencvaros and Ujpest. In 1916 the legendary English coach Jimmy Hogan arrived at MTK, discovered the first great Hungarian individual footballer in Gyorgy Orth, and prepared Hungarian football for the advance of professionalism in the 1920s and 1930s.

This era reached a climax in 1938 when Hungary progressed to the World Cup Final in Paris. Their inspiration came from the academic centre-forward or centre-half Gyorgy Sarosi. Hungary lost 4–2 in the Final to Italy but the disappointment was as nothing compared with the shock waves which went through the world game in 1954. Here again Hungary lost the World Cup Final, by 3–2 to West Germany in Switzerland.

This was the team built around goalkeeper Gyula Grosics, right-half Jozsef Bozsik and the inside-forward trio of Sandor Kocsis, Nandor Hidegkuti and Puskas. They had won the 1952 Olympic title; they had ended England's record of invincibility against continental opposition, winning 6–3 at Wembley; they had been unbeaten four years ... only to then lose the one match which mattered the most.

It was the beginning of the end. Two years later came the Hungarian Revolution. Honved, top club team which provided the nucleus for the national team, were touring abroad at the time. Some of the players decided to go home; some to stay in exile, including Puskas, Kocsis and left-winger Zoltan Czibor.

Hungary's national team have never been the same though they have reached the finals of the World Cup on six occasions and, in the European Championship, were third in 1964 and fourth in 1972.

The only occasion on which they have seriously threatened to break loose was at the 1966 World Cup finals in England. Then a fine side (managed by Lajos Baroti and starring Florian Albert and Ferenc Bene) scored a memorable 3–1 victory over Brazil only to fall to the Soviet Union

in the quarter-finals because of goal-keeping errors.

Twice since then Puskas, the old hero, has been recalled as national manager. But the collapse of communism condemned the domestic game to penury. Star players go abroad as soon as they can. The national team comes bottom of the priority list.

Hungary are now one of eastern Europe's weakest teams.

ICELAND

Knattspymusamband Islands
Founded: 1929
Joined FIFA: 1947

Iceland do not expect to be seen at the finals of the World Cup or European Championship. But their fans do expect more sophisticated and ambitious opponents to work hard for points and goals against their favourites.

Once considered Europe's last amateurs, Iceland have exported dozens of their best players south to the professional world with success. The national team have also numbered the likes Wales, Northern Ireland and East Germany among their victims.

Their most successful national manager was probably Englishman Tony Knapp though many other Englishmen – among them George Kirby – have worked with great domestic success at Icelandic clubs.

Football in Iceland can be traced back to 1894 when it was apparently introduced by James Ferguson, a Scottish printer and bookseller. An Athletic Union and championship were set up in 1912. This was on a knock-out basis and the first winners were KR Reykjavik. It was not until 1925 that a proper home-and-away league was set up. First winners – again – were KR.

Iceland's first international was played on July 17, 1946, and ended in a 3–0 defeat in Reykjavik by Denmark – the country from which Iceland had achieved independence only two years earlier. The first World Cup campaign was the 1958 competition. Iceland's qualifying debut was a match to forget: they lost 8–0 to a French side which would finish third. Playing inside left for Iceland that day was Albert Gudmundsson, for years rated Iceland's finest player and later a senior figure in both federation and government.

ISRAEL

Israel Football Association
Founded: 1928
Joined FIFA: 1929

Israel have reached the final stages of the World Cup only once, in 1970, but since being admitted to UEFA in 1991, they have made impressive progress. Certain proof was their 3–2 win over France in Paris in the World Cup qualifying competition in November, 1993.

Israel are the only country in the world to have played World Cup qualifiers on all five continents, a legacy of an era in which the Jewish state, which is geographically part of Asia, was kicked out of the Asian federation and regularly forced to compete in the Oceania group with

ON THE UP Israel beat France in the 1994 World Cup qualifiers.

play-offs against South American or European nations.

Now everything has changed. At a stroke, the collapse of the Soviet Union removed the bar to Israeli inclusion in Europe. Israeli teams now compete in all three European club competitions.

The development of Israeli football at international level has been helped by the steady movement of players – including English-based Rony Rosenthal and Eyal Berkovic – into European clubs since the mid-1980s. They have learned the game at the highest level and now that knowledge is starting to rub off on home-based players in the national squad.

ITALY

Federazione Italiana Gioco Calcio
Founded: 1898
Joined FIFA: 1905

Two gunmen once held up a ticket bureau in Naples but it was not money they wanted. Instead their desperate demand was for tickets to see Argentina's Diego Maradona make his first home appearance after joining the local club from Barcelona for a then world record £5million.

That exemplifies the mad passion which turned Italy into world football's El Dorado from the 1930s until the 1990s, when the television revolution offered big clubs in England and Spain financial parity in terms of transfer funds and pay rates. All the world's transfer records between Barcelona's £922,000 capture of Johan Cruyff in 1973 and Newcastle's £15million acquisition of Alan Shearer in 1996 saw Italian clubs behind the purchase counter.

The massive power of the Italian game is illustrated again by glancing through the European club competition record books. Italian clubs have won the World Club Cup on seven

occasions, the European Champions Cup on nine occasions, the Cup-Winners Cup six times, the UEFA Cup eight times and the European Supercup six times. All of those Italian victories depended to a significant extent on the extra qualities imported by Frenchmen, Argentines, Brazilians and Germans.

Imports have always played a central role in Italian football, right back to the closing years of the nineteenth century when visitors – particularly engineers, students and sailors from England, Scotland and Switzerland – first introduced the game.

In 1898 the first Italian championship featured just four teams and was all over and completed in just one day. By 1921 eight regions were involved and a professional, nation-wide top division was launched in 1929. Only Inter and Juventus can boast of never having been relegated – Juventus having won the championship a record 23 times.

Along the way Juventus became one of only four clubs to have won all three European club trophies. In nine remarkable months from May 1996 they won the Champions Cup, the

World Club Cup and then the European Supercup.

The power of Calcio is demonstrated most clearly in World Cup history. Italy were the first nation in Europe to host the finals and the first European nation to win the game's greatest prize three times.

In 1934 Italy, managed by the legendary Vittorio Pozzo, took advantage of their status as hosts. Pozzo included three Argentine stars in centre-half Luisito Monti and wingers Enrico Guaita and Raimundo Orsi in the team who defeated Czechoslovakia 2–1 after extra time in the Final in Rome in front of delighted dictator Benito Mussolini. Ruthless Pozzo rebuilt his team entirely for the World Cup defence in France in 1938. Only the inside forwards Giuseppe Meazza and Ferrari survived in the team who defeated Hungary 4–2 in the Final.

Disaster struck as Italy prepared to defend their crown in Brazil in the post-war world of 1950. Just over 12 months before the opening of the finals, the entire first-team squad of Italian champions Torino were wiped out in an air crash, including national captain Valentino Mazzola. The con-

HOME FROM HOME Gianfranco Zola outwits England's defence at Wembley.

sequence, in World Cup terms, was first-round elimination.

The big clubs spent ever more lavishly on foreign stars and the small clubs responded by perfecting the catenaccio defensive system. The Azzurri paid the penalty in terms of World Cup failure. Italy were beaten in the first round of the finals in 1954 and then, humiliatingly, by Northern Ireland in the 1958 qualifying competition. In Chile in 1962 Italy fell in the first round after a notoriously violent match against their hosts; in 1966 they were eliminated, again notoriously, by North Korea.

Even as European Championship hosts in 1968, Italy struggled to capitalize on home advantage. They beat the Soviet Union in the semi-finals on the toss of a coin and defeated Yugoslavia in the Final only after a replay. The nucleus of that team, under the managership of Ferruccio Valcareggi, went on to finish runners-up to a magnificent Brazil in the World Cup in Mexico two years later.

Valcareggi took Italy through to

first-round elimination in Germany in 1974 and was replaced by veteran coach Fulvio Bernardini. He, in turn, gave way to assistant Enzo Bearzot, who steered Italy to fourth place in 1978 in Argentina and then to victory in Spain in 1982, thus achieving Europe's first World Cup hat-trick.

Bearzot's men were past their best in Mexico in 1986 and his successor, Azeglio Vicini, was short on luck when Italy played hosts again in 1990 and went out to Argentina in the semi-finals in a penalty shoot-out.

More penalty pain followed four years later when Italy, having scraped through to the Final courtesy of the face-saving goals of Roberto Baggio, lost to Brazil in a penalty shoot-out in Pasadena after two hours without a "proper" goal. Failure to build on that achievement at Euro 96, where Italy crashed out in the first round, led to the departure of controversial theorist coach Arrigo Sacchi.

Italy's stuttering results and perfor-mances were a stark contrast to the manner in which Milan dominated European club football. But then, while Italy and Milan shared star defenders Franco Baresi and Paolo Maldini, the national team had no one quite like Ruud Gullit, Marco Van Basten, Dejan Savicevic and George Weah, in attack.

LATVIA

Latvian Football Federation
Founded: 1921
Joined FIFA: 1922

Latvia stand, alongside Lithuania and Estonia, among the Baltic states who regained their political independence in the early 1990s after 50 years "on ice".

The collapse of the Soviet empire allowed Latvia to reclaim their sporting identity. FIFA duly bent the World Cup rules to permit their late inclusion in the draw for the qualifying

competition for 1994. Those matches helped raise badly-needed funds for an impoverished federation.

Latvia were independent between the wars, their international experi-ence including a modest record victory by 4–1 over Sweden in 1932 in Riga. Their most notable result of that era was, however, a defeat. In Vienna, in 1937, Latvia lost only 2–1 in a World Cup qualifying tie to an Austrian side who were then one of the giants of the era.

Top club Skonto Riga won the league championship in the first five years of 1990s' independence, also won the cup twice and supplied the backbone of the national team. They have made little headway in European club competitions though, in 1994–95, they profited from the away goals rule to defeat Aberdeen, former holders of the Cup-Winners' Cup, in the preliminary round of the UEFA Cup.

LIECHTENSTEIN

Liechtensteiner Fussball-Verband
Founded: 1974
Joined FIFA: 1974

Liechtenstein have no national cham-pionship but that did not stop their entering the World Cup for the first time in 1990.

On the eve of the draw in New York in December, 1991, however, their officials got cold feet and pulled out at the last minute. When they did eventually make their World Cup debut, they were beaten 3–0 by Macedonia in Skopje in the qualifying competition in April, 1996.

Liechtenstein has an autonomous federation but its main clubs all compete in the Swiss regional leagues.

CLOSE-RUN *Latvia's Imants Bleidelis takes on Scotland's Tosh McKinlay in a 1996 World Cup Qualifying match.*

The main Liechtenstein competition is the knock-out cup whose winners now enter the European Cup-winners Cup regularly.

Liechtenstein's first outing at any sort of serious international level was in the President's Cup in South Korea in 1981, However, not all of the players used by Liechtenstein in that tournament – in which they drew 1–1 with Malta and beat Indonesia 3–2 – were Liechtenstein nationals and thus properly qualified for international status.

LITHUANIA

Lithuanian Football Federation
Founded: 1922
Joined FIFA: 1923/1992

As with Latvia and Estonia, so with Lithuania. They were independent during the inter-war years and competed, unsuccessfully, in the World Cup qualifying tournaments of 1934 and 1938, losing first to Sweden and then to Latvia.

After being reintegrated into international life, Lithuania began their football rehabilitation in the 1994 World Cup qualifying competition. Their start was promising as they took seven points from seven games, drawing twice – once away, in Northern Ireland, and once in a home match against Denmark – but then lost their last five fixtures and managed to finish only fifth of the seven nations in their group.

Striker Valdas Ivanauskas was their best-known player of the 1990s, having appeared with success in Germany with Hamburg. Later his mantle of Lithuanian No. 1 was taken over by Darius Maciulevicius, twice Footballer of the Year, from Inkaras Grifas Kaunas.

LUXEMBOURG

Luxembourgeoise de Football
Founded: 1908
Joined FIFA: 1910

The Grand Duchy are European football's original minnows. Luxembourg have had a federation, league, cup and national team structure all firmly in place long before the likes of Cyprus, Malta, Iceland (and of course the Faroes and San Marino) dipped their first toe in the international mainstream.

The federation was founded in 1908, just four years after FIFA, the first championship organized in 1910 and the first domestic cup in 1922. In 1956–57 Spora entered the second edition of the Champions Cup. They almost upset West German champions Borussia Dortmund in the first round. Spora lost 4–3 away, won 2–1 at home

but then crashed 7–0 in the play-off in Dortmund (the away goals rule was then undreamed of).

They have also shared some less impressive records. For example, Chelsea beat Jeunesse Hautcharage 21–0 on aggregate in the Cup-winners Cup in 1971–72 and US Rumelange crashed by the same overall margin to Feyenoord of Holland in the UEFA Cup in 1972–73 (Feyenoord's 12–0 win in Luxembourg in that tie remains a record away victory in Europe).

The national team compete regularly in the World Cup and European Championship without ever dreaming of reaching the finals. Their most historic result was in 1961, in the World Cup qualifiers, when they scored a

4–2 victory over a Portugal side built around European club champions Benfica and for whom Eusebio was making his debut.

MACEDONIA
(FORMER YUGOSLAV REPUBLIC OF)

Fudbalski Sojuz Makedonija
Founded: 1992
Joined FIFA: 1994

This is the country officially known as the Former Yugoslav Republic of Macedonia as a compromise to meet Greek complaints that this is not the "real" Macedonia of legend, from which Alexander the Great emerged.

This Macedonia is one of the four states to have gained independence from the bloody fragmentation in the Balkans. Like Slovenia, the separation

of Macedonia was comparatively peaceful when compared with events in Croatia and in Bosnia.

The national stadium, the Gradski in the city of Banja Luka, has a capacity of 25,000 though the volatility of the local fans meant it was shut for two matches by UEFA as punishment for hooliganism during the 1996 European Championship qualifying competition.

Vardar Skopje are the oldest and most successful of Macedonian teams, having three times competed in Europe as representatives of the former Yugoslavia. They also won the first three independent Macedonian championships in 1993, 1994 and 1995.

It was in 1993 that Macedonia, birthplace of many quality players, staged their first formal international, beating Slovenia 4–1.

MALTA

Malta Football Association
Founded: 1900
Joined FIFA: 1959

Malta has a special place in football history for it was on the George Cross island that the first referee's whistle was heard. That was in 1886 in a 1–1 draw between soldiers of the Shropshire Regiment and locals from Cospicua St Andrew's.

Thus Maltese football history most clearly stretches back before FIFA – the game having been imported by British servicemen under the Governorship of Sir Arthur Borton. Early records describe matches played in stockinged feet on rough ground.

The original Malta FA was set up

in 1900 and a league championship in 1901. These competitions were soon followed by the MFA Cup, the Cousis Shield and the Cassar Charity Shield. The FA Trophy, later to become one of the most prestigious domestic contests, was launched in 1934–35.

Clubs from mainland Europe were invited on guest tours in the mid-1920s but the first official international was not played until February 24, 1957 when Malta lost 3–2 at home to Austria. Even the status of this match remains in question because Malta had yet to join FIFA.

For years all important matches were played on the notorious Gzira stadium whose sand, grit and stones

SHADOW MAN Macedonia's Zoran Jovanovski struggles to find a way around Dennis Irwin.

intimidated many a visiting team. Later, however, after a great deal of political confusion, Maltese football took possession of the superb new Ta'Qali national stadium complex.

What the national team and clubs such as Sliema Wanderers, Floriana, Valletta and Hibernians lost in home advantage they gained in prestige from the impressive facilities which were now available.

MOLDOVA

Federatia Moldoveneasca de Fotbal

Founded: 1990
Joined FIFA: 1994

Moldova is another of the states which gained independence with the fragmentation of the old Soviet Union. Various ethnic groups expected Moldova to be moulded into either Romania or Ukraine. Instead the people decided to go their own way – refusing in their haste even to go through the route out offered to the

old Soviet states by the halfway house of the Commonwealth of the Independent States.

The main stadium in the capital, now known as Chisinau, is the Republic Stadium, with a capacity of 20,000, and the country's most famous footballing son is the Russian and former Soviet international, Igor Dobrovolski. He was born in Ukraine but was brought up in Moldova before being "discovered" and lured away as a teenager by Moscow Dynamo.

In the pre-independence days, Moldovan clubs competed in the regional structure of the old Soviet Supreme Championship. Zimbru became the first Moldovan club to compete in European club competition when they were allowed into the Champions Cup in 1993–94, but they went out on a 3–1 aggregate to Betar Jerusalem. Moldova's national team entered international competition in the 1996 European Championship qualifiers and opened sensationally by defeating Georgia 1–0 in Tbilisi and then Wales 3–2 in Chisinau.

NORTHERN IRELAND

Irish Football Association Ltd.

Founded: 1880
Joined FIFA: 1911

Football was launched back in the days of an Ireland united under British rule. The Irish Football Association was established in 1880. The first recorded match to take place was a friendly played in Belfast between Scottish clubs Caledonian FC and Queen's Park.

The immediate consequence was the formation of a locally based Ulster FC and then Cliftonville in Ballyclare at the instigation of J M McAlery, the so-called "Father of Irish Football". Belfast Celtic were founded in 1881 and Linfield in 1887.

Within two years of that first match, international fixtures were being undertaken. Initial signs were not promising. First came a 13–0 defeat by England in Belfast and then a 7–1 thrashing by Wales in Wrexham, both within seven days in 1882.

THE GREATEST George Best demonstrates his mastery of the football.

In due course, political developments cast a long shadow across the Irish game. A number of matches were marred by politically-influenced crowd disturbances in the run-up to partition. Ultimately, the Irish FA's influence was reduced to the Six Counties of Ulster or Northern Ireland. Up until the mid-1980s, however, its international achievements belied its size.

Northern Ireland shared the Home International Championship titles in 1956, 1958 and 1959 and achieved a historic first win over England at Wembley in 1957. Danny Blanchflower was the inspirational captain and right-half who then led the Irish to a shock victory over Italy in the 1958 World Cup qualifying competition.

A spirited team managed by Peter Doherty and spearheaded in attack by Aston Villa's Peter MacParland reached the quarter-finals in Sweden before – weakened by injury, fatigue and a lack of players – they went out 4–0 to the France of Just Fontaine and Raymond Kopa.

Northern Ireland have appeared in the finals on a further two occasions but, sadly, their greatest-ever player, George Best, never appeared on the World Cup stage. By the time Northern Ireland returned to the finals tournament, in Spain in 1982 (when they were again eliminated by France, this time 4–1) and in Mexico in 1986, Best's meteoric career had already burned out.

The mantle of leadership had fallen instead to players such as midfielder Sammy McIlroy and goal-keeper Pat Jennings – who, in the 1986 finals in Mexico, set a world record 119 caps.

NORWAY

Norges Fotballforbund
Founded: 1902
Joined FIFA: 1908

Norway were once considered a sort of inferior Sweden – a Scandinavian side with strength and commitment but lacking in finesse.

All that has changed completely now Norway is able to boast having twice out-thought, outplayed and beaten England in World Cup qualifying ties, reached the 1994 World Cup finals, sold a string of players to English clubs and seen champions Rosenborg Trondheim knock mighty Milan out of the 1996–97 UEFA Champions League.

Until the turn of the 1980s, to summon up Norwegian football's greatest exploit required a football history book going back to the 1936 Berlin Olympic Games. Here Norway caused a historic upset, beating their German hosts in front of an enraged Adolf Hitler. Italy took Axis revenge but even the ultimate gold medal-winners defeated Norway only 2–1 in the semi-finals.

Two years later Italy defeated Norway again, this time in the first round of the 1938 World Cup finals in France. Norway lost 3–1 in the Velodrome in Marseille but not until they had taken Italy to extra time.

Soccer was introduced to the Norwegian ports of Oslo and Bergen by students in the 1880s. The oldest surviving club is Odds BK, founded in Skien in 1894 but long out of the running for the major prizes. The club scene has been dominated more recently by Moss, Brann Bergen, Viking Stavanger – where Tony Knapp proved one of the many Brits to work successfully in Norway – and Rosenborg.

Ambitious players had to build their reputations in club football abroad. For goalkeeper Erik Thorstvedt that meant with Tottenham in England, which duly welcomed many other compatriots such as Henning Berg, Oyvind Leonhardsen, Steffen Iversen, Stig-Inge Bjornebye and Ole Gunnar Solskjar. Sweeper Rune Bratseth, a cornerstone of the Norwegian side which, in 1994,

ARM'S LENGTH Stig Bjornebye holds off Italy's Nicola Berti.

MILLION MAN Poland's Zbigniew Boniek.

and Jerzy Gorgon – guided Poland to third place in the World Cup finals in West Germany. Along the way they beat England in the qualifiers.

Poland finished third again in Spain in 1982 when the conveyor belt which had produced so many outstanding players in such a comparatively short time came up with the best of all in Zbigniew Boniek. "Zibi" later became the most expensive eastern European player when he joined Italy's Juventus for £1 million in 1982 on his way to winning 80 caps for his country.

Perhaps the greatest of Boniek's talents was the ability to rise to the occasion, such as the World Cup second round tie in 1982 when Solidarity union banners were unfurled on the Nou Camp terraces in Barcelona, and Boniek responded with a thrilling hat-trick against Belgium.

Boniek also produced Juventus' winner against FC Porto in the 1984 Cup-winners Cup Final and it was Boniek's pace which provoked the controversial penalty from which Michel Platini won the tragic 1985 Champions Cup Final against Liverpool in Brussels.

PORTUGAL

Federacao Portuguesa de Futebol
Founded: 1914
Joined FIFA: 1923

Portugal owed their introduction to football to the British but it is to Brazil, who share their language, that officials, coaches, players and fans have looked for their style. Sadly, Portuguese football has also suffered from the sort of administrative confusion which has been a hallmark of the Brazilian game, too.

Benfica, FC Porto and Sporting are among the most famous clubs in the world and Portugal among the most popular senior national teams and most successful junior teams. Yet all have been held back in recent years by a number of underlying structural problems.

For example, it was clearly unsatisfactory that, in the mid-1990s, Porto president Jorge Pinto da Costa was

reached the World Cup finals for only the second time, starred in Germany with Werder Bremen. He was voted best sweeper in the Bundesliga before returning home to become general manager of Rosenborg.

POLAND

Polski Zwiazek Noznij
Founded: 1919
Joined FIFA: 1923

Poland, in both political and naturally therefore sporting terms, was a creation of the fall-out from World War One. Football was popular from the turn of the century but a formal Polish federation had to wait until 1919 with a first international following in 1921 – a 1–0 defeat by Hungary in Budapest – FIFA membership in 1923 and a national league championship in 1927.

Poland made brief headlines at the 1938 World Cup finals, when Ernst Willimowski scored four goals in a remarkable 5–4 defeat by Brazil, but the country had to wait until the 1970s to come of football age.

Polish clubs were involved almost from the start in the development of the European competitions in the late 1950s when Ernst Pol emerged as Poland's next great player. But it was 1970 which was the watershed year. That was when the miners club from Silesia, Gornik Zabrze, became the first (and, so far, only) Polish club to reach a European final.

A 2–1 defeat by Manchester City in the rain in the Cup-Winners Cup Final in Vienna was disappointing in itself but signalled great things to come. Thus in 1972 Poland won the Olympic title in Munich and two years later the nucleus of that team – Kazimierz Deyna, Robert Gadocha

EXPORT SPECIAL Portuguese midfielder Rui Costa.

also president of the league and heading the referees' commission.

Simultaneously the domestic game was awash with rumours of match-fixing which undermined its credibility and drove away the fans. All very sad after the Portuguese national team had brought a flair and technical vigour to Euro 96 which deserved better than a quarter-final defeat by the Czech Republic.

The first officially recorded club match in Portugal was played in 1888, Benfica were founded in 1904, Sporting two years later, a league was set up in 1909, the federation in 1914 and the national team made their debut in 1921.

Portugal first entered the World Cup in 1934 and have entered every European Championship since the continental event was launched in 1959–60. In all that time their successes have been few and far between. Portugal's finest World Cup was 1966, when they reached the finals for the first time and finished third.

A team inspired by the attacking power of Eusebio scored a memorable quarter-final victory over North Korea – hitting back from 3–0 down – before losing 2–1 to England in a glorious semi-final. A Eusebio penalty and a goal by Jose Torres in the closing minutes provided victory against the Soviet Union in the Third Place Play-off.

Portugal's team was built around the attack of Benfica – European club champions in 1961 and 1962 – plus the defence of Sporting – Cup-winners Cup winners in 1962. Apart from Eusebio, players such as midfield general Mario Coluna, wingers Jose Augusto and Antonio Simoes and centre-forwards Jose Aguas and Torres wrote their names into the history books.

In 1984 Portugal enjoyed their finest European Championship campaign. Once again, the semi-final was as far as they went before Spain beat them in a penalty shoot-out. Two years later they were first-round failures in the World Cup finals but amends were made shortly afterwards. Under Carlos Queiros, Portugal were twice world youth champions with budding teenage superstars from goal-keeper Vitor Baia to midfielders Rui Costa and Paulo Sousa and striker Joao Vieira Pinto.

Then Romania reached the finals of the 1984 European Championship in France. The nucleus of that team came from the army club, Steaua Bucharest, who became eastern Europe's first European club champions when, in 1986, they beat Barcelona on penalties in Seville.

Outstanding players were strikers Dudu Georgescu and Rodion Camataru, both of whom won the Golden Boot awarded annually to Europe's top league goalscorer. Georgescu won with 47 goals in 1977; Camataru, in controversial circumstances, with 44 a decade later.

Steaua's coach, Emerich Jenei, was later appointed manager of the national team and steered Romania to the finals of the 1990 World Cup.

REPUBLIC OF IRELAND

Football Association of Ireland
Founded: 1921
Joined FIFA: 1923

Football was launched in Ireland in the late 1870s but the formal history of Irish Republic football began following the political division of 1921 and the establishment of the Football Association of Ireland.

Not bounded by the xenophobia which kept the four British associations out of the international football family, the Irish can boast a proud record of having entered all except the very first World Cup competition. Indeed, in the 1934 event Paddy Moore became the first player to score four goals in a single qualifying match. His feat was accomplished in a remarkable 4–4 draw with Belgium in Dublin.

Throughout the post-war years footballers from the Irish Republic contributed in significant numbers to top clubs in the English Football League. These ranged from defender Johnny Carey to midfield general Johnny Giles, just two of the considerable number of outstanding talents to shine for Manchester United.

It took an English manager, Jack Charlton, to harness Irish potential at international level. Charlton first took the Republic to the finals of the 1988 European Championship, where they opened with a memorable 1–0 victory over England. This was not the first time the Republic had beaten England: the most notable previous success was by 2–0 at Goodison Park, Liverpool, in 1949. Thus Ireland, rather than Hungary, became the first foreign team to win on English soil.

As for Charlton, England's World Cup-winning centre back in 1966, his ultimate managerial achievement followed in the World Cup. He guided the Republic to the quarter-finals in 1990 and the second round in 1994 before being succeeded by his one-time captain, Mick McCarthy.

ROMANIA

Federatia Romana de Fotbal
Founded: 1909
Joined FIFA: 1930

Romania secured a place in soccer history as one of the four European nations who competed at the inaugural World Cup finals in Uruguay in 1930. They did so thanks to the enthusiasm and generosity of King Carol, who offered to pay the wages of the leading players while they were away.

His regal gesture was rewarded, however, only by first-round elimination and Romania struggled for 50 years before asserting themselves on the international stage.

DANCING FOR JOY *Romanian World-Cup hero Gheorghe Hagi.*

Here a team inspired in attack by Gheorghe Hagi – the "Maradona of the Carpathians" – and Marius Lacatus reached the second round only to lose on a penalty shoot-out to the Republic of Ireland. Four years later they went one round better, defeating Argentina in the second round before losing unluckily on penalties to Sweden in the quarter-finals. Hagi was still their inspiration, superbly supported by defensive mid-fielder Gica Popescu both at USA'94 and at Euro 96.

In England they were again short of luck. This time Romania had a potentially vital goal disallowed against France because Danish referee Peter Mikkelsen did not see the ball bounce down from the bar, behind the goal-line and out again into play.

RUSSIA

Rossiiski Futbolnyi Soyuz
Founded: 1912
Joined FIFA: 1992

The story of Russian football is a tale of political complexity.

Popularly, football is recorded as having been introduced to Czarist Russia in 1887 by Britons Clement and Harry Charnock, whose family managed cotton mills in Orekhovo Zuyevo some 50 miles east of Moscow. Simultaneously, however, students were coming home to St Petersburg from Britain with the new craze and soon teams were starting to appear in the city's schools and military academies.

A Moscow league was formed in 1901 and in the succeeding years regional leagues sprang up throughout the territory and major cities of what would duly become, after all the revolutionary upheavals, the Soviet Union. Russia even entered a team at the 1912 Olympic Games in Stockholm.

In the turmoil of the 1920s, Russian or Soviet sports teams were barred from international contact. But that same decade saw the creation of clubs such as Moscow Dynamo, Spartak, Torpedo and CSKA which would become pillars of the commun-ist recreational structures. A national

TAKING OFF Midfielder Alexander Mostovoi.

LEADING BY EXAMPLE Scotland's Gary McAllister.

SAN MARINO

Federazione Sanmarinese Gioco Calcio
Founded: 1931
Joined FIFA: 1988

San Marino, Liechtenstein and Andorra are Europe's weakest three nations. Indeed San Marino is not so much a nation, rather it is an enclave within Italy, some 15 miles from the Adriatic seaside resort of Rimini.

Its history dates back to the 10th century but a football federation was set up little more than 60 years ago. Even then it was not until after the election of Giorgio Crescenti as president in 1985 that the possibility of full international independence was realized.

UEFA and FIFA membership ultimately followed in the summer of 1988. The first official match played by San Marino was a friendly against the Danish club, Odense BK. This was staged in the 7,000-capacity San Marino "national stadium" at Serravalle, in 1985, and ended in a 1–1 draw.

San Marino has produced only one top-class footballer: Massimo Bonini, a Champions Cup-winning midfielder with Juventus in 1985 who later became San Marino's national coach.

SCOTLAND

Scottish Football Association
Founded: 1873
Joined FIFA: 1910

Scottish football has always been, at international level, long on pride but comparatively short on achievement. The national team have regularly attended the World Cup finals – though they missed 1994 – and have been present at the last two European Championship finals tournaments. But they have never progressed beyond the first round and, at club level, only Celtic have ever won the Champions Cup (in 1967).

Rangers, for all their European league ambitions, won only the Cup-winners Cup and that back in 1972. Aberdeen also won the Cup-Winners Cup once. Yet Rangers and Celtic are two of the most famous clubs in the world and Scottish football has

league was set up in 1936 but it was not until a decade later, in the wake of World War Two, that Soviet soccer finally came in from the cold.

The Soviet Union won the Olympic title in Melbourne in 1956, reached the quarter-finals two years later on their first tilt at the World Cup and won the inaugural European Championship in 1960. They were European runners-up in 1964, 1972 and 1988 and fourth in 1968. As for

the World Cup, despite all their power and pretensions, their best finish was fourth in 1966.

In the 1970s and 1980s the Soviets turned away from the more physical Russian game to embrace the technical bravado of Kiev Dynamo, who were twice winners of the Cup-Winners Cup. But that, ultimately, produced no better results because the excessive number of fixtures wore down even stars such as European

Footballer of the Year Oleg Blokhin.

After the communist collapse, the Soviet Union transmogrified into the Commonwealth of Independent States at the 1992 European Championship finals. The newly independent Russian federation assumed the Soviet place in the international game. It also took over all those current international players from the other republics who wished to be Russian for, at least, professional purposes.

NEW COUNTRY, NEW STAR
Slovenia's Dzoni Novak.

produced a string of outstanding personalities from Alex James to Paul McStay via George Young, Jim Baxter, Dave Mackay, Jock Stein, Denis Law, Kenny Dalglish, Graeme Souness and Ally McCoist.

Scotland's general international path has matched that of England. They started together in the world's very first international (a 0–0 draw) in 1872, quit FIFA and the international competitive scene together in the 1920s over broken-time payments to amateurs, then returned together to the FIFA fold in 1946.

Scotland might also have travelled, along with England, to the 1950 World Cup finals in Brazil. The Home International Championship was the qualifying event and the top two nations had the right to go to the finals.

Scotland, for reasons never sensibly explained, insisted that they would go to the World Cup only if they finished top of the group. In the event, they finished runners-up to England, who beat them at Hampden Park in the last match, and stayed home.

Even when they qualified, controversy pursued them, as in 1978 when Scotland winger Willie Johnston tested positive in a dope check. Ally MacLeod's managerial reputation never quite recovered from that. But Jock Stein, Alex Ferguson, Andy Roxburgh and Craig Brown made good the damage in the years which followed – culminating in Scotland's appearances at the European finals of 1992, where they lost narrowly to both

SHOULDERS France's Lizarazu and Spain's Lopez clash.

Holland and Germany, and 1996, where they were unlucky to lose a dramatic Wembley showdown with England.

SLOVAKIA

Football Association of Slovak Republic
Founded: 1990
Joined FIFA: 1994

Slovakia were always poor relations in football terms before the split from the Czech Republic though Slovan Bratislava did once win the European Cup-Winners' Cup in the 1960s. Slovakia made their international competitive debut in the 1996 European Championship and were unlucky to find themselves drawn in a group due to be dominated by outstanding Romanian and French teams. In such company, third place added up to a promising start. Top Slovak player of the 1990s has been winger Peter Dubovsky who made his name with Slovan Bratislava before being lured away to Spain by Real Madrid. So far Slovakia have never looked like matching the ongoing achievements of their former political partners in the Czech Republic.

SLOVENIA

Nogometna Zveza Slovenija
Founded: 1920
Joined FIFA: 1992

Slovenia, first state to break free of the former Yugoslavia, finished a disappointing fifth (out of six countries) in their Euro 96 qualifying group on their competitive debut. Olimpija of Ljubljana have been the most successful club, winning the league title four years in a row following Slovenia's attainment of secure and peaceful independence. Italy-based Matjasz Florjancic has been the creative heart of Slovenia's national team efforts.

SPAIN

Real Federacion Espanola de Futbol
Founded: 1913
Joined FIFA: 1904

The big clubs, rather than the national team, hold responsibility for Spain's intimidating reputation as a football nation.

The European club scene in the 1950s was dominated by Real Madrid and Barcelona. Madrid won the Champions Cup five times in a row and Barcelona collected the old Fairs Cup (precursor of the UEFA Cup) twice. Along the way various of their foreign signings were pressed into service for Spain – such as Madrid's Alfredo Di Stefano and Hector Rial (ex-Argentina), Jose Santamaria (ex-Uruguay) and even Ferenc Puskas (ex-Hungary).

In later years economic realism compelled a greater concentration on youth and nursery team schemes. Thus Madrid's "second generation" for Spain were not imported but home-grown, such as Emilio Butragueno, Michel, Ricardo Gallego and Rafael Martin Vazquez. Today's Spanish heroes, apart from the remarkable young Brazilian, Ronaldo,

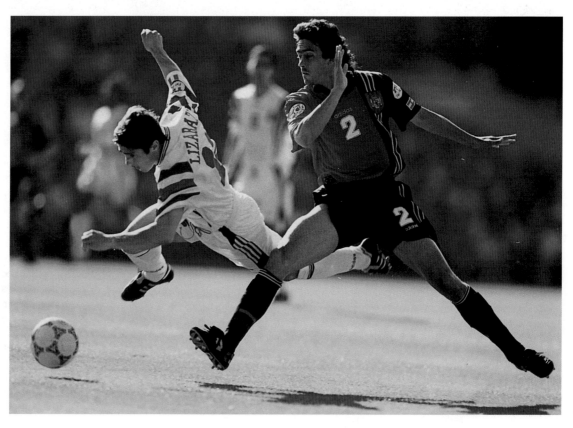

at Barcelona, are also home-grown: Real Madrid's Raul Gonzalez and Barcelona's Ivan de la Pena.

Their ability is underlined by the manner in which they have forced a way through despite the virtual collapse of foreign player restrictions, in the wake of the Bosman case, and the multi-million TV investment which has permitted the Madrids and Barcelonas to buy up just about anything which moves.

Yet, for all the club domination, the Spanish national team have also had their moments. For example it was Spain, in Madrid on May 15, 1929, who became the first continental team ever to defeat England; secondly, Spain won the European Championship in 1964 (also in Madrid) after disposing of Romania, Northern Ireland, the Republic of Ireland, Hungary and the Soviet Union, 2–1 in the final; thirdly, they won the 1992 Olympic Games title in Barcelona.

At World Cup level, Spain's best remains fourth place in Brazil in 1950 – the first and last time when the final round was played on a league basis.

Spain boasts some of the finest football stadia in the world and some of the most fanatical fans. Football in Spain served as a political vehicle, too. The number of clubs boasting the prefix Real (or Royal) stemmed from the support the sport gained from King Alfonso XIII in the early years of the century.

After the Spanish civil war, football offered people in the regions such as Catalunya and Vizcaya their only opportunity for protest and tacit opposition to the dictatorship of General Francisco Franco. Thus the traditional rivalry between Barcelona and Real Madrid is more than merely a sporting contest.

These two amazingly successful clubs compete against each other in the transfer market – sometimes having even signed players not because they wanted them but to stop their rivals buying them. Very few players have lined up for both clubs. Notable exceptions to the rule in the past 40 years have included Spaniards Luis Enrique and Justo Tejada, Brazilian centre-forward Evaristo de Macedo, French midfielder Lucien Muller, Belgian wing-half Ferdinand Goyvaerts and the temperamental German, Bernd Schuster.

SUNSHINE SWEDE Feyenoord forward Henrik Larsson.

SWEDEN

Svenska Fotboliforbundet
Founded: 1904
Joined FIFA: 1904

Football was brought to Sweden through the ports and it is the provincial centres of Gothenburg and Malmo which have generally proved more dynamic soccer centres than the capital, Stockholm.

Remarkably Sweden, a country whose domestic game has never been anything more than part-time, have a proud World Cup record which says much for the talent and pragmatism of players and coaches.

Sweden reached the quarter-finals of the World Cup in 1934 and finished fourth in 1938. After the war they won the 1948 Olympic Games in London to launch themselves upon further success at top level.

Managed by Englishman George Raynor, the Swedes produced several great players who were quickly lured away to Italy. The inside forward trio of Gunnar Gren, Gunnar Nordahl and Nils Liedholm became legendary with Milan as the Grenoli trio.

Raynor rebuilt his team for the 1950 World Cup where Sweden finished third. That success helped clinch for Sweden the right to stage the 1958 finals, when Raynor was allowed by the federation to recall the Italy-based mercenaries such as Liedholm and Gren and wingers Kurt Hamrin and Lennart "Nacka" Skoglund.

Sweden reached the Final before losing 5–2 in Stockholm to Pele's incomparable Brazilians.

In the European Championship Sweden did not reach the finals for the first time until 1992 and then only courtesy of their right as hosts. However, under Tommy Svensson, they proved worthy of the status and reached the semi-finals. Svensson used a simple tactical framework while concentrating his players' minds on doing the simple things well.

Solid defending, perceptive midfield control from Jonas Thern and Stefan Schwarz plus the attacking skills of Tomas Brolin then took Sweden on to third place at the 1994 World Cup.

That this was no fluke was underlined by the manner in which IFK Gothenburg, twice winners of the UEFA Cup in the 1980s, became virtual ever-presents in the UEFA Champions League.

SWITZERLAND

Schweizerische Fussball-Verband
Founded: 1895
Joined FIFA: 1904

Switzerland were effective secondary pioneers in spreading the football gospel at the start of the twentieth century. They took to the game back in the 1860s, then helped carry it south to Milan and Genoa as well as south-west where a Swiss émigré, Hans Gamper, founded Spanish giants Barcelona.

Grasshopper, the best known Swiss club on account of their picturesque name, were founded by the English in 1886, and represent the dominant power of the Swiss-German "school" of soccer. Only Servette, from "French" Geneva, have challenged that supremacy with much success. And the "Italian" clubs have achieved next to nothing.

In 1924, Switzerland reached the Olympic Games Final in Paris only to lose 3–0 to the emergent Uruguayans. Their clubs took part sporadically in the Mitropa Cup – the 1930s forerunner of today's European tournaments – and in 1934 and 1938 Switzerland reached the finals of the World Cup in Italy and France.

Switzerland owed much of their success either side of the Second World War to Karl Rappan, an Austrian and a shrewd manager and tactician who devized the Swiss bolt defensive system. This was the

foundation through which they reached the 1950 World Cup finals, and then got to the quarter-finals as hosts in 1954. An astonishing 7–5 defeat by Austria ended their dreams of success.

Switzerland fell in the first round of the finals in 1962 and 1966 and then were largely missing from the international top table until Englishman Roy Hodgson took over the national team in the 1990s. Hodgson created cohesion which brought the best out of a bright new generation of players led by

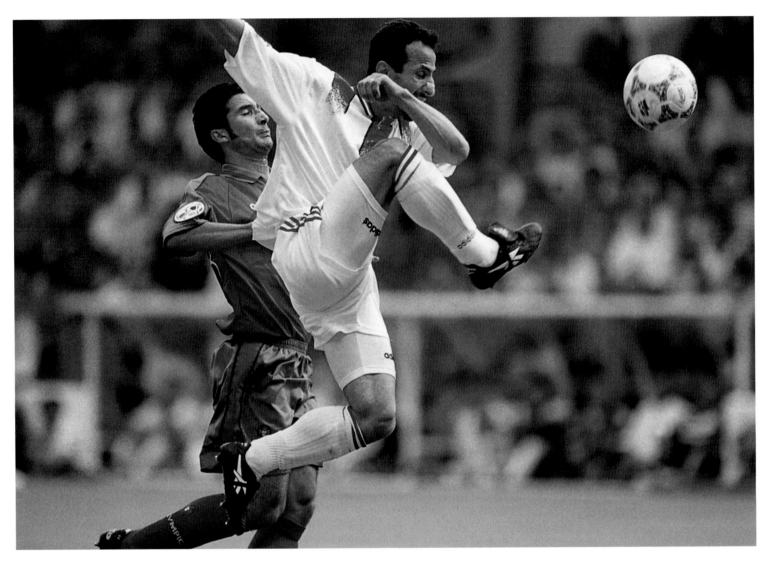

midfielder Ciri Sforza and striker Stephane Chapuisat.

Hodgson took Switzerland to the second round of the World Cup finals in 1994 and secured qualification for Euro 96 before his success encouraged an impossible-to-refuse offer from Italian club Internazionale. His players began well in the European Championship, holding England to a 1–1 draw, but then narrowly lost to Holland and Scotland, whose greater experience of top-level soccer proved too much for the Swiss to handle. Consolation was the emergence of midfielder Ciri Sforza and striker Kubilay Turkyilmaz – among others – as players of demonstrable international class.

Whatever the fluctuations of the national team's form, Switzerland has never been far from the centre of international action: its status as home to the headquarters of FIFA (Zurich) and UEFA (Nyon, near Geneva) has seen to that.

TURKEY

Turkiye Futbol Federasyonu
Founded: 1923
Joined FIFA: 1923

Turkish football has improved by leaps and bounds in the 1990s. The point was demonstrated emphatically when Galatasaray eliminated Manchester United from the European Champions Cup in 1993–94 and then again when the national team reached the finals of the 1996 European Championship.

They were eliminated in the first round but they did not disgrace themselves against Portugal, Denmark and Croatia. Anyway, as coach Fatih Terim insisted: "What is important is getting to the finals. This will do wonders for our players' confidence."

Football was played in secret, originally, in the early years of the century when such westernized team sports were considered undesirable. But the climate of opinion changed rapidly and the early years of the century saw the creation of the three Istanbul clubs which still dominate Turkish football today: Galatasaray, Besiktas and Fenerbahce.

Former West Ham and Blackburn forward Sydney Puddefoot had two spells coaching in Istanbul, but a "proper" national championship had to wait until 1960 and it was not long before foreign coaches and then players were hired in droves to help improve domestic standards.

One such pioneer was George Dick, a Scottish inside-forward who played for Blackpool, West Ham, Carlisle, Stockport and Workington in the 1940s and early 1950s. He was followed by other Britons who, with varying degrees of success, included Brian Birch, Don Howe, Malcolm Allison, Gordon Milne and Graeme Souness. The Turks have also

ALL CLEAR Turkey's Recep Cetin clears from Portugal's Antonio Folha.

employed Germans such as Sepp Piontek and Jupp Derwall.

Turkey have reached the World Cup finals on one occasion so far. That was in 1954 when they got to the finals after a play-off against Spain in Rome ended all-square and a blind boy, drawing lots, pulled their name out of the hat.

Two years later, Turkey made headlines again, this time beating Ferenc Puskas's Hungary 3–1 in Istanbul. It was only the Hungarians' second defeat in five years and 49 matches. The heroes were goalkeeper Turgay Seren and two-goal winger Kucukandonyadis Lefter. They remained the two most famous Turkish footballers until goal-scorer Hakan Sukur during the 1990s provided fans with a modern-day hero.

UKRAINE

Federatsija Futbola Ucrainy
Founded: 1991
Joined FIFA: 1992

Kiev Dynamo had been one of Europe's top clubs yet Ukraine's international competitive debut after the Soviet collapse was disappointing. They offered little threat to Croatia and Italy in the Euro 96 qualifying tournament.

Mafia attempts to infiltrate the domestic game did not help, nor did Kiev's expulsion from European competition for trying to bribe Spanish referee Antonio Lopez Nieto before a Champions League tie. Indeed, Ukraine football was in such a parlous state that UEFA later quashed Kiev's

THE "NEW BEST" Welsh winger Ryan Giggs.

three-year suspension on what might be termed "compassionate grounds".

WALES

Football Association of Wales
Founded: 1876
Joined FIFA: 1910

Wales appear very much nowadays as poor relations in the British football set-up. The national team have qualified for the World Cup finals only once and it is more than 30 years since Cardiff City appeared, and then only briefly, in the top division.

The sporting image of Wales remains more strongly identified with rugby union even though the National Stadium is used internationally now by both football codes. Certainly, the image of Welsh domestic football was not helped by the

wrangling over the creation of a national league championship.

Cardiff stayed in the English league system but remain the most famous Welsh club – though their greatest years were the 1920s. They missed out once on a League Championship only on goal average (the division of home goals by away goals) and then became the only club ever to take the FA Cup out of England thanks to a famous Wembley victory over favourites Arsenal.

Wales's only World Cup finals appearance was in 1958 after they won a lucky losers' play-off against Israel to reach Sweden. Outstanding Welsh players included goalkeeper Jack Kelsey, Ivor and Len Allchurch in attack and the great John Charles – at the height of his "Gentle Giant" prowess with Italy's Juventus. Wales reached the quarter-finals before

losing only 1–0 to Brazil, for whom the 17-year-old Pele scored the decisive goal.

YUGOSLAVIA

Fudbalski Savez Jugoslavije
Founded: 1919
Joined FIFA: 1919

Yugoslavia are now back in the international game after a four-year "freeze" imposed because of security concerns following the tragic outbreak of civil war which led to independence for Slovenia, Macedonia, Croatia and Bosnia-Herzegovina. What is left for the new Yugoslavia are the republics of Serbia (capital Belgrade) and Montenegro.

The war increased the flight of players and coaches to western Europe from a region which had always been Europe's leader in the talent export business. That image was first fostered in 1930, when Yugoslavia were one of only four European nations to brave the Atlantic crossing and attend the first World Cup finals in Uruguay. Exports then included inside forward Ivan Beck, who played for Sete in France. Beck scored one goal in a 2–1 defeat of Brazil which put Yugoslavia in the semi-finals. Other key players were forwards Alexander Tirnanic and Barne Sekulic – both later national managers.

Yugoslavia returned to the World Cup finals in 1950 with a squad full of future managerial talent, including Ivica Horvat, Zlatko Cajkowski, Bernard Vukas, Stjepan Bobek and Rajko Mitic. Luck was against them. Before the match against Brazil Mitic cut his head on a steel rail in the players' tunnel. By the time he had been bandaged up and joined the game, the Slavs were already a goal down.

Beaten in the quarter-finals by West Germany in both 1954 and 1958, they achieved their best finish in 1962, when they finished fourth in Chile.

In the European Championship Yugoslavia were runners-up in 1960 and 1968 and top club Red Star Belgrade won both the UEFA Cup and then the Champions Cup before the eruption of fighting in the early 1990s.

Yugoslavia would have been among the favourites to win the 1992 European Championship finals in Sweden had security concerns not led to their expulsion.

CLUB COMPETITIONS

It is impossible today to imagine European football without the glamour, excitement and constant controversy provided by the three major international club tournaments. Yet the Champions Cup, Cup-winners Cup and UEFA/Fairs Cup have been up and running together only since the early 1960s. Until then international football meant national teams.

CHAMPIONS CUP

Never mind politicians, it was sport in general – and association football in particular – which was the greatest unifying force in Europe in the second half of the 20th century.

Of course the communications revolution and the increasing ease of travel helped. But these were mere mechanics. It was the sporting ideal of peaceable, competitive interaction which channelled the historic antagonisms of Europe into more acceptable – and entertaining – confrontations.

In the late 1920s the associations of federal Europe had created, under the visionary impulse of Austria's Hugo Meisl, the Mitropa Cup (a contraction of the German Mittel Europa – Central Europe). Italy, Austria, Hungary and Czechoslovakia were the dominant partners though, as the competition's success grew, so their neighbours wanted to join in.

The Mitropa Cup pioneered the format later to become so familiar. It was a knock-out cup competition but each pair of teams played each other home and away with the aggregate score deciding who progressed into the next round. Rapid and FK Austria of Vienna, Slavia and Sparta of Prague, Bologna and Ambrosiana-Inter of Italy were the giants of the age.

The Mitropa staggered back into life after the World War II but the spirit had vanished just as the cold war barriers had gone up between old neighbours. Football's focus of club power shifted west as the top clubs of Italy, Spain, France and Portugal created the Latin Cup. This was an end-of-season tournament played – in a single venue and in a single-match knock-out format – between the newly-crowned champions of each country. "National" points were allocated and, every four years, they were totalled up to provide an overall winning country.

Real Madrid, Barcelona and Benfica achieved their initial taste for European competitive drama in the Latin Cup.

Elsewhere, the end was the same if the means were different. The fledgling fascination of continental football, sparked by the legendary Hungarians of Ferenc Puskas in 1953, provoked progressive Wolverhampton Wanderers into arranging a series of international friendly matches under their new-fangled floodlighting system.

They beat Honved, the Budapest club team which provided Hungary's national team nucleus, and they beat Moscow Spartak. The English newspapers, in their comfortable xenophobia, instantly proclaimed Wolves champions of Europe.

That was like a red rag to a bull for Gabriel Hanot, a former French international who had become editor of the Parisian sports newspaper *L'Equipe*. He had seen the developments at Real Madrid, as well as the thrilling power of a Milan team built around their Swedish Gre-No-Li trio (Gren, Nordahl, Liedholm) and he was thrilled by the potential of a "local" Reims club with a twinkle-toed creative centre forward named Raymond Kopa.

Hanot took out a page of his newspaper to propose a "real" European club cup. He invited representatives of leading clubs from all over Europe to a meeting in Paris, and they laid down the concept of a midweek knock-out competition based on the two-leg aggregate system. Some clubs were more enthusiastic than others.

Madrid, whose ambition knew no bounds under the leadership of president Santiago Bernabeu and secretary Raimundo Saporta, were signing some of the world's finest players and wanted a stage on which to parade them. This was it.

On the other hand Chelsea, league champions in 1955, were ordered by the English football authorities not to go near this disruptive, unauthorized, extra-curricular activity.

The race for glory

So, like most international football competitions, the English missed the start. That was, precisely, on September 4, in front of a crowd of 60,000 in Lisbon where Sporting Clube de Portugal drew 3–3 with Partizan of Belgrade. Four days later Real Madrid set their own ball rolling when they defeated Servette of Geneva 2–0 in Switzerland. Appropriately it was Madrid's right half and captain – and later long-serving coach – Miguel Muñoz who scored their first goal.

This was football in a different era. Television was a new technological toy which caught fading images of the first final but nothing else. There were no sponsors, no commercial side-shows. Football was king – and the glamour of Real Madrid, winning for the first five years in a row, provided the magical lustre which launched the European Champion Clubs' Cup on its journey into the sporting stratosphere.

Even now, with its format changed to incorporate a league system with million-pound bonuses on offer, it remains the most prestigious club event in the world.

The French having dreamed up the idea, the first final was staged, appropriately, in the old Parc des Princes in Paris. England did make one contribution – providing referee Arthur Ellis. Under his control Reims raced into a lead of 2–0 then 3–1. Madrid stormed back to win 4–3. Their Argentine-born centre forward Alfredo Di Stefano, inside forward compatriot Hector Rial and flying left winger Francisco Gento were on their way towards football immortality.

The next season, better late than never, the English joined up in the shape of Manchester United's Busby Babes. They, too, were ordered not to compete but manager Matt Busby shared the same internationalist vision as Madrid, and went his own way ... to both triumph and disaster.

United opened with a 10–0 thrashing of Belgian champions Anderlecht but were ultimately too inexperienced to cope with the semi-final sophistication of Madrid for whom Di Stefano covered huge tracts of the pitch – one

CLASS OF '97... Borussia Dortmund hold the Champions' Cup high.

KIDD'S STUFF ... Brian Kidd heads Man Utd's 3rd against Benfica.

moment clearing from his own penalty area the next shooting for goal at the other end.

Madrid's defence was not up to the standard of their attack – in fact, they needed a replay to defeat Rapid Vienna along the way and would have been eliminated had today's away goals rule then applied – but they could always summon up the necessary goals. Raymond Kopa, leading light with Reims in the first European Cup, starred in the victory over United by 3–1 at home and a 2–2 draw in Manchester.

The final, by initial decision, was to be hosted by the previous year's winners. Thus Madrid beat Italy's Fiorentina 2–0, with goals from Di Stefano (penalty) and Gento in their own Estadio Bernabeu in front of 110,000 delighted Spaniards.

Next season, 1957–58, was overshadowed by tragedy though it also produced a classic final and the first which went to extra time. Benfica of Portugal and Ajax Amsterdam from Holland, both future champions, competed for the first time – albeit Ajax lost to Vasas of Hungary in the quarter-finals while Benfica were beaten in the second round by Sevilla (invited as a second Spanish entry since they had finished league runners-up to Madrid, who benefited from the holders' automatic right of participation).

Munich air crash

Also in the quarter-finals Manchester United scored a thrilling victory over Red Star Belgrade only for their plane to crash on take-off after a refuelling stop in Munich on the way home. Eight players were killed, including England stalwarts Roger Byrne, Duncan Edwards and Tommy Taylor, and a weakened United duly lost to Milan in the semi-finals.

Milan, beaten by Madrid in the 1956 semi-finals, came within a whisker of revenge in the final in the Heysel stadium in Brussels. In the shadow of the Atomium, Di Stefano kept Madrid in the game virtually single-handed and also contributed one of the goals with which they triumphed 3–2 in extra time.

In 1958–59 Reims, returned to the attack with a forward line spearheaded by Just Fontaine, who had scored a record-breaking 13 goals at the World Cup finals in Sweden. He opened his European club account with a four-goal display away to Ards in Northern Ireland.

Two Madrid clubs competed this time, Real as holders and neighbours Atletico by special invitation after finishing runners-up to Real in the Spanish league. They came face to face, too, in the semi-finals. Under present rules, Atletico would have won on away goals. Instead, after winning 1–0 at home and losing 2–1 away across the city, they went down 2–1 in a replay in Zaragoza.

Madrid, despite having Kopa limping for much of the clash against his old club, defeated Reims 2–0 in the final and even permitted themselves the luxury of a penalty miss by Enrique Mateos.

England's challenge was represented by Wolves who proved a shadow of the team in competition that they had been in those famous friendlies. After being granted a first-round bye, they fell in the second round to West German champions Schalke. The gap between the English and top European clubs was brutally exposed the next season, 1959–60. Wolves were thrashed in the quarter-finals by Barcelona who were in turn swatted by Real Madrid in the semis.

The greatest Final

Madrid then exemplified all the class, excitement and drama of the event in the most famous match in its history – their 7–3 demolition of Eintracht Frankfurt at Hampden Park, Glasgow, in May, 1960, before a record crowd for a final. Di Stefano scored three of Madrid's goals with the other four all contributed by the great Hungarian Ferenc Puskas – who had been rescued from oblivion by Madrid after fleeing Hungary following the Soviet suppression of the 1956 revolution.

It was not that Frankfurt were a poor team – anything but. They had, after all, just put 12 goals past Scottish champions Rangers in the semi-finals and opened the scoring against Madrid in the final.

Looked at today, the final makes strange viewing, considering the space in which the players had time to work. But the flow of goals remains breathtaking with Di Stefano and Puskas, who set a then record with 12 goals in the season's competition, supported brilliantly by Gento, Santamaria and by the hard-working inside right from Betis, Luis Del Sol.

That was also the beginning of the end. Madrid were eliminated in the second round the following season by their Spanish rivals, Barcelona – led by a veteran Hungarian of their own in Ladislav Kubala and by possibly the greatest Spanish footballer of all time in Luis Suarez. He scored both Barcelona's goals in the 2–2 draw in Madrid in the first leg and the Catalans won the return 2–1 against a Madrid side who had defender Pachin at half-pace for much of the game and no luck with several refereeing decisions.

FOREST FIRE ... John McGovern celebrates after beating Malmo.

Barcelona then needed a play-off in Brussels to defeat Germany's Hamburg in the semi-finals. The semi-finals also saw the Cup's first serious crowd trouble when Austrian fans ran amok in Vienna as Rapid headed for defeat against Benfica.

Barcelona were favourites for the final in Bern but Benfica played magnificently to win 3–2 after Barcelona hit both posts and crossbar. Kocsis and left-winger Zoltan Czibor thus took away another bitter memory from the stadium where, seven years earlier, they had ended up as surprise losers with Hungary in the World Cup final.

For the following season, 1961–62, Benfica had reinforced their attack in formidable fashion with the addition of their new Mozambique-born striker, Eusebio. The quarter-finals provided some classic action. The Czech army team, Dukla, guided from midfield by Jozef Masopust, fell to a Tottenham double-winning side reinforced by Jimmy Greaves. Then Italy's Juventus (Omar Sivori, John Charles and all) went down to Real Madrid, though not until

after a play-off in Paris. Juventus had earned the extra chance after becoming the first team in Champions Cup history to beat Madrid in the Estadio Bernabeu.

The Tottenham bubble burst in the semi-finals. Manager Bill Nicholson used Tony Marchi, back from Torino, as an extra defender in away legs but the tactic failed in Lisbon where Spurs lost 3–1 to Benfica. The return was a typical White Hart Lane European special, but Spurs let physical hearts rule footballing heads and Benfica survived to go on and defeat Real Madrid – after being 3–1 down – in yet another fantastic final, this time in Amsterdam.

Season 1962–63 saw the first Italian success. Milan had been original entrants in the Champions Cup, lost one final (in 1958) and had no intention of losing another. They boasted a superb, cosmopolitan team but, for all the midfield wisdom of Brazil's Dino Sani, the goals of Brazil's Jose Altafini and the tight marking of Peru's Victor Benitez, it was Italy's own Gianni Rivera who was the No. 1.

The British challenge was provided by Ipswich for England and Dundee for Scotland and neither proved up to the Milan test. Ipswich were rolled over in the second round while Dundee, after fine victories over Köln, Sporting Lisbon and Anderlecht, fell to Milan in the semi-finals.

Benfica did not have an easy time reaching Wembley, the first English staging of Europe's top club event. Eusebio scored a second-round hat-trick against Norrkoping but then Dukla Prague, followed by Feyenoord, tested Portuguese creativity and resilience to the limits. Perhaps they came to face Milan at Wembley believing that the hardest part was behind them – especially after Eusebio outpaced Giovanni Trapattoni to shoot them ahead. But Milan had planned for a full 90 minutes and Rivera twice sent Altafini away for the two goals which earned him a one-season record of 14.

Pragmatism over flair

The nature of the game was changing. The free-flowing attacking football of the 1950s had given way to a much more pragmatic, physical style. The rewards for victory and the pressure for achievement were increasing all

the time and, in the circumstances, it was hardly surprising that Italian football dominated the Champions Cup in this era.

Helenio Herrera's Internazionale were the most adept exponents of this negative new football, marking tightly at the back and using a sweeper, in skipper Armando Picchi, who was never to be found anywhere except behind his own defenders.

Inter had also bought Luis Suarez from Barcelona to run midfield and revealed the youthful Sandro Mazzola – the equal of Rivera – in attack. Inter had too much all-round strength for Everton, Monaco, Partizan Belgrade and Borussia Dortmund and then too much physical resistance against an ageing, fading Real Madrid in the 1964 final in Vienna. Mazzola scored two of Inter's three goals in the final to finish as the competition's seven-goal joint-top scorer.

Liverpool announced their arrival on the Champions Cup scene by reaching the 1964–65 semi-finals. Bill Shankly's men beat Anderlecht home and away in the second round, but then needed the toss of a coin to beat Köln after a dramatic play-off in Rotterdam in the quarter-finals. They harboured brief ambitions of beating Inter in the semi-finals. But, after winning 3–1 at home, Liverpool were outmanoeuvred in Milan. Inter's Spanish forward, Joaquin Peiro, "stole" a bounced ball from keeper Tommy Lawrence for one goal and attacking full-back Giacinto Facchetti scored a brilliant winner.

In the final, also staged in the San Siro, Inter faced Benfica. The Portuguese, appearing in their fourth Final in five years, had everything against them. First the venue, secondly the crowd, thirdly the monsoon rain which wrecked their delicate interpassing and fourthly the injury which cost them the services of veteran goalkeeper Costa Pereira. Inter won with a single goal from Brazilian right winger Jair and appeared to possess the discipline and iron will to dominate Europe for years. However, the British challenge was growing ever stronger. Manchester United, in 1965–66, became favourites after a thrilling 5–1 victory over Benfica in Lisbon in the quarter-finals – only to blow up against Partizan Belgrade next time out. The Yugoslavs became the first eastern European team to

WITHE'S WINNER ... for Aston Villa against Bayern Munich.

reach the final where their opponents – surprising semi-final victors themselves over holders Inter – were a new Real Madrid.

Di Stefano and Puskas had gone, succeeded by a new youthful generation nicknamed the "Ye-ye" team. They certainly had too much rhythm for Partizan and hit back from 1–0 down to win 2–1 with two goals inside six second-half minutes from Amancio and Serena. That was Madrid's sixth – and, so far, last – Champions Cup.

Neither Liverpool nor Manchester United, surprisingly, achieved the first British success which had been on the cards for several years. Instead it was Scotland's Celtic who brought the Cup back for the first time when they defeated Inter 2–1 in Lisbon's Stadium of Light in 1967. Jock Stein's men overcame the shock of an early penalty by Mazzola to win with storming second-half goals from Tommy Gemmell and Steve Chalmers.

British domination was extended the following season when Manchester United – amid high emotion – marked the 10th anniversary of the Munich air disaster by securing the trophy their predecessors had been pursuing. This time there was no late slip-up, as against Partizan Belgrade at the semi-final stage in 1966, to stand between Matt Busby, Bobby Charlton, Bill Foulkes and destiny.

United beat Hibernians of Malta in the first round, Sarajevo in the second, Poland's Gornik Zabrze in the quarter-finals and then old friends and rivals

Real Madrid in the semi-finals. Indeed, in Madrid United appeared virtually eliminated when they went 3–1 down in the second leg. But they stormed back against all the odds and a goal from defender Bill Foulkes turned the aggregate tables.

Benfica beat Juventus in the semi-finals and resisted bravely against United and the pressure of the Wembley crowd for the first 90 minutes of the final. A late save by goalkeeper Alex Stepney from Eusebio earned United extra time when their superior fitness and ambition lifted them to three further goals and a 4–1 win. Munich survivor Bobby Charlton scored twice before being presented with the Cup as United's captain.

Holland takes over

Their reign, however, lasted less than a year. Milan beat them in the 1969 semi-finals and then thrashed a naive, youthful Ajax Amsterdam 4–1 in the final in the Estadio Bernabeu in Madrid. With hindsight, however, Milan's success was less significant than Ajax's presence in the final. A year later Feyenoord became the first Dutch champions of Europe when they defeated Celtic 2–1 in extra-time in Milan, then Ajax themselves embarked upon the three-year run in which their "total football" enthralled the world game.

In 1971 Ajax collected their first Cup by defeating Panathinaikos of Athens, first Greek finalists and coached by Ferenc Puskas, by 2–1 at Wembley. Their towering centre forward, Antoniadis, had scored freely on the way to the final, including two goals when Panathinaikos overcame a

4–1 first leg defeat by Red Star Belgrade in the semi-finals. But Ajax contained him easily and goals by Van Dijk and Haan did the rest.

"Total football" was perhaps the ultimate expression of modern football – involving footballers of high technical and intellectual competence switching and inter-changing to suit the state of the game. All of it was threaded together by the central genius of Johan Cruyff who also scored most of the goals – including the single effort which was, over 180 minutes, enough to defeat Benfica in the 1972 semi-finals.

Inter, with fortune on their side, qualified to meet Ajax in the final. In the second round the Italians had been thrashed 7–1 by Borussia Mönchengladbach in Germany but obtained a replay in Berlin after protesting that Roberto Boninsegna had been struck by a Coca-Cola can. While UEFA was deliberating, Inter won the second leg 4–2 and then held out for a 0–0 draw in the replayed first leg. They beat Celtic on a penalty shoot-out in the semi-finals but, in the final in Rotterdam, their luck ran out. Two more goals for Cruyff secured Ajax's second cup.

Next season, 1972–73, was Ajax's swan-song. But first they became the first team since Real Madrid to win the Champions Cup three years running. This they achieved thanks to a 1–0 win over Juventus in the final which was a much clearer victory than the result might indicate. Ajax scored through Johnny Rep after only four minutes and played such wonderful, sweeping football over the next quarter of an hour that they could have won by a hatful of goals. It was almost as if they became bored with their own domination.

But, while Ajax could not score any more goals, Juventus could not score any at all despite the presence in their ranks of the veteran Brazilian striker Jose Altafini, of £500,000 centre forward Pietro Anastasi and of German World Cup star Helmut Haller.

England's challenge had been carried by Brian Clough's Derby County, who beat Benfica before falling to Juventus in the semi-finals – where penalty expert Alan Hinton missed a decisive spot kick in the second leg at the Baseball Ground. Further controversy surrounded events in the first leg when Juve's Haller paid a "courtesy

call" on the German referee Tschenscher at half-time in Turin. Derby's protests were ignored.

Bayern's hat-trick

No German team had, up to now, won the Champions Cup. Indeed, Bayern Munich had been put very firmly in their place in the 1973 quarter-finals by Ajax. But now the Ajax bubble had been punctured. Cruyff had been sold to Barcelona for a world record £922,000, coach Stefan Kovacs had gone and Ajax were duly eliminated in the second round by CSKA Sofia.

Franz Beckenbauer's Bayern Munich immediately took over as new favourites – a status they ultimately vindicated though not without difficulty. Reaching the final in the Heysel stadium in Brussels was not so hard. But once there Bayern were within mere seconds of defeat in extra-time by Atletico Madrid. That was remarkable in itself since Atletico had had three players sent off in a battle of a semi-final against Celtic. But they held Bayern goalless through 90 minutes in Brussels then seized the lead through a free-kick from Luis Aragones. Bayern hit back, with a speculative low drive from centre-back Georg Schwarzenbeck, in the very last seconds of injury time.

That meant a replay – the first and last in the history of the event. This time fatigue caught up with Atletico and Bayern won with two goals apiece from Uli Hoeness and Gerd Müller who thus became the season's eight-goal top scorer.

Bayern retained the Cup in 1975 but the final was marred by the first major eruption of a decade of English

STEAUA'S HERO... Ducadam blocks Marcos' penalty in the '86 shoot-out.

hooligan violence in Europe. Angry fans of Leeds United ripped out seats and seat backs in the new Parc des Princes in Paris in the closing minutes of their 2–0 defeat by Bayern Munich.

They were furious that a "goal" by Peter Lorimer had been ruled out though referee Kitabdjian was later justified by film showing Billy Bremner in the centre of the goalmouth, offside and clearly interfering with play. Less easy to defend was Kitabdjian's refusal to award Leeds a penalty for a first-half trip by Beckenbauer.

Bayern, however, certainly earned whatever luck was going. Swedish defender Bjorn Andersson was injured in only the second minute by a "careless" tackle, and a gamble on Uli Hoeness' fitness was quickly exposed as well. Bayern brought on Klaus Wunder up front and withdrew Gerd Müller into midfield where he played with a poise and vision which surprised all those observers who had thought him nothing but a penalty-box poacher.

The Germans duly completed their hat-trick the following season though in unconvincing fashion. They beat Jeunesse d'Esch of Luxembourg 8–1 on aggregate in the first round only to squeeze past Malmo 2–1 in the second. They were then in turn magnificent and irresistible in disposing of Benfica 0–0, 5–1 in the quarter finals and Real Madrid 1–1, 2–0 in the semis. Gerd Müller's wonderful opportunism was the key. He scored two of the five goals against Benfica and all three against Madrid.

Bayern's final opponents were the

first French team to reach that exalted stage since Reims faced Real Madrid in Stuttgart in 1959. Saint-Etienne dominated the first half at Hampden Park, Glasgow, with left-winger Christian Sarramagna a particular thorn in the German defence. Yet the only goal fell to Bayern, 12 minutes into the second half when Franz Roth drove home a low 25-yard drive from a free-kick which caught goalkeeper Yvan Curkovic unsighted.

Bayern very nearly came apart in the last 10 minutes after Saint-Etienne brought on right-winger Dominique Rocheteau. He had been injured and unfit to start the 90 minutes. In the closing minutes he tore the left flank of the German defence to ribbons but all to no avail.

The English invasion

Spain, Portugal, Italy, Holland and Germany had all enjoyed their eras of dominance. Now it was the turn of English football – starting with Liverpool in 1977. Under Shankly and then Bob Paisley, Liverpool had been irresistible for more than a decade in England. It had been only a question of time before they translated that into European success.

Liverpool had already won the UEFA Cup and reached the final of the Cup-Winners Cup before taking the last step up – beating Borussia Mönchengladbach in Rome in what was Kevin Keegan's competitive farewell before his transfer to Hamburg. Allan Simonsen, of Denmark, was Borussia's inspiration but his goal in Rome's Olympic stadium proved mere consolation in a 3–1 defeat.

Liverpool went marching on a year later – better than ever – after filling the Keegan void with the very player best equipped for the challenge in Celtic's Kenny Dalglish. He had joined the Scottish club on the day they won the Champions Cup a decade earlier and completed the circle of achievement by scoring the goal which, for Liverpool, defeated Club Brugge in the 1978 final.

The Belgians had reached Wembley with victories over KuPa of Finland, Panathinaikos, Atletico Madrid and Juventus. But injuries upset all coach Ernst Happel's tactical planning and he opted, in the end, for a highly-defensive formation and a minimal attack in which Hungarian Lajos Ku was making his European debut for the club.

Liverpool's second defence was short-lived, upset in the autumn of 1978 by a Nottingham Forest now managed by former Derby boss Clough, who had become a football cult figure in England – a media super-star whose motivational powers turned losers into winners.

His reputation never travelled to the continent but at least Nottingham Forest's two Champions Cup victories at the turn of the decades ensured a place in the history books for his name.

Forest began with a gesture of intent which said everything by eliminating Liverpool. They won 2–0 at home then drew 0–0 at Anfield. AEK Athens fell next, then Grasshopper Zurich and Köln in the semi-finals. The Germans thought they had achieved most of their task when they drew 3–3 at the City Ground in the first leg but a single goal from Ian Bowyer did the trick for Forest in Germany.

One single goal was also enough in the final against Malmo, the first Swedish side ever to progress so far. The scorer was Trevor Francis, England's first million-pound player when Brian Clough signed him in mid-season from Birmingham City. A diving header shortly before half-time was all it took in Munich's Olympiastadion. For the first time, both managers in the final were English – Clough for Forest and Bob Houghton for Sweden's Malmo.

The opposition to Forest's title defence appeared top-rate the following term. Real Madrid, Ajax, FC Porto, Milan, Hamburg and Liverpool were all considered probably better all-round outfits. But the luck of the draw meant that Porto knocked out Milan and were then eliminated by Real Madrid – who, in turn, fell to Hamburg in the semi-finals. Madrid won 2–0 at home with goals from centre forward Carlos Santillana but then crashed 5–1 in West Germany. Madrid were furious at their failure since the final had already been allocated to their own Estadio Bernabeu.

Instead Hamburg, led by Kevin Keegan, took on Nottingham Forest there. Once again, Forest needed just

EUROPEAN PRESIDENT ... Milan owner Silvio Berlusconi in 1989.

one goal – scored after 19 minutes of the first half by their Scottish international left-winger John Robertson.

The Cup stayed in England for a fifth successive year in 1981 when Liverpool recovered to secure their third European triumph in five seasons with a goal from a most unexpected source – left-back Alan Kennedy bursting through a half-hearted tackle from Real Madrid's Garcia Cortes to thump an angled drive past goalkeeper Agustin in Paris.

Madrid's first appearance in the final for 15 years thus ended in anti-climax, with English winger Laurie Cunningham a fitness gamble and midfield fulcrum Uli Stielike driven deeper and deeper and ultimately out of creative contention by the terrier-like pursuit of Sammy Lee.

Holders Forest had fallen in the first round to the ever-threatening giant-killers of CSKA Sofia. CSKA won 1–0 both home and away but Liverpool ultimately wreaked English football's revenge in the quarter-finals and then defeated Bayern Munich on the away goals rule in the semi-finals.

Madrid defeated Limerick, Honved and Moscow Spartak before renewing, in the semi-finals, their great rivalry with Internazionale. Goals from Santillana and Juanito brought Madrid victory in the Bernabeu while one from sweeper Bini was not enough in the second leg for the Italian champions.

Aston Villa maintained the English grip in 1982. They had won their first league championship in 71 years under the management of Ron Saunders but he parted company with the club within months and Villa's European campaign was plotted by Tony Barton, his former assistant.

Barton, unprepossessing but popular, put together a side which was a team in the very sense of the word – players dedicated to the club and to each other out on the pitch. Gordon Cowans pulled the strings in midfield, Tony Morley provided fireworks out on the left wing and centre forward Peter Withe contributed power through the middle. It was Withe who scored the only goal in the final against Bayern Munich, though he very nearly fell over his own feet

before toe-poking the ball home from inside the six-yard box. Villa's success on the day in Rotterdam was even more remarkable considering they lost goalkeeper Jimmy Rimmer to injury only a few minutes into the game. Nigel Spink barely had time to say: "My mum will be pleased!" before sprinting off the bench and into the action. Bayern had been favourites against Aston Villa but such a role has often weighed too heavily.

Favourites fail again

The Athens Final of 1983 underlined the point that favouritism is a double-edged sword once more, as the galaxy of superstars from Juventus had been expected to run rings around the work-men of Hamburg. Juve were perhaps the most star-studded team of the era, with France's Michel Platini, Poland's Zbigniew Boniek and Italian World Cup-winners in Dino Zoff, Claudio Gentile, Antonio Cabrini, Gaetano Scirea, Marco Tardelli and Paolo Rossi. They beat holders Aston Villa 2–1 away and 3–1 at home in the quarter-finals. But, in the final, one single goal from Hamburg midfielder Felix Magath proved too much for them.

Hamburg's success meant yet another appearance at the peak of the club game for Austrian master coach Ernst Happel, who had won with Feyenoord in 1970 and finished runner-up with Club Brugge in 1978. His defeated opposite number on the Juventus bench was Giovanni Trapattoni who had won the Champions Cup as a player with Milan in 1963 and 1969.

Hamburg's victory was not, however, the precursor of a German revival – just a blip on the Anglo-Italian screen. Liverpool, in 1984, returned to Rome to win again where they had secured their first Champions Cup against Borussia Mönchengladbach.

This time it was nothing like as clear-cut as in 1977 and Liverpool, with Joe Fagan having succeeded the retired Bob Paisley as manager, needed a penalty shoot-out to defeat the home side. Roma, under Swedish coach Nils Liedholm, had beaten CSKA Sofia, Dynamo Berlin and Dundee United on their way to the final. They boasted Brazil's Toninho Cerezo and Paulo Roberto Falcao in midfield plus Italy's own Bruno Conti, Francesco Graziani and Roberto

Pruzzo in attack.

Roma hit back through Pruzzo just before half-time to square Phil Neal's goal. But the longer the match went on the more fragile the Roma confidence appeared. When it came to the shoot-out Falcao, great hero of the local fans, would not take a penalty and Bruce Grobbelaar's wobbly knees did the rest. Conti and Graziani were Roma's unlikely failures in the shoot-out.

Heysel tragedy

The 1985 Champions Cup Final is listed in the record books as having been won 1–0 by Juventus. It is an occasion frequently recalled … but never for the football.

May 29, 1985, was the day of the Heysel stadium disaster when 39 Juventus fans were killed, crushed against or falling through a weak retaining wall after being charged across the terracing by a mob of Liverpool fans. It was the most horrific international display of the evils of hooliganism since the awful scenes were beamed around the world by the television cameras present to broadcast the glories of European club football's most prestigious match.

Criminal charges were laid and proved against Belgian and UEFA officials, despite highly-debatable protests. Video film was used to track down some of the hooligans. Controversy reigned over whether UEFA had been correct in going ahead with the match amid such carnage. But it did keep the remainder of the crowd in the stadium, preventing more trouble on the streets of Brussels and not clogging up traffic lanes cleared for the emergency services.

The match was decided by a penalty converted by Michel Platini but this was not a night to be remembered with pride and provoked the removal of English clubs from Europe for five years.

Yet, oddly, in the first post-Heysel season there was English interest in the Champions Cup Final, in the presence of Barcelona's coach, Terry Venables.

Barcelona reached the 1986 final believing that they needed merely to turn up to win. The venue was also Spanish, the Sanchez Pizjuan stadium in Seville, and their opposition were the little-known, little-appreciated Steaua of Bucharest. No eastern

European club had ever won the Champions Cup and Steaua were not considered in the same class as, say, Red Star Belgrade or Kiev Dynamo. On the night, however, Barcelona's attack was swallowed up by a Romanian defence superbly marshalled by Miodrag Belodedici. Even when it went to a penalty shoot-out Barça could not put the ball in the net. Steaua duly made history.

In 1987 FC Porto became the first Portuguese club since Benfica 25 years earlier to win the Champions Cup when they hit back with style and panache against Bayern Munich in the Prater stadium in Vienna. This was not the Bayern of Beckenbauer and Müller, but a more prosaic team who, despite snatching an early lead through Ludwig Kogl, never controlled the match. Porto, weakened by injury before the kick-off, deserved victory, late as their two goals were.

Paulo Futre had now emerged as a major new force in the European game. He was sold to Atletico Madrid, however, within weeks of the success in Vienna, and Porto also lost the cup. PSV Eindhoven became the third Dutch club to see their name engraved on the Cup when, in 1988, they defeated Benfica in a penalty shoot-out after a goalless draw in Stuttgart.

PSV had been most observers' favourites for the trophy and the only surprise was that Benfica made them work so hard in the final. This was, after all, the year in which a second generation of Dutch football achieved a European monopoly with PSV winning the Champions Cup and then the national team winning the European

OLYMPIQUE GOLD … Marseille skipper Didier Deschamps against Milan.

Championship in West Germany. PSV provided goalkeeper Hans Van Breukelen, defenders Berry Van Aerle and Ronald Koeman as well as midfielder Gerald Vanenburg to the Dutch effort.

In the final Koeman converted PSV's first kick in the penalty shoot-out while Van Breukelen saved the decisive, last, penalty taken by Benfica's Veloso. But this was not the beginning of a new Dutch era, at least, not directly.

Milanese maestros

In the mid-1980s Milan, one of the original Champions Cup contestants back in 1955–56, had been taken over by the millionaire businessman and media magnate, Silvio Berlusconi. He was a long-standing fan of the club but, more, he had a grand commercial vision which would help reshape football as a business in its own right and as a commercial contributor.

Berlusconi poured £20 million into Milan initially to pay off the debts of the old regime and buy Dutch superstars Ruud Gullit and Marco Van Basten (joined a year later by Frank Rijkaard). Results were spectacular. In 1988 Milan won the Italian league, in 1989 they won the Champions Cup and their domination of the European game has extended into the late 1990s.

Milan were among the television stars of Berlusconi's electronic empire and he even flew in his own TV crews and equipment to Barcelona for the 1989 Final when Spanish technicians

went on strike. His investment was rewarded with Milan's sweeping 4–0 victory over Steaua. Gullit and Van Basten scored twice each though some controversy arose later over suggestions from the ruins of the Romanian regime that Steaua were beaten even before the match started.

Milan appeared bound to dominate the Champions Cup in the manner of Real Madrid in the early days. But they did not have it as easy as Berlusconi might have hoped. In 1989–90 they disposed of HJK Helsinki in the first round by 5–0 overall but squeezed past Real Madrid 2–1 in the second round and needed extra time against both Mechelen in the quarter-finals and Bayern Munich in the semis. In the final Milan met Benfica, with a goal from Frank Rijkaard after 67 minutes deciding the Portuguese club's fifth defeat at this stage.

Benfica's presence in the final infuriated French fans after their semi-final victory over Marseille. The French champions, owned by a millionaire businessman in Bernard Tapie who was as major a personality in his own land as Berlusconi in his, had believed they could become the first French club to win the Cup. They beat Benfica 2–1 at home in the semi-finals and, at 0–0 in the closing stages in Lisbon, appeared on the verge of reaching the final. Then Vata struck for Benfica, a goal which delighted the Portuguese fans … and infuriated the French since it had been preceded by a clear handball. The referee was unsighted. Benfica, and not Marseille, were in the final.

Tapie had to wait just one year before Marseille did pierce the semi-final barrier. But the 1991 Final will go down as a Champions Cup paradox. First, the venue. The San Nicola stadium in Bari had been built for the 1990 World Cup but appeared something of a white elephant on the fringe of the south-eastern Italian port. Then the match. Milan had walked off the pitch in Marseille in a sulk after a floodlight failure held up their quarter-final and lost their title virtually by default. In their absence, Marseille and Red Star Belgrade were the best finalists available.

Both were capable of glorious attacking football, as Marseille displayed regularly in France and Red Star achieved in Europe, most notably in their semi-final victory over Bayern Munich. The Final, however, was a negative, fear-ridden bore. Marseille's veteran Belgian coach, Raymond Goethals, used his midfielders to protect defence rather than support attack; Red Star's Ljubko Petrovic left Darko Pancev isolated upfield. Hardly surprisingly, it was 0–0 at the end of extra time and went to penalties – the fourth Champions Cup Final decided in this manner. Manuel Amoros, experienced World Cup veteran, missed Marseille's first kick and Red Star converted all theirs to win 5–3. Sweeper Miodrag Belodedici became the first player to win the Cup with two different clubs, after having collected a winner's medal in 1986 with Steaua Bucharest.

Barcelona at last

Another echo of 1986 was heard in 1992 when Barcelona, beaten finalists both then and in 1961, achieved their long-awaited Champions Cup success. The Catalan giants had appeared jinxed in the one competition they wanted to win above all others. To succeed they had to negotiate safely a new mini-league structure which UEFA had dropped, experimentally, into the spring slot previously taken up by the quarter and semi-finals.

In Group B of the mini-league Barcelona triumphed over Sparta Prague, Benfica and Kiev Dynamo while Group A saw Italy's Sampdoria outrun Red Star Belgrade (now homeless in European competition because of the Yugoslav conflict), Anderlecht and Panathinaikos.

The Final was a repeat of the 1988 Cup-Winners Cup showdown but the game ended without a goal despite some high-quality football. No need for penalties this time, though. Eight minutes before the end of extra-time Barcelona were awarded a free-kick almost 30 yards from goal. Ronald Koeman thundered his drive beyond keeper Gianluca Pagliuca.

Barcelona celebrated in style. They had brought their "real" kit to replace the change strip they had played in and it was in their traditional red and blue that they collected the Cup for which they had waited so long.

UEFA now formalized the mini-league system into the newly-baptized Champions League. The European governing body had called a special meet-

ing to reshape its statutes and secure authority to market the entire competition as it saw fit – with exclusive sponsorship and television contracts.

Rules and regulations played a role in the early rounds, too, when Stuttgart fielded one foreigner too many against Leeds. The English champions won the duly-ordered replay then fell to Rangers – who went on into the Champions League. The Scottish champions very nearly reached the final too but were pipped by Marseille, who faced Milan in Munich.

Marseille's match-fixing

A goal from Basile Boli brought France their first-ever Champions Cup but even that night whispers were circulating about Marseille's match-fixing past. The whispers were not developed for several weeks after what appears, with hindsight, to have been a media and official conspiracy to allow Marseille's players their triumph. Ultimately it emerged that Marseille had fixed the league match before the final, against Valenciennes, so that they could concentrate on facing Milan knowing that the French league title was once again safely theirs.

The ripples of corruption spread on

down the years. Marseille were immediately barred from defending their tarnished Cup but it was not until the spring of 1997 that the now-disgraced Tapie was jailed for match-fixing. By then it had become clear that Marseille had fixed far, far more than just the infamous match with Valenciennes.

The credibility of the Champions Cup was on the line in 1993–94. Milan rose to that challenge – defeating Barcelona in Athens in the final with one of the finest displays seen in the event for more than 20 years.

They did so, remarkably, despite the absences through suspension of key central defenders Alessandro Costacurta and Franco Baresi and the further absence, through injury, of spearhead Marco Van Basten. The exigencies of UEFA's foreigners rules meant, also, that coach Fabio Capello left Romania's Florin Raducioiu and Denmark's Brian Laudrup in the stand.

Barcelona, under Johan Cruyff, were renowned for some of the finest one-touch attacking football in Europe – their attack spearheaded by a fearsome partnership in Brazil's top striker of the time Romario and Bulgaria's Hristo Stoichkov.

Not that they ever saw much of the

ball. Milan took the game by the scruff of the neck with French international Marcel Desailly providing the power and Dejan Savicevic all the skill and inspiration. Daniele Massaro (two), Savicevic and Desailly scored the goals. English clubs were, by now, back in Europe but both they and their German cousins struggled to keep pace with the tactical and technical developments of the international club game. The Italo-Dutch domination of what was now formally entitled the UEFA Champions League – no longer the European Champion Clubs' Cup – continued. Milan's hopes of a record-equalling sixth Cup were wrecked in 1995 when they lost 1–0 to a revived Ajax in Vienna – Patrick Kluivert, ultimately to join Milan in the summer of 1997, scored the winner.

Ajax then surrendered the Cup a year later to Italy – losing on penalties to Juventus in Rome who were then beaten in the 1997 Final by Borussia Dortmund, a team driven by the 1997 European Footballer of the Year, Matthias Sammer.

DELIGHT ... for Ajax after their victory over Italian favourites Milan in the 1995 final.

CHAMPIONS CUP FINALS

1956
June 13 (Parc des Princes, Paris)

Real Madrid 4
(Di Stefano 15, Rial 30, 79, Marquitos 71)

Reims 3
(Leblond 6, Templin 10, Hidalgo 62)

HT: 2–2.
Att: 38,239.
Ref: Ellis (Eng).

Real: Alonso, Atienza, Lesmes, Muñoz*, Marquitos, Zarraga, Joseito, Marsal, Di Stefano, Rial, Gento. Coach: Villalonga.

Reims: Jacquet, Zimny, Giraudo, Leblond, Jonquet*, Siatka, Hidalgo, Glowacki, Kopa, Bliard, Templin. Coach: Batteux.

1957
May 30 (Bernabeu, Madrid)

Real Madrid 2
(Di Stefano 70pen, Gento 76)

Fiorentina 0

HT: 0–0.
Att: 120,000.
Ref: Horn (Hol).

Real: Alonso, Torres, Lesmes, Muñoz*, Marquitos, Zarraga, Kopa, Mateos, Di Stefano, Rial, Gento. Coach: Villalonga.

Fiorentina: Sarti, Magnini, Cervato*, Scaramucci, Orzan, Segato, Julinho, Gratton, Virgili, Montuori, Prini. Coach: Bernardini.

1958
May 29 (Heysel, Brussels)

Real Madrid 3
(Di Stefano 74, Rial 79, Gento 107)

Milan 2
(Schiaffino 59, Grillo 78)

HT: 0–0. After extra-time (90 min: 2–2).
Att: 70,000.
Ref: Alsteen (Bel).

Real: Alonso*, Atienza, Lesmes, Santisteban, Santamaria, Zarraga, Kopa, Joseito, Di Stefano, Rial, Gento. Coach: Carniglia.

Milan: Soldan, Fontana, Beraldo, Bergamaschi, C Maldini, Radice, Danova, Liedholm*, Schiaffino, Grillo, Cucchiaroni. Coach: Puricelli.

1959
June 3 (Neckar, Stuttgart)

Real Madrid 2
(Mateos 2, Di Stefano 47)

Reims 0

HT: 1–0.
Att: 72,000.
Ref: Dusch (Fr).

Real: Dominguez, Marquitos, Zarraga*, Santisteban, Santamaria, Ruiz, Kopa, Mateos, Di Stefano, Rial, Gento. Coach: Carniglia.

Reims: Colonna, Rodzik, Giraudo, Penverne, Jonquet*, Leblond, Lamartine, Bliard, Fontaine, Piantoni, Vincent. Coach: Batteux.

1960
May 18 (Hampden Park, Glasgow)

Real Madrid 7
(Di Stefano 27, 30, 73, Puskas 36, 48 pen, 58, 63)

Eintracht Frankfurt 3
(Kress 18, Stein 72, 76)

HT: 3–1.
Att: 127,621.
Ref: Mowat (Scot).

Real: Dominguez, Marquitos, Pachin, Vidal, Santamaria, Zarraga*, Canario, Del Sol, Di Stefano, Puskas, Gento. Coach: Mutteux

Eintracht: Loy, Lütz, Höfer, Weilbächer, Eigenbrodt, Stinka, Kress, Lindner, Stein, Pfaff*, Meier. Coach: Osswald.

1961
May 31 (Wankdorf, Bern)

Benfica 3
(Aguas 30, Ramallets og 31, Coluna 54)

Barcelona 2
(Kocsis 20, Czibor 75)

HT: 2–1.
Att: 33,000.
Ref: Dienst (Swz).

Benfica: Costa Pereira, Mario Joao, Angelo, Neto, Germano, Cruz, Jose Augusto, Santana, Aguas*, Coluna, Cavem. Coach: Guttmann.

Barcelona: Ramallets*, Foncho, Gracia, Verges, Garay, Gensana, Kubala, Kocsis, Evaristo, Suarez, Czibor. Coach: Orizaola.

1962
May 2 (Olympic, Amsterdam)

Benfica 5
(Aguas 25, Cavem 34, Coluna 61, Eusebio 68pen, 78)

Real Madrid 3
(Puskas 17, 23, 38)

HT: 2–3.
Att: 68,000.
Ref: Horn (Hol).

Benfica: Costa Pereira, Mario Joao, Angelo, Cavem, Germano, Cruz, Jose Augusto, Eusebio, Aguas*, Coluna, Simoes. Coach: Guttmann.

Real: Araquistain, Casado, Miera, Felo, Santamaria, Pachin, Tejada, Del Sol, Di Stefano, Puskas, Gento*. Coach: Muoach.

1963
May 22 (Wembley)

Milan 2
(Altafini 58, 66)

Benfica 1
(Eusebio 18)

HT: 0–1.
Att: 45,000.
Ref: Holland (Eng).

Milan: Ghezzi, David, Trebbi, Benitez, C Maldini*, Trapattoni, Pivatelli, Dino Sani, Altafini, Rivera, Mora. Coach: Rocco.

Benfica: Costa Pereira, Cavem, Cruz, Humberto, Raul, Coluna*, Jose Augusto, Santana, Torres, Eusebio, Simoes. Coach: Riera.

1964
May 27 (Prater, Vienna)

Internazionale 3
(Mazzola 43, 76, Milani 62)

Real Madrid 1
(Felo 69)

HT: 1–0.
Att: 72,000.
Ref: Stoll (Aus).

Inter: Sarti, Burgnich, Facchetti, Tagnin, Guarneri, Picchi*, Jair, Mazzola, Milani, Suarez, Corso. Coach: Herrera.

Real: Vicente, Isidro, Pachin, Muller, Santamaria, Zoco, Amancio, Felo, Di Stefano, Puskas, Gento*. Coach: Murrera

1965
May 27 (San Siro, Milan)

Internazionale 1
(Jair 42)

Benfica 0

HT: 1–0.
Att: 80,000.
Ref: Dienst (Swz).

Inter: Sarti, Burgnich, Facchetti, Bedin, Guarneri, Picchi*, Jair, Mazzola, Peiro, Suarez, Corso. Coach: Herrera.

Benfica: Costa Pereira, Cavem, Cruz, Neto, Germano, Raul, Jose Augusto, Eusebio, Torres, Coluna*, Simoes.Coach: Schwartz.

1966
May 11 (Heysel, Brussels)

Real Madrid 2
(Amancio 70, Serena 76)

Partizan Belgrade 1
(Vasovic 55)

HT: 0–0.
Att: 55,000.
Ref: Kreitlein (WG).

Real Araquistain, Pachin, Sanchis, Pirri, De Felipe, Zoco, Serena, Amancio, Grosso, Velazquez, Gento*. Coach: Muhwart

Partizan: Soskic, Jusufi, Mihajlovic, Becejac, Rasovic, Vasovic*, Bajic, Kovacevic, Hasanagic, Galic, Pirmajer. Coach: Gegic.

1967
May 25 (Lisbon)

Celtic 2
(Gemmell 62, Chalmers 83)

Internazionale 1
(Mazzola 6 pen)

HT: 0–1.
Att: 55,000.
Ref: Tschenscher (WG).

Celtic: Simpson, Craig, Gemmell, Murdoch, McNeill*, Clark, Johnstone, Wallace, Chalmers, Auld, Lennox. Manager: Stein.

Inter: Sarti, Burgnich, Facchetti, Bedin, Guarneri, Picchi*, Domenghini, Bicicli, Mazzola, Cappellini, Corso. Coach: Herrera.

1968
May 29 (Wembley)

Manchester United 4
(Charlton 54, 98, Best 92, Kidd 95)

Benfica 1
(Jaime Graca 78)

HT: 0–0. After extra-time (90 min: 1–1).
Att: 100,000.
Ref: Lo Bello (It).

United: Stepney, Brennan, A Dunne, Crerand, Foulkes, Stiles, Best, Kidd, Charlton*, Sadler, Aston. Manager: Busby.

Benfica: Henrique, Adolfo, Humberto, Jacinto, Cruz, Jaime Graca, Jose Augusto, Coluna*, Eusebio, Torres, Simoes. Coach: Gloria.

From this season teams level on aggregate after 90 minutes of the second leg were split by the new away goals counting double rule. If the aggregate was still level, extra-time was played in the first two rounds, with a play-off maintained from the quarter-finals onwards.

1969
May 28 (Bernabeu, Madrid)

Milan 4
(Prati 7, 39, 74, Sormani 66)

Ajax Amsterdam 1
(Vasovic 61pen)

HT: 2–0.
Att: 50,000.
Ref: Ortiz de Mendibil (Sp).

CHAMPIONS CUP FINALS

Milan: Cudicini, Anquilletti, Schnellinger, Malatrasi, Rosato, Trapattoni, Hamrin, Lodetti, Sormani, Rivera*, Prati. Coach: Rocco.

Ajax: Bals, Suurbier (Muller 46), Van Duivendobe, Vasovic*, Hulshoff, Pronk, Groot (Nuninga 46), Swart, Cruyff, Danielsson, Keizer. Coach: Michels.

1970
May 6 (San Siro, Milan)

Feyenoord 2
(Israel 29, Kindvall 116)

Celtic 1
(Gemmell 31)

HT: 1–1. After extra-time (90min: 1–1).
Att: 53,187.
Ref: Lo Bello (It).

Feyenoord: Pieters Graafland, Romeijn (Haak 107), Van Duivendobe, Jansen, Israel*, Hasil, Wery, Laseroms, Kindvall, Van Hanegem, Moulijn. Coach: Happel.

Celtic: Williams, Hay, Gemmell, Murdoch, McNeill*, Brogan, Johnstone, Wallace, J Hughes, Auld (Connelly 77), Lennox. Manager: Stein.

1971
June 2 (Wembley)

Ajax Amsterdam 2
(Van Dijk 5, Haan 87)

Panathinaikos 0

HT: 1–0.
Att: 90,000.
Ref: Taylor (Eng).

Ajax: Stuy, Suurbier, Neeskens, Vasovic*, Rijnders (Blankenburg 46), Hulshoff, Swart (Haan 46), Van Dijk, Cruyff, G Muhren, Keizer. Coach: Michels.

Panathinaikos: Ekonomopoulos, Tomaras, Vlahos, Elefterakis, Kamaras, Sourpis, Gramos, Filakouris, Antoniadis, Domazos*, Kapsis. Coach: Puskas.

From this season, if aggregate scores and away goals were level at the end of 90 minutes of the second leg, then extra-time was played and, if the scores were still level, a penalty shoot-out determined the winners. A drawn Final would go to a replay until 1975.

1972
May 31 (De Kuijp, Rotterdam)

Ajax Amsterdam 2
(Cruyff 48, 77)

Internazionale 0

HT: 0–0.
Att: 61,000.
Ref: Helies (Fr).

Ajax: Stuy, Suurbier, Krol, Blankenburg, Hulshoff, Neeskens, Swart, G Muhren, Cruyff, Haan, Keizer*. Coach: Kovacs.

Inter: Bordon, Burgnich, Facchetti, Bellugi, Giubertoni (Bertini 12), Oriali, Jair (Pellizzaro 58), Bedin, Boninsegna, Mazzola*, Frustalupi. Coach: Invernizzi.

1973
May 30 (Belgrade)

Ajax Amsterdam 1
(Rep 4)

Juventus 0

HT: 1–0.
Att: 93,000.
Ref: Gugulovic (Yug).

Ajax: Stuy, Suurbier, Krol, Blankenburg, Hulshoff, Neeskens, Haan, G Muhren, Cruyff, Rep, Keizer*. Coach: Kovacs.

Juventus: Zoff, Longobucco, Marchetti, Furino, Morini, Salvadore*, Causio (Cuccureddu 78), Altafini, Anastasi, Capello, Bettega (Haller 63). Coach: Vycpalek.

1974
May 15 (Heysel, Brussels)

Bayern Munich 1
(Schwarzenbeck 120)

Atletico Madrid 1
(Luis Aragones 113)

HT: 0–0. After extra-time (90 min: 0–0).
Att: 65,000.
Ref: Loraux (Bel).

Bayern: Maier, Hansen, Breitner, Schwarzenbeck, Beckenbauer*, Roth, Torstensson (Dürnberger 76), Zobel, G Müller, Hoeness, Kapellmann. Coach: Lattek.

Atletico: Reina, Melo, Capon, Adelardo*, Heredia, Eusebio, Ufarte (Becerra 69), Luis, Garate, Irureta, Salcedo (Alberto 91). Coach: Lorenzo.

REPLAY
May 17 (Heysel, Brussels)

Bayern Munich 4
(Hoeness 28, 81, Müller 57, 70)

Atletico Madrid 0

HT: 1–0.
Att: 23,000.
Ref: Delcourt (Bel).

Bayern: Maier, Hansen, Breitner, Schwarzenbeck, Beckenbauer*, Roth, Torstensson, Zobel, G Müller, Hoeness, Kapellmann. Coach: Lattek.

Atletico: Reina, Melo, Capon, Adelardo* (Benegas 61), Heredia, Eusebio, Ufarte (Becerra 65), Luis, Garate, Irureta, Salcedo (Alberto). Coach: Lorenzo.

1975
May 28 (Parc des Princes, Paris)

Bayern Munich 2
(Roth 71, Muller 81)

Leeds United 0

HT: 0–0.
Att: 48,000.
Ref: Kitabdjian (Fr).

Bayern: Maier, B Andersson (Weiss 4), Dürnberger, Schwarzenbeck, Beckenbauer*, Zobel, Torstensson, Roth, G Müller, Hoeness (Wunder 42), Kapellmann. Coach: Cramer.

Leeds: Stewart, Reaney, F Gray, Bremner*, Madeley, Hunter, Lorimer, A Clarke, Jordan, Giles, Yorath (E Gray 80). Manager: Armfield.

1976
May 12 (Hampden Park, Glasgow)

Bayern Munich 1
(Roth 57)

Saint-Etienne 0

HT: 0–0.
Att: 54,684.
Ref: Palotai (Hun).

Bayern: Maier, Hansen, Horsmann, Schwarzenbeck, Beckenbauer*, Roth, Kapellmann, Dürnberger, G Müller, Hoeness, Rummenigge. Coach: Cramer.

Saint-Etienne: Curkovic, Janvion, Repellini, Piazza, Lopez, Bathenay, Santini, Larque*, P Revelli, H Revelli, Sarramagna (Rocheteau 82). Coach: Herbin.

1977
May 25 (Olimpico, Rome)

Liverpool 3
(McDermott 27, Smith 65, Neal 82 pen)

Borussia Mönchengladbach 1
(Simonsen 51)

HT: 1–0.
Att: 57,000.
Ref: Wurtz (Fr)

Liverpool: Clemence, Neal, Jones, Smith, R Kennedy, E Hughes*, Keegan, Case, Heighway, McDermott, Callaghan. Manager: Paisley.

Mönchengladbach: Kneib, Vogts*, Klinkhammer, Wittkamp, Bonhof, Wohlers (Hannes 79), Simonsen, Wimmer (Kulik 24), Stielike, Schäfer, Heynckes. Coach: Lattek.

1978
May 10 (Wembley)

Liverpool 1
(Dalglish 64)

Club Brugge 0

HT: 0–0.
Att: 92,000.
Ref: Corver (Hol)

Liverpool: Clemence, Neal, E Hughes*, Thompson, Hansen, Dalglish, Case (Heighway 63), Fairclough, McDermott, Souness. Manager: Paisley.

Brugge: Jensen, Bastijns*, Maes (Volders 70), Krieger, Leekens, Cools, De Cubber, Vandereycken, Simoen, Ku (Sanders 60), Sorensen. Coach: Happel.

1979
May 30 (Olympia, Munich)

Nottingham Forest 1
(Francis 44)

Malmo 0

HT: 1–0.
Att: 57,500.
Ref: Linemayr (Aus).

Forest: Shilton, V Anderson, Clark, McGovern*, Lloyd, Burns, Francis, Bowyer, Birtles, Woodcock, Robertson. Manager: Clough.

Malmo: Moller, R Andersson, Jonsson, M Andersson, Erlandsson, Tapper* (Malmberg 34), Ljungberg, Prytz, Kinnvall, Hansson (T Andersson 82), Cervin. Coach: Houghton.

1980
May 28 (Bernabeu, Madrid)

Nottingham Forest 1
(Robertson 19)

Hamburg 0

HT: 1–0.
Att: 51,000.
Ref: Garrido (Por).

Forest: Shilton, V Anderson, F Gray (Gunn 84), McGovern*, Lloyd, Burns, O'Neill, Bowyer, Birtles, Mills (O'Hare 68), Robertson. Manager: Clough.

Hamburg: Kargus, Kaltz, Nogly*, Jakobs, Buljan, Hieronymus (Hrubesch 46), Keegan, Memering, Milewski, Magath, Reimann. Coach: Zebec.

1981
May 27 (Parc des Princes, Paris)

Liverpool 1
(A Kennedy 82)

Real Madrid 0

HT: 0–0.
Att: 48,360.
Ref: Palotai (Hun).

Liverpool: Clemence, Neal, A Kennedy, R Kennedy, Thompson*, Hansen, Dalglish (Case 87), Lee, Johnson, McDermott, Souness. Manager: Paisley.

CHAMPIONS CUP FINALS

Real: Agustin, Garcia Cortes (Pineda 87), Camacho, Angel, Sabido, Garcia Navajas, Juanito, Del Bosque, Santillana, Stielike, Cunningham. Coach: Boskov.

1982

May 26 (De Kuyp, Rotterdam)

Aston Villa 1
(Withe 67)

Bayern Munich 0

HT: 0–0.
Att: 45,000.
Ref: Konrath (Fr).

Villa: Rimmer (Spink 10), Swain, Williams, Mortimer*, Evans, McNaught, Bremner, Shaw, Withe, Cowans, Morley. Manager: Barton.

Bayern: Müller, Dremmler, Horsmann, Dürnberger, Augenthaler, Weiner, Kraus (Niedermayer 79), Breitner, D Hoeness, Mathy (Güttler 52), Rummenigge. Coach: Csernai.

1983

May 25 (Olympic, Athens)

Hamburg 1
(Magath 9)

Juventus 0

HT: 1–0.
Att: 73,500.
Ref: Rainea (Rom).

Hamburg: Stein, Kaltz, Wehmeyer, Jakobs, Hieronymus, Rolff, Milewski, Groh, Hrubesch*, Magath, Bastrup (Von Heesen 56). Coach: Happel.

Juventus: Zoff, Gentile, Cabrini, Bonini, Brio, Scirea*, Bettega, Tardelli, P Rossi (Marocchino 56), Platini, Boniek. Coach: Trapattoni.

1984

May 30 (Olimpico, Rome)

Liverpool 1
(Neal 15)

Roma 1
(Pruzzo 38)

Liverpool 4–2 on pens.

HT: 1–1. After extra-time (90 mins: 1–1).
Att: 69,693.
Ref: Fredriksson (Swe).

Liverpool: Grobbelaar, Neal, A Kennedy, Lawrenson, Whelan, Hansen, Dalglish (Robinson 94), Lee, Rush, Johnston (Nicol 72), Souness*. Manager: Fagan.

Roma: Tancredi, Nappi, Bonetti, Righetti, Falcao, Nela, Conti, Toninho Cerezo (Strukely 115), Pruzzo (Chierico 64), Di Bartolomei*, Graziani. Coach: Liedholm.

1985

May 29 (Heysel, Brussels)

Juventus 1
(Platini 57 pen)

Liverpool 0

HT: 0–0.
Att: 60,000.
Ref: Daina (Swz).

Juventus: Tacconi, Favero, Cabrini, Bonini, Brio, Scirea, Briaschi (Prandelli 84), Tardelli, P Rossi (Vignola 89), Platini, Boniek. Coach: Trapattoni.

Liverpool: Grobbelaar, Neal, Beglin, Lawrenson (Gillespie 3), Nicol, Hansen, Dalglish, Whelan, Rush, Walsh (Johnston 46), Wark. Coach: Fagan.

1986

May 7 (Sanchez Pizjuan, Seville)

Steaua Bucharest 0

Barcelona 0

Steaua 2–0 on pens.
HT: 0–0.
After extra-time (90 min: 0–0).

Att: 75,000.
Ref: Vautrot (Fr).

Steaua: Ducadam, Belodedici, Iovan*, Bumbescu, Barbulescu, Balint, Balan (Iordanescu 72), Boloni, Majaru, Lacatus, Piturca (Radu 107). Coach: Jenei.

Barcelona: Urruti, Gerardo, Migueli, Alexanco*, Julio Alberto, Victor, Marcos, Schuster (Moratalla 85), Pedraza, Archibald (Pichi Alonso 106), Carrasco. Coach: Venables.

1987

May 27 (Prater, Vienna)

FC Porto 2
(Madjer 77, Juary 81)

Bayern Munich 1
(Kogl 25)

HT: 0–1.
Att: 62,000.
Ref: Ponnet (Bel).

Porto: Mlynarczyk, Joao Pinto*, Eduardo Luis, Celso, Ignacio (Frasco 66), Quim (Juary 46), Jaime Magalhaes, Sousa, Andre, Futre, Madjer. Coach: Jorge.

Bayern: Pfaff, Winkelhofer, Nachtweih, Eder, Pflugler, Flick (Lunde 82), Brehme, Hoeness, Matthäus, Kogl, Rummenigge*. Coach: Lattek.

1988

May 25 (Neckar, Stuttgart)

PSV Eindhoven 0

Benfica 0

PSV 6–5 on pens.

HT: 0–0. After extra-time (90 mins: 0–0).
Att: 68,000.
Ref: Agnolin (It).

PSV: Van Breukelen, Gerets*, Nielsen, R Koeman, Heintze, Lerby, Linskens, Van Aerle, Kieft, Vanenburg, Gillhaus (Janssen 107). Coach: Hiddink.

Benfica: Silvino, Veloso, Dito, Mozer, Alvaro, Chiquinho, Sheu*, Elzo, Pacheco, M Magnusson (Hajri 112), Rui Aguas (Valdo 56). Coach: Toni.

1989

May 24 (Nou Camp, Barcelona)

Milan 4
(Gullit 18, 38, Van Basten 27, 46)

Steaua Bucharest 0

HT: 3–0.
Att: 100,000.
Ref: Tritschler (WG).

Milan: G Galli, Tassotti, P Maldini, Colombo, Costacurta (F Galli 74), F Baresi*, Donadoni, Rijkaard, Van Basten, Gullit (Virdis 60), Ancelotti. Coach: Sacchi.

Steaua: Lung, Petrescu, Ungureanu, Bumbescu, Stoica*, Iovan, Lacatus, Minea, Piturca, Hagi, Rotariu (Balint 46). Coach: Iordanescu.

1990

May 23 (Prater, Vienna)

Milan 1
(Rijkaard 67)

Benfica 0

HT: 0–0.
Att: 58,000.
Ref: Kohl (Aus).

Milan: G Galli, Tassotti, P Maldini, Colombo (F Galli 89), Costacurta, F Baresi*, Ancelotti (Massaro 67), Rijkaard, Van Basten, Gullit, Evani. Coach: Sacchi.

Benfica: Silvino, Jose Carlos, Ricardo, Samuel, Aldair, Thern, Vitor Paneira (Vata 78), Jaime Pacheco* (Cesar Brito 59), Hernani, Valdo, M Magnusson. Coach: Eriksson.

1991

May 29 (San Nicola, Bari)

Red Star Belgrade 0

Marseille 0

Red Star 5–3 on pens.

HT: 0–0
After extra-time (90 min: 0–0).
Att: 58,000.
Ref: Lanese (It).

Red Star: Stojanovic*, Jugovic, Marovic, Sabanadzovic, Belodedici, Najdovski, Mihajlovic, Savicevic (Dodic 84), Pancev, Prosinecki, Binic. Coach: Petrovic.

Marseille: Olmeta, Amoros, Di Meco (Stojkovic 112), Boli, Mozer, Germain, Casoni, Waddle, Papin*, Pele, Fournier (Vercruysse 75). Coach: Goethals.

1992

May 20 (Wembley)

Barcelona 1
(Koeman 111)

Sampdoria 0

HT: 0–0. After extra-time (90 min: 0–0).
Att: 70,827.
Ref: Schmidhuber (Ger).

Barcelona: Zubizarreta*, Nando, Ferrer, R Koeman, Juan Carlos, Bakero, Salinas (Goikoetxea 64), Stoichkov, M Laudrup, Guardiola (Alexanco 113), Eusebio. Coach: Cruyff.

Sampdoria: Pagliuca, Mannini, Katanec, Pari, Vierchowod, Lanna, Lombardo, Toninho Cerezo, Vialli (Buso 100), Mancini*, Bonetti (Invernizzi 72). Coach: Boskov.

1993

May 26 (Olympia, Munich)

Marseille 1
(Boli 43)

Milan 0

HT: 1–0.
Att: 64,400.
Ref: Rothlisberger (Swz).

Marseille: Barthez, Angloma (Durand 64), Boli, Desailly, Pele, Eydelie, Sauzee, Deschamps*, Di Meco, Boksic, Völler (Thomas 78). Coach: Goethals.

Milan: S Rossi, Tassotti, Costacurta, F Baresi*, P Maldini, Donadoni (Papin 56), Albertini, Rijkaard, Lentini, Van Basten (Eranio 85), Massaro. Coach: Capello.

1994

May 18 (Olympic, Athens)

Milan 4
(Massaro 22, 45, Savicevic 47, Desailly 59)

Barcelona 0

HT: 2–0.
Att: 70,000.
Ref: Don (Eng).

Milan: S Rossi, Tassotti*, Panucci, Desailly, F Galli, P Maldini (Nava 84), Donadoni, Albertini, Boban, Savicevic, Massaro. Coach: Capello.

Barcelona: Zubizarreta*, Ferrer, Guardiola, R Koeman, Nadal, Bakero, Sergi (Quique 73), Stoichkov, Amor, Romario, Beguiristain (Eusebio 51). Coach: Cruyff.

CHAMPIONS CUP FINALS

1995
May 24 (Ernst-Happel-stadion, Vienna)

Ajax 1
(Kluivert 83)

Milan 0

HT: 0–0.
Att: 49,500.
Ref: Craciunescu (Rom).

Ajax: Van der Sar, Reiziger, Blind*, F de Boer, Seedorf (Kanu 52), Rijkaard, Litmanen (Kluivert 65), Davids, George, R de Boer, Overmars. Coach: Van Gaal.

Milan: S Rossi, Panucci, Costacurta, F Baresi*, P Maldini, Donadoni, Albertini, Desailly, Boban (Lentini 83), Massaro (Eranio 89), Simone. Coach: Capello.

1996
May 22 (Olimpico, Rome)

Juventus 1
(Ravanelli 12)

Ajax 1
(Litmanen 40)

Juventus 4–2 on pens.

HT: 1–1. After extra-time (90 min: 1–1).
Att: 70,000.
Ref: Diaz Vega (Spain).

Juventus: Peruzzi, Torricelli, Ferrara, Vierchowod, Pessotto, Conte (Jugovic 43), Paulo Sousa (Di Livio 56), Deschamps, Vialli*, Del Piero, Ravanelli (Padovano 76). Coach: Lippi.

Ajax: Van der Sar, Silooy, Blind*, F de Boer (Scholten 67), Bogarde, George, R de Boer (Wooter 91), Litmanen, Davids, Kanu, Musampa (Kluivert 46). Coach: Van Gaal.

1997
May 28 (Olimpia, Munich)

Borussia Dortmund 3
(Riedle 29, 34, Ricken 71)

Junventus 1
(Del Piero 65)
Att: 55,500.
Ref: Puhl (England).

Dortmund: Klos, Sammer*, Kree, Kohler, Reuter, Sousa, Lambert, Heinrich, Moller (Zorc 89), Chapuisat (Ricken 70), Reidle (Herrlich 67).

Juventus: Peruzzi*, Ferrara, Montero, Porrini (Del Piero 46), Juliano, Di Livio, Deschamps, Zidane, Jugovic, Boksic (Tacchinardi 87), Vieri (Amoruso 72).

CUP-WINNERS' CUP

The Champions Cup was such a sensational success from the outset it was inevitable that further developments on the theme would follow.

In the winter of 1959–60 representatives from a number of European federations began discussing, informally, the launching of a competition for national cup-winners. On February 13, 1960, the European Cup-Winners Cup was officially set up at a meeting in Vienna involving the federations of Austria, Belgium, West Germany, France, Italy, Yugoslavia, Switzerland, Spain, Czechoslovakia and Hungary.

At that time only half the federations in Europe organized cup competitions following the traditional direct-elimination formal which had been established in the 19th century within English football. But the launching of the Cup-Winners Cup galvanized every country in Europe into launching or raising the status of its own domestic event.

Just 10 clubs entered the first Cup-Winners Cup which was won by

LONDON PRIDE ... West Ham's first and only European trophy-winners.

Fiorentina of Italy, who defeated Rangers of Scotland in a two-leg final. The competition was then brought formally under the control of UEFA and finals ever since have been single-match events.

Three times in the first 10 years a replay was needed, seven finals have gone to extra time but – so far – only once has a penalty shoot-out been needed. That was in 1980 when Valencia of Spain beat Arsenal of England 5–4 on penalties after a 0–0 draw in Brussels.

It was in the Cup-Winners Cup that Tottenham Hotspur, Arsenal's North London rivals, made British football history in 1963. The event was only three years' old but that did not cast any sort of shadow over the celebrations which followed Spurs' 5–1 victory over Atletico Madrid in Rotterdam – since this was the first time an English or Scottish club had won a European competition.

Bad breaks for Spurs

Spurs had reached the Champions Cup semi-finals the previous season before losing narrowly to Benfica. The experience stood them in good stead in the Cup-Winners Cup and they overcame Atletico – the cup-holders – in the Feyenoord stadium despite the injury absence of powerful left-half Dave Mackay.

The Cup-Winners Cup offered Mackay more bad luck the following season. When Spurs were drawn against English FA Cup-winners Manchester United, Mackay broke his leg and – with substitutions not possible at the time – the holders went out. United were duly taken apart by Sporting from Lisbon who ultimately needed a replay to beat MTK of Hungary in the 1964 Final.

This was a decade in which English clubs came to dominate the Cup-Winners Cup. West Ham United claimed a second victory for England in 1965 when they defeated Munich 1860 2–0 at Wembley. A match of outstanding football – and sportsmanship – was decided by two goals in three minutes from Alan Sealey. Victory also contributed to the legend of the late Bobby Moore. The previous year he had captained West Ham to FA Cup victory at Wembley; 1965 brought Cup-Winners Cup success on the same pitch; and 1966 saw Moore hold aloft the World Cup on England's behalf, again at Wembley.

Liverpool were favoured to provide a third English victory in the Cup-Winners Cup in 1966 but they lost in extra time to Borussia Dortmund at Hampden Park. A remarkable extra-time goal from right winger "Stan" Libuda – lofted beyond goalkeeper Tommy Lawrence and skipper Ron Yeats from way out on the right wing – provided Dortmund with a first-ever European club triumph for German football.

Germany needed extra-time to beat Britain again the following year. This time Bayern Munich were the winners and Rangers the losers by 1–0 in Nuremberg. Bayern were laying the foundations for their Champions Cup takeover of the mid-1970s: goalkeeper Sepp Maier, sweeper and skipper Franz Beckenbauer, goal-scoring midfielder Franz Roth and supreme goal-grabber Gerd Müller already made up the backbone of the team.

The German hegemony was broken a year later when Milan

defeated Hamburg with two goals from the Swedish veteran Kurt Hamrin. With hindsight it is clear Milan were one of the most outstanding of Cup-Winners Cup holders. A year later they went on to win the Champions Cup: players of the quality of Hamrin, Germany's Karl-Heinz Schnellinger and home-based Giovanni Trapattoni, Pierino Prati and Gianni Rivera demanded the greatest stages in Europe.

British clubs regained control at the start of the 1970s through Manchester City, Chelsea and Rangers but Leeds United failed against Milan in 1973. That final, in Salonika, was a bad-tempered affair decided by a fifth-minute goal from Luciano Chiarugi – and some highly-controversial refereeing by Greek official Giorgios Michas, who was later suspended by his own federation. That defeat was a sad farewell to international club football for Leeds manager Don Revie, who was appointed manager of England and it was his successor, Jimmy Armfield, who took Leeds on to another European final defeat the following season – in the Champions Cup in Paris.

Eastern bloc champions

Milan were, in 1974, runaway favourites to hold onto the Cup-Winners Cup. To everyone's surprise they failed, losing 2-0 in Rotterdam to

WINNER ... Sampdoria's Gianluca Vialli with "his" Cup in 1990.

Magdeburg of East Germany. This was the peak year in the "other" Germany's brief, awkward football history. A few weeks after the triumph in Rotterdam, Magdeburg stars such as Jurgen Sparwasser were starring in their national team's victory over neighbours West Germany in the World Cup finals.

But East German football remained an uncomfortable, unfashionable cousin, right the way through to the reintegration after the collapse of the Berlin Wall. Only 4,000 fans, for example, turned out in Rotterdam

to watch Magdeburg defeat Milan.

A far finer representative of Warsaw Pact football emerged to carry off the Cup-Winners Cup a year later. Kiev Dynamo were a class above most of the rest of Europe. They despatched Ferencvaros of Hungary 3–0 in the 1975 final with a mixture of skill, pace and tactical intelligence which drew comparisons with the impact made by the Moscow Dynamo side of the late 1940s. Kiev went on to claim the European Supercup, barely raising a sweat in victory over Bayern Munich. But their prospects of achieving greater things were undermined by the Soviet federation which demanded Kiev turn out, en bloc, as the national team in the World Cup qualifiers and even the Olympic Games.

Even outstanding players such as midfield general Viktor Kolotov and striker Oleg Blokhin could not withstand the physical and mental pressures and Kiev quickly ran out of steam.

Belgium's Anderlecht filled the void in the Cup-Winners Cup. They reached the final three years in a row in the late 1970s, defeat by Hamburg in 1977 being sandwiched between entertaining victories over West Ham United and FK Austria. Anderlecht's dominance owed much to their Dutch neighbours from whom they had acquired goalkeepers Jan Ruiter and Nico De Bree, centre back Johnny Dusbaba, midfield fulcrum Arie Haan and goal-scoring left winger Rob Rensenbrink.

One of the most exciting finals was that of 1979, in which Barcelona defeated unfancied Fortuna Dusseldorf 4–3 in extra time. Barcelona thus made amends for their surprising defeat in 1969 by Slovan Bratislava of the former Czechoslovakia. They would return to win again in 1982, beating Standard Liege in their own Nou Camp, and Sampdoria 2–0 in Berne in 1989. That was a poignant victory: it was in the same Wankdorf stadium that Barcelona had lost the 1961 Champions Cup Final to Benfica.

Unrepeatable

Remarkably, no club have ever retained the Cup-Winners Cup. Arsenal came close to breaking the jinx. They beat Parma of Italy in 1994

PRESSURE ... Everton's Graeme Sharp with Rapid's Kurt Gargeri.

then lost in the final the following year when Nayim scored an astonishing last-minute winner for Zaragoza with a lob from out by the right-wing touchline.

Previously, those who came closest were Atletico Madrid, Milan, Anderlecht and Ajax Amsterdam who all reached successive finals but won the first only to lose the second. Two clubs, Milan in 1968 and Juventus in 1984, followed their success in the Cup-Winners Cup by winning the Champions Cup the following year.

As for Zaragoza, they also failed the title defence challenge. They lost to their fellow Spaniards from La Coruna in the 1996 quarter-finals. One round later and La Coruna succumbed to Paris Saint-Germain who went on to beat Rapid Vienna 1–0. PSG then succumbed to Barcelona and the holders' jinx the following year.

Diluting the talent

The Cup-Winners Cup remains, officially, the second competition in status in Europe behind the Champions League and ahead of the UEFA Cup. But how long that may last is open to

question. The absence of a third round (in November-December) makes the Cup-Winners Cup financially unpopular compared with the UEFA Cup.

Also, the admission from 1997–98 of second-placed teams from eight countries into the Champions League will further reduce the already-erratic

quality of the Cup-Winners Cup. UEFA had always accepted that entry to the competition had to be kept open for domestic cup runners-up when the winners had also won the league (and thus entered the Champions Cup). In future, UEFA will accept even domestic cup semi-finalists if necessary. Like

the Champions League, the title of the Cup-Winners Cup is being undermined by the inexorable march towards an eventual European Super League.

SPOT ON ... Ronaldo's winner against Paris Saint-Germain in 1997.

CUP-WINNERS CUP FINALS

1961
May 17 (Ibrox, Glasgow) 1st leg

Rangers 0

Fiorentina 2
(Milani 12, 88)

HT: 0–1.
Att: 80,000.
Ref: Steiner (Aus).

Rangers: Ritchie, Shearer, Caldow, Davis, Paterson, Baxter, Wilson, McMillan, Scott, Brand, Hume.

Fiorentina: Albertosi, Robotti, Castelletti, Gonfiantini, Orzan, Rimbaldo, Hamrin, Micheli, Da Costa, Milani, Petris.

May 27 (Comunale, Florence) 2nd leg

Fiorentina 2
(Milani 12, Hamrin 88)

Rangers 1
(Scott 60)

Fiorentina 4–1 on aggregate.

HT: 1–0.
Att: 50,000.
Ref: Hernadi (Hun).

Fiorentina: Albertosi, Robotti, Castelletti, Gonfiantini, Orzan, Rimbaldo, Hamrin, Micheli, Da Costa, Milani, Petris.

Rangers: Ritchie, Shearer, Caldow, Davis, Paterson, Baxter, Scott, McMillan, Millar, Brand, Wilson.

1962
May 10 (Hampden Park, Glasgow)

Atletico Madrid 1
(Peiro 11)

Fiorentina: 1
(Hamrin 27)

HT: 1–1.
Att: 27,000.
Ref: Wharton (Scot).

Atletico: Madinabeytia, Rivilla, Calleja, Ramirez, Griffa, Glaria, Jones, Adelardo, Mendonça, Peiro, Collar.

Fiorentina: Albertosi, Robotti, Castelletti, Malatrasi, Orzan, Marchesi, Hamrin, Ferretti, Milan, Dell'Angelo, Petris.

REPLAY
September 5 (Neckarstadion, Stuttgart)

Atletico Madrid 3
(Jones, 8, Mendonca 27, Peiro 59)

Fiorentina 0

HT: 2–0.
Att: 38,000.
Ref: Tschenscher (WG).

Atletico: Madinabeytia, Rivilla, Calleja, Ramirez, Griffa, Glaria, Jones, Adelardo, Mendonça, Peiro, Collar.

Fiorentina: Albertosi, Robotti, Castelletti, Malatrasi, Orzan, Marchesi, Hamrin, Ferretti, Milani, Dell'Angelo, Petris.

1963
May 15 (Feyenoord, Rotterdam)

Tottenham Hotspur 5
(Greaves 16, 80, White 35, Dyson 67, 85)

Atletico Madrid 1
(Collar 47)

HT: 2–0.
Att: 49,000.
Ref: Van Leuwen (Hol).

Tottenham: Brown, Baker, Henry, Blanchflower, Norman, Marchi, Jones, White, Smith, Greaves, Dyson.

Atletico: Madinabeytia, Rivilla, Griffa, Rodriguez, Ramiro, Glaria, Jones, Adelardo, Chuzo, Mendonça, Collar.

1964
May 13 (Heysel, Brussels)

Sporting Clube 3
(Mascarenhas 40, Figueiredo 45, 80)

MTK Budapest 3
(Sandor 18, 75, Kuti 73)

HT: 2–1.
Att: 30,000.
Ref: Van Nuffel (Bel).

Sporting: Carvalho, Gomes, Peridis, Battista, Carlos, Geo, Mendes, Oswaldo, Mascarenhas, Figueiredo, Morais.

MTK: Kovalik, Keszei, Dansky, Jenei, Nagy, Kovacs, Sandor, Vasas, Kuti, Bodor, Halapi.

REPLAY
May 15 (Antwerp)

Sporting Clube 1
(Morais)

MTK Budapest 0

HT: 1–0.
Att: 19,000.
Ref: Versyp (Bel).

Sporting: Carvalho, Gomes, Peridis, Battista, Carlos, Geo, Mendes, Oswaldo, Mascarenhas, Figueiredo, Morais.

MTK: Kovalik, Keszei, Dansky, Jenei, Nagy, Kovacs, Sandor, Vasas, Kuti, Bodor, Halapi.

1965
May 19 (Wembley)

West Ham United 2
(Sealey 70, 72)

TSV 1860 Munich 1860 0

HT: 0–0.
Att: 100,000.
Ref: Zsolt (Hun).

West Ham: Standen, Kirkup, Burkett, Peters, Brown, Moore, Sealey, Boyce, Hurst, Dear, Sissons.

TSV 1860: Radenkovic, Wagner, Kohlars, Reich, Bena, Luttrop, Heiss, Küppers, Brunnenmeier, Grosser, Rebele.

1966
May 5 (Hampden Park, Glasgow)

Borussia Dortmund 2
(Held 62, Libuda 109)

Liverpool 1
(Hunt 68)

HT: 0–0. After extra-time (90 min: 1–1).
Att: 41,000.
Ref: Schwinte (Fr).

Borussia: Tilkowski, Cyliax, Redder, Kurrat, Paul, Assauer, Libuda, Schmidt, Held, Sturm, Emmerich.

Liverpool: Lawrence, Lawler, Byrne, Milne, Yeats, Stevenson, Callaghan, Hunt, St John, Smith, Thompson.

1967
May 31 (Franke, Nuremberg)

Bayern Munich 1
(Roth 108)

Rangers 0

HT: 0–0. After extra-time (90 min: 0–0).
Att: 69,000.
Ref: Lo Bello (It).

Bayern: Maier, Nowak, Kupferschmidt, Beckenbauer, Olk, Roth, Koulmann, Nafziger, Ohlhauser, G Müller, Brenniger.

Rangers: Martin, Johansen, Provan, Greig, McKinnon, Jardine, D Smith, Henderson, Hynd, A Smith, Johnston.

1968
May 23 (Feyenoord, Rotterdam)

Milan 2
(Hamrin 3, 19)

Hamburg 0

HT: 2–0.
Att: 53,000.
Ref: De Mendibil (Sp).

Milan: Cudicini, Anquilletti, Schnellinger, Scala, Rosato, Trapattoni, Hamrin, Lodetti, Sormani, Rivera, Prati.

Hamburg: Özcan, Sandmann, Schulz, Horst, Kurbjuhn, Dieckmann, Krämer, B Dörfel, Seeler, Hönig, G Dörfel.

1969
May 21 (St Jakob, Basle)

Slovan Bratislava 3
(Cvetler 2, Hrivnak 30, Jan Capkovic 42)

Barcelona 2
(Zaldua 16, Rexach 52)

HT: 3–1.
Att: 19,000.
Ref: Van Raven (Hol).

Slovan: Vencel, Filo, Horvath, Hrivnak, Zlocha, Hrdlicka, Josef Capkovic, Cvetler, Moder (Hatar 67), Jokl, Jan Capkovic.

Barcelona: Sadurni, Franch (Pereda 11), Eladio, Rife, Olivella, Zabalza, Pellicer, Castro (Mendonça 46), Zaldua, Fuste, Rexach.

1970
May 29 (Prater, Vienna)

Manchester City 2
(Young 11, Lee 43)

Gornik Zabrze 1
(Oslizlo 70)

HT: 2–0.
Att: 8,000.
Ref: Schiller (Aus).

Manchester City: Corrigan, Book, Pardoe, Booth, Heslop, Doyle (Bowyer 23), Towers, Oakes, Bell, Lee, Young.

Gornik: Kostka, Oslizlo, Florenski (Kuchta 85), Gorgon, Olek, Latocha, Szoltysik, Wilczek (Skowronek 75), Szarynski, Banas, Lubanski.

1971
May 19 (Karaiskaki, Piraeus)

Chelsea 1
(Osgood 55)

Real Madrid 1
(Zoco 30)

HT: 0–1. After extra-time (90 min: 1–1).
Att: 42,000.
Ref: Scheurer (Swi).

Chelsea: Bonetti, Boyle, Dempsey, Webb, Harris, Hollins (Mulligan 91), Hudson, Cooke, Weller, Osgood (Baldwin 86), Houseman.

Real: Borja, Jose Luis, Benito, Zoco, Zunzunegui, Pirri, Grosso, Velazquez, Miguel Perez (Fleitas 65), Amancio, Gento (Grande 70).

REPLAY
May 21 (Karaiskaki, Piraeus)

Chelsea 2
(Dempsey 31, Osgood 39)

Real Madrid 1
(Fleitas 75)

HT: 2–0.
Att: 19,917.
Ref: Bucheli (Swz).

Chelsea: Bonetti, Boyle, Dempsey, Cooke, Harris, Weller, Baldwin, Webb, Hudson, Osgood (Smethurst 73), Houseman.

Real: Borja, Jose Luis, Benito, Zoco, Zunzunegui, Pirri, Velazquez (Gento 75), Fleitas, Amancio, Grosso, Bueno (Grande 60).

CUP-WINNERS CUP FINALS

1972
May 24 (Nou Camp, Barcelona)

Rangers 3
(Stein 23, Johnston 40, 49)

Dynamo Moscow 2
(Estrekov 60, Makovikov 87)

HT: 2–0.
Att: 24,000.
Ref: De Mendibil (Sp).

Rangers: McCloy, Jardine, Johnstone, Smith, Mathieson, Greig, Conn, MacDonald, McLean, Stein, Johnston.

Dynamo: Pilgui, Basalev, Dolmatov, Zikov, Dobonosov (Gershkovich 69), Zhukov, Yakubik (Estrekov 56), Sabo, Baidachni, Makovikov, Yevreshukin.

1973
May 16 (Kaftantzoglio, Salonica)

Milan 1
(Chiarugi 5)

Leeds United 0

HT: 1–0.
Att: 45,000.
Ref: Michas (Gre).

Milan: Vecchi, Sabadini, Zignoli, Anquilletti, Turone, Rosato (Dolci 59), Rivera, Benetti, Sogliano, Bigon, Chiarugi.

Leeds: Harvey, Reaney, Cherry, Bates, Madeley, Hunter, F Gray (McQueen 54), Yorath, Lorimer, Jordan, Jones.

1974
May 8 (Feyenoord , Rotterdam)

Magdeburg 2
(Lanzi og 40, Seguin 74)

Milan 0

HT: 1–0.
Att: 4,000.
Ref: Van Gemert (Hol).

Magdeburg: Schülze, Enge, Zapf, Tyll, Abraham, Seguin, Pommerenke, Gaube, Raugust, Sparwasser, Hoffmann.

Milan: Pizzaballa, Sabadini, Anquilletti, Lanzi, Schnellinger, Benetti, Maldera, Rivera, Tresoldi, Bigon, Bergamaschi (Turini 60).

1975
May 14 (St Jakob, Basle)

Dynamo Kiev 3
(Onischenko 18, 39, Blokhin 67)

Ferencvaros 0

HT: 2–0.
Att: 10,000.
Ref: Davidson (Scot).

Dynamo: Rudakov, Troshkin, Matvienko, Reshko, Fomenko, Muntian, Konkov, Buryak, Kolotov, Onischenko, Blokhin.

Ferencvaros: Geczi, Martos, Megyesi, Pataki, Rab, Nyilasi (Ohnhaus 60), Juhasz, Mucha, Szabo, Magyar, Mate.

1976
May 5 (Heysel, Brussels)

Anderlecht 4
(Rensenbrink 42, 73, Van der Elst 48, 87)

West Ham United 2
(Holland 28, Robson 68)

HT: 1–1.
Att: 58,000.
Ref: Wurtz (Fr).

Anderlecht: Ruiter, Lomme, Van Binst, Thissen, Broos, Dockx, Coeck (Vercauteren 32), Haan, Van der Elst, Ressel, Rensenbrink.

West Ham: Day, Coleman, Lampard (A Taylor 47), T Taylor, McDowell, Bonds, Brooking, Paddon, Holland, Jennings, Robson.

1977
May 11 (Olympisch, Amsterdam)

Hamburg 2
(Volkert 78, Magath 88)

Anderlecht 0

HT: 0–0.
Att: 66,000.
Ref: Partridge (Eng).

Hamburg: Kargus, Kaltz, Ripp, Nogly, Hidien, Memering, Magath, Keller, Steffenhagen, Reimann, Volkert.

Anderlecht: Ruiter, Van Binst, Van den Daele, Thissen, Broos, Dockx (Van Poucke 81), Coeck, Haan, Van der Elst, Ressel, Rensenbrink.

1978
May 3 (Parc des Princes, Paris)

Anderlecht 4
(Rensenbrink 13, 41, Van Binst 45, 80)

FK Austria 0

HT: 2–1.
Att: 48,000.
Ref: Alginder (WG).

Anderlecht: De Bree, Van Binst, Thissen, Dusbaba, Broos, Van der Elst, Haan, Nielsen, Coeck, Vercauteren (Dockx 87), Rensenbrink.

Austria: Baumgartner, R Sara, J Sara, Obermayer, Baumeister, Prohaska, Daxbacher (Martinez 60), Gasselich, Morales (Dragan 74), Pirkner, Parits.

1979
May 16 (St Jakob, Basle)

Barcelona 4
(Sanchez 5, Asensi 34, Rexach 104, Krankl 111)

Fortuna Düsseldorf 3
(K Allofs 8, Seel 41, 114)

HT: 2–2. After extra-time (90 min: 2–2).
Att: 58,000.
Ref: Palotai (Hung).

Barcelona: Artola, Zuviria, Migueli, Costas (Martinez 66), Albaledejo (De la Cruz 57), Sanchez, Neeskens, Asensi, Rexach, Krankl, Carrasco.

Fortuna: Daniel, Baltes, Zewe, Zimmermann (Lund 84), Brei (Weikl 24), Kohnen, Schmitz, T Allofs, Bommer, K Allofs, Seel.

1980
May 15 (Heysel, Brussels)

Valencia 0

Arsenal 0

Valencia 5–4 on pens.

HT: 0–0. After extra-time (90 min: 0–0).
Att: 36,000.
Ref: Christov (Czech).

Valencia: Pereira, Carrete, Botubot, Arias, Tendillo, Solsona, Saura, Bonhof, Subirats (Castellanos 112), Kempes, Pablo.

Arsenal: Jennings, Rice, Nelson, O'Leary, Young, Rix, Talbot, Price (Hollins 105), Brady, Sunderland, Stapleton.

1981
May 13 (Rheinstadion, Düsseldorf)

Tbilisi Dynamo 2
(Gutsayev 67, Daraselia 86)

Carl Zeiss Jena 1
(Hoppe 63)

HT: 0–0.
Att: 9,000.
Ref: Lattanzi (It).

Dynamo: Gabelia, Kostava, Chivadze, Khisanishvili, Tavadze, Svanadze (Kakilashvili 67), Sulakvelidze, Daraselia, Gutsayev, Kipiani, Shengalia.

Carl Zeiss: Grapenthin, Bräuer, Kurbjuweit, Schnüphase, Schilling, Hoppe (Overmann 88), Krause, Lindemann, Bielau (Topfer 76), Raab, Vogel.

1982
May 12 (Nou Camp, Barcelona)

Barcelona 2
(Simonsen 44, Quini 63)

Standard Liege 1
(Vandersmissen 7)

HT: 1–1.
Att: 100,000.
Ref: Eschweller (WG).

Barcelona: Urruti, Gerardo, Migueli, Alesanco, Manolo, Sanchez, Moratalla, Estaban, Simsonsen, Quini, Carrasco.

Standard: Preud'Homme, Gerets, Poel, Meeuws, Plessers, Vandersmissen, Daarden, Haan, Botteron, Tahamata, Wendt.

1983
May 11 (Nya Ullevi, Gothenburg)

Aberdeen 2
(Black 4, Hewitt 112)

Real Madrid 1
(Juanito 15)

HT: 1–1. After extra-time (90 min: 1–1).
Att: 17,000.
Ref: Menegali (It).

Aberdeen: Leighton, Rougvie, McLeish, Miller, McMaster, Cooper, Strachan, Simpson, McGhee, Black (Hewitt 87), Weir.

Real: Agustin, Juan Jose, Metgod, Bonet, Camacho, Angel, Gallego, Stielike, Isidro (Salguero 103), Juanito, Santillana.

1984
May 16 (St Jakob, Basle)

Juventus 2
(Vignola 12, Boniek 41)

FC Porto 1
(Sousa 29)

HT: 2–1.
Att: 60,000.
Ref: Galler (Swi).

Juventus: Tacconi, Gentile, Brio, Scirea, Cabrini, Tardelli, Bonini, Vignola (Caricola 89), Platini, Rossi, Boniek.

Porto: Ze Beto, Joao Pinto, Lima Pereira, Enrico, Eduardo Luis (Costa 82), Jaime Magalhaes (Walsh 65), Frasco, Pacheco, Sousa, Gomes, Vermelinho.

1985
May 15 (Feyenoord, Rotterdam)

Everton 3
(Gray 57, Steven 72, Sheedy 85)

Rapid Vienna 1
(Krankl 85)

HT: 0–0
Att: 50,000.
Ref: Casarin (It).

Everton: Southall, Stevens, Van Den Hauwe, Ratcliffe, Mountfield, Reid, Steven, Bracewell, Sheedy, Gray, Sharp.

Rapid: Konsel, Lainer, Weber, Garger, Brauneder, Hrstic, Kranjcar, Kienast, Weinhofer (Panenka 67), Pacult (Gross 60), Krankl.

1986
May 2 (Gerland, Lyon)

Kiev Dynamo 3
(Zavarov 4, Blokhin 85, Yevtushenko 87)

Atletico Madrid 0

HT: 1–0.
Att: 50,000.
Ref: Wohrer (Aus).

CUP-WINNERS CUP FINALS

Dynamo: Chanov, Bessonov, Baltacha (Bal 38), Kuznetsov, Demianenko, Yaremchuk, Yakovenko, Zavarov (Yevtushenko 70), Rats, Belanov, Blokhin.

Atletico: Fillol, Tomas, Arteche, Ruiz, Clemente, Julio Prieto, Landaburu (Quique Setien 61), Marina, E R Quique, Da Silva, Cabrera.

1987
May 13 (Olympic, Athens)

Ajax 1
(Van Basten 21)

Lokomotive Leipzig 0

HT: 1–0.
Att: 35,000.
Ref: Agnolin (It).

Ajax: Menzo, Silooy, Rijkaard, Verlaat, Boeve, Wouters, Winter, A Muhren (Scholten 83), Van't Schip, Van Basten, Rob Witschge (Bergkamp 66).

Lokomotive: Müller, Kreer, Baum, Lindner, Zötzsche, Scholz, Liebers (Kühn 76), Bredow, Marschal, Richter, Edmond (Leitzke 55).

1988
May 11 (Meinau, Strasbourg)

Mechelen 1
(Den Boer 53)

Ajax 0

HT: 0–0.
Att: 40,000.
Ref: Pauly (WG).

Mechelen: Preud'Homme, Clijsters, Sanders, Rutjes, Deferm, Hofkens, (Theunis 73), Emmers, Koeman, De Wilde (Demesmaeker 60), Den Boer, Ohana.

Ajax: Menzo, Blind, Wouters, Larsson, Verlaat (Meijer 73), Van't Schip (Bergkamp 57), Winter, A Muhren, Scholten, Bosman, Rob Witschge.

1989
May 10 (Wankdorf, Berne)

Barcelona 2
(Salinas 4, Lopez Rekarte 79)

Sampdoria 0

HT: 1–0.
Att: 45,000.
Ref: Courtney (Eng).

Barcelona: Zubizarreta, Aloisio, Alexanco, Urbano, Milla (Soler 61), Amor, Eusebio, Roberto, Lineker, Salinas, Beguiristain (Lopez Rekarte 74).

Sampdoria: Pagliuca, L Pellegrini (Bonomi 54), Mannini (S Pellegrini 27), Lanna, Salsano, Pari, Victor, Toninho Cerezo, Dossena, Vialli, Mancini.

1990
May 9 (Nya Ullevi, Gothenburg)

Sampdoria 2
(Vialli 105, 107)

Anderlecht 0

HT: 0–0. After extra-time (90 min: 0–0).
Att: 20,000.
Ref: Galler (Swz).

Sampdoria: Pagliuca, L Pellegrini, Mannini, Vierchowod, Carboni, Pari, Katanec (Salsano 92), Invernizzi (Lombardo 55), Dossena, Vialli, Mancini.

Anderlecht: De Wilde, Grun, Marchoul, Keshi, Kooiman, Vervoot, Musonda, Gudjohnson, Jankovic (Oliveira 116), Degryse (Nilis 104), Van der Linden.

1991
May 15 (Feyenoord, Rotterdam)

Manchester United 2
(Bruce 67, Hughes 74)

Barcelona 1
(Koeman 79)

HT: 0–0.
Att: 48,000.
Ref: Karlsson (Swe).

United: Sealey, Irwin, Bruce, Pallister, Blackmore, Phelan, Robson, Ince, Sharpe, Hughes, McClair.

Barcelona: Busquets, Alexanco (Pinilla 72), Nando, R Koeman, Ferrer, Goikotxea, Eusebio, Bakero, Beguiristain, Salinas, M Laudrup.

1992
May 6 (Benfica, Lisbon)

Werder Bremen 2
(K Allofs 41, Rufer 54)

Monaco 0

HT: 1–0.
Att: 15,000.
Ref: D'Elia (It).

Werder: Rollmann, Bockenfeld, Borowka, Bratseth, Wolter (Schaaf 34), Eilts, Votava, Bode, Neubarth (Kohn 75), Rufer, K Allofs.

Monaco: Ettori, Valery (Djorkaeff 62), Mendy, Sonor, Gnako, Rui Barros, Dib, Petit, Passi, Fofana (Clement 59), Weah.

1993
May 12 (Wembley)

Parma 3
(Minotti 9, Melli 30, Cuoghi 83)

Antwerp 1
(Severeyns 11)

HT: 2–1.
Att: 37,000.
Ref: Assenmacher (Ger).

Parma: Ballotta, Benarrivo, Di Chiara, Minotti, Apolloni, Grun, Zoratto (Pin 25), Cuoghi, Osio (Pizzi 65), Melli, Brolin.

Antwerp: Stojanovic, Brockaert, Taeymans, Smidts, Van Rethy, Segers (Moukrim 85), Kiekens, Jakovljevic (Van Veirdeghem 57), Lehnoff, Severeyns, Czerniatynski.

1994
May 4 (Parkstadion, Copenhagen)

Arsenal 1
(Smith 19)

Parma 0

HT: 1–0.
Att: 33,765.
Ref: Krondl (Czech).

Arsenal: Seaman, Dixon, Winterburn, Davis, Bould, Adams, Campbell, Morrow, Smith, Merson (McGoldrick 86), Selley.

Parma: Bucci, Benarrivo, Di Chiara, Minotti, Apolloni, Sensini, Brolin, Pin (Melli 70), Crippa, Zola, Asprilla.

1995
May 10 (Parc des Princes, Paris)

Zaragoza 2
(Esnaider 68, Nayim 119)

Arsenal 1
(Hartson 77)

HT: 0–0
After extra-time (90 min: 1–1). Att: 42,424.
Ref: Ceccarini (It).

Real: Cedrun, Belsue, Solana, Caceres, Aragon, Nayim, Aguado, Poyet, Esnaider, Higuera (Garcia Sanjuan 66; Geli 114), Pardeza.

Arsenal: Seaman, Dixon, Schwarz, Winterburn (Morrow 47), Adams, Linighan, Keown (Hillier 46), Parlour, Merson, Wright, Hartson.

1996
May 8 (King Baudouin, Brussels)

Paris Saint-Germain 1
(N'Gotty 28)

Rapid Vienna 0

HT: 1–0.
Att: 37,500.
Ref: Pairetto (Italy).

PSG: Lama, Roche, Le Guen, N'Gotty, Fournier (Llacer 76), Bravo, Guerin, Colleter, Djorkaeff, Loko, Rai (Dely Valdes 11).

Rapid: Konsel, Hatz, Ivanov, Schöttel, Heraf, Guggi, Stöger, Kühbauer, Marasek, Jancker, Stumpf (Barisic 46).

1997
May 14 (Feyenoord, Rotterdam)

Barcelona 1
(Ronaldo 35 pen)

Paris Saint-Germain 0

HT: 1–0.
Att: 50,000.
Ref: Merk (Ger)

Barcelona: Vitor Baia, Ferrer, Fernando Couto, Abelardo, Sergi, Guardiola, Luis Enrique (Pizzi 88), De la Pena (Stoichkov 83), Popescu (Amor 46), Luis Figo, Ronaldo.

PSG: Lama, Fournier (Algerino 58), Ngotty, Le Guen, Domi, Leroy, Rai (Dely Valdes 68), Cauet, Leonardo, Loko (Pouget 77).

UEFA CUP

The competition now known as the UEFA Cup is, in origins, the oldest of the present triumvirate of European club tournaments.

It was the brainchild of the Swiss vice-president of FIFA, Ernst Thommen, who in 1950 first proposed the creation of an international competition between clubs – or city select teams – from those cities which hosted industrial fairs.

Thommen found allies in top officials such as prospective FIFA president Sir Stanley Rous (who drafted the initial regulations) and Italy's Ottorino Barassi and they eventually launched their project – totally independently from the European Champion Clubs' Cup – in 1955.

In April of that year 12 representatives from European trade fair cities from 10 countries met in Basle to lay down the rules. They decided that each city should be represented by a local club or by a city select team, or by both – as long as no more than two teams competed simultaneously from any one city. It was also proposed – and agreed – that the matches should ideally be timed to coincide with the cities' trade fairs.

That was one reason why the first edition of the Industrial Inter-City Fairs Cup took three years to complete! Yet, oddly enough, it foreshad-

HISTORY ... London (right) versus Lausanne in the first Fairs Cup.

owed by nearly 40 years the UEFA Champions League in that the first round of the first competition was organized in four mini-leagues. The group winners would qualify for two-leg knock-out semi-finals, followed by a two-leg final.

The first match took place on June 4, 1955, when Basle lost 5–0 at home to London who went on to reach the semi-finals along with Barcelona, Lausanne and Birmingham City.

Barcelona needed a play-off in Basle to beat Birmingham City and then thrashed London 2–2, 6–0 in the final in 1958. The Spanish club's cosmopolitan line-up included superstars of the era such as Hungary's Ladislao Kubala, Spain's Luiz Suarez, Brazil's Evaristo de Macedo and Paraguayan striker Eulogio Martinez.

Some 13 years later, in 1971, UEFA formally took over organization of the event from the Fairs Cup committee.

The original trophy, named after Noel Beard, was put up for competition between first winners Barcelona and last winners Leeds. Barcelona, appropriately, won 2–1.

Confusion over entry regulations – the trade fair idea had quickly gone out of the window – and disciplinary control had contributed towards the demise of the Fairs Cup. The European governing body's formal adoption of the event produced a new trophy and a new title – the UEFA Cup. Entry was specifically allocated to highest-placed clubs who did not qualify for the Champions or Cup-Winners Cup.

Stepping stone

The history of the Fairs/UEFA Cup is full of clubs using it as a springboard to greater glory in the Champions Cup. No fewer than 12 clubs (Barcelona, Roma, Juventus, Leeds United, Liverpool, Borussia Mönchengladbach, Club Brugge, PSV Eindhoven, Red Star Belgrade,

Hamburg, Benfica and Ajax) followed up a place in the Fairs/UEFA Cup Final with a later victory or runners-up spot in the senior competition.

Notable among them were Liverpool, who beat Brugge in 1976 after being 2–0 down in the first half of the first leg at Anfield, and Borussia Mönchengladbach under master coach Hennes Weisweiler. Some nine clubs (Barcelona, Liverpool, Feyenoord, Juventus, PSV Eindhoven, Real Madrid, Internazionale, Ajax and Bayern Munich) of the Fairs/UEFA Cup winners have also won the Champions Cup at one stage or another.

Four clubs (Barcelona, Ajax, Juventus and Bayern Munich) have won all three European club competitions and two of those (Ajax and Juventus) have achieved the Grand Slam of the three mainstream European cups plus the Supercup and the World Club Cup. An exclusive band indeed.

Barcelona dominated the first decade. They won against English entries in the first competitions – against a representative London team in 1958 and then against Birmingham City in 1960. Birmingham were also runners-up, this time to a Roma side spearheaded by Argentine marksman Pedro Manfredini, in 1961. How might the history of that football club have changed if City had won either of those finals and thus become the first British club to win a European trophy? They have but one win of a major trophy in England – and that was the League Cup when it was a lesser event.

Birmingham were defied, however, by Roma's goalkeeper Fabio

Cudicini who later claimed a record as the first man to win all three European club trophies. Having collected a winner's medal in the Fairs Cup with Roma, he later won the Cup-Winners Cup in 1968 and then Champions Cup in 1969 with Milan. Oddly enough, however, the talents of this early hero of the European club tournaments were never recognized by selection for the Italian national team.

Spanish football remained the dominant early force in the Fairs Cup. Valencia won in 1962 and 1963 then lost the 1964 final to Zaragoza who were, in turn, beaten in the 1966 final by a revived Barcelona. In between, Ferencvaros collected Hungary's only European prize when they defeated Juventus in a single-leg final in Turin. The academic left-winger, Dr Mate Fenyvesi, scored the decisive goal. Swiss referee Gottfried Dienst waved away Italian protests – just as he would wave away German protests a year later in the 1966 World Cup Final.

The late 1960s saw English clubs take over the Fairs Cup. Leeds United were surprised to lose to Dinamo Zagreb in 1967, but made amends a year later against Ferencvaros. Newcastle United then produced a flamboyant victory both home and away against another Hungarian club, Ujpest Dozsa, in 1969. Skipper Bobby Moncur, never previously on the scoresheet for the north-easterners, hit two goals in the first leg at St James' Park and another in Budapest. Arsenal and Leeds United maintained the

TOP MAN ... Leeds' Mick Jones climbs the Juventus defence.

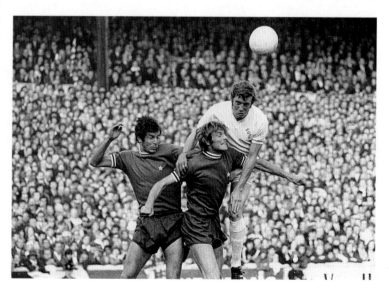

English stranglehold before UEFA decided to bring the Fairs Cup into the fold, took full administrative responsibility and substituted the trophy with the newly-entitled UEFA Cup.

UEFA coefficient

Entrance to the UEFA Cup is available on a multiple-entry system, based on a ranking list of success rates of a country's clubs in European competitions. This was computed by adding up the points gained by a country's clubs over the previous five years – based on a notional two points for a win, one for a draw. The total number of points was then divided by the total number of games played – arriving thus at the so-called UEFA coefficient.

The top three countries were rewarded with four entries, the next best countries with three, and so on. This, of course, allied to a seeded draw in the early rounds, assisted the top countries in maintaining their high coefficient.

Tottenham and Liverpool carried on in the UEFA Cup where English clubs had left off in the Fairs Cup but in due course German clubs such as

Borussia Mönchengladbach and Bayer Leverkusen and then Italians – Napoli, Juventus, Internazionale and Parma – took over. They were assisted, of course, by the post-Heysel ban which barred English entry between 1985 and 1991.

By the time English clubs returned to the UEFA Cup, technical and tactical developments meant there was a lot of catching-up to do. A palpable gap between English and continental football was evident as far down the line as 1997 when Newcastle United were outclassed by French league leaders Monaco in the quarter-finals of the UEFA Cup.

By this time, qualification for the event had been further expanded to produce a 100-plus entry – with a preliminary round as early as July – to take account of the increase in entries following the fragmentation of eastern Europe and the Balkan region. A handful of countries had also long been permitted to enter the winners of their domestic league cup. But this right is likely to be scrapped from 1998–99 for all countries which oper-

ate a top division comprising more than 16 clubs – a clumsy attempt at UEFA coercion into a reduction of league sizes.

New way in

Also allowed in during the mid-1990s were the winning clubs from a reorganized Intertoto Cup.

This had been launched in the early 1960s to provide a summer break fixtures schedule for the state-run central and eastern European pools. Its expansion, under UEFA auspices, to cover all of Europe led to controversy. England's Sheffield Wednesday, Tottenham and Wimbledon attracted disciplinary action for not taking the competition seriously enough i.e. not playing matches in their own stadia and not fielding full-strength teams. The fact that hardly anyone else did, either, appeared to pass UEFA by. The only outcome of such heavy-handed "encouragement" was to dissuade other top countries, such as Italy and Spain, from entering teams.

Not that the Intertoto experiment was bad for everyone. French club

ELBOW GREASE ... Schalke's Olaf Thon and Inter's Ciri Sforza.

Bordeaux qualified through the Intertoto for the 1995–96 UEFA Cup and duly went right the way through to the final where they lost only to Bayern Munich.

The backlash was felt, however, by the French national team. Bordeaux's Zinedine Zidane had been expected to be a key man for France in the 1996 European Championship finals. He was, however, so tired by then that he could do little more than totter out on to the pitches in England – and toothless France fell in the semi-finals.

Schalke maintained German control of the UEFA Cup. In 1997 when they beat hot favourites Inter Milan in a penalty shoot-out at the San Siro. It was Schalke's first appearance in a European final.

Clearly, all this expansion has been good for European football democracy but bad for quality. More and more "minnow country" entrants were to be found clogging up the bottom rungs of the UEFA Cup ladder. That downward trend will continue now that the runners-up from Europe's top eight countries have been creamed off into the Champions League.

SHOWDOWN ... Juventus' Sousa shoots before Parma's Apolloni can get the tackle in.

INDUSTRIAL INTER-CITIES' FAIRS CUP FINALS

1955-58

March 5 (Stamford Bridge, London)
1st leg

London Select XI 2
(Greaves 10, Langley 88 pen)

Barcelona 2
(Tejada 7, Martinez 35)

HT: 1–2.
Att: 45,466.
Ref: Dusch (WG).

London: Kelsey, Sillett, Langley, Blanchflower, Norman, Coote, Groves, Greaves, Smith, Haynes, Robb.

Barcelona: Estrems, Olivella, Segarra, Gracia, Gensana, Ribelles, Basora, Evaristo, Martinez, Villaverde, Tejada.

May 1 (Nou Camp, Barcelona) 2nd leg

Barcelona 6
(Suarez 6, 8, Evaristo 52, 75, Martinez 43, Verges 63)

London Select XI 0

Barcelona 8–2 on aggregate.

HT: 3–0.
Att: 62,000.
Ref: Dusch (WG).

Barcelona: Ramallets, Olivella, Segarra, Verges, Brugue, Gensana, Tejada, Evaristo, Martinez, Suarez, Basora.

London: Kelsey, Wright, Cantwell, Blanchflower, Brown, Bowen, Medwin, Groves, Smith, Bloomfield, Lewis.

1958-60

March 29 (St Andrew's, Birmingham) 1st leg

Birmingham City 0

Barcelona 0

HT: 0–0.
Att: 40,000.
Ref: Van Nuffel (Bel).

Birmingham: Schofield, Farmer, Allen, Watts, Smith, Neal, Astall, Gordon, Weston, Orritt, Hooper.

Barcelona: Ramallets, Olivella, Gracia, Segarra, Rodri, Gensana, Coll, Kocsis, Martinez, Ribelles, Villaverde.

May 4 (Nou Camp, Barcelona) 2nd leg

Barcelona 4
(Martinez 3, Czibor 6, 48, Coll 78)

Birmingham City 1
(Hooper 82)

Barcelona 4–1 on aggregate.

HT: 2–0.
Att: 70,000.
Ref: Van Nuffel (Bel).

Barcelona: Ramallets, Olivella, Gracia, Verges, Rodri, Segarra, Coll, Ribelles, Martinez, Kubala, Czibor.

Birmingham: Schofield, Farmer, Allen, Watts, Smith, Neal, Astall, Gordon, Weston, Murphy, Hooper.

1960-61

September 27 (St Andrew's, Birmingham)
1st leg

Birmingham City 2
(Hellawell 78, Orritt 85)

Roma 2
(Manfredini 30, 56)

HT: 0–1.
Att: 21,000.
Ref: Davidson (Scot).

Birmingham: Schofield, Farmer, Sissons, Hennessy, Foster, Beard, Hellawell, Bloomfield, Harris, Orritt, Auld.

Roma: Cudicini, Fontana, Corsini, Giuliano, Losi, Carpanesi, Orlando, Da Costa, Manfredini, Angelillo, Menichelli.

October 11 (Olimpico, Rome) 2nd leg

Roma 2
(Farmer og 56, Pestrin 90)

Birmingham City 0

Roma 4–2 on aggregate.

HT: 0–0.
Att: 60,000.
Ref: Schwinte (Fr).

Roma: Cudicini, Fontana, Corsini, Carpanesi, Losi, Pestrin, Orlando, Angelillo, Manfredini, Lojacono, Menichelli.

Birmingham: Schofield, Farmer, Sissons, Hennessy, Smith, Beard, Hellawell, Bloomfield, Harris, Singer, Orritt.

1962

August 9 (Luis Casanova, Valencia) 1st leg

Valencia 6
(Yosu 14, 42, Guillot 35, 54, 67, Nunez 74)

Barcelona 2
(Kocsis 4, 20)

HT: 3–2.
Att: 65,000.
Ref: Barberan (Fr).

Valencia: Zamora, Piquer, Mestre, Sastre, Quincoces, Chicao, Nunez, Ribelles, Waldo, Guillot, Yosu.

Barcelona: Pesudo, Benitez, Rodri, Olivella, Verges, Gracia, Cubilla, Kocsis, Re, Villaverde, Camps.

September 9 (Nou Camp, Barcelona)
2nd leg

Barcelona 1
(Kocsis 46)

Valencia 1
(Guillot 87)

Valencia 7–3 on aggregate.

HT: 0–0.
Att: 60,000.
Ref: Campanati (It).

Barcelona: Pesudo, Benitez, Garay, Fuste, Verges, Gracia, Cubilla, Kocsis, Goyvaerts, Villaverde, Camps.

Valencia: Zamora, Piquer, Mestre, Sastre, Quincoces, Chicao, Nunez, Urtiago, Waldo, Guillot, Yosu.

1963

June 12 (Zagreb) 1st leg

Dinamo Zagreb 1
(Zambata 13)

Valencia 2
(Waldo 64, Urtiaga 67)

HT: 1–0.
Att: 40,000.
Ref: Adami (It).

Dinamo: Skoric, Belin, Braun, Biscam, Markovic, Perusic, Kobesnac, Zambata, Knez, Matus, Lamza.

Valencia: Zamora, Piquer, Chicao, Paquito, Quincoces, Sastre, Mano, Sanchez Lage, Waldo, Ribelles, Urtiaga.

June 26 (Luis Casanova, Valencia) 2nd leg

Valencia 2
(Mano 68, Nunez 78)

Dinamo Zagreb 0

Valencia 4–1 on aggregate.

HT: 0–0.
Att: 55,000.
Ref: Howley (Eng).

Valencia: Zamora, Piquer, Chicao, Paquito, Quincoces, Sastre, Mano, Sanchez Lage, Waldo, Ribelles, Nunes.

Dinamo: Skoric, Belin, Braun, Matus, Markovic, Perusic, Kobesnac, Lamza, Raus, Zambata, Knez.

1964

June 25 (Nou Camp, Barcelona)
single match

Real Zaragoza 2
(Villa 40, Marcelino 83)

Valencia 1
(Urtiaga 41)

HT: 1–1.
Att: 50,000.
Ref: Campos (Por).

Zaragoza: Yarza, Cortizo, Santamaria, Reija, Isasi, Pais, Canario, Duca, Marcelino, Villa, Lapetra.

Valencia: Zamora, Arnal, Videgany, Paquito, Quincoces, Roberto, Suco, Guillot, Waldo, Urtiaga, Ficha.

1965

June 23 (Comunale, Turin) single match

Ferencvaros 1
(Fenyvesi 74)

Juventus 0

HT: 0–0.
Att: 25,000.
Ref: Dienst (Swz).

Ferencvaros: Geczi, Novak, Horvath, Juhasz, Matrai, Orosz, Karaba, Varga, Albert, Rakosi, Fenyvesi.

Juventus: Anzolin, Gori, Sarti, Bercellino, Castano, Leoncini, Stacchini, Del Sol, Combin, Mazzia, Menichelli.

1966

September 14 (Nou Camp, Barcelona)
1st leg

Barcelona 0

Real Zaragoza 1
(Canario 30)

HT: 0–1.
Att: 70,000.
Ref: Zsolt (Hung).

Barcelona: Sadurni, Benitez, Eladio, Montesinos, Gallego, Torres, Zaballa, Muller, Zaldua, Fuste, Vidal.

Zaragoza: Yarza, Irusquieta, Reija, Pais, Santamaria, Violeta, Canario, Santos, Marcelino, Villa, Lapetra.

September 21 (La Romareda, Zaragoza) 2nd leg

Real Zaragoza 2
(Marcelino 24, 87)

Barcelona 4
(Pujol 3, 86, 119, Zaballa 89)

Barcelona 4–3 on aggregate.

HT: 1–1. After extra-time (90 min: 2–3).
Att: 70,000.
Ref: Lo Bello (It).

Zaragoza: Yarza, Irusquieta, Reija, Pais, Santamaria, Violeta, Canario, Santos, Marcelino, Villa, Lapetra.

Barcelona: Sadurni, Foncho, Eladio, Montesinos, Gallego, Torres, Zaballa, Mas, Zaldua, Fuste, Pujol.

1967

August 30: (Dinamo Stadion, Zagreb),
1st leg

Dinamo Zagreb 2
(Cercek 39, 59)

Leeds United 0

HT: 1–0.
Att: 40,000.
Ref: Bueno Perales (Sp).

Dinamo: Skoric, Gracanin, Brncic, Belin, Ramljak, Blaskovic, Cercek, Piric, Zambata, Gucmirtl, Rora.

FAIRS CUP/UEFA CUP

Leeds: Sprake, Reaney, Cooper, Bremner, Charlton, Hunter, Bates, Lorimer, Belfitt, Gray, O'Grady.

September 6: (Elland Road, Leeds), 2nd leg

Leeds United 0

Dinamo Zagreb 0

Dinamo Zagreb 2–0 on aggregate.

HT: 0–0.
Att: 35,000.
Ref: Lo Bello (It).

Leeds: Sprake, Bell, Cooper, Bremner, Charlton, Hunter, Reaney, Belfitt, Greenhoff, Giles, O'Grady.

Dinamo: Skoric, Gracanin, Brncic, Belin, Ramljak, Blaskovic, Cercek, Piric, Zambata, Gucmirtl, Rora.

1968

September 7 (Elland Road, Leeds) 1st leg

Leeds United 1
(Jones 41)

Ferencvaros 0

HT: 1–0.
Att: 25,000.
Ref: Scheurer (Swz).

Leeds: Sprake, Reaney, Cooper, Bremner, Charlton, Hunter, Lorimer, Madeley, Jones (Belfitt), Giles (Greenhoff), E Gray.

Ferencvaros: Geczi, Novak, Pancsics, Havasi, Juhasz, Szucs, Szoke, Varga, Albert, Rakosi, Fenyvesi (Balint).

September 11 (Nep, Budapest) 2nd leg

Ferencvaros 0

Leeds United 0

Leeds 1–0 on aggregate.

HT: 0–0.
Att: 25,000.
Ref: Schulenburg (WG).

Ferencvaros: Geczi, Novak, Pancsics, Havasi, Juhasz, Szucs, Rakosi, Szoke (Karaba), Varga, Albert, Katona.

Leeds: Sprake, Reaney, Cooper, Bremner, Charlton, Hunter, O'Grady, Lorimer, Jones, Madeley, Hibbitt (Bates).

1969

May 29 (St James Park, Newcastle) 1st leg

Newcastle United 3
(Moncur 63, 72, Scott 83)

Ujpest Dozsa 0

HT: 0–0.
Att: 60,000.
Ref: Hannet (Fr).

Newcastle: McFaul, Craig, Clark, Gibb, Burton, Moncur, Scott, Robson, Davies, Arentoft, Sinclair (Foggon, 75).

Ujpest: Szentmihalyi, Kaposzta, Solymosi, Bankuti, Nosko, E Dunai, Fazekas, Gorocs, Bene, A Dunai, Zambo.

June 11 (Nep, Budapest) 2nd leg

Ujpest Dozsa 2
(Bene 31, Gorocs 44)

Newcastle United 3
(Moncur 46, Arentoft 50, Foggon 74)

Newcastle Utd 6–2 on aggregate.

HT: 2–0.
Att: 37,000.
Ref: Heymann (Swit).

Ujpest: Szentmihalyi, Kaposzta, Solymosi, Bankuti, Nosko, E Dunai, Fazekas, Gorocs, Bene, A Dunai, Zambo.

Newcastle: McFaul, Craig, Clark, Giles, Burton, Moncur, Scott (Foggon, 76), Arentoft, Robson, Davies, Sinclair.

1970

April 22 (Parc Astrid, Brussels) 1st leg

Anderlecht 3
(Devrindt 25, Mulder 30, 74)

Arsenal 1
(Kennedy 82)

HT: 2–0.
Att: 37,000.
Ref: Scheurer (Swz).

Anderlecht: Trappeniers, Heylens, Velkeneers, Kialunda, Cornelis (Peeters, 68), Nordahl, Desanghere, Puis, Devrindt, Van Himst, Mulder.

Arsenal: Wilson, Storey, McNab, Kelly, McLintock, Simpson, Armstrong, Sammels, Radford, George (Kennedy, 77), Graham.

April 28 (Highbury, London) 2nd leg

Arsenal 3
(Kelly 25, Radford 75, Sammels 76)

Anderlecht 0

Arsenal 4–3 on aggregate.

HT: 1–0.
Att: 37,000.
Ref: Scheurer (Swz).

Arsenal: Wilson, Storey, McNab, Kelly, McLintock, Simpson, Armstrong, Sammels, Radford, George, Graham.

Anderlecht: Trappeniers, Heylens, Velkeneers, Kialunda, Martens, Nordahl, Desanghere, Puis, Devrindt, Mulder, Van Himst.

1971

May 26 (Comunale, Turin) 1st leg

Juventus 0

Leeds United 0

Att: 65,000.
Ref: Van Ravens (Hol).

Abandoned 57 mins, waterlogged pitch.

Juventus: Piloni, Spinosi, Marchetti, Furino, Morini, Salvadore, Haller, Causio, Anastasi, Capello, Bettega.

Leeds: Sprake, Reaney, Charlton, Hunter, Cooper, Bremner, Giles, Clarke, M Jones, Lorimer, Madeley.

May 28 (Communale, Turin) lst leg

Juventus 2
(Bettega 27, Capello 55)

Leeds United 2
(Madeley 48, Bates 77)

HT: 1–0.
Att: 65,000.
Ref: Van Ravens (Hol).

Juventus: Piloni, Spinosi, Salvadore, Marchetti, Furino, Morini, Haller, Capello, Causio, Anastasi (Novellini, 72), Bettega.

Leeds: Sprake, Reaney, Cooper, Bremner, Charlton, Hunter, Lorimer, Clarke, Jones (Bates, 72), Giles, Madeley.

June 3 (Elland Road, Leeds) 2nd leg

Leeds United 1
(Clarke 12)

Juventus 1
(Anastasi 20)

Leeds on away goals, 3–3 aggregate.

HT: 1–1.
Att: 42,000.
Ref: Glöckner (EG).

Leeds: Sprake, Reaney, Cooper, Bremner, Charlton, Hunter, Lorimer, Clarke, Jones, Giles, Madeley (Bates, 56).

Juventus: Tancredi, Spinosi, Salvadore, Marchetti, Furino, Morini, Haller, Capello, Causio, Anastasi, Bettega.

A one-off, single-leg match was organized between the first and last winners of the Fairs Cup. Barcelona, as first winners, were granted home advantage.

September 22 (Nou Camp, Barcelona)

Barcelona 2
(Duenas 51, 83)

Leeds United 1
(Jordan 53)

HT: 0–0.
Att: 35,000.
Ref: Zsolt (Hun).

Barcelona: Sadurni, Rife, Gallego, Torres, Eladio, Costas, Juan Carlos, Rexach, Marcial, Duenas, Asensi (Fuste 46).

Leeds: Sprake, Reaney, Charlton, Hunter, Darey, Bremner, Giles, Belfitt, Lorimer, Jordan, Galvin.

From this season the competition was renamed the UEFA Cup, the words 'Industrial', then 'Inter-Cities' having been dropped gradually through the 1960s as qualification became based on football exploits.

1972

May 3 (Molineux, Wolverhampton) 1st leg

Wolverhampton Wanderers 1
(McCalliog 72)

Tottenham Hotspur 2
(Chivers 57, 87)

HT: 0–0.
Att: 38,000.
Ref: Bakhramov (SU).

Wolves: Parkes, Shaw, Taylor, Hegan, Munro, McAlle, McCalliog, Hibbitt, Richards, Dougan, Wagstaffe.

Tottenham: Jennings, Kinnear, Knowles, Mullery, England, Beal, Gilzean, Perryman, Chivers, Peters, Coates (Pratt, 68).

May 17 (White Hart Lane, London) 2nd leg

Tottenham Hotspur 1
(Mullery 30)

Wolverhampton Wanderers 1
(Wagstaffe 41)

Tottenham Hotspur 3–2 on aggregate.

HT: 1–1.
Att: 54,000.
Ref: Van Ravens (Hol).

Tottenham: Jennings, Kinnear, Knowles, Mullery, England, Beal, Gilzean, Perryman, Chivers, Peters, Coates.

Wolves: Parkes, Shaw, Taylor, Hegan, Munro, McAlle, McCalliog, Hibbitt (Bailey, 55), Richards, Dougan (Curran, 84), Wagstaffe.

1973

May 9 (Anfield, Liverpool) 1st leg

Liverpool 0

Borussia Mönchengladbach 0

Att: 44,900.
Ref: Linemayr (Aus).

Abandoned 27 mins, waterlogged pitch.

Liverpool: Clemence, Lawler, Lindsay, Lloyd, Smith, Hughes, Keegan, Cormack, Heighway, Hall, Callaghan.

Borussia: Kleff, Vogts, Michallik, Netzer, Bonhof, Danner, Wimmer, Kulik, Jensen, Rupp, Heynckes.

UEFA CUP FINALS

May 10 (Anfield, Liverpool) 1st leg

Liverpool 3
(Keegan 21, 32, Lloyd 61)

Borussia Mönchengladbach 0

HT: 2–0.
Att: 41,000.
Ref: Linemayr (Aus).

Liverpool: Clemence, Lawler, Lindsay, Smith, Lloyd, Hughes, Keegan, Cormack, Toshack, Heighway (Hall, 83), Callaghan.

Borussia: Kleff, Michallik, Netzer, Bonhof, Vogts, Wimmer, Danner, Kulik, Jensen, Rupp (Simonsen, 82), Heynckes.

May 23 (Bokelberg, Mönchengladbach) 2nd leg

Borussia Mönchengladbach 2
(Heynckes 29, 40)

Liverpool 0

Liverpool 3–2 on aggregate.

HT: 2–0.
Att: 35,000.
Ref: Kasakov (SU).

Borussia: Kleff, Surau, Netzer, Bonhof, Vogts, Wimmer, Danner, Kulik, Jensen, Rupp, Heynckes.

Liverpool: Clemence, Lawler, Lindsay, Smith, Lloyd, Hughes, Keegan, Cormack, Heighway (Boersma, 77), Toshack, Callaghan.

1974

May 21 (White Hart Lane, London) 1st leg

Tottenham Hotspur 2
(England 39, Van Daele og 64)

Feyenoord 2
(Van Hanegem 43, De Jong 85)

HT: 2–1.
Att: 46,000.
Ref: Scheurer (Swz).

Tottenham: Jennings, Evans, Naylor, Pratt, England, Beal (Dillon, 79), McGrath, Perryman, Peters, Chivers, Coates.

Feyenoord: Treytel, Rijsbergen, Van Daele, Israel, Vos, De Jong, Jansen, Van Hanegem, Ressel, Schoenmaker, Kristensen.

May 29 (Feyenoord, Rotterdam) 2nd leg

Feyenoord 2
(Rijsbergen 43, Ressel 84)

Tottenham Hotspur 0

Feyenoord 4–2 on aggregate.

HT: 1–0.
Att: 59,000.
Ref: Lo Bello (It).

Feyenoord: Treytel, Rijsbergen (Boskamp, 76; Wery, 86), Van Daele, Israel, Vos, Ramljak, Jansen, De Jong, Ressel, Schoenmaker, Kristensen.

Tottenham: Jennings, Evans, Naylor, Pratt (Holder, 77), England, Beal, McGrath, Perryman, Peters, Chivers, Coates.

1975

May 7 (Rheinstadion, Düsseldorf) 1st leg

Borussia Mönchengladbach 0

Twente Enschede 0

HT: 0–0.
Att: 21,000.
Ref: Palotai (Hung).

Borussia: Kleff, Wittkamp, Stielike, Vogts, Surau, Bonhof, Wimmer, Danner (Del'Haye, 75), Kulik (Schäffer, 78), Simonsen, Jensen.

Twente: Gross, Drost, Van Iersel, Overweg, Oranen, Thijssen, Palhplatz, Van der Vall, Bos, Jeuring (Achterberg, 86), Zuidema.

May 21 (Diekman, Enschede) 2nd leg

Twente Enschede 1
(Drost 76)

Borussia Mönchengladbach 5
(Simonsen 2, 86, Heynckes 9, 50, 60)

Borussia 5–1 on aggregate.

HT: 2–0.
Att: 21,000.
Ref: Schiller (Aus).

Twente: Gross, Drost, Van Iersel, Overweg, Oranen, Bos (G. Muhren, 53), Thijssen, Pahlplatz (Achterberg, 75), Van der Vall, Jeuring, Zuidema.

Borussia: Kleff, Wittkamp, Vogts, Surau (Schäffer, 13), Klinkhammer, Bonhof, Wimmer (Köppel, 75), Danner, Simonsen, Jensen, Heynckes.

1976

April 28 (Anfield, Liverpool) 1st leg

Liverpool 3
(Kennedy 59, Case 61, Keegan 65)

Club Brugge 2
(Lambert 5, Cools 15)

HT: 0–2.
Att: 49,000.
Ref: Biwersi (Aus).

Liverpool : Clemence, Smith, Neal, Thompson, Hughes, Keegan, Kennedy, Callaghan, Fairclough, Heighway, Toshack (Case, 46).

Brugge: Jensen, Bastijns, Krieger, Leekens, Volders, Cools, Vandereycken, Decubber, Van Gool, Lambert, Lefevre.

May 19 (Olympiastadion, Bruges) 2nd leg

Club Brugge 1
(Lambert 11)

Liverpool 1
(Keegan 15)

Liverpool 4–3 on aggregate

HT: 1–1.
Att: 32,000.
Ref: Glöckner (EG).

Brugge: Jensen, Bastijns, Kriger, Leekens, Volders, Cools, Vandereycken, Decubber (Hinderyckx, 68), Van Gool, Lambert (Sanders, 75), Lefevre.

Liverpool: Clemence, Smith, Neal, Thompson, Hughes, Keegan, Kennedy, Callaghan, Case, Heighway, Toshack (Fairclough, 62).

1977

May 4 (Comunale, Turin) 1st leg

Juventus 1
(Tardelli 15)

Athletic Bilbao 0

HT: 1–0.
Att: 75,000.
Ref: Corver (Hol).

Juventus: Zoff, Cuccureddu, Gentile, Scirea, Morini, Tardelli, Furino, Benetti, Causio, Boninsegna (Gori, 39), Bettega.

Athletic: Iribar, Onaederra, Escalza, Goicoechea, Guisasola, Villar, Irureta, J.A. Rojo, Churruca, Dani, J.F. Rojo.

May 18 (San Mames, Bilbao) 2nd leg

Athletic Bilbao 2
(Churruca 11, Carlos 78)

Juventus 1
(Bettega 7)

Juventus on away goals, 2–2 aggregate.

HT: 1–1.
Att: 43,000.
Ref: Linemayr (Aus).

Athletic: Iribar, Lasa (Carlos, 63), Guisasola, Alexanco, Escalza, Villar, Churruca, Irureta, Amorrortu, Dani, J.F. Rojo.

Juventus: Zoff, Cuccureddu, Morini, Scirea, Gentile, Causio, Tardelli, Furino, Benetti, Boninsegna (Spinosi, 59), Bettega.

1978

April 26 (Furiani, Bastia) 1st leg

Bastia 0

PSV Eindhoven 0

HT: 0–0.
Att: 15,000.
Ref: Maksimovic (Yug).

Bastia: Hiard, Burkhard, Guesdon, Orlanducci, Cazes, Papi, Lacuesta (Felix, 56), Larios, Rep, Krimau, Mariot.

PSV: Van Beveren, Van Kraay, Krijgh, Stevens, Brandts, Poortvliet, Van der Kuijlen, W Van de Kerkhof, Deijkers, R Van de Kerkhof, Lubse.

May 9 (Philips, Eindhoven) 2nd leg

PSV Eindhoven 3
(W Van de Kerkhof 24, Deijkers 67, Van der Kuijlen 69)

Bastia 0

PSV 3–0 on aggregate.

HT: 1–0.
Att: 27,000.
Ref: Rainea (Rom).

PSV: Van Beveren, Krijgh, Stevens, Van Kraay (Deacy, 79), Brandts, W Van de Kerkhof, Poortvliet, Van der Kuijlen, Lubse, Deijkers, R Van de Kerkhof.

Bastia: Hiard (Weller, 75), Marchioni, Orlanducci, Guesdon, Cazes, Lacuesta, Larios, Papi, Rep, Krimau, Mariot (De Zerbi, 67).

1979

May 9 (Crvena Zvezda, Belgrade) 1st leg

Red Star Belgrade 1
(Sestic 21)

Borussia Mönchengladbach 1
(Jurisic og 60)

HT: 1–0.
Att: 87,000.
Ref: Foote (Eng).

Red Star: Stojanovic, Jovanovic, Miletovic, Jurisic, Jovin, Muslin (Krmpotic, 88), Petrovic, Blagojevic, Milosavljevic (Milovanovic, 88), Savic, Sestic.

Borussia: Kneib, Vogts, Hannes, Schäffer, Ringels, Schäfer, Kulik, Nielsen (Danner, 75), Wohlers (Gores, 80), Simonsen, Lienen.

May 23 (Rheinstadion, Düsseldorf) 2nd leg

Borussia Mönchengladbach 1
(Simonsen 15)

Red Star Belgrade 0

Borussia Mönchengladbach 2–1 on aggregate.

HT: 1–0.
Att: 45,000.
Ref: Michelotti (It).

Borussia: Kneib, Vogts, Hannes, Schäffer, Ringels, Schäfer, Kulik (Köppel, 58), Gores, Wohlers, Simonsen, Lienen.

Red Star: Stojanovic, Jovanovic, Miletovic, Jurisic, Jovin, Muslin, Petrovic, Blagojevic, Milovanovic (Sestic, 46), Savic, Milosavljevic.

UEFA CUP FINALS

1980

May 7 (Bokelberg, Mönchengladbach) 1st leg

Borussia Mönchengladbach 3
(Kulik 44, 88, Matthäus 76)

Eintracht Frankfurt 2
(Karger 37, Hölzenbein 71)

HT: 1–1.
Att: 25,000.
Ref: Gureceta (Sp).

Borussia: Kneib, Hannes, Schäfer, Schäffer, Ringels, Matthäus, Kulik, Nielsen (Thychosen, 86), Del'Haye (Bodecker, 72), Nickel, Lienen.

Eintracht: Pahl, Pezzey, Neuberger, Korbel, Ehrmanntraut, Lorant, Hölzenbein (Nachtweih, 79), Borchers, Nickel, Cha Bum-kun, Karger (Trapp, 81).

May 21 (Waldstadion, Frankfurt) 2nd leg

Eintracht Frankfurt 1
(Schaub 81)

Borussia Mönchengladbach 0

Eintracht on away goals, 3–3 on aggregate.

HT: 0–0.
Att: 59,000.
Ref: Ponnet (Belg).

Eintracht: Pahl, Pezzey, Neuberger, Korbel, Ehrmanntraut, Lorant, Hölzenbein, Borchers, Nickel, Cha Bum-kun, Nachtweih (Schaub, 77).

Borussia: Kneib, Bodecker, Hannes, Schäfer, Ringels, Matthäus (Thychosen, 86), Fleer, Kulik, Nielsen (Del'Haye, 68), Nickel, Lienen.

1981

May 6 (Portman Road, Ipswich) 1st leg

Ipswich Town 3
(Wark 28, Thijssen 46, Mariner 56)

AZ Alkmaar 0

HT: 1–0.
Att: 27,000.
Ref: Prokop (EG).

Ipswich: Cooper, Mills, Osman, Butcher, McCall, Thijssen, Wark, Muhren, Mariner, Brazil, Gates.

Alkmaar: Treytel, Van der Meer, Spelbos, Metgod, Hovenkamp, Peters, Arntz, Jonker, Nygaard (Welzl, 75), Tol, Kist.

May 20 (Alkmaar) 2nd leg

AZ Alkmaar 4
(Welzl 7, Metgod 25, Tol 40, Jonker 74)

Ipswich Town 2
(Thijssen 4, Wark 32)

Ipswich 5–4 on aggregate.

HT: 3–2.
Att: 28,500.
Ref: Eschweiler (WG).

Alkmaar: Treytel, Reinders, Spelbos, Metgod, Hovenkamp, Peters, Arntz, Jonkers, Nygaard, Welzl (Talan, 79), Tol (Kist, 46).

Ipswich: Cooper, Mills, Osman, Butcher, McCall, Thijssen, Wark, Muhren, Mariner, Brazil, Gates.

1982

May 5 (Nya Ullevi, Gothenburg) 1st leg

IFK Gothenburg 1
(Tord Holmgren 87)

Hamburg 0

HT: 0–0.
Att: 42,000.
Ref: Carpenter (Ire).

IFK: Wernersson, Svensson, Hysen, C Karlsson, Fredriksson, Tord Holmgren, J Karlsson, Stromberg, Corneliussen, Nilsson (Sandberg, 19), Tommy Holmgren (Schiller, 46).

Hamburg: Stein, Kaltz, Hieronymus, Groh, Wehmeyer, Hartwig, Jakobs, Magath, Von Heesen (Memering, 82), Hrubesch, Bastrup.

May 19 (Volksparkstadion, Hamburg) 2nd leg

Hamburg 0

IFK Gothenburg 3
(Nilsson 6, Corneliusson 26, Fredriksson 63)

Gothenburg 4–0 on aggregate.

HT: 0–2.
Att: 60,000.
Ref: Courtney (Eng).

Hamburg: Stein, Kaltz (Hidien, 75), Hieronymus, Groh, Wehmeyer, Hartwig, Memering, Magath, Von Heesen, Hrubesch, Bastrup.

IFK: Wernersson, Svensson, Hysen (Schiller, 19), C Karlsson, Fredriksson, Tord Holmgren, Stromberg, J Karlsson, Corneliussen (Sandberg, 68), Nilsson, Tommy Holmgren.

1983

May 4 (Heysel, Brussels) 1st leg

Anderlecht 1
(Brylle 29)

Benfica 0

HT: 1–0.
Att: 55,000.
Ref: Dochev (Bul).

Anderlecht: Munaron, Hofkens, Peruzovic, Olsen, De Groot, Frimann, Coeck, Vercauteren, Lozano, Vandenbergh (Czeriatynski, 78), Brylle.

Benfica: Bento, Pietra, Alvaro, Humberto Coelho, Jose Luis, Sheu (A Bastos Lopes, 78), Frederico, Carlos Manuel, Chalana (Nene, 68), Diamantino, Filipovic.

May 18 (Benfica, Lisbon) 2nd leg

Benfica 1
(Sheu 36)

Anderlecht 1
(Lozano 38)

Anderlecht 2–1 on aggregate.

HT: 1–1.
Att: 80,000.
Ref: Corver (Hol).

Benfica: Bento, Pietra, Humberto Coelho, Bastos Lopes, Veloso (Alves, 62), Carlos Manuel, Stromberg, Sheu (Filipovic, 50), Chalana, Nene, Diamantino.

Anderlecht: Munaron, Peruzovic, De Gref, Broos, Olsen, De Groot, Frimann, Lozano, Coeck, Vercauteren, Vandenbergh (Brylle, 78).

1984

May 9 (Parc Astrid, Brussels) 1st leg

Anderlecht 1
(Olsen 85)

Tottenham Hotspur 1
(Miller 57)

HT: 0–0.
Att: 35,000.
Ref: Galler (Swz).

Anderlecht: Munaron, Grun, De Greef, M Olsen, De Groot, Hofkens, Vandereycken, Scifo, Brylle, Vandenbergh (Arnesen, 81), Czerniatynski (Vercauteren, 85).

Tottenham: Parks, Thomas, Roberts, Hughton, Perryman, Miller, Stevens (Mabbutt, 80), Hazard, Galvin, Archibald, Falco.

May 23 (White Hart Lane, London) 2nd leg

Tottenham Hotspur 1
(Roberts 84)

Anderlecht 1
(Czerniatynski 60)

Tottenham 4–3 on pens, 2–2 aggregate.

HT: 0–0. After extra-time (90 min: 1–1).
Att: 46,000.
Ref: Roth (WG).

Tottenham: Parks, Thomas, Hughton, Roberts, Miller (Ardiles, 78), Mabbutt (Dick, 74), Hazard, Stevens, Galvin, Archibald, Falco.

Anderlecht: Munaron, Hofkens, Grun, De Greef, M Olsen, De Groot, Arnesen (Gudjohnsen, 77), Vercauteren, Scifo, Czerniatynski (Brylle, 103), Vandereycken.

1985

May 8 (Sostol, Szekesfehervar) 1st leg

Videoton 0

Real Madrid 3
(Michel 31, Santillana 77, Valdano 89)

HT: 0–1.
Att: 30,000.
Ref: Vautrot (Fr).

Videoton: P Disztl, Borsanyi, L Disztl, Csushay, Horvath, Palkovics, Vegh, Wittman, Vadasz, Novath (Gyenti, 62), Burcsa.

Madrid: Miguel Angel, Chendo, Sanchis, Stielike, Camacho, San Jose, Michel, Gallego, Butragueño (Juanito, 80), Santillana (Salguero, 86), Valdano.

May 22 (Bernabeu, Madrid) 2nd leg

Real Madrid 0

Videoton 1
(Majer 86)

Real Madrid 3–1 on aggregate.

HT: 0–0.
Att: 90,000.
Ref: Ponnet (Bel).

Real: Miguel Angel, Chendo, Sanchis, Stielike, Camacho, San Jose, Michel, Gallego, Butragueño, Santillana, Valdano (Juanito, 57)

Videoton: P Disztl, Csushay, L Disztl, Vegh, Horvath, Burcsa, Csongradi (Wittman, 57), Vadasz, Szabo, Majer, Novath (Palkovics, 51).

1986

April 30 (Bernabeu, Madrid) 1st leg

Real Madrid 5
(Sanchez 38, Gordillo 42, Valdano 51, 84, Santillana 89)

Köln 1
(K Allofs 29)

HT: 2–1.
Att: 85,000.
Ref: Courtney (Eng).

Real: Agustin, Salguero, Solana, Camacho, Martin Vazquez (Santillana, 83), Michel, Juanito, Gordillo, Butragueño, Sanchez, Valdano.

Köln: Schumacher, Geils, Gielchen, Steiner, Prestin, Geilenkirchen, Hönerbach, Bein (Hässler, 71), Janssen, Littbarski (Dickel, 84), K Allofs.

May 6 (Olympiastadion, Berlin) 2nd leg

Köln 2
(Bein 22, Geilenkirchen 72)

Real Madrid 0

Real Madrid 5–3 on aggregate.

UEFA CUP FINALS

HT: 1–0.
Att: 15,000.
Ref: Valentine (Sc).

Köln: Schumacher, Prestin, Gielchen, Geils (Schmitz, 82), Geilenkirchen, Steiner, Bein, Hönerbach, Janssen (Pisanti, 51), Littbarski, K Allofs.

Real: Agustin, Chendo, Maceda, Solana, Camacho, Michel, Gallego, Valdano, Gordillo, Butragueño, (Juanito), Sanchez, (Santillano).

1987
May 6 (Nya Ullevi, Gothenburg) 1st leg

IFK Gothenburg 1
(Pettersson 38)

Dundee United 0

HT: 1–0.
Att: 50,000.
Ref: Kirschen (EG).

IFK: Wernersson, C Karlsson, Hysen, Larsson, Fredriksson, Jonsson (R Nilsson, 68), Tord Holmgren (Zetterlund, 89), Andersson, Tommy Holmgren, Pettersson, L Nilsson.

Dundee United: Thompson, Malpas, Narey, Hegarty (Clark, 55), Holt, McInally, Kirkwood, Bowman, Bannon, Sturrock (Beaumont, 89), Redford.

May 20 (Tannadice Park, Dundee) 2nd leg

Dundee United 1
(Clark 60)

IFK Gothenburg 1
(Nilsson 22)

IFK 2–1 on aggregate.

HT: 0–1.
Att: 21,000.
Ref: Igna (Rom).

Dundee United: Thompson, Malpas, Clark, Narey, Holt (Hegarty, 46), McInally, Ferguson, Kirkwood, Sturrock, Redford (Bannon, 72), Gallacher.

IFK: Wernersson, C Karlsson, Hysen, Larsson, Fredriksson, R Nilsson (Johansson, 78), Tord Holmgren, Andersson, Tommy Holmgren (Mordt, 70), Pettersson, L Nilsson.

1988
May 4 (Sarria, Barcelona) 1st leg

Español 3
(Losada, 44, 57, Soler 49)

Bayer Leverkusen 0

HT: 1–0.
Att: 42,000.
Ref: Krchnak (Cz).

Español: N'Kono, Job, Miguel Angel, Gallart, Soler, Orejuela (Golobart, 66), Urquiaga, Iñaki, Valverde, Pichi Alonso (Lauridson, 71), Losada.

Bayer: Vollborn, Rolff, De Kayser, A Reinhardt, Hinterberger, Cha Bum-kun (Götz, 18), Tita, Buncol, Falkenmayer (K Reinhardt, 78), Waas, Tauber.

May 18 (Ulrich Haberland Stadion, Leverkusen) 2nd leg

Bayer Leverkusen 3
(Tita 57, Götz 63, Cha Bum-kun 81)

Español 0

Bayer 3–2 on pens, 3–3 aggregate.

HT: 0–0. After extra-time (90 min: 3–0).
Att: 22,000. 90min: 0–0.
Ref: Keizer (Hol).

Bayer: Vollborn, Rolff, Seckler, A Reinhardt, K Reinhardt, Schreier (Waas, 46), Buncol, Falkenmayer, Cha Bum-kun, Götz, Tita (Täuber, 62).

Español: N'Kono, Miguel Angel, Golobart, (Zuniga, 73), Urquiaga, Job, Orejuela (Zubillaga, 67), Iñaki, Soler, Pichi Alonso, Gallart, Losada.

1989
May 3 (San Paolo, Naples) 1st leg

Napoli 2
(Maradona 68, Careca 87)

Stuttgart 1
(Gaudino 17)

HT: 0–1.
Att: 83,000.
Ref: Germanakos (Gr).

Napoli: Giuliani, Renica, Ferrara, Francini, Corradini (Crippa, 46), Alemão, Fusi, De Napoli, Careca, Maradona, Carnevale.

Stuttgart: Immel, Allgöwer, N Schmäler, Hartmann, Buchwald, Schäfer, Katanec, Sigurvinnsson, Schröder, Walter (Zietsch, 75), Gaudino.

May 17 (Neckarstadion, Stuttgart) 1st leg

Stuttgart 3
(Klinsmann 27, De Napoli og 70, O Schmäler 89)

Napoli 3
(Alemão 18, Ferrara 39, Careca 62)

Napoli 5–4 on aggregate.

HT: 1–2.
Att: 67,000.
Ref: Sanchez Arminio (Sp).

Stuttgart: Immel, Allgöwer, N Schmäler, Hartmann, Schäffer, Katanec, Sigurvinnsson, Schröder, Walter (O Schmäler,77), Klinsmann, Gaudino.

Napoli: Giuliani, Renica, Ferrara, Francini, Corradini, Alemão (Carranante, 31), Fusi, De Napoli, Careca (Bigliardi, 70), Maradona, Carnevale.

1990
May 2 (Comunale, Turin) 1st leg

Juventus 3
(Galia 3, Casiraghi 59, De Agostini 73)

Fiorentina 1
(Buso 10)

HT: 1–1.
Att: 45,000.
Ref: Soriano Aladren (Sp).

Juventus: Tacconi, Napoli, De Agostini, Galia, Brio (Alessio, 46), Bonetti, Aleinikov, Barros, Marocchi, Casiraghi, Schillaci.

Fiorentinia: Landucci, Dell'Oglio, Volpecina, Pin, Battistini, Dunga, Nappi, Kubik (Malusci, 46), R Baggio, Buso, Di Chiara.

May 16 (Partenio, Avellino) 2nd leg

Fiorentina 0

Juventus 0

Juventus 3–1 on aggregate.

Att: 32,000.
Ref: Schmidhuber (WG).

Fiorentina: Landucci, Dell'Oglio, Volpecina, Pin, Battistini, Dunga, Nappi (Zironelli, 72), Kubik, R Baggio, Buso, Di Chiara.

Juventus: Tacconi, Napoli, De Agostini, Galia, Bruno, Alessio, Aleinikov, Barros (Avallone, 72), Marocchi, Casiraghi (Rosa, 78), Schillaci.

1991
May 8 (Giuseppe Meazza, Milan) 1st leg

Internazionale 2
(Matthäus 55, Berti 67)

Roma 0

HT: 0–0.
Att: 75,000.
Ref: Spirin (SU).

Inter: Zenga, Bergomi, Brehme, Battistini, Ferri, Paganin (G Baresi, 64), Bianchi, Berti, Matthäus, Klinsmann, Serena (Pizzi, 89).

Roma: Cervone, Tempestilli, Nela, Berthold, Aldair (Carboni, 72), Comi (Muzzi, 74), Gerolin, Di Mauro, Giannini, Völler, Rizzitelli.

May 22 (Olimpico, Rome) 2nd leg

Roma 1
(Rizzitelli 81)

Internazionale 0

Inter 2–1 on aggregate.

HT: 0–0.
Att: 71,000.
Ref: Quiniou (Fr).

Roma: Cervone, Tempestelli (Salsano, 56), Gerolin, Berthold, Aldair, Nela, Desideri (Muzzi, 69), Di Mauro, Giannini, Völler, Rizzitelli.

Inter: Zenga, Bergomi, Brehme, Battistini, Ferri, Paganin, Bianchi, Berti, Matthäus, Klinsmann, Pizzi (Mandorlini, 66).

1992
April 29 (Delle Alpi, Turin) 1st leg

Torino 2
(Casagrande 65, 82)

Ajax 2
(Jonk 17, Pettersson 73)

HT: 0–1.
Att: 65,000.
Ref: Worrall (Eng).

Torino: Marchegiani, Bruno, Annoni, Cravero (Bresciani, 77), Mussi (Sordo, 80), Benedetti, Scifo, Martin Vasquez, Venturin, Lentini, Casagrande.

Ajax: Menzo, Silooy, Blind, Jonk, F De Boer, Winter, Kreek, Bergkamp, Van't Schip, Pettersson, Roy (Groenendijk, 83).

May 13 (Olympisch Stadion, Amsterdam) 2nd leg

Ajax 0

Torino 0

Ajax on away goals, 2–2 aggregate.

HT: 0–0.
Att: 42,000.
Ref: Petrovic (Yug).

Ajax: Menzo, Silooy, Blind, Jonk, F De Boer, Winter, Kreek (Vink, 80), Alflen, Van't Schip, Pettersson, Roy (Van Loen, 65).

Torino: Marchegiani, Mussi, Cravero (Sordo, 58), Benedetti, Fusi, Policano, Martin Vazquez, Scifo (Bresciani, 62), Veturin, Casagrande, Lentini.

1993
May 5 (Westfalenstadion, Dortmund) 1st leg

Borussia Dortmund 1
(M Rummenigge 2)

Juventus 3
(D Baggio 27, R Baggio 31, 74)

HT: 1–2.
Att: 37,000.
Ref: Puhl (Hung).

Borussia: Klos, Grauer, Reuter, Schmidt, Lusch, Frank (Mill, 46), Zorc (Karl, 75), M Rummenige, Poscher, K Reinhardt, Chapuisat.

Juventus: Peruzzi, Julio Cesar, Carrera, Kohler, De Marchi, Conti, D Baggio, R Baggio (Di Canio, 80), Marocchi, Vialli, Möller (Galia, 86).

May 19 (Delle Alpi, Turin) 2nd leg

UEFA CUP FINALS

Juventus 3
(D Baggio 5, 40, Möller 65)

Borussia Dortmund 0

Juventus 6–1 on aggregate.

HT: 2–0.
Att: 60,000.
Ref: Blankenstein (Hol).

Juventus: Peruzzi, Carrera, Torricelli (Di Canio, 66), De Marchi, Kohler, Julio Cesar, Möller, D Baggio, R Baggio, Vialli (Ravanelli, 79), Marocchi.

Dortmund: Klos, Reinhardt, Schmidt, Schulz, Zelic, Poscher, Reuter (Lusch, 65), Karl, Mil, Rummenige (Frank, 43), Sippel.

1994

April 26 (Ernst-Happel-Stadion, Vienna) 1st leg

Austria Salzburg 0

Internazionale 1
(Berti 35)

HT: 0–1.
Att: 47,000.
Ref:Nielsen (Den).

Salzburg: Konrad, Lainer, Weber, Winklhofer (Steiner, 61), Fürstaller, Aigner, Amerhauser (Muzek, 64), Artner, Marquinho, Pfeifenberger, Stadler.

Inter: Zenga, A Paganin, Orlando, Jonk, Bergomi, Battistini, Bianchi, Manicone, Berti, Bergkamp (Dell'Anno, 89), Sosa (Ferri, 74).

May 11 (Giuseppe Meazza, Milan) 2nd leg

Internazionale 1
(Jonk 63)

Austria Salzburg 0

Inter 2–0 on aggregate.

HT: 0–0.
Att: 80,000.
Ref: McCluskey (Scot).

Inter: Zenga, A Paganin, Fontolan (Ferri 23), Jonk, Bergomi, Battistini, Orlando, Manicone, Berti, Bergkamp (M Paganin, 90) Sosa.

Salzburg: Konrad, Winklhofer (Amerhauser, 68), Lainer, Weber, Fürstaller, Aigner, Jurcevic, Artner (Steiner), Hütter, Marquinho, Feiersinger.

1995

May 3 (Tardini, Parma) 1st leg

Parma 1
(D Baggio 5)

Juventus 0

HT: 1–0.
Att: 22,000.
Ref: Lopez Nieto (Sp).

Parma: Bucci, Benarrivo (Mussi, 8), Minotti, Apolloni, Fernando Couto, Di Chiara, Pin, D Baggio, Sensini, Zola (Fiore, 89), Asprilla.

Juventus: Rampulla, Fusi (Del Piero, 72), Tacchinardi, Carrera (Marocchi, 46), Jarni, Paulo Sousa, Di Livio, Deschamps, Vialli, R Baggio, Ravanelli.

May 17 (Giuseppe Meazza, Milan) 2nd leg

Juventus 1
(Vialli 33)

Parma 1
(D Baggio 54)

Parma 2–1 on aggregate.

HT: 1–0.
Att: 80,000.
Ref: Van der Wijngaert (Bel).

Juventus: Peruzzi, Ferrara, Porrini, Torricelli, Jarni, Paulo Sousa, Di Livio (Carrera, 80), Marocchi (Del Piero, 73), R Baggio, Vialli, Ravanelli.

Parma: Bucci, Benarrivo (Mussi, 46), Susic, Minotti, Di Chiara (Castellini, 79), Fernando Couto, Fiore, D Baggio, Crippa, Zola, Asprilla.

1996

May 1 (Olympia, Munich) 1st leg

Bayern Munich 2
(Helmer 35, Scholl 60)

Bordeaux 0

HT: 1–0.
Att: 62,500.
Ref: Mühmenthaler (Swz).

Bayern: Kahn, Matthäus (Frey 53), Babbel, Ziege, Kreuzer, Helmer, Hamann, Scholl, Sforza, Klinsmann, Papin (Witeczek 70).

Bordeaux: Huard, Grenet, Lizarazu, Friis-Hansen, Dogon, Lucas, Croci, Dutuel, Tholot (Anselin 89), Richard Witschge, Bancarel.

May 15 (Bordeaux) 2nd leg

Bordeaux 1
(Dutuel 75)

Bayern Munich 3
(Scholl 53, Kostadinov 65, Klinsmann 79)

Bayern 5–1 on aggregate.

HT: 0–0.
Att: 36,000.
Ref: Zhuk (Bela).

Bordeaux: Huard, Bancarel, Lizarazu (Anselin 32), Friis-Hansen, Dogon, Lucas (Grenet 79), Zidane, Croci (Dutuel 57), Tholot, Richard Witschge, Dugarry.

Bayern: Kahn, Babbel, Ziege, Strunz, Helmer, Frey (Zickler 60), Scholl, Sforza, Klinsmann, Matthäus, Kostadinov (Witeczek 75).

1997

1st leg, May 7 (Park, Gelsenkirchen)

Schalke 1
(Wilmots 69)

Internazionale 0

HT: 0-0.
Att: 56,824.
Ref: Batta (Fr)

Schalke: Lehmann, de Kock, Thon, Linke, Muller, Nemec, Buskens (Max 69), Anderbrugge, Eigenrauch, Wilmots, Latal.

Inter: Pagliuca, Pistone, Galante, Fresi (Berti 61), M Paganin, Bergomi, Zanetti, Winter, Sforza, Ganz, Zamorano.

2nd leg, May 21 (Meazza, Milan)

Internazionale 1
(Zamorano 84)

Schalke 0

HT: 0-0. 90min: 1–0.
Att: 81,675
Schalke 4–1 on pens, 1–1 aggregate
Fresi sent off, 90min.

Inter: Pagliuca, Bergomi (Angloma 71), M Paganin, Fresi, Pistone, Ince, Sforza (Winter 81), Zanetti (Berti 120), Djorkaeff, Zamorano, Ganz. *Fresi sent off, 89min.*

Schalke: Lehmann, Thon, Linke, de Kock, Eigenrauch, Latal (Held 96), Nemec, Muller (Anderbrugge 96), Buskens, Max.

Indeed, yet another metamorphosis may soon be necessary for the competition originally conceived by Ernst Thommen all of 50 years ago.

EUROPEAN SUPERCUP

The European Supercup was created to fill a gap which arose out of repulsion at the violent course taken by the original Inter-continental (or World Club) Cup.

Ajax, European champions in 1971, had been so horrified by events at the previous year's clash between their fellow Dutchmen from Feyenoord and Estudiantes de La

DANGER MAN ... Milan's Gianni Rivera teasing Ajax defenders.

Plata, the champions of South America. Accordingly, they refused to play the world club tie and found Rangers, holders of the Cup-Winners Cup, eager to launch a European club play-off between the holders of the two top titles. The Dutch, under the inspiration of Johan Cruyff, won both in Holland and Scotland, then thrashed Milan the following year even though Cruyff had been sold to Barcelona. Milan's revenge, over the succeeding years, has been to win the Supercup as often – three times – as Ajax.

The Supercup has never been a major crowd-puller, the two-leg, home format is usually squashed into mid-season. On three occasions the clubs involved could only find time for a single-match event. Juventus beat Liverpool in Turin in 1984, Steaua Bucharest saw off Dynamo Kiev in 1986 then Manchester United squeezed a victory over Red Star Belgrade in the early 1990s. Political problems con-

ROMANIAN MASTER ... Gheorghe Hagi with 1986 cup and medal.

EASY ... Juventus celebrate another of their six goals in Paris.

fused the meeting between United and Red Star; UEFA judged it too risky for United to travel to the capital of the violently-unravelling former Yugoslavia. Typical of the interest taken in it was the remark in January 1997 of Bernard Lama, goalkeeper of Paris Saint-Germain, that the Supercup "is just a piece of business for the club." Bad business, as it turned out, for Paris, 1996 winners of the Cup-Winners Cup, were duly thrashed 6–1 at home and 3–1 away by Juventus. Juve' had to take the second leg to Palermo to lure a decent crowd. The soccer-saturated Turin public would have ignored it had it gone ahead, as scheduled, in their own Delle Alpi stadium.

So far then, the Champions Cup holders lead 13-8 overall (discounting 1993 when Milan replaced Marseille, who had been barred after match-fixing revelations). UEFA wants to upgrade status of the Supercup which is likely to switch, from 1998, to a "proper" single match final at a neutral venue. How that may persuade the paying public – increasingly spoiled by televised football – to come out to watch such a hybrid event has yet to be explained.

EUROPEAN SUPERCUP RESULTS

1972
Glasgow:

Rangers 1 (MacDonald)

Ajax 3 (Rep, Cruyff, Haan).
Att: 57,000

Amsterdam:

Ajax 3 (Haan, G Muhren, Cruyff)

Rangers 2 (MacDonald 2)
Att: 37,000

*Ajax 6–3 on agg

1973
Milan:

Milan 1 (Chiarugi)

Ajax 0
Att: 15,000

Amsterdam:

Ajax 6 (Mulder, Keizer, Neeskens, Muhren 2, Haan),

Milan 0.
Att: 40,000

*Ajax 6–1 on agg

1974
Not held

1975
Munich:

Bayern Munich 0,

Kiev Dynamo 1 (Blokhin).
Att: 30,000

Kiev:

Kiev Dynamo 2 (Blokhin 2) 2

Bayern Munich 0.
Att: 100,000

Kiev Dynamo 3–0 on agg

1976
Munich:

Bayern Munich 2 (Muller 2),

Anderlecht 1 (Haan).
Att: 41,000

Brussels:

RSC Anderlecht 4 (Rensenbrink 2,
Van der Elst, Haan),

Bayern Munich 1 (Muller).
Att: 35,000

Anderlecht 5–3 on agg

1977
Hamburg:

Hamburg 1 (Keller),

Liverpool 1 (Fairclough).
Att: 16,000

Liverpool:

Liverpool 6 (Thompson, McDermott 3,
Fairclough, Dalglish),

Hamburg 0.
Att: 34,931

*Liverpool 7–1 on agg

1978
Brussels:

RSC Anderlecht 3 (Vercauteren, Vander Elst, Resenbrink),

Liverpool 1 (Case).
Att: 35,000

Liverpool:

Liverpool 2 (Hughes, Fairclough),

RSC Anderlecht 1 (Van Der Elst).
Att: 23,598

Anderlecht 4–3 on agg

1979
Nottingham:

Nottingham Forest 1 (George),

Barcelona 0.
Att: 23,807

Barcelona:

Barcelona 1 (Roberto),

Nottingham Forest 1 (Burns).
Att: 80,000

*Nottingham Forest 2–1 on agg

1980
Nottingham:

Nottingham Forest 2 (Bowyer 2),

Valencia 1 (Felman).
Att: 12,463

Valencia:

Valencia 1 (Morena),

Nottingham Forest 0.
Att: 45,000

*Nottingham Forest on away goals, agg 2–2

1981
Not held

1982
Barcelona:

Barcelona 1 (Marcos),

Aston Villa 0.
Att: 50,000

Birmingham:

Aston Villa 3 (Shaw, Cowans, McNaught),

Barcelona 0.
Att: 32,570

*Aston Villa 3–1 on agg

1983
Hamburg:

Hamburg 0,

Aberdeen 0.
Att: 12,000

Aberdeen:

Aberdeen 2 (Simpson, McGhee),

Hamburg 0.
Att: 24,000

Aberdeen 2–0 on agg

1984
Turin:

Juventus 2 (Boniek 2),

***Liverpool 0.**
Att: 60,000 (single match in Turin)

1985
Not held

1986
Monte Carlo:

***Steaua Bucharesti 1** (Hagi),

Kiev Dynamo 0 .
Att: 8,456 (single match in Monaco)

1987
Amsterdam:

Ajax 0,

FC Porto 1 (Rui Barros).
Att: 27,000

Oporto:

FC Porto 1 (Sousa),

Ajax 0.
Att: 50,000

*FC Porto 2–0 on agg

1988
Mechelen:

Mechelen 3 (Bosman 2, De Wilde),

PSV Eindhoven 0.
Att: 7,000

Eindhoven:

PSV Eindhoven 1 (Gilhaus),

Mechelen 0.
Att: 17,100

Mechelen 3–1 on agg

1989
Barcelona:

Barcelona 1 (Amor),

Milan 1 (Van Basten).
Att: 70,000

Milan:

Milan 1 (Evani),

Barcelona 0.
Att: 50,000

*Milan 2–1 on agg

1990
Genoa:

Sampdoria 1 (Mikhailichenko 31),

Milan 1 (Evani).
Att: 25,000

Milan:

Milan 2 (Gullit, Rijkaard),

Sampdoria 0.
Att: 25,000

*Milan 3–1 on agg

1991
Manchester:

Manchester United 1 (McClair),

***Red Star Belgrade 0.**
Att: 22,110 (single match)

1992
Bremen:

Werder Bremen 1 (Allofs),

Barcelona 1 (Salinas).
Att: 22,098

Barcelona:

Barcelona 2 (Stoichkov, Goikoetxea),

Werder Bremen 1 (Rufer).
Att: 75,000

*Barcelona 3–2 on agg

1993
Parma:

Parma 0,

Milan 1 (Papin).
Att: 8,083

Milan:

Milan 0,

Parma 2 (Sensini, Crippa).
Att: 24,074

Parma 2–1 on agg

1994
London:

Arsenal 0,

Milan 0.
Att: 38,044

Milan:

Milan 2 (Boban, Massaro),

Arsenal 0.
Att: 23,953

*Milan 2–0 on agg

1995
Zaragoza:

Zaragoza 1 (Aguado),

Ajax 1 (Kluivert).
Att: 23,000

Amsterdam:

Ajax 4 (Bogarde, George, Blind 2),

Zaragoza 0.
Att: 22,000

*Ajax 5–1 on agg

1996
Paris:

Paris Saint-Germain 1 (Rai),

Juventus 6 (Porrini, Padovano 2, Ferrara, Lombardo, Amoruso).
Att: 29,519

Palermo:

Juventus 3 (Del Piero 2, Vieri),

Paris Saint-Germain 1 (Rai).
Att: 35,100

*Juventus 9–2 on agg

* = Champions Cup winners

WORLD CLUB CUP

The days of the World Club Cup – properly called either the Intercontinental Club Cup or the Europe-South America Club Cup – appear to be numbered.

Real Madrid set the event off to a spectacular start in 1960 when they held Peñarol of Uruguay, inaugural South American champions, 0–0 in Montevideo and thrashed them 5–1 back in Spain.

The next two events maintained the quality level. Peñarol returned to

WORLD IN ACTION Forest take on Nacional in 1980's World Club Cup.

the event in 1961 to see off new European champions Benfica – but only after a play-off in Montevideo which saw the explosive arrival on the competitive international scene of a youthful Portuguese discovery… named Eusebio.

Benfica lost in 1962 as well – in memorable circumstances. Two late goals in Brazil meant they lost the first leg to Santos by only 3–2.

But Pele and his strike partner Coutinho went to work in wondrous style in Lisbon.

Benfica were sliced to pieces 5–2 in front of their own shocked fans who could do little but marvel at the

Brazilian master class. The event went downhill from there on.

The concept had come from South America – indeed the Copa Libertadores (the South American club cup) had been created to produce a contestant to meet Europe's top team. But the South American (and, more specifically, Argentine) pursuit of a result at all costs spiralled into a series of ever more violent confrontations.

Santos of Brazil started the rot in 1963 when – unnerved by the absence through injury of their star and stella influence, Pele – kicked their way to a brutal play-off victory over Milan.

The Italians flew home battered,

bruised and furious with the controversial Argentine referee, Juan Brozzi, who awarded the decisive penalty.

The nadir was reached in 1967 when no fewer than five players were ordered off in the play-off between Racing of Argentina and Celtic of Scotland in Montevideo.

In 1980 the Toyota the Japanese car giant entered the world of football as sponsors on condition that the match be staged as a one-off each year in neutral Tokyo – which is where the event has rested peacefully ever since.

South America currently lead Europe 20–15 overall and produced probably the best single-match perfor-

WORLD CLUB CUP RESULTS

1960
Montevideo:

Peñarol 0

Real Madrid 0
Att: 75,000

Madrid:

Real Madrid 5 (Puskas 2, Di Stefano, Herrera, Gento),

Peñarol 1 (Borges)
Att: 125,000

1961
Lisbon:

Benfica 1 (Coluna),

Peñarol 0
Att: 50.000

Montevideo:

Peñarol 5 (Sasia, Joya 2, Spencer 2),

Benfica 0.
Att: 56,000

Montevideo:
(play-off)

Peñarol 2 (Sasia 2),

Benfica 1 (Eusebio),
Att: 62,000

1962
Rio de Janeiro:

Santos 3 (Pele 2, Coutinho),

Benfica 2 (Santana 2).
Att: 90,000

Lisbon:

Benfica 2 (Eusebio, Santana),

Santos 5 (Pele 3, Coutinho, Pepe).
Att: 75,000

1963
Milan:

Milan 4 (Trapattoni, Amarildo 2, Mora),

Santos 2 (Pele 2).
Att: 80,000

Rio de Janeiro:

Santos 4 (Pepe 2, Almir, Lima),

Milan 2 (Altafini, Mora).
Att: 150,000

Rio de Janeiro (play-off):

Santos 1 (Dalmo),

Milan 0.
Att: 121,000

1964
Avellanada:

Independiente 1 (Rodriguez),

Internazionale 0.
Att: 70,000

Milan:

Internazionale 2 (Mazzola, Corso),

Independiente 0.
Att: 70,000

Milan (play-off):

Internazionale 1 (Corso),

Independiente 0 (aet).
Att: 45,000

1965
Milan:

Internazionale 3 (Peiro, Mazzola 2),

Independiente 0.
Att: 70,000

Avellanada:

Independiente 0,

Internazionale 0.
Att: 70,000

1966
Montevideo:

Peñarol 2, (Spencer 2)

Real Madrid 0.
Att: 70,000

Madrid:

Real Madrid 0,

Penarol 2 (Rocha, Spencer)
Att: 70,000

1967
Glasgow:

Celtic 1 (McNeill),

Racing Club 0.
Att: 103,000.

Avellanada:

Racing Club 2 (Raffo, Cardenas),

Celtic 1 (Gemmell).
Att: 80,000

Montevideo (play-off):

Racing Club 1 (Cardenas),

Celtic 0.
Att: 65,000.

1968
Buenos Aires:

Estudiantes 1 (Conigliaro),

Manchester United 0.
Att: 65,000

Manchester:

Manchester United 1 (Morgan),

Estudiantes 1 (Veron).
Att: 60,000

From this season the result was decided on aggregate. Previously if both teams had won one leg or both legs were drawn, a playoff decided the Cup.

1969
Milan:

Milan 3 (Sormani 2, Combin),

Estudiantes 0.
Att: 80,000

Buenos Aires:

Estudiantes 2 (Conigliaro, Aguirre-Suarez),

Milan 1 (Rivera).
Att: 65,000.

Milan won 4–2 on aggregate

1970
Buenos Aires:

Estudiantes 2 (Echecopar, Veron),

Feyenoord 2 (Kindvall, Van Hanegem).
Att: 65,000

Rotterdam:

Feyenoord 1 (Van Deale),

Estudiantes 0.
Att: 70,000.

Feyenoord won 3–2 on aggregate.

1971
Athens:

Panathinaikos 1 (Filakouris),

Nacional (Uru) 1 (Artime).
Att: 60,000

Montevideo:

Nacional 2 (Artime 2),

Panathinaikos 1 (Filakouris).
Att: 70,000.

Nacional won 3–2 on aggregate

1972
Avellanada:

Independiente 1 (Sa),

Ajax 1 (Cruyff).
Att: 65,000.

Amsterdam:

Ajax 3 (Neeskens, Rep 2),

Independiente 0.
Att: 60,000.

Ajax won 4–1 on aggregate

1973
Rome (single match):

Independiente 1 (Bochini 40),

Juventus 0.

Att: 35,000

1974
Buenos Aires:

Independiente 1 (Balbuena 33),

Atletico Madrid 0.
Att: 60,000

Madrid:

Atletico Madrid 2 (Irureta 21, Ayala 86),

Independiente 0.
Att: 45,000.

Atletico won 2–1 on aggregate

1975
Not held (Bayern Munich and Independiente failed to agree dates).

1976
Munich:

Bayern Munich 2 (Müller, Kapellmann),

Cruzeiro 0.
Att: 22,000

Belo Horizonte:

Cruzeiro 0,

Bayern Munich 0.
Att: 114,000.

Bayern won 2–0 on aggregate

1977
Buenos Aires:

Boca Juniors 2 (Mastrangelo, Ribolzi),

Borussia Monchengladbach 2 (Hannes, Bonhof).
Att: 50,000

Karlsruhe:

Borussia Mönchengladbach 0,

Boca Juniors 3 (Zanabria, Mastrangelo, Salinas).
Att: 21,000.

Boca Juniors won 5–2 on aggregate

1978
Not held.

1979
Malmö:

Malmö 0,

Olimpia 1 (Isasi).
Att: 4,000

Asuncion:

Olimpia 2 (Solalinde, Michelagnoli),

Malmö 1 (Earlandsson).
Att: 35,000.

Olimpia won 3–1 on aggregate

WORLD CLUB CUP RESULTS

From this season the Cup was a one-off match with penalties to decide the result if the match was drawn after 90 minutes. The venue has always been Tokyo, Japan.

1980

Nacional (Uru) 1 (Victorino),

Nottingham Forest 0.
Att: 62,000

1981

Flamengo 3 (Nunes 2, Adilio),

Liverpool 0.
Att: 62,000

1982

Peamengo 3 (Nunes 2, Adilio),

Liverpool 0.
Att: 62,000

1983

Gremio 2 (Renato 2),

Hamburg 1 (Schröder).
Att: 62,000

1984

Independiente 1 (Percudani),

Liverpool 0.
Att: 62,000

1985

Juventus 2 (Platini, Laudrup M.),

Argentinos Juniors 2 (Ereros, Castro)

(after extra-time).
Att: 62,000

(Juventus won 4–2 on penalties)

1986

River Plate 1 (Alzamendi),

Steaua Bucharest 0.
Att: 62,000

1987

FC Porto 2 (Gomes, Madjer),

Peñarol 1 (Viera) (aet).
Att: 45,000

1988

Nacional (Uru) 2 (Ostolaza 2),

PSV Eindhoven 2 (Romario, R Koeman)

(Nacional won 7–6 on pens after extra-time).
Att: 62,000

1989

Milan 1 (Evani),

Nacional (Col) 0 (aet).
Att: 62,000

1990

Milan 3 (Rijkaard 2, Stroppa),

Olimpia 0.
Att: 60,000

1991

Red Star Belgrade 3 (Jugovic 2, Pancev),

Colo Colo 0.
Att: 60,000

1992

São Paulo 2 (Rai 2),

Barcelona 1 (Stoichkov).
Att: 80,000

1993

São Paulo 3 (Palinha, Cerezo, Muller),

Milan 2 (Massaro, Papin).
Att: 52,000

1994

Velez Sarsfield 2 (Trott, Abad),

Milan 0.
Att: 65,000

1995

Ajax 0,

Gremio 0

(Ajax won 4–3 on pens after extra-time).
Att: 62,000

1996

Juventus 1 (Del Piero),

River Plate 0.
Att: 55,000

mance when Flamengo despatched Liverpool 3–0 in 1981. centre forward Nunes (two) and midfield general Adilio scored the goals but the man of the match was Zico who created all three goals.

That was the start of a mutual love affair between Zico and Japanese football which led to him later returning to play a key role in the successful launch of the J.League.

Two clubs from each continent have won the World Club Cup twice in succession – Santos then Sao Paulo for South America and Internazionale then neighbours Milan on behalf of Europe.

In bid to extend the reach of soccer, FIFA is considering the creation of a "real" world club cup which would feature the champion clubs of all six regional confederations. However, with rapidly over-played club calendars already causing managers and players to complain of match-weariness, the biggest task here could be simply organising a mutually acceptable timetable for the event.

TOPS ... Del Piero shoots Juventus' winner against River Plate.

THE GREAT CLUBS

Clubs are the bedrock of the game. They play in the central competitions providing a stage on which players display their abilities and are the prime focus for support from the fans. The professional clubs have grown ever more important and powerful since the advent first of the European club competitions then of television – with all its allied attraction for commercial sponsors. But what matters most remains the opportunity to capture one of the ultimate prizes – whether a domestic league or cup or an international trophy. Not all the international winners have been able to maintain their success, of course. The following clubs are those who have won a European trophy – and maintained their top division presence.

ABERDEEN
SCOTLAND
Founded: 1903
Stadium: Pittodrie (21,634)
Colours: Red/white
Honours: Cup-Winners' Cup 1983; Supercup 1983; League Champions 4; Cup 7; League Cup 5.

Aberdeen, thanks to their successful years under Alex Ferguson in the early 1980s, are considered the third force in Scottish club football. Events since then, however, have reopened the significant gap between the club from the Granite City and Glasgow's Rangers and Celtic.

In the 1980s Aberdeen's key role as a centre for the North Sea oil industry was seen as having been reflected on the football pitch by victory over Real Madrid in the 1983 Cup-Winners' Cup final.

Ferguson's team well deserved to win, maintaining a remarkable tempo in the rain in Gothenburg. Eric Black's early goal was wiped out by a Juanito penalty and only eight minutes remained in extra-time when John Hewitt grabbed the winner. To reach the final Aberdeen had beaten Sion, Dinamo Tirana, Lech Poznan, Bayern and Waterschei running up a remarkable 23 goals and stealing the European thunder of the Old Firm.

Success in Gothenburg was not the end of the matter. At the end of 1983 Aberdeen faced Champions Cup-winners Hamburg for the Supercup. The first leg was played in West Germany and ended goalless. At Pittodrie it was a different story. Goals from Paul Simpson and Mark McGhee in the first 20 minutes of the second half provided Aberdeen's second European prize inside a year.

Aberdeen followed up with league championship triumphs in 1984 and 1985 including the league and cup Double in 1984. In 1990 they won both Scottish Cup and League Cup. But Ferguson had, by now, been lured away to Manchester United and further European success proved beyond his successors. Not only that but power in Scotland swung back to Glasgow's Rangers in particular, their 1996 "9-in-a-row" proving this.

AJAX
AMSTERDAM, HOLLAND
Founded: 1900
Stadium: Arena (50,000)
Colours: White with a broad red stripe/white
Honours: World Club Cup 1972, 1995; Champs Cup 1971, 1972, 1973, 1995; Cup-Winners' Cup 1987; UEFA Cup 1992; Supercup 1972, 1973, 1995; League 26; Cup 12.

Ajax Amsterdam initiated a football revolution when they won the Champions Cup three times in succession in the early 1970s with "total football" – a style in which players of high technical ability, fitness and football intellect inter-changed position at will.

The style was still in its infancy the first time Ajax had reached the Champions Cup final in 1969, but they crashed 4–1 to Milan, for whom Pierino Prati scored a hat-trick. The foreign player restrictions then in force limited the movement of players across national boundaries and meant this Ajax team, built around the genius of Johan Cruyff, stayed together to mature into a Europe-dominating force in 1971, 1972 and 1973. Six members of the team who dominated Europe were born within two miles of the club. Cruyff himself was born and grew up in a street next to Ajax's stadium.

Ajax had shot to international prominence after nearly 70 years of domestic success. The start was a meeting of half a dozen young football enthusiasts and a few interested businessmen in top hats at the East India Restaurant in Kalverstraat, now the Dutch capital's main shopping street, in March 1900.

Two years later the fledgling club were promoted to the Dutch third division, gained entry to the top flight by 1911, and won league titles in 1918 and 1919. During the 1920s English trainer Jack Reynolds made his mark, found-

DUTCH DUET ... Ronald de Boer outwits Peter Van Vossen.

ENGLISH HERITAGE ... Arsenal's Paul Merson (right) shooting for goal.

ing the Ajax side which dominated the Golden 1930s when Ajax won the Dutch title five times in nine years.

The arrival of professional soccer in the mid-1950s revolutionized the Dutch domestic scene and Ajax helped set up the premier league in 1956. In 1958 the Amsterdam club entered the Champions Cup for the first time, but fortunes dipped and only the arrival of Rinus Michels – their former centre-forward – as coach helped beat off the threat of relegation in 1964–65.

Michels created the all-conquering Ajax side of the 1970s. They won the league in 1966, 1967 and 1968 as the young Cruyff's skills blossomed. In Europe, too, Ajax were becoming a force to be reckoned with, their exploits including a sensational 5–1 Champions Cup win over Liverpool on a famous foggy night in Amsterdam in 1966.

Three years later Ajax became the first Dutch side to reach the Champions Cup final, crashing to

Milan. But they were soon back in the final to triumph over Panathinaikos (1971), Inter Milan (1972) and Juventus (1973) with a side built around Cruyff, Ruud Krol, Johan Neeskens, Arie Haan, Piet Keizer and Johnny Rep. They went on to be crowned World Club champions by beating South American champions Independiente in 1972.

Neeskens and Cruyff were lured away to Spain but Ajax replaced them from within their own, highly-refined youth system. This produced a new generation including Frank Rijkaard, Marco Van Basten, John Bosman, Dennis Bergkamp, Bryan Roy and, later, the De Boer twins (Frank and Ronald), Clarence Seedorf and Patrick Kluivert.

Cruyff returned briefly as trainer and, in 1987, Ajax beat Lokomotiv Leipzig to capture the Cup-Winners' Cup and then the UEFA Cup in 1992. By now the Ajax youth policy had become world-famous and its master, Louis Van Gaal, was promoted to boss of the first-team – whom he guided to victory in the Champions Cup in 1995. Kluivert, latest product of the Ajax

conveyor belt, scored the winner against Milan in Vienna.

To match their high-profile status, Ajax left behind their old De Meer home in the summer of 1996 – although their big nights in Europe were played at the equally old Olympisch Stadion – to take over the 50,000-capacity new Arena stadium.

ANDERLECHT
BRUSSELS, BELGIUM

Founded: 1908
Stadium: Constant Vanden Stock (28,063)
Colours: White with mauve/white
Honours: Cup-Winners' Cup 1976, 1978; UEFA Cup 1983; Supercup 1976, 1978; League 24; Cup 8

Anderlecht are the most famous club in Belgium with a proud record in European competition which includes two victories in the Cup-Winners' Cup in 1976 and 1978. Their greatest past players include Paul Van Himst, who later managed the Belgian national team at the 1994 World Cup finals.

The shadow of scandal fell across

the club, however, in early 1997 when it was revealed that long-time president Constant Vanden Stock had been the subject of blackmail over claims that Anderlecht had sought to fix matches in the 1983–84 UEFA Cup campaign.

All of that was unthinkable when Sporting Club Anderlecht were founded in 1908. The club joined the national federation a year later and moved in 1919 to the Parc Astrid – still their home. It took another 16 years to qualify for the top division by which time Anderlecht had been honoured by royal decree with the right to describe themselves as a Société Royale, allowing them to include a crown in their club badge.

Albert Roosens and Constant Vanden Stock were members of the team who won promotion to the top division. Roosens later became president of the club, and then general secretary of the Belgian football association while brewery boss Vanden Stock became club president.

In 1947 Anderlecht won the championship for the first time, coached by a former Blackburn Rovers goalkeeper, Englishman Bill Gormlie. In the late 1940s and the early 1950s, Anderlecht owed much to their powerful centre-forward Jef Mermans. Later it was the subtle skills of bespectacled midfield general Jef Jurion and the great Van Himst up front which proved decisive.

In the 1960s Anderlecht won the championship five years in a row. Under French coach Pierre Sinibaldi, they practised a highly-effective zone defence system which relied heavily on the offside trap and upset a string of top-rank rivals. Among them were Real Madrid, over whom Anderlecht scored a famous victory in the 1962–63 Champions Cup. When Belgium beat Holland 1–0 in 1964, all the players in the Belgian line-up were from Anderlecht.

"Sporting" had been among the founders of the inaugural Champions Cup in 1955–56. Then, in 1970, they became the first Belgian club to reach a European final, losing 4–3 on aggregate to Arsenal in the Fairs Cup. The following year Vanden Stock succeeded Roosens as president and led the club into a new era which brought three successive appearances in the Cup-Winners' Cup final. Anderlecht defeated West Ham in 1976, lost to Hamburg in 1977, then thrashed FK Austria 4–0 in 1978. Star player now was the Dutch World Cup winger Rob Rensenbrink.

In 1980 Michel Verschueren joined the club as general manager to initiate another golden era. The stadium was redeveloped – with the first executive boxes in Belgium – while another European prize was secured. This was the 1983 UEFA Cup which Anderlecht won by defeating Benfica. They reached the final again the following season, losing to Tottenham after a penalty shoot-out – but amid ultimate controversy.

A decade later it emerged that Vanden Stock had paid more than £300,000 in "hush money" to an agent who claimed to have recorded telephone calls concerning an attempt to fix the semi-final second leg against Nottingham Forest – which Anderlecht won 3–0.

ARSENAL
LONDON, ENGLAND
Founded: 1886
Stadium: Highbury (38,500)
Colours: Red with white sleeves/white
Honours: Cup-Winners' Cup 1994; Fairs Cup 1970; League 10; Cup 6; League Cup 2.

Arsenal are one of the most famous clubs in the game – as proved by the number of teams throughout the world who adopted that illustrious title in the hope it might bring them the same glory.

The Gunners' nickname owes everything to their original foundation in south London, in the vicinity of Woolwich and its naval arsenal. In 1913, however, they moved from south to north London in the search for greater support.

The inter-war years were sensational. Legendary manager Herbert Chapman arrived from Huddersfield Town, where he had created a highly-successful team in the early 1920s, and made all the difference in London, leading Arsenal to one success after another and laying the foundations for one of the game's enduring legends.

Until the Liverpools and Manchester Uniteds of recent years, no club had dominated a decade in English football as completely as Arsenal in the 1930s. Using the innovative stopper centre-half, they won the league championship five times, finished runners-up once, and won the FA Cup twice, again finishing runners-up once. The great players of those days – wingers Joe Hulme and Cliff Bastin, attacking general Alex James and immaculate full-back Eddie Hapgood are still, today, legends of British football.

The 1930s' aura survived both the premature death of Chapman and World War Two, so that Arsenal, now under the guidance of Tom Whittaker, won the league again in 1948 and

1953. Veteran wing-half Joe Mercer was an inspirational captain.

Yet the greatest achievement of all came in 1970–71, when Arsenal became only the second English team of the twentieth century to complete the celebrated Double – winning both the league championship and the FA Cup in the same season.

A first European success had come in the Fairs Cup in 1970, when Arsenal beat Belgian club Anderlecht in the two-leg final. The Belgian capital of Brussels was not such a happy venue a decade later, however, when Arsenal lost the Cup-Winners' Cup final to Spain's Valencia on a penalty shoot-out.

Great players of the modern era included England's 1966 World Cup-winner Alan Ball, Irishmen Liam Brady, David O'Leary and Frank Stapleton and Northern Ireland's great goalkeeper Pat Jennings. In the early 1970s Arsenal were guided from midfield by George Graham who then returned in 1986 as manager to re-ignite the flames of success.

The most dramatic came in May 89, when Arsenal became London's first league champions in 18 years thanks to a last-minute, final-match goal scored by Michael Thomas to deny Liverpool – a club he later joined – at a shocked Anfield. Two years later the wing magic of Sweden's Anders Limpar helped inspire another championship success before Graham parted company with the club following a row over transfer "bungs".

ASTON VILLA
BIRMINGHAM, ENGLAND
Founded: 1874
Stadium: Villa Park (39,341)
Colours: Claret with blue sleeves/white
Honours: Champions Cup 1982; Supercup 1982; League 7; Cup 7; League Cup 5.

Aston Villa mean Tradition with a capital "T". Few clubs anywhere in England, let alone the world, boast a timeline of success which runs right-back to the pioneering days of 1874.

In the 1880s and 1890s Villa, founder members of the Football League, won five of their seven cham-

RECORD MEN ... Aston Villa with their 7th FA Cup win in 1957.

GENIUS? ... Ronaldo, Barcelona's 1996–97 season star, signed for Inter.

pionships and two of their seven FA Cups. They established a reputation for entertaining, positive football which was enhanced when they set a scoring record for the old First Division by running up no fewer than 128 goals in the 1930–31 league season ... yet finished runners-up to Arsenal.

In 1957 Villa won the FA Cup for a then record seventh time when they defeated Manchester United's Busby Babes amid controversy by 2–1 at Wembley. United had to play most of the match with 10 men after goalkeeper Ray Wood was felled by a shoulder charge by Villa's top-scoring left-winger Peter MacParland.

In the early 1960s Villa drew admirers from far and wide with an attacking team managed by former England wing-half Joe Mercer and spearheaded by the England World Cup leader Gerry Hitchens. They were

inaugural winners of the Football League Cup in 1961.

In the 1970s Villa suffered the humiliation of sliding down into the old Third Division. But Vic Crowe, a wing-half stalwart of both Villa and Wales in the 1960s, returned as manager to undertake a rebuilding programme.

Steady progress was rewarded with the double glory of League Championship success under manager Ron Saunders in 1981. This was followed by triumph in the Champions Cup a year later under former assistant, Tony Barton.

The greatest moment in Villa's history was achieved with a 1–0 victory over Germany's Bayern Munich. South African-born Peter Withe stabbed home the winner from close range in the Feyenoord stadium in Rotterdam.

Such standards proved impossible to maintain. Not until 1990, when Villa finished league runners-up under Graham Taylor, did they challenge again for honours. Their "reward" was

to see Taylor snatched away by the Football Association to become manager of England.

ATLETICO MADRID
SPAIN

Founded: 1903
Stadium: Vicente Calderon (62,000)
Colours: Red and white stripes/blue
Honours: World Club Cup 1974; Cup-Winners' Cup 1962; League 9; Cup 9.

Atletico Madrid's star name over the past decade had not been that of a player or coach. Instead, whatever the identity of the coach or the star players, the personality which has dominated the club has been that of president Jesus Gil.

Gil is a millionaire, a builder, a politician, who has owned Atletico since 1987 and went through more than a dozen team managers in his search for the guru who could depose neighbours Real Madrid as the Spanish capital's top team. Eventually he found his man in Radomir Antic, who guided Atletico to the league and cup double in 1996.

Such ambition is not new for an Atletico president. It was the driving force behind the club in the late 1950s and early 1960s under a previous president, Vicente Calderon. But somehow, although Atletico won the occasional domestic championship and cup and even the Cup-winners' Cup once, they never stayed the pace for long.

That appeared to be the club's destiny. Back in the late 1930s, after the Spanish civil war, it had taken a merger with the air force club to keep Atletico in business; in the early 1960s they had to borrow the use of Real's Estadio Bernabeu because Atletico's Metropolitano had been sold to developers before the club's new stadium could be completed.

In 1966, Atletico toppled Real in a thrilling run-in to pip their neighbours to the championship. Yet even then their moment of glory was overshadowed as Real won the Champions Cup.

Atletico spent heavily trying to compete with Real and Barcelona in the domestic transfer market. When, in 1973, the federation eased a ban on import restrictions, Atletico picked up a string of fine players such as the Argentines Ruben Hugo Ayala, Ramon Heredia and Ruben 'Panadero' Diaz.

Their reward was the 1973 league title and in 1974 they reached the Champions Cup final. But, facing Bayern Munich, Atletico were pushed to the brink of glory, then slapped in the face. Goal-less at 90 minutes, it seemed the outcome was resolved when inside-forward Luis curled a textbook free kick beyond Sepp Maier but, with seconds remaining, Bayern centre-back Hans-Georg Schwarzenbeck tried a low, speculative shot which somehow skimmed into the bottom corner of the net for an equaliser. There was not even time to restart the game. Atletico were well beaten in the replay.

Controversial coach Juan Carlos Lorenzo was dismissed early the next season. As caretaker the club appointed former midfield star Luis and he led them to victory in the World Club Cup (Bayern having refused to compete).

Luis later returned for two stints as club coach under Gil, who had spent around £130,000 of his private fortune in campaigning to win the presidential election in 1987. New signings swiftly followed. Top of the list was Portuguese star Paulo Futre, who cost £2 million plus the yellow Porsche which was Futre's personal dream; Cesar Luis Menotti, Argentina's 1978 World Cup-winning coach was the first of the string of managers; later Gil swooped in spectacular style to sign Bernd Schuster when the controversial German veteran fell out with Real Madrid.

For all that, it took nine years before Atletico finally made his dream come true.

BARCELONA
SPAIN

Founded: 1899
Stadium: Camp Nou (115,000)
Colours: Blue and red stripes/blue
Honours: Champions Cup 1992; Cup-Winners' Cup 1979, 1982, 1989; 1997; Fairs Cup 1958, 1960, 1966; Supercup 1992; League 14; Cup 22.

Barcelona are more than a football club. They are the flagship of the Catalan region, and a vast multi-sports organization which caters for a European record 108,000 members and runs its own bank and radio station.

Barcelona have frequently been described, not surprisingly, as the world's richest club. Precise comparisons are awkward because of their "private club" status but such a claim cannot be far from the truth with average attendances hovering around 80,000 – the average even topped 100,000 in the 1981–82 season – and with no need to use tacky commercialization as shirt advertising.

The club's explosion would have amazed Hans Gamper, the Swiss emigrant who founded the club in 1899 and whose name is perpetuated in the club's prestigious annual pre-season tournament. Barcelona were the first Spanish league champions in 1929 and share with Athletic Bilbao and Real Madrid the honour of never having been relegated.

Their international status was achieved in the 1950s and early 1960s. In 13 years from 1948 Barcelona won the league six times, the cup five times, the Fairs Cup twice and the Latin Cup twice. They were also desperately unlucky to lose 3–2 to Benfica in the 1961 Champions Cup final in Berne.

At one time – long before Bosman! – they boasted 20 internationals from seven countries. Three of the greatest were Hungarians. Ladislav Kubala escaped to Spain in the late 1940s while Sandor Kocsis and Zoltan Czibor fled Hungary after the 1956 Revolution.

Coach in the late 1950s was Helenio Herrera, the charismatic trainer who later went on to win the Champions Cup with Internazionale. Herrera rarely fielded the same line-up for two matches running – often switching inside-forwards to wing-half for home matches when Barcelona were expected to run up the goals. Apart from a glittering array of foreign players, Herrera's squad also boasted some of Spain's finest in goalkeeper Antonio Ramallets, wing-halves Juan Segarra, Jesus Garay and Martin Verges and inside-forward Luis Suarez.

In the early 1960s Barcelona had their wings clipped when the Spanish federation banned imports, but after that barrier was lifted in 1973 Barcelona immediately splashed a world record £922,000 on Holland's Johan Cruyff.

He led them, within six months, from relegation zone to league title in an astonishing revival which included a 5–0 away win over Real Madrid. But for all the talents of Cruyff and later Diego Maradona, it was not until after

Cruyff had returned as coach that Barcelona attained their long-sought goal of winning the Champions Cup.

An extra-time goal from Ronald Koeman broke down Sampdoria's resistance at Wembley. But Cruyff's touchy relationship with the board deteriorated after a 4–0 thrashing by Milan in the 1994 European final and he was subsequently dismissed among a flurry of fans protests and legal battles.

Ex-England coach Bobby Robson found putting the pieces back together a thankless task despite success in teh 1996-97 Cup-Winners Cup.

BAYER LEVERKUSEN
GERMANY
Founded: 1904
Stadium: Ulrich Haberland (26,500)
Colours: All red
Honours: UEFA Cup 1988; Cup 1.

Six clubs in the German top division in 1996–97 can boast a European club success. Bayer Leverkusen were the unfashionable contributors, having secured the UEFA Cup in dramatic fashion in 1988 against Español of Spain. Leverkusen reached the final by defeating FK Austria, Toulouse, Feyenoord, Barcelona and their fellow Germans Werder Bremen. The quarter-final success over Barcelona was notable for the fact that Leverkusen were held 0–0 at home yet won the tie with a 1–0 success in Nou Camp thanks to a goal from Brazilian import Tita.

The final, against Barcelona's "poor" neighbours, Español, was a topsy-turvy affair. Leverkusen lost 3–0 in Spain then won by the same margin in Germany: Tita scored their first goal and South Korea's Cha Bum-kun their aggregate equaliser. After extra-time proved goal-less, Leverkusen then triumphed 3–2 in the ensuing penalty shoot-out.

It is, perhaps, more surprising that no further successes have been recorded. The sponsor/owner support of the Bayer chemical corporation led many experts to predict that Leverkusen would take a leading role in German football in the same way as the Philips offshoot, PSV Eindhoven, in Holland. Leverkusen's comparative failure may have been due, in part, to Bayer's simultaneous support for Bayer Uerdingen (now KSC Uerdingen). However, in 1995, Bayer decided to concentrate on Leverkusen

and this paid off in 1997 with qualification for the Champions League.

BAYERN MUNICH
GERMANY
Founded: 1900
Stadium: Olympiastadion (64,000)
Colours: All red
Honours: World Club Cup 1976; Champions Cup 1974, 1975, 1976; Cup-Winners' Cup 1967; UEFA Cup 1996; League 14; Cup 8.

Bayern Munich are Germany's greatest modern football club and the only one to have climbed every peak of the international football mountain: domestic championship and cup, Champions Cup, Cup-Winners' Cup, UEFA Cup and World Club Cup.

The Bavarian club had achieved little before the introduction of the unifying Bundesliga in 1963. Until then German league competition had been organized on a regional basis with the "local" winners playing off for the national title. Bayern triumphed once in the championship, in 1932, and once in the cup, in 1957.

Their record did not earn Bayern a place in the inaugural Bundesliga, so they had to fight their way up through the promotion play-offs in 1965. Once in the top flight, however, there was no looking back. In 1966 Bayern won the cup by defeating MSV Duisburg 4–2 in the final to qualify for the Cup-Winners' Cup. The final was played not far north of Munich, in Nuremberg,

PRIZE ... Bayern Munich get their hands on the UEFA Cup in 1996.

where Bayern overcame Rangers 1–0 after extra-time.

Already Bayern had the nucleus of the team which would conquer Europe and the world at both club and national team level. Sepp Maier was the goalkeeper, Paul Breitner a left-back whose creative talent was so pronounced he later converted into midfield general, Gerd Müller one of the all-time great strikers and Franz Beckenbauer simply one of the greatest footballers of all time.

Beckenbauer played midfield for West Germany in the late 1960s but was already developing, at Bayern, the revolutionary attacking sweeper role from which he captained his country to victory in the 1972 European Championship and 1974 World Cup.

That year, 1974, saw Bayern at their most brilliant as they defeated Atletico Madrid 4–0 in a replayed final to win the Champions Cup for the first time. Müller and Uli Hoeness – later to become general manager – scored two goals apiece. The next year a side battered by injury defeated Leeds 2–0 in a controversial Champions Cup final in Paris then, in 1975, Bayern squeaked past Saint-Etienne 1–0 at Hampden Park, Glasgow. A 2–0, 0–0 win over Cruzeiro of Brazil brought Bayern the World Club Cup as well.

Then it was time to rebuild. Breitner had already gone to Real Madrid and Beckenbauer went off to join New York Cosmos. The new hero of the fans was flying forward Karl-Heinz Rummenigge who led Bayern to two more Champions Cup finals – and defeats against Aston Villa in 1982, and FC Porto in 1987. As the commercial balance of football changed, so it became obvious that Bayern, financially, were head and shoulders above the rest of German football. Beckenbauer returned, successively, as director, championship-winning coach then club president. Rummenigge joined him on the board in the mid-1990s when Bayern brought Lothar Matthäus back from Italy and Jürgen Klinsmann home from England.

It took another superstar to manage such big egos which is why Beckenbauer himself had to step back in as coach in May 1996 to steer Bayern to victory in the UEFA Cup – lining them up with Ajax, Barcelona and Juventus as the only clubs to have won all three major European club prizes.

BENFICA
LISBON, PORTUGAL

Founded: 1904
Stadium: Sport Lisboa e Benfica (92,385)
Colours: Red/white
Honours: Champions Cup 1961, 1962; League 30; Cup 26.

Benfica, for all the recent success of FC Porto, remain Portugal's most successful and renowned club. A statue of their greatest footballer, Eusebio, stands at the entrance to the largest football stadium in Europe to intimidate each and every rival.

Their story is synonymous with that of Portuguese football since founder Cosme Damiao learned the game from English residents in Lisbon at the turn of the century. It was Damiao who laid down the tradition that Benfica should use only Portuguese citizens. This, of course, included players from the African colonies. The club's victories in the 1961 and 1962 Champions' Cup finals would have been unthinkable without the presence of goalkeeper Costa Pereira and centre-forward Jose Aguas from Angola as well as schemer Mario Coluna and Eusebio from Mozambique.

Benfica cater, as a club, for two dozen sports but football is by far the most important, and finances the other sections. It was in 1910 that Benfica landed their first title, the Lisbon championship, and from then on they have dominated domestic football. Typically, Benfica have also built the most well-appointed Portuguese stadium, the Estadio da Luz or Stadium of Light. This is the club's fifth permanent home, to which they moved in December 1954, just in time for the European explosion.

Benfica were, perhaps, lucky to win the 1961 Champions' Cup final against Barcelona. But under Hungarian coach Bela Guttmann they well deserved a brilliant 5–3 victory over Real Madrid a year later. However, losses in the World Club final in both years have been followed by a hat-trick of defeats in the Champions Cup finals.

Benfica, with Eusebio winning the domestic goalscorer's title seven times, remained the dominating force at home. But despite the emergence of later stars such as goalkeeper Manuel Bento, centre-back Humberto Coelho and forwards Nene and Chalana, Benfica have not found it as easy abroad any more.

The African option was ended by the colonies' independence in the mid-1970s. So, in the summer of 1978, Benfica members voted by a majority of two-to-one to break with tradition and enter the foreign market. The fruits could be seen in the team which reached the 1983 UEFA Cup final with the Yugoslav Zoran Filipovic and the Swedish midfielder Glenn Stromberg.

But further appearance success proved beyond them. An increasing reliance on player imports led to controversy which undermined their resistance the rise of FC Porto.

**THOROUGHLY modern sweeper ...
Dortmund's Matthias Sammer.**

LION OF LISBON ... Celtic's skipper Billy McNeill.

BORUSSIA DORTMUND
GERMANY

Founded: 1909
Stadium: Westfalenstadion (42,800)
Colours: Yellow shirts, black shorts, yellow and black hooped socks
Honours: Champions Cup 1997, Cup-Winners' Cup 1966; League 5; Cup 2.

Borussia hold a particular place in history because they were the first German club to win a European trophy. That was in 1966, when they beat Liverpool 2–1 after extra-time in the final of the Cup-Winners' Cup in Glasgow.

Pride in that achievement extended almost to superstition when the members of that team were taken by Dortmund to the final of the 1997 Champions Cup against Juventus.

The pride paid off when Dortmund won by 3-1 with two goals from Kerlheinz Riedle and from sub-stitute Lars Ricken – with his first touch.

Dortmund have been German champions on five occasions and cup-winners twice but the 1995 and 1996 triumphs were their first since the inception of the Bundesliga in the early 1960s.

The foundations had been laid several years earlier. Evidence was clear when Dortmund finished runners-up in 1992 then, again, in January 1993 when they paid £3 million to bring home attacking sweeper Matthias Sammer from Internazionale of Italy. Sammer, a former East German international, had been sold to Inter only the previous summer by Stuttgart, but he failed to adapt to football, life and the language in Italy and Dortmund's enterprise in bringing him home was fully rewarded.

The financial profit on the expanded sponsorship and television interest provided the club with the funds to surround Sammer with international stars such as Brazilian central defender Julio Cesar, Swiss striker Stephane Chapuisat and Germany's own top defenders such as Jürgen Kohler and Stefan Reuter plus striker Karlheinz Riedle.

The Westfalenstadion, built for the 1974 World Cup finals, is one of the few modern German stadia created specifically for football. There is no athletics track surrounding the pitch and every player survey has Dortmund as one of their favourite venues.

BORUSSIA MÖNCHENGLADBACH
GERMANY

Founded: 1900
Stadium: Bökelberg (34,500)
Colours:
Honours: UEFA Cup 1975, 1979; League 5; Cup 3.

Borussia Mönchengladbach are struggling to regain the position of pre-eminence they enjoyed not so long ago in both Germany and Europe. They won the West German championship five times between 1970 and 1977, added the German cup in 1995 to two previous successes in the 1960s and 1970s and collected the UEFA Cup in 1975 and 1979.

Those were the years in which all the progressive management of master coach Hennes Weisweiler earned its due reward. Borussia became renowned as a football academy in the same way as West Ham in England – with one difference: Borussia not only played superb football, they were consistently successful at the highest level.

Indeed, they very nearly crowned it all with the Champions Cup but were beaten by Liverpool in an outstanding final in Rome in 1977.

Many of Weisweiler's pupils – most notably Berti Vogts (Germany's 1996 European Championship-winning boss) and Jupp Heynckes (later of Bayern Munich, Bilbao and Eintracht Frankfurt) – became successful coaches in their own right. Even when Weisweiler himself was tempted away to Spain, to Barcelona, the foundations he had laid proved firm for his successors to build further success.

Borussia were founded on August 1, 1900. They first won the western region German title in 1920. But it was then 40 years before they topped that, with a first victory in the West German cup. Under coach Bernd Oles, Borussia beat Karlsruhe 3–2 in the 1960 final, the goals being shared among the inside-forward trio of Brulls, Kohn and Muhlhausen.

Albert Brulls was the first major star Borussia ever had. He played 25 times for West Germany and was a member of their World Cup finals squads both in Chile in 1962 and England in 1966 before transferring to Italy's Brescia.

CELTIC
GLASGOW, SCOTLAND

Founded: 1888
Stadium: Celtic Park (50,500)
Colours: Green and white hoops/white
Honours: Champions Cup 1967; League 35; Cup 30; League Cup 9.

Celtic and Rangers are Scottish football's dominant clubs, their financial power having multiplied beyond all expectations following the television and sponsor-driven awakening of the 1990s.

That created its own problems and frustrations. However much the Old Firm invested in high-quality players, they needed the stimulus of top-class competition to stay sharp to achieve matching success in European competition. The greater the power of Celtic and Rangers, the more distance they put between themselves and the rest of Scottish football – and the more obviously they pined for top-level competition.

Rangers have had the better of the past decade but Celtic boast the historic achievement of having become the first British club – and, still, the only Scottish club – to have won the Champions Cup in 1967. It was a measure of the way they swept all before them that season that they won everything at home as well: the league, the cup and the league cup. No other team in Europe has ended a season with a 100 per cent record in all four major competitions.

The 1967 "Lisbon Lions" had been assembled shrewdly by manager Jock Stein, a former Celtic player. As well as new Scottish stars he included veterans such as goalkeeper Ronnie Simpson and inside-left and schemer

Bertie Auld. In the final in Lisbon they beat former holders Internazionale from Italy by 2–1, with goals from full-back Tommy Gemmell and centre-forward Steve Chalmers. They did it with dash and style despite having gone behind to an early penalty.

Sadly, Celtic's golden touch did not last long at international level. Only months later they fell to Kiev Dynamo at the start of their Cup defence. They were then dragged down in the infamous World Club Cup final against Racing of Argentina – a clash which saw five players ordered off in a play-off in Montevideo, ultimately won by Racing by 1–0.

Celtic remained a Champions Cup power in the early 1970s. They returned to the final in 1970, in Milan, only to lose 2–1 to Feyenoord in extra-time. In

MAGIC TOUCH ... Chelsea's Dutch player-manager Ruud Gullit.

1971 they reached the quarter-finals, losing to eventual winners Ajax, and in 1972 they came close to a third final appearance – losing on penalties to Internazionale in the semi-finals after two goal-less draws. Celtic were beaten semi-finalists again in 1974 before being overtaken by Rangers and by the force of boardroom uncertainty.

Fergus McCann's seizure of control in the mid-1990s proved a new turning point. Parkhead was redeveloped and manager Tommy Burns was given the financial support to trawl Europe for new faces – Andreas Thom, Pierre Van Hooijdonk, Paulo Di Canio and Jorge Cadete proving among the most successful and popular.

CHELSEA
LONDON, ENGLAND
Founded: 1905
Stadium: Stamford Bridge (31,791)
Colours: All blue
Honours: Cup-Winners' Cup 1971; League 1; Cup 2; League Cup 1.

Chelsea's honours list may be comparatively modest compared with other English sides, but the West London outfit have been one of the most continually fascinating of clubs.

Chelsea should have been England's first competitors in the Champions Cup. They were invited to enter the inaugural competition in 1955–56 but withdrew on the orders of the Football League, which feared a fixtures snarl-up. The next year Manchester United did compete and thus, ironically, opened the way for Chelsea to accept an invitation into the 1968–69 Fairs' Cup.

They reached the quarter-finals then and went a step further in 1966, reaching the semi-finals – beating Milan on the way in a thriller decided on the toss of a coin after a drawn play-off in San Siro – and Munich 1860 before losing to Barcelona.

Manager Tommy Docherty had brought a wind of change blowing through English football with a young team featuring the likes of Peter Osgood, Bobby Tambling and Terry Venables. But it required the more pragmatic approach of Dave Sexton to steer the team to a European title.

Chelsea won the FA Cup in a memorable, if physical, replay against Leeds in 1970, to earn a shot at the Cup-Winners' Cup. Chelsea began with a 6–2 aggregate victory over Aris Salonika, which proved a good omen as the final was back in Greece. There, they beat Real Madrid after a replay.

Inside 10 years, however, Chelsea were in grave financial difficulties and it took all the business ingenuity new chairman Ken Bates could muster could turn the club around. This he did with such success that, in the mid-1990s, Chelsea had become London's most fashionable club to watch.

Just as in the "Swinging Sixties" Chelsea were a glamorous club, attracting high-profile fans who were entertained by an imaginative transfer policy which brought in first Glenn Hoddle as player-manager then, in his

wake, Ruud Gullit. The Dutchman took charge after Hoddle's departure for the England job he imported Italy's Gianluca Vialli, Roberto Di Matteo and Gianfranco Zola and was rewarded with FA Cup succes in 1997.

EVERTON
LIVERPOOL, ENGLAND
Founded: 1878
Stadium: Goodison Park (42,200)
Colours: Blue/white
Honours: Cup-Winners' Cup 1985; League 9; Cup 5.

Everton have lived – too long, say their fans – in the domestic and European shadow of neighbours Liverpool. Luck has not always been with them. Everton hit the European heights themselves in 1985 when they defeated Rapid Vienna 3–1 in Rotterdam in the Cup-Winners' Cup final. Sadly, the hooligan horror of Heysel two weeks later brought a European ban on all English clubs for the next five years. Everton were neither allowed to defend the Cup-Winners' Cup nor to compete against Juventus in the European Supercup.

The talents at the disposal of manager Howard Kendall were beyond dispute. Gary Lineker was, in 1986, not only top scorer in the World Cup finals in Mexico (with six goals) but leading marksman in the league with 30. Everton finished runners-up, three points behind Liverpool.

Lineker's departure for Barcelona did not weaken Everton one iota. Indeed, they won the league championship for the ninth (and, so far, last) time a year later. Then the Goodison Park faithful had to wait a further eight years, until 1995, for the next celebration. But the delight of FA Cup success was in sharp contrast to simultaneous struggles at the wrong end of the Premiership.

Everton had been league founder members in 1888 and Lineker and £4.4 million Duncan Ferguson have been only the more recent in a long line of outstanding attackers to grace the "School of Science". Joe Parker and Bert Freeman were free-scoring forwards in the early years of the century, followed by the record-breaking Bill "Dixie" Dean in the 1920s and 30s. For an outlay of £3,000, Everton secured the 17-year-old who would total 349 league goals – a record 60 in 1927–28.

He was succeeded in the No 9 shirt, in due course, by Tommy Lawton – for many an even greater centre-forward – and then Scotland's Alex Young. Subsequent heroes included England's World Cup-winning midfield dynamo Alan Ball, who was bought and sold for then club record fees. He cost £110,00 from Blackpool in 1966 but Everton collected £225,000 when he joined Arsenal in 1971.

FERENCVAROS
BUDAPEST, HUNGARY
Founded: 1899
Stadium: Ulloi ut (17,743)
Colours: Green and white stripes/white
Honours: Fairs Cup 1965; League 26; Cup 18.

Ferencvaros Club – Athletic Club of Ferencvaros – are the one Hungarian club who have stood their European ground at a time when the domestic game appears to be falling apart.

But then, Ferencvaros have been defending a reputation and pride built up since their foundation under Dr Ferenc Springer in 1899. Even then the club's colours were green and white, arranged in five green and four white stripes symbolizing the Notn district of Budapest, the Hungarian capital. The three letters on the emblem refer to the motto of the club which, translated, is: Strength, Understanding, Morality.

Ferencvaros' football section has its own emblem which dates back to 1928 and features a bronze eagle gripping a football. Also known in the inter-war years as FTC, they are the only club to have taken part in every Hungarian top division championship and their 25 league titles is a record.

The most remarkable season was 1931–32 when Ferencvaros won every game. They were also European competition pioneers and were twice winners of the Mitropa Cup in its heyday of the 1920s and 1930s. Ferencvaros' record in modern international affairs is also a proud one, winning the Fairs Cup in 1965, being runners-up to Leeds in 1968, and losing to Kiev Dynamo in the Cup-Winners' Cup final of 1975.

DIXIE DEAN ... 60 goals in a season for Everton remains a record.

Great players have featured down the years. The first was Imre Schlosser who scored a record 48 goals for Hungary in the early 1900s. Gyorgy Sarosi and Geza Toldi were World Cup heroes in the 1930s; Sarosi scored 613 goals in 607 matches for the club – both records. Ferenc Deak set a one-season record with 59 goals in 1948–49 while Laszlo Budai, Sandor Kocsis and Zoltan Czibor – members of the great Hungarian national team of the 1950s – first made their names with Ferencvaros. In more recent times Florian Albert became, in 1967, the only Hungarian player so far to win the European Footballer of the Year award, while Tibor Nyilasi was runner-up in 1981.

In 1996–97 Ferencvaros became one of the first teams to play in two different European competitions in the same season. First, as champions of Hungary they played in the Champions League preliminary round, but lost out to IFK Gothenburg of Sweden and were thus relegated into the UEFA Cup; here they were knocked out convincingly in the second round by England's Newcastle United.

FEYENOORD
ROTTERDAM, HOLLAND
Founded: 1908
Stadium: Feyenoord (52,000)
Colours: Red and white halves/black
Honours: World Club Cup 1970; Champions Cup 1970; UEFA Cup 1974; League 13; Cup 10.

It is Feyenoord, and not Ajax, who hold the honour of being the first Dutch club to capture the Champions Cup. They triumphed in 1970 – one year before Ajax won the first of three back-to-back titles.

The Rotterdam club also gained success in the UEFA Cup before hitting financial problems in the late 1980s and early 1990s. Major investment was backed by the signing of former World Cup finalist Arie Haan as coach and Ronald Koeman returned from Spain to reorganize the defence.

Feyenoord were the first Dutch club to make an international mark in the early 1960s courtesy of the talents of players such as goalkeeper Eddy Pieters Graafland and outside-left Coen Moulijn. Later, under Austrian coach Ernst Happel, they won the Champions Cup by defeating Celtic

2–1 in extra-time in Milan. Swedish striker Ove Kindall scored the decisive goal and Feyenoord went on to add the World Club Cup by defeating Estudiantes de La Plata.

In the 1980s and 1990s, however, Feyenoord's star was overshadowed by those of Ajax and PSV. They won the league only once in each decade and found more success in the cup which they won six times between 1980 and 1995.

In the mid-1990s Feyenoord mounted their most serious league title challenge for years with the appointment of ex-World Cup star Arie Haan as coach and acquisitions of Swefish World Cup forward Henrik Larsson and veteran Dutch defender Ronald Koeman.

Sadly Feyenoord's reputation has been tarnished by a hooligan fringe attached to the club. In 1996 Rotterdam's mayor, Bram Peper, demanded that their league match against Ajax should be moved from an evening kick-off to the afternoon so that up to 400 police could control fans.

Six years earlier, a teenage Feyenoord fan had been jailed for hurling a home-made bomb which injured

over a dozen rival fans at an Ajax-Feyenoord game. In the spring of 1997 fans from both clubs fought a pitched battle on a motorway near Volendam.

FIORENTINA
FLORENCE, ITALY
Founded: 1926
Stadium: Artemio Franchi (47,350)
Colours: All violet
Honours: Cup-Winners' Cup 1961; League 2; Cup 5.

Fiorentina's reputation over the years has been for skilful, inventive football – thanks to the contributions of the likes of Giancarlo Antognoni, Daniel Bertoni,

Kurt Hamrin and Julinho in the ranks – yet they owed their most famous success to an iron defence.

This was the team with which they won their first league title in 1956. Fiorentina conceded a then record of only 20 goals in their 34 league games and remained unbeaten until the last day of the season, when they went down 3–1 to Genoa.

Coach Fulvio Bernardini, a former Italian international, created a watertight unit at the back. Goalkeeper Giuliano Sarti, left-back Sergio Cervato, wing-halves Beppe Chiappella and Armando Segato and the inside-right Guido Gratton were

the Italian foundations on which the outstanding Brazilian right-wing Julinho and Chilean inside-left Miguel Montuori built the incisive counterattacks. This team reached the 1957 Champions' Cup final, but unluckily had to face Real Madrid in the Spanish capital, and lost 2–0. Fiorentina, however, gained the consolation of becoming the first winners of the Cup-Winners' Cup in 1961, and lost to Atletico Madrid only after a replay in the following year's final.

In the mid-1960s former star Chiappella became coach and built a fine young team which was later guided to the league title by the Swedish manager, Nils Liedholm. A key figure was Brazil's 1962 World Cup star Amarildo while midfielder Giancarlo De Sisti later became coach.

The "Viola" reached a further European final when they lost to Juventus in the UEFA Cup in 1990. But three years later they suffered the ignominy of relegation for the first time in more than 50 years.

An instant revival owed much to the financial power of film-maker Vittorio Cecchi Gori and the acquisition of international stars such as Portuguese midfielder Rui Costa, Sweden's Stefan Schwarz and Gabriel Batistuta, the record-breaking Argentine centre-forward.

Batistuta scored twice as Fiorentina defeated Atalanta 1–0, 2–0 in the 1996 cup final – their first trophy in 21 years.

HAMBURG
GERMANY
Founded: 1887
Stadium: Volksparkstadion (61,234)
Colours: White/red
Honours: Champions Cup 1983; Cup-Winners' Cup 1977; League 6; Cup 3.

Hamburg are the second most successful German side in Europe after Bayern Munich. No other club have won two of Europe's three prizes and the Hamburg trophy room boasts replicas of both the Champions Cup (from 1983) and the Cup-Winners' Cup (from 1977).

The club first made their European mark in the Champions' Cup of

EUROPE'S NUMBER ONE ... IFK goalkeeper Thomas Ravelli.

1960–61. Those were the days of the great centre-forward Uwe Seeler, allied with his brother Dieter at wing-half and a fine left-wing partnership in Klaus Sturmer and Gerd Dorfel. They came within a minute of beating Barcelona in the 1961 semi-finals but had to settle instead for a play-off, which they lost 1–0.

Seven years later they reached a European final, but Seeler's men went down 2–0 to Milan in Rotterdam in the Cup-Winners' Cup. Nine years later Hamburg were back. Again the final was in Holland – but in Amsterdam – and this time Hamburg defeated holders Anderlecht 2–0. Their second goal was scored by midfield general Felix Magath, who was also the match-winning hero in 1983 when Hamburg, against all expectations, defeated Michel Platini's Juventus 1–0 in the Champions Cup final in the new Olympic stadium in Athens.

"I think I deserved that," said Magath later. He had also been a member of the Hamburg squad which – despite the presence of Kevin Keegan – lost the 1980 Champions Cup final to Nottingham Forest and then lost the 1982 UEFA Cup final to IFK Gothenburg.

Remarkably Hamburg have, since then, won only one other trophy – the German cup in 1987. Somehow, the club lost their way both on and off the pitch. Not until the second coming of Uwe Seeler in 1995 – this time as president, with Magath as coach – did Hamburg start to pull their weight once more within the Bundesliga.

IFK GOTHENBURG
SWEDEN
Founded: 1904
Stadium: Nya Ullevi (43,000)
Colours: Blue and white stripes/blue
Honours: UEFA Cup 1982, 1987; League 17; Cup 4.

IFK, founded in 1904 by a group of sports enthusiasts gathered at a cafe in Annedal, one of Gothenburg's working-class areas, are the only Swedish club to have won a European prize – the UEFA Cup.

The first members of IFK played not only football but also athletics and winter sports, but it did not take long for IFK to became one of Sweden's leading football clubs. Apart from eight seasons in the second division since the

**STRIKING SUCCESS ... Juventus'
Del Piero and Boksic.**

start of the national league, the Blaavit (Blue/white) – as the club are nicknamed – have belonged to the elite.

After winning the league in 1969, they were immediately relegated – underlining their reputation for entertaining, if erratic football – and it took them six years to return to the top flight. Once they were back, IFK invested heavily in experience. Ove Kindvall, Bjorn Nordqvist and Ralf Edstrom were all brought back from Holland. Yet this crowd-pleasing team did not win any honours. The turning point came in 1979, when Sven-Goran Eriksson was signed from Degerfors as coach. He immediately guided IFK to their first-ever triumph in the Cup – defeating Aatvidaberg 6–1 in the final.

In 1982 IFK, also nicknamed the Angels, became the first Swedish club to win a European club prize, when they beat Hamburg of Germany both home (1–0) and away (3–0) in the UEFA Cup final. In 1986 IFK reached the Champions Cup semi-final, losing only on penalties to Barcelona. The following year, they once again won the UEFA Cup, beating Dundee United 1–0 in Gothenburg and drawing 1–1 in Scotland.

Many Swedish football legends have played for IFK, including 1950s inside-forward Gunnar Gren, 1970s striker Torbjorn Nilsson, 1980s stars Glenn Stromberg and Glenn Hysen and then goalkeeper Thomas Ravelli, the most-capped European player of all time.

IFK play in the Nya Ullevi stadium – sharing with fellow Allsvenska teams Orgryte and GAIS – which was built for the 1958 World Cup finals and hosted Denmark's remarkable victory over Germany in the 1992 European Championship final.

INTERNAZIONALE
MILAN, ITALY
Founded: 1908
Stadium: Giuseppe Meazza (85,443)
Colours: Blue and black stripes/black
Honours: World Club Cup 1964, 1965; Champions Cup 1964, 1965; UEFA Cup 1991, 1994; League 13; Cup 3.

One of the greatest of inter-city rivalries is that in Milan between Internazionale and AC (Associazione Calcio) Milan – a rivalry which goes back more than 90 years since the Inter club was founded directly because of a dispute within the Milan club. Some 45 members, led by committee man Giovanni Paramithiotti, broke away in protest at the authoritarian way Milan was being run by the powerful Camperio brothers.

That was not the end of the politics. In the 1930s, fascist laws forced Internazionale into a name change to rid the club of the foreign associations of their title. So they took the name of the city of Milan's patron saint and became Ambrosiana.

Under this title they led the way in continental club competition – being one of the leading lights in the pre-war Mitropa Cup (the 1930s' forerunner of today's European competitions).

After the war, the club reverted to the Internazionale name and led the way in a tactical revolution. So many star foreign forwards were being introduced into the Italian league that the old defensive systems were no longer effective. Alfredo Foni, a World Cup-winning full-back before the war and Inter's coach after it, devised a new tactical system. He pulled right-winger Gino Armani back into midfield to help improve the defensive cover – and Inter won the Italian league titles in both 1953 and 1954.

The brilliance of Milan (with Nils Liedholm and Juan Schiaffino) and then Juventus (Omar Sivori and John Charles) overpowered even Inter in the late 1950s and early 1960s. But then Angelo Moratti became president and brought in coach Helenio Herrera who, in turn, built an outstanding team around Spanish midfield general Luis Suarez. In defence Herrera constructed the most formidable unit in club football. Goalkeeper Giuliano Sarti – a championship-winner with Fiorentina in 1956 – sweeper Armando Picchi and backs Tarcisio Burgnich, Aristide Guarneri and Giacinto Facchetti were as near water-tight as possible.

They were the foundation on which outstanding forwards such as Brazil's Jair da Costa, Spain's Joaquim Peiro and Italy's own Sandro Mazzola built success. Inter won the World Club and European Cups in both 1964 and 1965 – beating Real Madrid and Benfica in Europe, and Argentina's Independiente twice for the world crown. But even they could not soak up pressure indefinitely. In 1966 Real Madrid toppled Inter in the Champions' Cup semi-finals and

Celtic repeated the trick a year later in a memorable Lisbon final.

Moratti retired and Herrera was lured away to Roma. But the elegant Mazzola remained in attack to lead Inter back to the Champions' Cup final in 1972, when they lost 2–0 to Ajax in Rotterdam – Johan Cruyff scoring both goals. The Italian federation's ban on foreign players restricted Inter's ambitions for the rest of the 1970s. But the 1980 championship triumph coincided with the reopening of the borders and the following season Austrian midfielder Herbert Prohaska guided them to the Champions' Cup semi-finals. Later, in the ranks of illustrious foreigners, came West German midfield general Hansi Müller, then Ireland's Liam Brady, before Lothar Matthäus drove Inter to their 1989 league title and 1991 UEFA Cup triumph.

JUVENTUS
TURIN, ITALY
Founded: 1897
Stadium: Delle Alpi (71,012)
Colours: Black and white stripes/white
Honours: World Club Cup 1985, 1996; Champions Cup 1985, 1996: Cup-Winners' Cup 1984: UEFA Cup 1977, 1990, 1993; Supercup 1984, 1996; League 24: Cup 9.

Juventus were founded by a group of Italian students who decided originally to adopt red as the colour for their shirts. However in 1903, when the club was six years old, one of the committee members was so impressed on a trip to England by Notts County's black-and-white stripes that he bought a set of shirts to take home to Turin.

In the 1930s Juventus laid the foundations for their legend, winning the Italian league championship five times in a row. Simultaneously they also reached the semi-finals of the Mitropa Cup on four occasions and supplied Italy's World Cup-winning teams with five players in 1934 and three in 1938. Goalkeeper Gianpiero Combi, from Juventus, was Italy's Cup-lifting captain in 1934 just as another Juve 'keeper, Dino Zoff, would be in 1982.

After the war the Zebras (after the colours of their shirts) scoured the world for talent to battle the imported foreign contingent. First came the Danes, John and Karl Hansen, then the

LEEDS' LEADER ... Irish midfield general Johnny Giles.

Argentine favourite Omar Sivori and Wales' "Gentle Giant", John Charles, followed by Spanish inside-forward Luis Del Sol and French inspiration Michel Platini. In 1971 they lost the Fairs Cup final to Leeds United on the away goals rule but, six years later, it was the same regulation which brought Juventus victory over Athletic Bilbao in the UEFA Cup final.

In 1982 no fewer than six Juventus players featured in Italy's World Cup-winning line-up and the likes of Antonio Cabrini, Marco Tardelli, Gaetano Scirea, Claudio Gentile and Paolo Rossi went on to help Juve win the 1984 Cup-Winners' Cup and the 1985 Champions Cup. Seeking new magic Juventus paid huge fees for Italy's Roberto Baggio and Gianluca Vialli who helped Juve secure a record 23rd league title – before Baggio was transferred to Milan. Without him Juventus went on to win the Champions Cup – beating Dutchmen Ajax in Rome – then ripped up their team again, bringing in Frenchman Zinedine Zidane and Croat Alen Boksic, while shipping out both Vialli and Fabrizio Ravanelli to English clubs Chelsea and Middlesbrough respectively. The pace of change may have contributed to their subsequent Champions Cup defeat by Borussia Dotrmund in 1997.

KIEV DYNAMO
UKRAINE

Founded: 1927
Stadium: Republic (100,169)
Colours: White/blue
Honours: Cup-Winners' Cup 1975, 1986: Supercup 1975: League 18 (5 Ukraine, 13 USSR); Cup 11 (2 Ukraine, 9 USSR).

Ukraine is now an independent nation with Kiev Dynamo acknowledged as the top team. Originally the club was formed as a subsidiary of police organizations which inaugurated the USSR-wide network of Dynamo clubs in the late 1920s.

Kiev Dynamo, for example, were founded in 1927 but quickly earned recognition as one of the best in the Soviet Union. A national league was introduced in 1936, with Kiev founding members of the top division. They were never relegated.

In 1961, Dynamo became the first club from outside Moscow to win the national championship. In 1975, they went on to become the first Soviet side to win a European prize, when they defeated Ferencvaros of Budapest 3–0 in the Cup-Winners' Cup final in Basle. Later that year, Dynamo beat Bayern Munich in the European Super Cup, which helped earn success for left-wing Oleg Blokhin in the European Footballer of the Year poll.

Valeri Lobanovski was the head coach then and he was still the boss

when Dynamo regained the Cup-Winners' Cup in 1986, this time defeating Atletico Madrid 3–0 in front of a 40,000 crowd in Lyon and millions of television viewers throughout Europe. Experts described the performance as "football of the next century", and Igor Belanov followed in Blokhin's footsteps as European Footballer of the Year.

Kiev's skilled, thoughtful and entertaining approach was a breath of fresh air compared with the unimaginative, stereotyped teams which had been coming out of the Soviet Union for many years. Unfortunately the Soviet federation tried to make too much of a good thing.

It turned Kiev Dynamo into the national team, and the combined weight of domestic and international fixtures took the sparkle from their play. They might, otherwise, have won more European trophies. Dynamo won the Soviet Supreme Championship 13 times (a record) and were runners-up 11 times. They also won the Cup nine times before the dissolution of the USSR and the foundation of the independent state of Ukraine.

Life in independent Ukraine was not easy. Football fought a long battle to try to resist mafia infiltration. In 1995 Kiev were expelled from the Champions League after a clumsy attempt to bribe Spanish referee Antonio Lopez Nieto on the eve of their tie against Panathinaikos of Greece.

Kiev were barred from Europe, initially, for three years. But UEFA, considering the financial pressures on the Ukraine game, later took pity and allowed them back in to the Champions League the following season.

LEEDS UNITED
ENGLAND

Founded: 1919
Stadium: Elland Road (39,775)
Colours: All white
Honours: Fairs Cup 1968, 1971; League 3; Cup 1; League Cup 1.

Leeds United attained a reputation for the ultimate in disciplined, effective English football in the late 1960s and early 1970s under the managership of Don Revie, a former England inside-forward. He instilled these qualities, plus an immense pride, which made Leeds feared opponents at home and abroad.

Yet the extent to which Leeds set the agenda in English football is hardly demonstrated by the trophies they won. Leeds were more often runners-up than winners: five times in the league, three times in the FA Cup, once each in the Champions Cup (in 1975), Cup-Winners' Cup (in 1973) and Fairs Cup (in 1967).

Later, after Revie's spell as England manager had ended amid controversy, it became fashionable to carp at the dossiers on opponents, at the organized games of carpet bowls for the players. But few "teachers" inspired so many pupils to go into football management – among them Billy Bremner, Eddie Gray, Norman Hunter, Allan Clarke, Johnny Giles and, most notably, Jack Charlton.

Leeds first earned international headlines in 1957 when they sold Welshman John Charles to Juventus for a then British record £57,000. The club itself did not enter Europe until 1965 in the Fairs Cup – a competition they won after finals against Ferencvaros in 1968 and Juventus in 1971. They were permanent fixtures then in Europe until the UEFA-imposed suspension in 1975 after rioting Leeds fans ripped out seats in the Champions Cup final in Paris. Leeds had lost 2–0 against an injury-weakened Bayern Munich. By then Revie had already gone to the England job and Jimmy Armfield was manager. It was a sad end to an era.

Relegation followed in 1982 and

Leeds stayed down eight long years before Howard Wilkinson not only brought them back up but turned them – thanks to the fleeting inspiration of Eric Cantona – into league champions once more.

LIVERPOOL
ENGLAND

Founded: 1892
Stadium: Anfield (41,210)
Colours: All red
Honours: Champions Cup 1977, 1978, 1981, 1984; UEFA Cup 1973, 1976; Supercup 1977; League 18; Cup 5; League Cup 5.

Successful sportsmen the world over tell the same tale: reaching the top is tough, but not as tough as staying at the top. The enormous pressures generated by success even wore down the cogs of the Liverpool machine in the end – but only after a remarkable 28 years of unprecedented achievement.

The modern adventure began in

MERSEY MESSIAH ... Liverpool's legendary manager, Bill Shankly.

1954 when Liverpool, with a proud history behind them, slipped into the old second division. They remained there for eight years until Bill Shankly's unrivalled enthusiasm and football insight guided them back to the top division in 1962. Shankly had arrived in 1959, just after the club had reached its nadir, an exit from the FA Cup at the hands of Southern League Worcester City.

In 1964 – surfing the waves of Beatlemania – Liverpool won the first of their modern championships. In the next 26 years, Liverpool were to win the league 13 times (adding up to a record 18 in all), the FA Cup five times, the League Cup four times and the league and Cup double once.

Such drive proved relentlessly successful in Europe. Shankly and successors Bob Paisley and Joe Fagan managed to create a style which incorporated the physically-based strengths of the English game with the more technically thoughtful school of the best continental sides.

It worked like a dream. Four times Liverpool won the Champions Cup

and twice the UEFA Cup. They were runners-up in the Champions Cup once and the Cup-Winners' Cup once. The only occasion on which Liverpool were comprehensively put to the sword on a mainline occasion was the 1981 World Club Cup final in Tokyo. Zico's Flamengo, from Brazil, were well-deserved 3–0 winners.

Borussia Mönchengladbach and Brugge suffered worst from Liverpool. Borussia were the victims of Liverpool's first UEFA Cup triumph – losing 5–0 on aggregate, and were the victims again in Rome in 1977 when Kevin Keegan bowed out of the Anfield scene with the club's first Champions Cup secured. Brugge were beaten by Liverpool in both the UEFA Cup final in 1976 and the Champions Cup final at Wembley in 1978. The winning goal second time around was scored by Kenny Dalglish, who had arrived from Celtic to fill – seamlessly – the gap left by Keegan's departure for Hamburg.

Dalglish, wherever his career may subsequently have taken him, will always be considered – at least in

England – as a legend of Anfield. He took over as manager in the awful wake of the Heysel tragedy in 1985 and later had to bear the burden of pain of the city after the 1989 Hillsborough disaster. At Heysel, 39 Juventus fans died; at Hillsborough 96 Liverpool fans were crushed to death.

In between, Dalglish became the only player-manager to have guided his team to the league and cup double in 1986 and there were further honours. The league title trophy returned in 1988 and 1990 and the FA Cup in 1989 – the second final victory over city neighbours Everton in four years – before Dalglish stepped out from beneath the combined stress of triumph and tragedy.

Successor Graeme Souness won "only" the FA Cup before Liverpool went back to the old "Boot Room" regime and promoted long-time servant Roy Evans to the manager's chair. A League Cup win in 1995 and the emergence of new heroes such as Steve McManaman and Robbie Fowler promised an imminent return to the glory days.

MANCHESTER UNITED
ENGLAND

Founded: 1878
Stadium: Old Trafford (55,800)
Colours: Red/white
Honours: Champions Cup 1968; Cup-Winners' Cup 1991; Supercup 1991; League 11; Cup 9; League Cup 1.

Matt Busby may stand as the most charismatic of Manchester United managers. But even Sir Matt's record of achievement cannot compare with that of Alex Ferguson in the 1990s which saw United – a commercial as well as footballing monolith – hailed as the richest club in the world as their share value rocketed.

United had been founded in 1878 as Newton Heath by employees of the Lancashire and Yorkshire Railway Company. Ironically, considering events of 90 years later, Newton Heath went bankrupt in 1902 and it was out of that commercial failure that a new club, entitled Manchester United, was formed.

The club floated in and out of the top division between the wars but it was the 1948 Cup final victory which provided the spark for the future. United twice hit back from a goal down to defeat Stanley Matthews' Blackpool 4–2 in what is considered one of the great FA Cup finals.

This was the first outstanding team built by manager Busby, who had played before the war for neighbour Manchester City. His second outstanding team were the so-called "Busby Babes" of the mid-1950s. United defied Establishment orders and entered the European Champions Cup in 1956–57. They opened with a 10–0 thrashing of Belgium's Anderlecht and never looked back – not even in the bleak days of February 1958, after eight players, including England internationals Roger Byrne, Tommy Taylor and Duncan Edwards, died in the Munich air disaster.

It took United 10 years to recover, in international terms. Thus it was in May 1968 that United's European quest was rewarded as they defeated Benfica 4–1 in extra-time at Wembley. Bobby Charlton, a Munich survivor

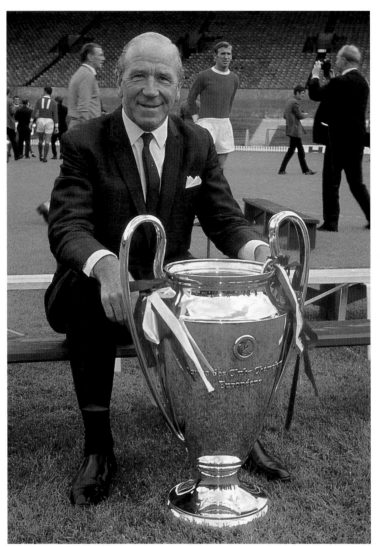

THE ULTIMATE PRIZE ... Matt Busby with the European Champions Cup.

along with defender Bill Foulkes and manager Busby, scored twice to secure the club's most emotional triumph. Foulkes himself had scored the match-winner in a dramatic semi-final against Real Madrid.

The club became synonymous with entertaining, attacking soccer as epitomized by the talents of Charlton, Denis Law and the wayward but mesmeric Northern Irishman, George Best. Later came England's long-serving skipper Bryan Robson, who was still in harness in 1993 when United, under Alex Ferguson, regained the English league title for the first time in 26 years.

Ferguson – brought south from Aberdeen to put United back on track after the managerial ups and downs wrought by Frank O'Farrell, Tommy Docherty and Ron Atkinson – had managed on a knife-edge in his early days.

Victory in the European Cup-Winners Cup in 1991 – United were first back, appropriately, after the five-year post-Heysel ban – proved that Ferguson was on the right lines. Events in the next five years underlined the point. Between 1993 and 1996 United won the league title three times in four seasons, including an unprecedented "double Double" of

TARNISHED ... Marseille before the match-fixing revelations.

league and FA Cup in 1994 and 1996.

Danish goalkeeper Peter Schmeichel and French forward Eric Cantona contributed the cosmopolitan icing to the most successful English club recipe of the 1990s. But the new United's dominance was not merely the product of big-money purchases. Home-grown youngsters such as Wales' Ryan Giggs and England's David Beckham added an extra dimension in terms of both skill and public fascination.

MARSEILLE
FRANCE

Founded: 1898
Stadium: Velodrome (46,000)
Colours: All white
Honours: Champions Cup 1993 (disqualified); League 9 (1993 revoked); Cup 10.

September 6, 1993, was the blackest day in the history of Olympique Marseille. That was the date on which UEFA decided to bar Marseille from defending the Champions Cup – won against Milan just over three months earlier – and opened up the path for an avalanche of match-fixing revelations which scandalized French football.

Some 16 days later, the French federation stripped Marseille of their league title and suspended former secretary Jean-Pierre Bernes and three of the four players involved in the bribery scandal – Jean-Jacques Eydelie and Valenciennes' Christophe Robert and Argentine international Jorge Burruchaga. No action was taken immediately against Marseille president Bernard Tapie but, in due course he too stood trial in court for match-fixing, and was imprisoned for corruption. Marseille had played Valenciennes in May 1993, just before their Champions Cup final against Milan, and by winning 2–0 had claimed the title, or so they thought.

European exclusion cost Marseille an estimated £14 million and they were duly punished by the French federation with enforced relegation. Only in 1996 did Marseille, now under the direction of new owners, led by Adidas boss Robert Louis-Dreyfus, regain top division status.

All of this was a sad comedown for a club which had been renowned as one of the richest in France, with perhaps the most loyal and fanatical fans.

Marseille are one of the oldest of French clubs, but their history has been chequered with controversy. Their 1971 and 1972 league championship successes were tarnished after they had lured away top goalkeeper Georges Carnus and defender Bernard Bosquier from closest rivals Saint-Etienne in mid-season.

Marseille boasted other great players such as Yugoslav striker Josip Skoblar, who was the league's top scorer for three years in a row, but their most enduring talent has proved to be one for courting controversy.

MECHELEN
BELGIUM

Founded: 1904
Stadium: Achter de Kazerne (14,131)
Colours: Yellow shirts with thin red stripes, black shorts, black socks
Honours: Cup-Winners' Cup 1988; Supercup 1988; League 4; Cup 1.

Mechelen won the Belgian championship – when the domestic game was amateur – on three occasions in the 1940s but were unrated as an international force when they shocked Europe in general and Ajax Amsterdam in particular to win the 1988 Cup-Winners' Cup.

The previous season they had won the Belgian cup for the first time to earn their first-ever European qualification and they reached the final in Strasbourg without having lost a game. Dinamo Bucharest were beaten 1–0 home and 2–0 away, St Mirren 2–0 away, Dynamo Minsk 1–0 at home and Italy's Atalanta 2–1 both home and away in the semi-finals.

Ajax were holders of the Cup-Winners' Cup and overwhelming favourites to become the first club to retain the trophy. But defender Danny Blind was sent off after 17 minutes and Mechelen, coached by Dutchman Aad de Mos, won with a 53rd-minute goal from Pieter Den Boer. Mechelen midfielder Erwin Koeman, yet another Dutchman, set up a rare family double that year because, two weeks after his triumph, Erwin's brother Ronald collected a winner's medal in the Champions Cup with PSV Eindhoven. Mechelen beat PSV 3–1 in the 1988 Supercup. Mechelen, with whom goalkeeper Michel Preud'homme was resurrecting his career after a match-fixing scandal with Standard Liege, won the championship in 1989 but lost their grip on the Cup-Winners' Cup in the semi-final against Sampdoria.

CHAMPIONS ... Milan celebrate their 1993 Italian league triumph.

MILAN
ITALY

Founded: 1898
Stadium: Giuseppe Meazza (85,443)
Colours: Red and black stripes/black
Honours: World Club Cup 1969, 1989, 1990; Champions Cup 1963, 1969, 1989, 1990, 1994; Cup-Winners' Cup 1968, 1973; Supercup 1989, 1990, 1995: League 15; Cup 4.

Milan have been the dominant club in Europe over the past 10 years. The era began when the club signed Holland's Ruud Gullit and Marco Van Basten in 1987. The next year they won the Italian championship and then, two years in a row, the Champions Cup. In 1993 Milan lost 1–0 in the final to Marseille, defeated Barcelona in thrilling style by 4–0 in 1994, then lost to Ajax by 1–0 in Vienna in 1995.

Milan's reign was constructed on a futuristic commercial blueprint laid down by the media magnate Silvio Berlusconi. He had come to the rescue in 1986 – investing £20 million to save Milan from bankruptcy and turn the club into a key player in his commercial empire.

Milan had been one of the founders of the Italian championship back in 1898 but most of the pre-World War Two years were spent in

the shadows of neighbours Internazionale – or Ambrosiana as they were then called. After the War Milan achieved spectacular success thanks to their forays into the international transfer market – at that stage virtually uncontrolled by the Italian league authorities.

Sweden had won the 1948 Olympic title thanks to the inside-forward skills of Gunnar Gren, Gunnar Nordahl and Nils Liedholm so Milan signed them *en bloc* and then followed up by paying a then world record £72,000 for Juan Schiaffino – hero of Uruguay's shock World Cup victory in 1950.

Milan were the first major rivals to Real Madrid in the new European Champions Cup – losing to the Spanish club in the 1956 semi-finals, then only after extra-time in the 1958 final. That was also the year Milan discovered the teenaged Gianni Rivera, whose inside-forward genius inspired Milan to their first Champions Cup victory in 1963.

His partnership with Brazilian centre-forward Jose Altafini destroyed Benfica in the final and skipper and sweeper Cesare Maldini held the Cup aloft at Wembley – where he would later enjoy another significant success, this time as manager of Italy, in the 1998 World Cup qualifying event. Rivera was Milan's figurehead in the 1960s and early 1970s, winning the

Champions Cup again in 1969 and the Cup-Winners' Cup. But even his charisma could not save the club from the scandals and financial disasters inflicted by a string of presidents. Twice Milan were relegated – once as punishment for a match-fixing scandal – before the club found itself on the brink of bankruptcy in the mid-1980s.

That was where Berlusconi came in, providing the money and the men – coaches Arrigo Sacchi and Fabio Capello, Dutch superstars Ruud Gullit, Marco Van Basten, Frank Rijkaard as well as Italy's Franco Baresi and Paolo Maldini (son of Cesare) – to Milan into a "new media" football club for the 21st century.

NAPOLI
ITALY
Founded: 1904
Stadium: San Paolo (72,810)
Colours: Blue/white
Honours: UEFA Cup 1989; League 2; Cup 3.

Napoli were, for years, a club with more passion than purpose. The original Naples club – English language style, of course – were founded in 1904 then underwent a series of mergers before taking the present Associazione Calcio Napoli title in 1926. In the further inter-war years they held their place in Serie A but could make little headway against the giants of the era, Juventus, Bologna and Ambrosiana-Inter.

Relegated in the penultimate pre-war season – 1941–42 – Napoli spent much of the first 20 post-war years hopping between divisions. They also collected a string of ground suspensions whenever the pas-

sion of their huge following boiled over.

The "new era" began in 1965. Napoli had just regained their Serie A place when the club found new investors able to fund the sensational purchases of Jose Altafini from Milan and Omar Sivori from Juventus. Both superstars were past their best and had squabbled their way out of their previous clubs. But their presence revolutionized the atmosphere around Fuorigrotta.

In the next decade Napoli established themselves as virtual ever-presents in the league's top four but they had only two Italian cups to show for it. The step up to European achievement demanded a further coup – which president Corrado Ferlaino provided in 1984 when he signed Diego Maradona from Barcelona for a world record £5 million.

Within a fortnight of the transfer, Napoli had recouped most of the fee in season-ticket sales. Maradona played to sell-out 85,000 crowds and inspired Napoli to win the league title twice, the UEFA Cup and the Italian cup. The money Napoli made, however, was frittered away. After Maradona's dope-ban exit in 1991, the club collapsed to the brink of bankruptcy. It took Ferlaino's return to the helm to steer the club back off the financial rocks.

NEWCASTLE UNITED
ENGLAND
Founded: 1881
Stadium: St James' Park (36,610)
Colours: Black and white stripes/black
Honours: Fairs Cup 1969; League 4; Cup 6.

Newcastle's revival in the 1990s had everything to do with Kevin Keegan. He was given financial carte blanche by chairman Sir John Hall, but far more managers have squandered cash than invested wisely. Keegan's achievement was to breathe life and soul back into an apparently moribund club.

In his first half-season he saved Newcastle from relegation from the old second division; in his first full season he achieved promotion to the Premiership; in the next he guided Newcastle to third place and into the UEFA Cup; his third full season culminated in sixth place; in 1996 Newcastle finished second. Keegan then splashed

MAGIC MARADONA ... he brought Napoli their first Italian league title.

was the 1969 Fairs Cup, which they captured by defeating Hungary's Ujpest Dozsa 3–0 at home then 3–2 away after being 2–0 down. Skipper Bobby Moncur scored three of Newcastle's six goals from wing-half – his opener in the first leg of the final being his first for Newcastle in nine years!

NOTTINGHAM FOREST
ENGLAND

Founded: 1865
Stadium: City Ground (30,602)
Colours: Red/white
Honours: Champions Cup 1979, 1980; Supercup 1979; League 1; Cup ·2; League Cup 4.

Nottingham Forest joined illustrious company when they defeated Malmo 1–0 in Munich in 1979 to win the Champions Cup. Only Real Madrid (in the inaugural tournament in 1955–56) and Internazionale (in 1963–64) had ever won Europe's most prestigious club prize at the first attempt.

Forest won it again the following year, defeating Hamburg this time by the same minimal margin, in Madrid. This double only further enshrined the legend of Brian Clough in English football folklore, although such was the particular style of the man that his aura made little impression abroad – despite the achievements of his team.

Forest, when Clough took over in the mid-1970s, were a famous old club in the middle of what was then the second division and apparently going nowhere. They had never won the league title and had won the FA Cup only twice – in 1898 and then again in

PRODIGAL SON ... Newcastle United's England striker Alan Shearer.

a world record £15 million on England spearhead Alan Shearer before bailing out in mid-season and handing over to Kenny Dalglish.

The sky appears to be the limit. The north-east of England had known nothing like it since the Magpies dominated English football in the early years of the century. Then, with such heroes as defender Bill McCracken – the man who forced the offside law change from three defenders to two – they won the league three times and reached the cup final five times (albeit

winning only once).

In the early 1950s Newcastle became the first club of the twentieth century to win the FA Cup twice in a row – beating Blackpool 2–0 in 1951 then Arsenal 1–0. Centre-forward "Wor Jackie" Milburn was one hero, left-winger Bobby Mitchell another, tough-tackling right-half Jimmy Scoular another.

After four years in the old second division, Newcastle returned to achieve the feat of winning a European prize at first attempt. This

WINNER ... Forest's Champions Cup-winning goal against Malmo.

1959, when they beat Luton 2–1 despite losing right-winger Roy Dwight with a broken leg.

Clough had made his managerial name at Derby County, with whom he gained his first taste of the Champions Cup, reaching the semi-finals in 1973. With Forest he went one step better, in double-quick time. Forest came up into the top division in 1977, won the league a year later then the Champions Cup followed by a Supercup victory over Barcelona later in 1979.

Along the way Forest invested some of their new-found riches by turning Trevor Francis, from Birmingham City, into English football's first £1 million player.

Francis's European debut for Forest was a dream – the 1979 Champions Cup final in which he headed the only goal. A year later, against Hamburg in Madrid, it was the turn of Scotland's John Robertson to decide matters, single-handed. Forest were also four-times winners of the League Cup, although FA Cup success eluded them under Clough, who finally stepped down amid the depression of relegation in 1993. After bouncing back in 1994, Forest were relegated in 1997 amidst boardroom wranglings.

PARIS SAINT-GERMAIN
FRANCE

Founded: 1970
Stadium: Parc des Princes (148,712)
Colours: Blue with broad red stripe/blue
Honours: Cup-Winners' Cup 1996: League 2: Cup 4.

Paris Saint-Germain, remarkably, became the very first club from the French capital to win a European prize when they defeated Rapid Vienna 1–0 in the Cup-Winners' Cup final in 1996.

Yet PSG had been founded only 26 years earlier – by Parisien fans anxious to fill the gap left by the collapse of professional football in the French capital. They did not turn formally full professional until 1973, by which time they had risen to the brink of promotion to the French top division under the enthusiastic presidency of the couturier, Daniel Hechter. He spent money on players the same way his fashions encouraged women to spend money on clothes, signing Yugoslav goalkeeper Ilija Pantelic and midfielder Safet Susic, record-breaking Argentine centre-forward Carlos Bianchi and French World Cup internationals Dominique Rocheteau, Dominique Bathenay and Luis Fernandez.

The trophy breakthrough arrived with Paris' French cup successes in 1982 and 1983 and was extended in 1986 when, under former English teacher Gerard Houllier, Paris won their first league title. Amazingly, it was the first time a Paris club had won the national championship since Racing Club exactly 50 years earlier in 1936.

In due course Houllier was spirited away to become assistant and then full manager of the French national team and Paris had to look for new resources and backers. They found them in 1995, in the ambitious television station Canal-Plus. Michel Denisot invested heavily in a string of new star players – such as Liberian George Weah, Frenchman David Ginola and Brazilians Ricardo, Valdo and Rai – and the results are now plain to see.

PSG reached European semi-finals in four successive seasons: losing in the UEFA Cup in 1993, the Cup-Winners' Cup in 1994 and the Champions League in 1995, but this hurdle was finally cleared in the 1996 Cup-Winners' Cup. However, their final victory over Rapid was followed by the departures of coach Luis Fernandez and attacking key Youri Djorkaeff – provoking wide-ranging changes among both playing staff and management.

PARMA
ITALY

Founded: 1913
Stadium: Ennio Tardini (29,048)
Colours: All white
Honours: Cup-Winners' Cup 1993: UEFA Cup 1995; Supercup 1993; Cup 1.

The town of Parma is world famous for its ham and as the birthplace of the great composer Giuseppe Verdi. Now it is also famous world-wide as the home of one of European football's fastest-growing clubs. This particular Parma have produced plenty of star names in the past. One was coach Arrigo Sacchi, who took Italy to the 1994 World Cup final; others include players such as Nicola Berti (later Inter) and Carlo Ancelotti (one-time Milan).

But plenty has changed in a few short years. Now Parma can hold on to

ESCAPE TO VICTORY ... PSG won the 1996 Cup-winners Cup Final.

TINO! ... Asprilla in triumph after the 1995 UEFA Cup victory.

their star men if they wish. The financial backing of sponsors Parmalat, the dairy produce company, means Parma have become transfer raiders themselves. In 1990 they bought Sweden's baby-faced World Cup star Tomas Brolin; later came Colombian talent Faustino Asprilla, then Italy's own Gianfranco Zola and Enrico Chiesa as well as Argentina's Hernand Crespo.

Parma were founded on July 27, 1913 – originally under the name of Verdi Foot Ball Club. Five months later the composer disappeared from view as the club committee voted to change titles to Parma Foot Ball Club. Most of the years up until the early 1950s were spent in the fourth, third and second

divisions. In the 1950s Parma appeared to establish themselves in the second division but were relegated in 1965 and slipped right on down into the fourth division and had to merge with another local club to survive.

finally, in 1986, under Sacchi they gained promotion back to Serie B and, four years later, were in Serie A for the first time in their history. They finished fifth in their first season and earned entry to the UEFA Cup, falling unluckily on the away goals rule in the first round to CSKA Sofia. That same season they beat Juventus 0–1, 2–0 in the Italian cup final, returned to Europe in the Cup-Winners' Cup and triumphed thanks to a 3–1 victory over Belgian club Antwerp at Wembley.

Against Arsenal a year later, Parma narrowly failed to become the

first club to retain the Cup-Winners' Cup but their European consolation, a year later, was to beat fellow Italians Juventus in the UEFA Cup final.

FC PORTO
OPORTO PORTUGAL

Founded: 1893
Stadium: Das Antas (53,069)
Colours: Blue and white stripes/blue
Honours: World Club Cup 1987; Champions Cup 1987; Supercup 1987; League 15; Cup 12.

FC Porto had always been always considered the "third club" in the Portuguese football hierarchy until their thrilling Champions Cup victory over Bayern Munich in Vienna in 1987. Events then and since have ensured that Porto, while their trophy count may not

ANY PORTO ... Porto with the 1987 European Champions Cup trophy.

WAITING ... PSV Eindhoven before their 1988 Champions Cup triumph.

yet match that of Benfica and Sporting, are considered an alternative centre of power in the domestic game. Indeed, Porto are now *the* club in Portugal, having won the league championship six times in the 1990s.

Their basic pattern of tactics and style means that the team can withstand whatever changes may be enforced by the uncertainties of the transfer market. In the summer of 1996, for instance, Porto lost coach Bobby Robson and international goalkeeper Vitor Baia (both to Barcelona), defender Carlos Secretario (to Real Madrid) and Brazilian midfielder Emerson (to Middlesbrough). Yet they went on to complete a hat-trick of league championships with such command that one newspaper wrote of the "Scottishization" of Portuguese football – only Porto, Sporting and Benfica have won the league title since Belenenses in 1945.

Certainly, no-one who witnessed

the Brazilian-style skill and movement of their national team at Euro 96 can doubt the outstanding quality of the top Portuguese teams.

Foreign imports have always played an important role in Porto football. But that was entirely appropriate since, in the early 1930s, Porto had been pioneers in the international transfer market.

They began by bringing in two Yugoslavs, and that ambition was reflected in Porto's initial championship successes in 1938 and 1939. Almost 40 years later, Porto beat Bayern in the Champions Cup final with a Polish goalkeeper Jozef Mlynarczyk, Brazilians Celso and Juary and Algerian winger Rabah Madjer supporting Portugal's own wonder-boy, Paulo Futre.

Originally, Porto's home was the old, rundown Campo da Constituciao. Now, as befits a club with such a good European cup-winning pedigree, home is the impressive, Estadio das Antas. Though its original 70,000 capacity has had to be scaled down.

PSV EINDHOVEN
HOLLAND

Founded: 1913
Stadium: Philips (30,000)
Colours: Red and white stripes/white
Honours: Champions Cup 1988; UEFA Cup 1978; League 14; Cup; 7.

PSV have gained international kudos not merely as the sporting arm of the Philips electronics corporation but through their own achievements. They have won the Dutch championship 14 times – one fewer than Feyenoord and 12 less than Ajax – and the cup on seven occasions. On four occasions they were domestic cup runners-up while at international level they won the European Champions Cup in 1988 and the UEFA Cup in 1978.

Along the way, PSV have also benefited from the services of some of the most outstanding Dutch footballers of the modern era, including Ruud Gullit and Ronald Koeman.

In the 1960s Feyenoord took the international eye on behalf of Holland, an era which they climaxed by winning

the Champions Cup and the World Club Cup in 1970. Then came Ajax Amsterdam's three-year domination of the Champions Cup and PSV took their cue in style in 1978. They won the UEFA Cup in 1978 with a team built around the intuitive attacking partnership of midfielder Willy Van der Kerkhof and his wing twin, Rene.

Both were regulars in the Dutch national squad at the 1974 and 1978 World Cups while combative defensive midfielders Jan Poortvliet and Ernie Brandts were also among Holland's World Cup stalwarts in Argentina.

It needed a 10-year gap and the development of a new generation of star players before PSV again made headlines in Europe. In 1987–88 they were virtually irresistible at club level. Hans Van Breukelen was an outstanding personality in goal, Ivan Nielsen a Danish rock at the heart of defence, Jan Heintze a dangerous raiding left-back and Soren Lerby – another Dane – a feisty, energetic midfield dynamo. Mix in the power-packed shooting of the young Ronald Koeman and the attacking talent of Wim Kieft and PSV presented a virtually unbeatable force.

It took a penalty shoot-out, however, for PSV to defeat the experienced old campaigners of Portugal's Benfica in the Champions Cup final in Stuttgart. Weeks later, Van Breukelen, full-back Berry Van Aerle, midfielder Gerald Vanenburg and Koeman completed an international double as members of the Dutch team which won the European Championship final by 2–0 against the Soviet Union in Munich.

At one stage the Philips corporation allowed the sports club to exist almost as an autonomous entity. But as football grew ever more important as a promotional vehicle, so the company invested more money into both the impressive Philips stadium – with, naturally, its state-of-the-art floodlighting system – and the coaching and playing staff.

One of the club's major coups was to sign up Bobby Robson to take over immediately after he had led England to the semi-finals and fourth place in the 1990 World Cup. Robson stayed two years, winning the championship both times, before moving on to Portugal with Sporting of Lisbon.

His star player was the Brazilian striker Romario, whom PSV had picked up at a virtual bargain price after he starred at the 1988 Olympic Games football tournament in South Korea. Romario later transferred to Barcelona – the same path followed in due course by PSV's next Brazilian discovery, Ronaldo.

RANGERS
GLASGOW, SCOTLAND

Founded: 1873
Stadium: Ibrox (50,411)
Colours: Blue/white
Honours: Cup-Winners' Cup 1972;
League 47; Cup 27; League Cup 20.

Rangers represent one half – and, in recent years, the more successful half – of the "Old Firm".

Their rivalry with Glasgow neighbours Celtic has dominated Scottish football for a century. Yet the 'Gers have never been able to extend their power into Europe. Their only prize from virtual non-stop international competition has been the 1972 Cup-Winners' Cup, which they won by defeating Moscow Dynamo in Barcelona.

DYNAMITE ... Rangers' Brian Laudrup was twice voted Scottish Footballer of the Year.

Not that Rangers' history is short on proud moments. One particular era of legend was the 1920s when Rangers' heroes included the legendary "Wee Blue Devil", Alan Morton. His career overlapped with that of Bob McPhail, whose record of 233 goals in 354 league matches was only recently overtaken by Ally McCoist.

After World War Two Rangers' success was built on the so-called "Iron Curtain" defence starring George Young and Willie Woodburn, with the goals created by Willie Waddell for Willie Thornton. But in Europe in the 1960s Rangers were brought down to earth by heavy defeats at the hands of Eintracht Frankfurt, Tottenham and Real Madrid.

The start of the 1970s was a time of mixed emotions: 1971 saw the Ibrox disaster, when 66 fans died in a stairway crush at the end of a game against Celtic. Less than 18 months later, there was European glory in that Cup-Winners Cup game, but the Old Firm's grip was loosened by Aberdeen and Dundee United

Rangers' upturn began in November, 1985, when Lawrence Marlboro, a Nevada-based businessman and grandson of a previous club chairman, bought control of the club. The following April came stage two, when he brought in Graeme Souness as player-manager. In 1988 steel magnate David Murray bought the club and Souness revolutionized Rangers' image and the transfer market by buying no fewer than 18 English players and smashing the club's traditional Protestants-only ethic with his £1.5 million capture of striker "Mo" Johnston, a Roman Catholic.

Souness' successor, Walter Smith, brought in Denmark's Brian Laudrup and England's Paul Gascoigne to help lift Rangers towards a championship-winning decade. Both men won Scottish Footballer of the Year awards but European success remained as elusive as ever. In the 1996–97 Champions League, Rangers finished bottom of their four-team first round group with only one win in six games. The club's 1996-97 elague title was their ninth in a row – equalling Celtic's.

REAL MADRID
SPAIN

Founded: 1902
Stadium: Santiago Bernabeu (105,000)
Colours: All white
Honours: World Club Cup 1960; Champions Cup 1956, 1957, 1958, 1959, 1960, 1966; UEFA Cup 1985, 1986; League 27; Cup 17.

Real Madrid have won it all: they are record six-times champions of Europe and record 27-times champions of Spain. They also boast one World Club Cup, two UEFA Cups and 17 Spanish cups plus a host of other trophies and awards from around the world. All of which goes to make Madrid's trophy room one of the wonders of world football.

Madrid were founded by students

ROYALTY ... Real Madrid's Dutch midfielder, Clarence Seedorf.

in 1898 but did not become an "official" entity until 1902. Their first manager was an Englishman, Arthur Johnson, who was so fanatical about football that he even arranged his wedding for a morning so he could play football for Madrid FC – the Real title, meaning Royal, was later granted by special permission of King Alfonso XIII – in the afternoon.

Madrid were not only among the founders of cup and then league competition of Spain: it was also the Madrid president, Carlos Padros, who represented Spain at the inaugural meeting of FIFA in Paris in 1904. In the late 1920s Madrid launched a policy of buying big. They paid a then Spanish record fee of £2,000 for

Ricardo Zamora, still revered as the greatest Spanish goalkeeper of all time.

The Spanish civil war left Madrid's Chamartin stadium in ruins. The club had no money but boasted one of the greatest visionaries in European football history. He was Santiago Bernabeu, a lawyer who had been, by turn, player, team manager, secretary and now club president. Bernabeu found the funds to build both the great stadium which now bears his name and then a team worthy of it.

Bernabeu scoured Europe and South America for stars. The greatest of these was centre-forward Alfredo Di Stefano from Argentina – for many experts the greatest footballer of all time. He inspired Madrid to victory in the first five Champions Cup finals and scored in them all. Most notable was the 7–3 demolition of Germany's Eintracht Frankfurt at Hampden Park, Glasgow, in 1960. Di Stefano scored three goals with Madrid's other four being snapped up by another legend of the game, Hungarian Ferenc Puskas.

Of course, the standards those players and that team set, could never be maintained. Outstanding players who have tried include Spanish superstars Pirri and Amancio in the 1960s, Germany's Gunter Netzer and Paul Breitner in the 1970s, Spain's Emilio Butragueno and Michel and Mexico's Hugo Sanchez in the 1980s and most recently Croatia's Davor Suker, Holland's Clarence Seedorf and Brazil's Roberto Carlos.

It is generally accepted that the legacy of the legends is an enormous one to bear. Thus, in 1996, Madrid president Lorenzo Sanz "borrowed" Milan coach Fabio Capello for one season to bring some Italian know-how to the challenge of turning the European clock back.

REAL ZARAGOZA
SPAIN

Founded: 1932
Stadium: La Romareda (43,554)
Colours: Blue and white/blue
Honours: Cup-Winners' Cup 1995; Fairs Cup 1964; Cup 4.

Zaragoza are proof that football in Spain is about much more than Real Madrid and Barcelona.

They have never won the Spanish league – second in 1975 remains their best finish. But they have landed the

Spanish Cup on four occasions and twice conquered Europe. The first time was in the 1964 Fairs Cup with a superb forward line known as the Cincos Magnificos (Magnificent Five); the second time was in winning the Cup-Winners' Cup against Arsenal in Paris in 1995.

Zaragoza were founder members of the Spanish second division in 1928 and took their present full title after a merger with the Iberia Club de Futbol in 1932. They gained access to the top division in 1936 – the year the Civil War put an end to sporting matters for three years. Zaragoza were relegated two seasons after the restart and vacillated between the top divisions before establishing themselves at last after the 1956–57 promotion campaign.

In 1962 new president Waldo Marco shocked the fans by selling star Peruvian forward Juan Seminario to Italy's Fiorentina and midfielder or full-back Julio Benitez to Barcelona. But the cash financed the finishing touches to the team of the Magnificent Five forward line: Brazilian right-wing pair Canario and Santos, centre-forward Marcelino, Spanish inside-left Juan Villa (a Real Madrid cast-off) and left-wing Carlos Lapetra.

In 1962 left-back Severino Reija became the first Zaragoza player ever capped by Spain. From 1963 to 1966, Zaragoza played in six finals all against native opposition in Spain, twice in the Fairs Cup. In 1963 and 1965 Zaragoza were Spanish cup runners-up but in 1964 and 1966 its winners. Their first cup victory became a double when they also won the Fairs Cup, beating Valencia 2–1 in a single match final in Barcelona. Zaragoza were runners-up in 1966, losing by 1–0 and 2–4 to Barcelona.

In the middle of all that Marcelino and Lapetra were both members of the Spanish national team which won the 1964 European championship against the Soviet Union. However defeat by Barcelona in the 1966 Fairs Cup final sparked a long slide from glory which was not reversed for almost 30 years when Zaragoza achieved Cup-winners success against Arsenal. Midfielder Nayim – who had spent time in England playing for the Gunners' fiercest rivals Tottenham – lobbed an astonishing winning goal from out on the right touchline in the dying moments of extra-time.

RED STAR BELGRADE
YUGOSLAVIA

Founded: 1945
Stadium: Crvena Zvezda (Red Star) (97,422)
Colours: Red and white stripes/red
Honours: World Club Cup 1991; Champions Cup 1991; League 20; Cup 16.

The name Crvena Zvezda means next to nothing outside their own country. Instead it is as Red Star that Yugoslavia's greatest club are known in England; as Estrella Roja in Spain; as Stella Rossa in Italy; as Etoile Rouge in France; and as Roter Stern in Germany.

Their achievements really speak for themselves: a record 20 league championships, a record 15 national cups. And then, to top it all off, Red Star won the Champions Cup in 1991, just before the Balkans exploded in the sort of conflict Europe thought it had left behind in the 1940s.

Red Star were among the great clubs who created the glamour and fascination of the Champions Cup in the late 1950s. It was against Red Star that Manchester United played their last match before the Munich air disaster. United won – but not before players such as fierce-shooting Bora Kostic and artistic schemer Dragoslav Sekularac had stamped their seal of quality on the international game.

Dragan Dzajic was one of the world's greatest left-wingers in the 1960s before exporting his talents to France then bringing his experience to bear back with Red Star as general manager.

Dzajic was a senior executive when Red Star achieved their greatest success. They had already reached one European final when they finished runners-up in the UEFA Cup in 1979. Twelve years later, under coach Ljubko Petrovic, Red Star swept through the Champions Cup with an even finer team. Players such as Vladimir Jugovic, Robert Prosinecki, Dejan Savicevic, Sinisa Mihajlovic and Darko Pancev went on to stardom elsewhere in Europe after defeating Marseille in the final in a penalty shoot-out.

ROMA
ITALY

Founded: 1927
Stadium: Olimpico (82,922)
Colours: All burgundy
Honours: Fairs Cup 1961; League 2; Cup 7.

All the fuss afforded the clubs of Milan and Turin over the years has obscured the fact that Roma were one of the first two Italians clubs to win a European trophy. That was in 1961 when Roma beat Birmingham City over two legs to win the Fairs Cup; that same year Fiorentina defeated Rangers to land the Cup-Winners' Cup.

Roma's team included two highly popular Argentine forwards in Pedro Manfredonia and Antonio Valentin Angelillo and an Italian goalkeeper in Fabio Cudicini who later became the first player to collect a winner's medal

BLOC'D ... Red Star, Yugoslav winners of the Champions Cup.

in all three European club competitions.

Roma came closest to a European prize again in 1984. They were favourites to beat Liverpool in the Champions Cup final since the venue was their own Stadio Olimpico. But the match ended 1–1 after extra-time and Roma proved more nervy in the penalty shoot-out, which they lost 4–2. Brazilian midfielder Paulo Roberto Falcao, one of the outstanding personalities in Italian football in the 1980s, stayed aloof from the shoot-out and his relationship with Roma fans was never quite the same again.

The club possessed enormous potential which went largely unfulfilled. In 13 years after the Champions Cup final defeat Roma won only the Italian cup twice and finished runners-up in the UEFA Cup in 1991. Three times Nils Liedholm – scudetto-winning coach in 1993 – had to be called out of retirement to steady the ship,

SAMPDORIA
GENOA, ITALY
Founded: 1946
Stadium: Luigi Ferraris (43,868)
Colours: Blue/white
Honours: Cup-Winners' Cup 1990; League 1; Cup 4.

Sampdoria have built a reputation, since the take-over by the oil-rich Mantovani family in the early 1980s, as one of Italy's most attractive teams. That has not been reflected in as much success as perhaps they deserved despite having won the Cup-Winners' Cup once and finished runners-up once in the Champions Cup.

Sampdoria had been founded only in 1946 from the merger of two unsuccessful local clubs, Sampierdaranese and Andrea Doria. Hence the club title, Sampdoria. Where neighbours Genoa were the "establishment" club, Sampdoria resorted to the cheque book as a short cut to success and popularity. One of the biggest early signings was Eddie Firmani, from Charlton Athletic. In 1958 Firmani was second in the Italian scoring charts, behind only John Charles of Juventus.

A string of famous coaches failed to prevent Sampdoria's gradual slide towards relegation in 1966. They bounced straight up at first attempt, but went back down in 1975. Tycoon Paolo Mantovani was then a director, and on becoming president in 1979, he launched a one-man revolution.

His drive steered Sampdoria back to Serie A in 1982. Mantovani also provided the finance to purchase English league stars Liam Brady, Trevor Francis and Graeme Souness. The first tangible sign of success was a cup victory in 1985, which Samp repeated in 1988 and 1989.

Attacking "twins" Roberto Mancini and Gianluca Vialli were overawed by the occasion. But the experience stood them in good stead a year later. Sampdoria returned to the Cup-winners' Cup final and triumphed, this time, by 2–0 over Anderlecht. Vialli scored both goals, in extra-time in Gothenburg.

The peak of the Mantovani years was Sampdoria's appearance in the Champions Cup final in 1992. But an extra-time thunderbolt from Barcelona's Ronald Koeman was the only goal of the game. Sampdoria had finished out of the UEFA Cup frame

in the Italian league and thus dropped out of the European mainstream. Vialli moved to Juventus – leaving a gap which not even the later acquisitions of England's David Platt and Dutch veteran Ruud Gullit could quite fill.

SLOVAN BRATISLAVA
SLOVAKIA
Founded: 1919
Stadium: Tehelne Pole (32,000)
Colours: All blue
Honours: Cup-Winners' Cup 1969; League 11 (3 Slovakia, 8 Czechoslovakia; Cup 6 (1 Slovakia, 5 Czechoslovakia).

Slovan Bratislava are the one major Slovakian club from the former Czechoslovakia. Founded in 1919 as S K Bratislava, the club first made an impact after becoming N K Bratislava in the late 1940s. They won the Czechoslovakian championship three years in succession before changing their name yet again to the present form, Slovan.

Financial and logistical support from the town's major chemical works helped Slovan to maintain a high-profile presence in the Czech championship.

In 1969, they became the only club from Czechoslovakia (Czech Republic or Slovakia, for that matter) to win a modern European club prize. Sparta and Slavia of Prague had been prime forces in the Mitropa Cup in pre-World War Two days, but that was the end of Czech/Slovak club power in Europe – until 1968–69 when Slovan won the Cup-Winners' Cup.

Their success was hugely ironic since every other Eastern Bloc club had – under Soviet orders – withdrawn from the three European club cups that season. The reason was to protest at the re-drawing of the opening rounds to keep eastern and western European clubs apart for a political cooling-off period following the Warsaw Pact invasion of Czechoslovakia.

Somehow Slovan slipped through the net of anger, defeated Bor (Yugoslavia), Porto, Torino and Dunfermline before defeating odds-on favourites Barcelona 3–2 in the final in Basle.

They never regained that pre-eminence in Europe. Slovan remained the top club in Slovakia and attracted the best young players – including Peter

most recently after the failed experiment with Argentine coach Carlos Bianchi in 1996–97.

Roma were founded from a merger of four city clubs – Alba, Fortitudo, Roman and Pro Patria. They were members of the inaugural first division in 1929–30, finishing sixth. Runners-up in 1931 and 1936 they rose to surprise championship winners in 1942 – inspired by the goals of Amadeo Amadei.

"TWIN" ... Roberto Mancini of Sampdoria, and later in his career, Lazio.

The club were nearly bankrupted by relegation in 1951 and then again a decade later after miscalculating the high cost of signing German striker Jürgen Schutz and the Italo-Brazilian centre-forward Angelo Benedetto Sormani for a then world record £250,000.

Dubovsky, who was ultimately lured away to Spain by Real Madrid. Even without him Slovan dominated football in the newly-formed Slovakia in the mid-1990s.

SPORTING CLUBE
LISBON, PORTUGAL

Founded: 1906
Stadium: Jose Alvalade (52,411)
Colours: Green and white hoops/green
Honours: Cup-Winners' Cup 1964; League 16; Cup 16.

Sporting Clube are, with neighbours Benfica and FC Porto, Portuguese football's "Big Three". Yet remarkably, for all their power and fame and perpetual presence in European competitions, fans have to look back to 1964 for the last time they triumphed in an international final. That was when they won the Cup-Winners' Cup in a replay against MTK Budapest.

Despite raising their fans' hopes time and again, Sporting have never quite managed to regain the pre-eminence at home and abroad of those years. Indeed, Sporting's 2–0 victory over Maritimo in the 1995 Portuguese cup final was the first trophy they had secured since winning the league and cup double 13 years earlier under English coach Malcolm Allison.

Back in the 1950s, Sporting rivalled Benfica as the country's top club and took the championship seven times in eight years. The tables were turned for most of the 1960s, with Benfica dominating at home and reaching the Champions Cup final five times, winning two, losing three. The pressure to match this success drew Sporting into a Barcelona-Manchester United-like syndrome (competing against more successful compatriots Real Madrid and Liverpool respectively) and they spent a great deal of money for comparatively minimal return.

Signs of progress emerged in the early 1990s, however, when Sporting reached the semi-final of the UEFA Cup before losing 0–0, 0–2 to eventual winners Internazionale of Milan.

Top coaches such as ex-England boss Bobby Robson and Portugal's World Youth Cup-winning manager Carlos Queiros were hired and fired at high speed – their attempts to rebuild a successful team undermined by financial problems which demanded the regular sale of Sporting's best players.

STEAUA
BUCHAREST, ROMANIA

Founded: 1947
Stadium: Steaua (30,000)
Colours: Red/blue
Honours: Champions Cup 1986; Supercup 1986; League 19; Cup 20.

Steaua of Bucharest were typical of an entire generation of clubs created or converted in eastern Europe after World War Two. Each country within the Eastern Bloc organized its sports clubs along similar subsidized, "state amateur" lines. The different state sectors had their own teams with the army club being traditionally the strongest.

That meant CSKA Moscow in the Soviet Union itself; CSKW Legia in Poland; CDNA (later CSKA) Sofia in Bulgaria; Dukla in Czechoslovakia; Vorwärts in East Germany; and AS Armata, later CSCA then CCA then, from 1961, Steaua (or Star) in Romania. The club was an umbrella sports body comprising facilities for football, volleyball, rugby, target shooting, athletics, tennis – Ilie Nastase was discovered playing football! – and basketball.

Up until the revolution of Christmas 1989, the balance of power in Romanian football was held between Steaua and Dinamo, the team of the secret police. As time went on, so Steaua got the upper hand thanks largely to the influential support of Valentin Ceaucescu, son of the dictator Nicolae Ceaucescu, who ordered the transfers of the country's best players to the army sports complex to the west of Bucharest.

Coached by Emerich Jenei, Steaua became the first eastern Europe team to win the Champions Cup when, in 1986, they defeated Terry Venables' Barcelona in Seville. A goal-less draw after extra-time was followed by a penalty shoot-out in which Steaua goalkeeper Helmut Ducadam proved unbeatable and the Romanians won 2–0.

Sweeper Miodrag Belodedici and striker Marius Lacatus were among Romania's finest players and Steaua had added midfielder Gheorghe Hagi – the country's greatest player – to their squad by the time they returned to the Champions Cup final in 1989. Not that his presence did them a lot of good in Barcelona as an out-of-sorts Steaua crashed 4–0 to Milan.

They maintained their domestic domination after the 1989 revolution but lacked the power to hold on to their star players. By the late 1990s officials were seriously considering severing all links with the army and "privatizing" the club.

TBILISI DYNAMO
GEORGIA

Founded: 1925
Stadium: Boris Paichadze (75,000)
Colours: All blue
Honours: Cup-Winners' Cup 1981; League 8 (Georgia 6, USSR 2 – Cup 8 (Georgia 6, USSR 2).

The political fragmentation of the Soviet Union in the early 1990s was felt in many ways in eastern European football. One was financial, with the ending of government subsidies; another was qualitative. The rigid police states had been able to prevent

players from transferring abroad. Without that protection, many clubs lost significant ground compared to their western European rivals.

Georgia had early warning of these developments, having seceded within the Soviet political and administrative structure two years before the ultimate collapse. Tbilisi's Dynamo club were both favourites and victims of the systems. In the 1950s and 1960s they travelled abroad frequently to earn hard currency through international friendly matches. Later they formalized that success by winning the European Cup-Winners' Cup courtesy

of a 2–1 victory over East Germany's Carl Zeiss Jena in Düsseldorf. Players such as centre-back Alexander Chivadze, midfielders David Kipiani and Vitali Daraselia and forward Ramaz Shengelia ranked among the finest in their positions in Europe. But Tbilisi could not build on their Dusseldorf foundations. Kipiani suffered a serious leg fracture in a friendly against Real Madrid then Daraselia was killed in a car crash.

Tbilisi dropped out of the international scene in the late 1980s when the Georgian federation seceded from the Soviet soccer system. Only after the

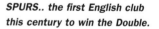

SPURS.. the first English club this century to win the Double.

Soviet collapse did Georgian football re-emerge. But in an era of open borders Tbilisi could not hold their players and outstanding talents such as schemer Georgi Kinkladze were quickly lost to cash-rich western Europe.

TOTTENHAM HOTSPUR
LONDON, ENGLAND

Founded: 1882
Stadium: White Hart Lane (33,083)

Colours: White/blue

Honours: Cup-Winners' Cup 1963; UEFA Cup: 1972, 1984; League 2; Cup 8; League Cup 2.

Since 1984 Tottenham Hotspur have not appeared in a European final, yet it says everything about the enduring romance of European football that Spurs' adventures between 1961 and 1963 should still retain a magical aura.

Danny Blanchflower was Spurs' captain leader from right-half; he had guided the team to the first English league and cup Double of the century. A team boasting Scotland left-half Dave Mackay, will o' the wisp inside-right John White and – later – deadly goalscorer Jimmy Greaves expected the onward march to continue untroubled through Europe.

But, in the first round of the 1961–62 Champions Cup, Spurs nearly came unstuck in Poland. Gornik Zabrze led them 4–0 before goals from Cliff Jones and Terry

Dyson hauled Spurs back from the brink. At White Hart Lane it was a different story. Spurs hit eight goals with three coming from Jones.

Feyenoord were beaten 3–1, 1–1 in the second round and Dukla Prague 0–1, 4–1 in the quarter-finals. The away leg in Prague saw Spurs bolster their defence by including defensive wing-half Tony Marchi instead of a forward. Manager Bill Nicholson used similar cautious tactics in the first leg of the semi-final away to holders Benfica but could not avert a 3–1 defeat. Spurs won the blood-and-thunder return 2–1 and narrowly went out of the competition.

It actually proved to have been good practice for the following season's Cup-Winners' Cup campaign, which ended in a triumphant 5–1 victory over Atletico Madrid in Rotterdam. Spurs thus became the first British team to win a European trophy.

Nine years later, at the expense of fellow English club Wolves, Spurs became the first holders of the newly-

presented UEFA Cup. They were runners-up to old foes Feyenoord in 1974, but regained the UEFA Cup, after a penalty shoot-out victory over holders Anderlecht in 1984. Along the way Tottenham electrified English football with an innovative transfer policy which included signing Argentine World Cup-winners Osvaldo Ardiles and Ricardo Villa in the summer of 1978. Domestic favourites such as Glenn Hoddle, Chris Waddle, Paul Gascoigne and Gary Lineker kept the fans' attention – as did a series of boardroom skirmishes.

It was chairman Alan Sugar who masterminded the signing in 1994 of German striker Jürgen Klinsmann who made an enormous impact on the English game in just one season. However, for all their occasional successes in the FA Cup remained as far away as ever from regaining the championship for the first time since the halcyon days of Blanchflower, White and Mackay.

VALENCIA
SPAIN

Founded: 1919

Stadium: Luis Casanova (49,291)

Colours: All white

Honours: Cup-Winners' Cup 1980: Fairs Cup 1962, 1963; Supercup 1980; League 4; Cup 5.

Valencia won the Spanish league championship three times in the post-civil war 1940s, but international recognition had to wait until the early 1960s. Then Valencia, seeking to emulate Real Madrid and Barcelona, underlined Spain's status as the top European nation at club level.

Real Madrid had won the European Champions Cup five times; Barcelona had won the Fairs Cup twice and Valencia stepped straight into their footsteps by reaching the Fairs Cup final themselves in three

HERO ... Argentina's Mario Kempes takes on Arsenal.

BEST OF ... Werder Bremen (left) outpaces Monaco in 1992.

consecutive years, 1962–64.

Valencia defeated Barcelona and Dinamo Zagreb respectively in the first two. The 1962 victory over Barcelona was an explosive occasion, Valencia winning the first leg 6–2, with a hat-trick from Spanish international Vicente Guillot, then drawing 1–1 in the Catalan capital.

A year later Valencia won both legs against Zagreb – 2–1 away and 2–0 at home. But it was not to be third time lucky for them, losing in the 1964 final to compatriots Zaragoza in a single-match tournament in Barcelona.

At domestic level, Valencia gave their fans little to celebrate. They won the league for the fourth time in 1971, then the cup for a fifth time in 1979. A year later Valencia regained European allure by winning the Cup-Winners' Cup.

The final against Arsenal in the Heysel stadium was a disappointment. Even Argentina's 1978 World Cup hero, Mario Kempes, was unable to engineer a breakthrough, but at least Valencia had the consolation of winning on penalties. They followed up this triumph by defeating another English club in the form of Brian Clough's Nottingham Forest on away goals to take the European Supercup.

Since then, absolutely nothing – despite the acquisitions of international stars such as Chilean striker Ivan Zamorano and Spain goalkeeper Andoni Zubizarreta.

WERDER BREMEN
GERMANY

Founded: 1899
Stadium: Weserstadion (29,850)
Colours: Green shirts (with white central panel), green shorts, white socks
Honours: Cup-Winners' Cup 1992; League 3; Cup 3.

Werder Bremen are one of the least fashionable clubs in Germany. However, over the years, they have been one of the most consistent.

Not for Bremen the big splash in the transfer market or the constant changing of coaches. Otto Rehhagel was boss for a decade before being lured away to Bayern Munich in 1995 and his wife was almost as well-known a figure around the Weserstadion.

Bremen won the cup for the first time in 1961, and then again in 1991 and 1994. As for the league championship, that was taken home to North Germany in 1965, 1988 and 1993.

The 1965 team's strength lay in defence where full-backs Horst-Dieter Hottges and Sepp Piontek were members of the West German squad who finished runners-up at the 1966 World Cup. Piontek went on to greater fame as the manager who turned Denmark's national team, in the 1980s, from an acorn into an oak – reaching the semi-finals of the 1984 European Championship and the second round of the 1986 World Cup finals.

In 1992 Bremen won their first European trophy when they defeated Monaco of France in the Cup-Winners' Cup final in the Benfica stadium in Lisbon. German veteran Klaus Allofs and New Zealander Wynton Rufer scored the goals in Bremen's 2–0 win but their success owed quite as much to the defensive command of Norway's Rune Bratseth. Their talents were later supplemented by Austrian schemer Andreas Herzog.

WEST HAM UNITED
LONDON, ENGLAND

Founded: 1895
Stadium: Upton Park (25,985)
Colours: Claret shirts with blue sleeves/white
Honours: Cup-Winners' Cup 1965; Cup 3.

West Ham have long been known as the "Football Academy", not only for the class of footballer they turn out but also for the class of football they play.

Never was that image better illustrated than on the day they won the Cup-Winners' Cup at Wembley in 1965 defeating Munich 1860 by 2–0 with both goals coming from Tony Sealey on a night which was a credit to English football.

Many of West Ham's heroes that night went on to greater things. Manager Ron Greenwood would take up the same post with England and lead them to the finals of both the 1980 European Championship and the 1982 World Cup. Left-half Bobby Moore captained England to victory in the 1966 World Cup triumph, supported by Martin Peters and Geoff Hurst. Hurst, of course, made history as the only man to score a hat-trick in a World Cup final.

It's an odd feature of West Ham's career in Europe that they have competed only in the Cup-Winners' Cup. In 1964–65 as FA Cup holders, the following season as defending champions. However, defeat both home and away at the hands of eventual winners Borussia Dortmund ended their European dream for nearly a decade.

After winning the FA Cup against Fulham in 1975 – this time with Moore playing against the at which he had justifiably become a legned – West Ham returned to Europe only to lose to Anderlecht in the Cup-Winners Cup final in Brussels.

THE KISS ... Bobby Moore with the FA Cup at Wembley in 1964.

EURO SOCCER STARS OF THE '90s

The game, as so many managers and coaches never tire of repeating, is all about players. That is more than ever true today with the advent of pan-European sports television followed by the Bosman Verdict's destruction of import/export restrictions. The fame of today's star players spreads far beyond their own national borders.

Abdullah Ercan
Turkey (born December 8, 1971)
Midfielder
Clubs: Fenerbahce, Trabzonspor.

Abdullah Ercan – known, Turkish-style, by his first name – was Turkey's best player in the finals of the 1996 European Championship. He had begun in the Fenerbahce youth sections but they did not think he would make the grade, so he was transferred to Trabzonspor with whom he made his league debut in 1991. Abdullah was a gold-medal winner with the Turkish Olympic under-21 team at the 1993 Mediterranean Games. His superb form in the run-up to Euro 96 for Trabzonspor attracted numerous scouts from foreign clubs, but he decided to stay in Turkey.

Tony Adams
England (born October 10, 1966)
Central defender
Club: Arsenal.

As a boy Adams always dreamed of playing for Arsenal and his dream came true at the age of 15. He made his league debut at 17 and his England debut in 1987 against Spain. Adams missed the 1990 World Cup finals in Italy, then displayed enormous strength of character to become captain of both Arsenal and England after serving a prison sentence for a motoring offence. He has captained Arsenal to two league championships, and to victories in finals of the FA Cup, League Cup and European Cup-Winners' Cup.

Demetrio Albertini
Italy (born August 23, 1971)
Midfielder
Clubs: Padova, Milan.

Albertini has proved an exemplary central midfielder both for Italy and for Milan – able to keep command of the ball deep in his own territory but find time for the creative passing which has offered so many counter-attacking opportunities for the likes of Savicevic and Weah. Albertini made his league debut for Milan, aged 17, in a 4–0 home win against Como in January 1989, and won his first cap in 1991 against Cyprus. It was only the second game in charge for former Milan coach Arrigo Sacchi, who called Albertini "the player who makes the side tick over".

Alfonso
(Full name: Alfonso Perez Muñoz)
Spain (born September 26, 1972)
Forward
Clubs: Castilla, Real Madrid, Real Betis, Real Madrid, Real Betis.

Alfonso has had a more complicated career than had appeared likely when

VICTORY SMILE for Arsenal's Tony Adams after the 1993 FA Cup Final replay.

he joined Real Madrid at 13 and later made an instant impact with Castilla, Madrid's nursery team. A powerful and direct striker, he played a starring role in Spain's gold-medal 1992 Olympic campaign. Two months later he made his full international debut, scoring his first goal three months later when Spain beat Latvia 5–0 in Seville. His career had a major setback when he suffered a cruciate ligament injury by inadvertently treading on the ball during Real Madrid's 5–0 defeat in Barcelona in January 1994. He thus missed the 1994 World Cup finals and, at the start of the following season, suffered an ankle injury which cost him another four months out. Madrid could not wait for him to get fit and bought Chilean striker Ivan Zamorano. When Alfonso was fit there was no place for him and he was sold to ambitious Betis for £3.5 million in 1995 with a buy-back clause which Madrid duly activated in 1996. Betis then offered Alfonso a significantly higher wage than Madrid were paying and, just two months later, bought him back.

Aljosa Asanovic

Croatia (born December 14, 1965)
Midfielder
Clubs: Hajduk Split, Metz (France), Cannes (France), Montpellier (France), Hajduk Split, Valladolid (Spain), Hajduk Split, Derby County (England).

Asanovic, a former youth, Olympic and full international for the former Yugoslavia, had to wait until his early 30s for recognition of his talents, at Euro 96. His first successes were in winning two Croat league championships and national cup competitions with Hajduk Split. He also scored one of modern Croatia's first international goals in a 2–1 win over the United States in Zagreb in 1990 – having chartered a private jet at his own expense to ensure he reached the match in time. Asanovic moved to France, but returned to Hajduk in 1994 even though the club were still, at the time, trying to recover £100,000 they claimed to have been owed under the terms of his original transfer to Metz. He joined newly-promoted Derby County in England after Euro 96.

MAN IN DEMAND Spanish Olympic title-winning striker Alfonso.

much more than a defender, having used his pace and vision to launch Milan into attack. Franco Baresi joined Milan in the summer of 1977 while elder brother Giuseppe joined local rivals Inter. Baresi made his international debut against Romania in 1982 and was a (non-playing) member of the World Cup-winning squad in Spain that same year. Suspension meant he missed Milan's wonderful European Champions Cup final victory over Barcelona in 1994, but he led the club to all their other modern triumphs including World Club Cup, Champions Cup and European Supercup as well as domestic league championship. Baresi had an incident-packed World Cup in 1994 – undergoing knee surgery in the middle of the finals yet returning to play superbly in the final against Brazil. Unfortunately, Baresi was one of the two Italians (Roberto Baggio was the other) who missed their penalties in the dramatic shoot out.

IN THE CLEAR *Croatia's Asanovic leaves Portugal's Tavares behind.*

Dino Baggio

Italy (born July 24, 1971)
Midfielder
Clubs: Torino, Internazionale, Parma.

Dino Baggio is no relation to star striker Roberto though his contribution, in a steadying midfield role, has been almost as important since he made his national team debut against Cyprus in 1991. Baggio is predominantly a ball-winner but he can also move forward to effect – as he demonstrated at the 1994 World Cup finals with important goals against Spain and Norway. He originally turned down the offer of a move from Juventus to Parma in the summer of 1994 – then thought better of it. Had he not had the change of heart, it would have been the teenaged Alex Del Piero who moved to Parma instead!

Krasimir Balakov

Bulgaria (born March 29, 1966)
Midfielder
Clubs: Etar Veliko Tarnovo, Sporting Clube (Portugal), Stuttgart (Germany).

Balakov was a boy wonder in Bulgaria where he made his top league debut at the age of 16 in 1982. He made his senior international debut against Denmark six years later, after overcoming a serious injury. Balakov was briefly suspended in 1990 when the Bulgarian Football Union found he had signed for both Etar and CSKA Sofia. Etar won the wrangle, but almost immediately they sold him on to Sporting Lisbon. Despite his midfield role, he was Sporting's 15-goal top scorer in the 1993–94 season. He and Petar Hubchev were then the only Bulgarians to play right through all their seven matches at the 1994 World Cup finals. Many observers at USA'94 put Balakov into their "Team of the Tournament", and German club Stuttgart duly took the transfer hint.

Franco Baresi

Italy (born May 8, 1960)
Sweeper
Club: Milan.

Baresi, now coming to the end of a wonderful one-club career, has been generally acknowledged as the best sweeper in the world for much of the 1980s and 1990s. But he has been

ONE-CLUB INSPIRATION *Milan's veteran sweeper Franco Baresi.*

Mario Basler

Germany (born December 18, 1968)
Midfielder
Clubs: VfL Neustadt-Weinstrasse,
Kaiserslautern, Rot-Weiss Essen,
Hertha Berlin, Werder Bremen,
Bayern Munich.

Basler may be one of the characters of
the German game but he has also
proved to be something of a late developer. As a youngster Kaiserslautern
did not rate him highly and let him go
to Rot-Weiss Essen on a free transfer
in 1989. Basler's determination to
make the grade eventually paid off
when he joined Werder Bremen from
Hertha Berlin in 1993 for £850,000.
Basler won the German cup in 1994
at the end of his first season with
Bremen. He was then the Bundesliga's
joint-top scorer in 1995 – with Heiko
Herrlich – on 20 goals. A specialist at
dead ball situations, Basler – nicknamed "Super Mario" – joined Bayern
Munich after the 1996 European
Championship finals.

NEW GENERATION
David Beckham is the
latest hero of Old
Trafford.

David Beckham

England (born May 2, 1975)
Midfielder
Clubs: Preston North End,
Manchester United.

Beckham was the outstanding discovery of the 1996–97 season in England
– right from the moment, on the opening day of the season, when he scored
an extraordinary goal from his own
half against Wimbledon. A hatful of
powerful long-range goals secured a
place in England's World Cup squad
while, simultaneously, Beckham
starred in Manchester United's
Champions League campaign.
Although Beckham was born in
Leytonstone, east London, and
had been on Tottenham Hotspur's
books as a youth player, he had
always wanted to play for United
and turned professional at Old
Trafford in 1992. He had a brief
spell on loan to Preston North End,
before returning to establish himself
in the United first team following the sale of Andrei
Kanchelskis to

Everton in the summer of 1995.
Beckham's form for Manchester
United won him the Professional
Footballers Association Young Player
of the Year 1997.

Radek Bejbl

Czech Republic (born August 29,
1972)
Midfielder
Clubs: Slavia Prague, Atletico
Madrid (Spain).

Bejbl was one of the international
discoveries of the 1996 European
Championship finals in England.
Although he lacked the pace and creativity of team-mate Patrik Berger,
Bejbl offered, by contrast, strength in
the tackle and reliability which were
key factors in the Czech Republic's
progress to runners-up spot at Euro 96.
Having just helped Slavia Prague to
win the league title for the first time in
49 years, Bejbl was lured away to
Spain by that country's champions,
Atletico Madrid.

Miodrag Belodedici

Romania (born May 20, 1964)
Sweeper
Clubs: Steaua, Crvena Zvezda
Beograd [Red Star Belgrade]
(Yugoslavia), Valencia (Spain), Real
Valladolid (Spain), Villarreal (Spain).

Belodedici's family comes from a
Romanian town which was on the
Serbian border. He played sweeper for

Steaua Bucharest, who became the first Eastern European club to win the European Champions Cup against Barcelona in Seville in 1986. Increasing unrest in Romania led to Belodedici going into exile in Belgrade, capital of the former Yugoslavia, in 1988 and his fine form with Crvena Zvezda (Red Star) led to both Romania and Yugoslavia wanting to select him for the 1990 World Cup finals, but he rejected both offers. In 1991, Belodedici became the first player to win the Champions Cup with two clubs when he added success with Crvena Zvezda to his victory with Steaua. He spent three-and-a-half seasons in international exile before resuming his career with Romania.

Patrik Berger

Czech Republic (born November 10, 1973)
Midfielder
Clubs: Slavia Prague, Borussia Dortmund (Germany), Liverpool (England).

The greatest natural talent discovered in Czech football in the 1990s. Berger

played originally in the youth sections of Sparta Prague, but they did not offer him a professional contract and old cross-city rivals Slavia did. He was twice a league championship runner-up with Slavia, but the top spot just eluded them. In the summer of 1995, Berger was transferred to Borussia Dortmund and he made an immediate impact in his first season, helping the German title-winners to reach the quarter-finals of the European Champions Cup. He scored four times in the Czech Republic's Euro 96 qualifying campaign and then their goal in the final defeat by Germany. After the finals, Berger was in great demand around Europe and he decided to sign for English club Liverpool.

Dennis Bergkamp

Holland (born May 10, 1969)
Forward
Clubs: Ajax, Internazionale (Italy), Arsenal (England).

Bergkamp was named after his father's football hero, Denis Law; however, the registrar refused to accept the spelling with one 'n' because it was considered

too similar to the girl's name Denise. He made his league debut for Ajax at 17 in a 2–0 home win against Roda in December 1986, and played for Ajax

RECORDS AHEAD for Arsenal striker Dennis Bergkamp.

MAKING NO MISTAKE Patrik Berger's penalty puts the Czech Republic ahead in the Euro 96 Final.

in the 1986–87 Cup-Winners' Cup while still a student. Bergkamp enjoyed great success at Ajax, winning the Dutch cup in 1987 and 1993, the European Cup-Winners' Cup in 1987 and the UEFA Cup in 1992. He was named Dutch Young Player of the Year in 1990 and made Youth and B international appearances before stepping up to the full side. Bergkamp played in the 1992 European Championship in Sweden and the following year signed – along with Wim Jonk – for Internazionale. He had trouble adapting to the football and lifestyle in Milan, although he collected a second UEFA Cup-winners' medal there, and was a member of the Dutch squad in the 1994 World Cup. In 1995, he moved to Arsenal and settled happily in London, forming a sharp striking partnership with Ian Wright. Bergkamp is expected to become Holland's leading international goalscorer, surpassing the 35 set by 1940s and 1950s star Faas Wilkes.

Vladimir Beschastnykh

Russia (born April 1, 1974)
Forward
Clubs: Moscow Spartak, Werder
Bremen (Germany) Santander (Spain).

Beschastnykh burst on to the scene at the age of 18 with two goals for Moscow Spartak in the 1992 Russian cup final against CSKA Moscow. It was one of his first games for the club, who became Russian champions in 1993 and 1994. Vladimir has a twin brother, Mikhail, who was sold by Spartak to Nizhni Novograd, while he left Spartak in 1994 for Werder Bremen in Germany. He scored 10 goals in his first season there, but found it difficult to adapt to the coaching change at Bremen when Otto Rehhagel left. Personal difficulties added to Beschastnykh's problems in adapting to both the football and lifestyle in Germany.

Oliver Bierhoff

Germany (born May 1, 1968)
Centre forward
Clubs: Essener SG, Schwarz-Weiss

Essen, Bayer Uerdingen, Hamburg, Borussia Mönchengladbach, Austria Salzburg (Austria), Ascoli (Italy), Udinese (Italy).

Germany's golden goal hero in the final of the 1996 European Championship against the Czech Republic, Bierhoff had also scored the Germans' first goal after appearing as a second-half substitute. Capped eight times at under-18 level, four times at under-19 and 10 times at under-21, Bierhoff earned selection with his goalscoring successes in Austria and Italy rather than in Germany, most notably when he was top scorer in Italy's Serie B in 1993–94 with Ascoli.

Slaven Bilic

Croatia (born September 11, 1968)
Defender
Clubs: Hajduk Split, Sibenik, Hajduk Split, Karlsruhe (Germany), West Ham United (England), Everton (England).

Bilic was the only university graduate in the Croatian squad at the 1996

European finals – having qualified as a lawyer. He won one national championship and two national cups while with Hajduk Split and, after being transferred, was appointed team captain during his first season with Karlsruhe because of his energy and positive attitude. The defender was voted into the 1994–95 Bundesliga "Team of the Season" by the German media. In the middle of the following season he moved countries again, joining England's West Ham United.

Joachim Bjorklund

Sweden (born March 15, 1971)
Central defender
Clubs: IFK Gothenburg, Brann Bergen (Norway), Vicenza (Italy), Rangers (Scotland).

Bjorklund was a member of the Swedes' under-21 side which lost narrowly to Italy in the 1992 European final 2–1 on aggregate. Quick to cover and firm in the tackle, Bjorklund is a nephew of national manager Tommy Svensson. His favourite film is *The Godfather* and his favourite football

CELEBRATION TIME for Germany's Oliver Bierhoff (left) and Matthias Sammer.

club as a boy was Leeds United. A key member of the Rangers team who achieved their record-equalling ninth successive league title in 1997.

Laurent Blanc

France (born November 19, 1965)
Sweeper
Clubs: Ales, Montpellier, Napoli (Italy), Nimes, Saint-Etienne, Auxerre, Barcelona (Spain).

Although Larent Blanc is now one of the most accomplished defenders in Europe, he began his career as an attacking midfielder – and it was in that position that he made his France debut in 1989 against the Republic of Ireland. His most prolific goal-scoring season was 1986–87, with 18 goals in 34 games for Montpellier. Blanc made his top division debut in July 1987, was a European under-21 championship winner with France in 1988 and also won the French cup in 1990 with

Montpellier. He had a spell in Italy – with Napoli – then returned home, to Auxerre, in July 1995, before joining Barcelona after Euro 96. Blanc scored the goal which gave France an impressive victory over Germany in Stuttgart on the eve of Euro 96.

Danny Blind

Holland (born August 1, 1961)
Sweeper
Clubs: Racing Club Souburg, Sparta Rotterdam, Ajax.

Blind is an experienced central defender whose career took off as a right-back with Sparta Rotterdam. Since his transfer to Ajax, Blind has won 14 titles including the Dutch championship four times, Dutch cup twice and Dutch Supercup three times and captained Ajax to victory in the 1995 European Champions Cup Final against Milan in Vienna. He has been unlucky in the European Cup-Winners' Cup: he missed Ajax's final victory in 1987 through injury and was sent off in their 1988 defeat by Mechelen. However, Blind was considered fortunate to have been available for the 1995 Champions Cup final, when he was shown only a yellow card for a handball offence in the second semi-final against Bayern Munich. With Ajax he also won the UEFA Cup in 1992, the Champions Cup and World Club Cup in 1995 and the European Supercup in 1996. For many years, Blind was

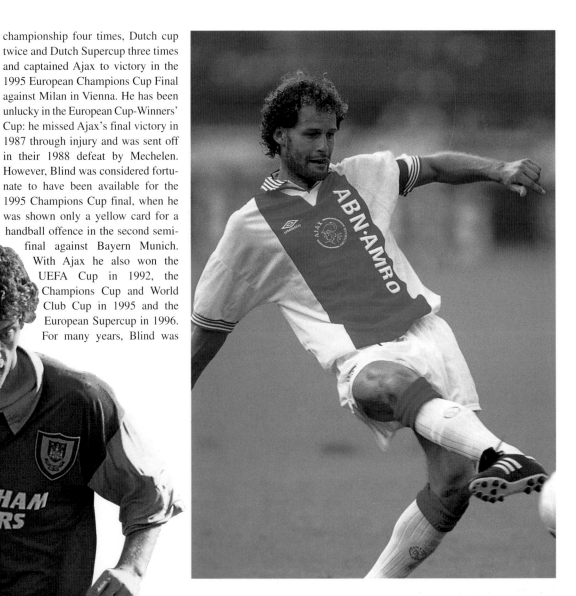

HEART OF THE ACTION The Ajax centre back Danny Blind.

Ronald Koeman's deputy as sweeper in the national team.

Jesper Blomqvist

Sweden (born February 5, 1974)
Forward
Clubs: Umea, IFK Gothenburg, Milan (Italy).

One of the most exciting players discovered in Sweden for years – until injury disrupted his career – Blomqvist, from the north of Sweden, was voted Young Player of the Year in 1993 when he joined IFK from minor club Umea. He was a member of the Swedish squad which finished third at the 1994 World Cup finals and followed up with crucial UEFA Champions League goals the following season against both Barcelona and Manchester United. Scored a superb goal for IFK in a 4–2 away defeat by Milan in the Champions League – which duly earned him a transfer to the Italian club.

Zvonimir Boban

Croatia (born October 8, 1968)
Midfielder
Clubs: Dinamo (later FC Croatia) Zagreb, Bari (Italy), Milan (Italy).

Boban was a member of the former Yugoslavia national team which won the 1987 World Youth Cup in Chile, and became Dinamo Zagreb's youngest-ever captain at 18. He became a national hero after he came to the defence of Croatian fans being manhandled by police at a high-tension match in the former Yugoslav league between Dinamo (now FC Croatia) and Crvena Zvezda (Red Star). Boban's intervention led to a

DEGREE OF CLASS Croatia's key defender, Slaven Bilic.

Rotterdam, but became a defender at Ajax, although he had to revert to his old position in the 1995–96 UEFA Champions League because of Marc Overmars' knee injury and the ineligibility of Peter Hoekstra. Bogarde enjoyed great success at Ajax, especially in 1995, when the club won the World Club Cup, European Supercup, European Champions Cup, Dutch league championship and Dutch Supercup. A year after Ajax had retained the Dutch league title and lost in the final of the Champions Cup, Bogarde moved to Milan on a free transfer, courtesy of the Bosman ruling.

Alen Boksic

Croatia (born January 31, 1970)
Striker
Clubs: Hajduk Split, Cannes (France), Marseille (France), Lazio (Italy), Juventus (Italy), Lazio (Italy).

Boksic's international career – and ambition to play in Italy – began early. He travelled to Rome at the age of 12 to play for Hajduk in a youth tournament and the only souvenir he bought was a Lazio shirt – the club for whom he later played. Boksic won one Yugoslav cup with Hajduk, scoring the only goal in a 1–0 win over Crvena Zvezda [Red Star] in Belgrade. Complications arising from a move to France – originally he was to join Marseille – meant that Boksic was suspended for a year. He finally joined the French giants from Cannes and, with Marseille, won the European Champions Cup, French league and French cup. Boksic was Footballer of the Year in Croatia for 1993, when he was also top scorer in France with 23 goals. In the wake of the match-fixing scandal in Marseille, he left the club to join Lazio. Boksic moved to Juventus in the summer of 1996, succeeding England-bound Fabrizio Ravanelli and Gianluca Vialli, but returned to Lazio after less than a year.

six-month suspension from the Belgrade-based Yugoslav federation, which cost him a place in the Yugoslavia squad at the 1990 World Cup finals. He remains the most expensive Croatian player, having cost £8 million when he left Croatia Zagreb for Milan, with whom he won three Italian championships and the European Champions Cup in 1994.

Winston Bogarde

Holland (born October 22, 1970)
Left-back
Clubs: SVV, Excelsior, SVV, Sparta, Ajax, Milan (Italy).

SLEIGHT OF FOOT as demonstrated at Euro 96 by Croatia's Zvonimir Boban.

Bogarde was a teenage talent who made his league debut at 17 for SVV in a 2–2 draw away to Heracles. He played as a left-winger at Sparta

Bulent Korkmaz

Turkey (born November 24, 1968)
Central defender
Club: Galatasaray.

Bulent Korkmaz – like compatriot Abdullah Ercan he is more frequently known by his first name – has been the

most consistent Turkish international in the 1990s having made his national team debut in 1990 against the Republic of Ireland. Domestic honours include multiple league cup and president's cup successes with Galatasaray, his only club. Bulent burst on to the scene as a 20-year-old member of the Galatasaray team which reached the European Champions Cup semi-finals in 1989.

Jorge Cadete

Portugal (born August 27, 1968)
Forward
Clubs: Santarem, Sporting Clube, Brescia (Italy), Sporting Clube, Celtic (Scotland).

Cadete rose to fame at Sporting under the coaching direction of former England team manager Bobby Robson, who appointed him club captain. He responded by becoming the league's top scorer with 18 goals in 1992–93. Cadete moved to play in Italy in 1994–95 but could not save Brescia from relegation and he then returned to Sporting. Strangely, he played in only one of Portugal's matches in the 1996 European Championship qualifying competition – appearing as a 66th-minute substitute for Domingos in Portugal's last game and scored the final goal in the final minute of the 3–0 win over the Irish Republic. Cadete left Portugal again, this time for Scotland, where he became Celtic top-scorer despite a drawn-out contract wrangle.

Jose Caminero

Spain (born November 8, 1967)
Midfielder
Club: Real Madrid, Castilla, Real Valladolid, Atletico Madrid.

Caminero began his career with Real Madrid, but they sold him to Valladolid because his route from nursery side Castilla to the first team was blocked by Michel. He was then converted to sweeper at Valladolid by Colombian coach Francisco Maturana. Caminero, signed for Atletico by president Jesus Gil for a £1 million fee in 1993, made his international debut in the September of that year as a substitute in a 2–0 friendly win over Chile in Alicante. He followed up by scoring Spain's first goal in his next match against

Albania. Despite being suspended from the second-round win over Switzerland, Caminero was Spain's three-goal top scorer at the 1994 World Cup finals.

Eric Cantona

France (born May 24, 1966)
Forward
Clubs: Martigues, Auxerre, Marseille, Bordeaux, Montpellier, Leeds United (England), Manchester United (England).

Cantona has been arguably the most successful foreign import into English football – winning league championships with both Leeds United and Manchester United, whom he captained to their 1996 league and cup double. Not only that, but Cantona

also scored the winning goal in the cup final against Liverpool, having scored twice against Chelsea in the 1994 cup final which clinched Manchester United's first double. His success in England was in marked contrast to his stormy career in France where a string of disciplinary incidents led to his being kicked around from one club to another. Not that Cantona has not shown in England why he is his own worst enemy. First he incurred a lengthy European ban for insulting a referee after the final whistle of a game against Galatasaray in Turkey, then he drew a seven-month suspension – plus a criminal court sentence – for attacking a Crystal Palace "fan" with a kung-fu kick at Selhurst Park after having been sent off. At one stage Cantona was also captain of France, but his falling out of favour with national coach Aimé Jacquet may have contributed to his sudden retirement in the summer of 1997.

Pierluigi Casiraghi

Italy (born March 4, 1969)
Centre forward
Clubs: Monza, Juventus, Lazio.

Casiraghi made his international debut in 1991 against Belgium but had to wait to establish himself because of a long-running rivalry with Fabrizio Ravanelli. A favourite of former national coach Arrigo Sacchi, he was picked for Italy without being a regular in the Lazio starting line-up. His height and strength earned him many comparisons with a traditional English centre forward and he has been frequently linked with possible transfers to the Premier League. His power both in the air and on the ground made him an unpopular opponent for defenders throughout the 1980s for Monza as a teenager then during four seasons apiece with Juventus – includein a UEFA Cup success – and Lazio.

Stephane Chapuisat

Switzerland (born June 28, 1969)
Striker
Clubs: Red Star Zurich, Lausanne-Sports, Malley, Lausanne-Sports, Bayer Uerdingen (Germany), Borussia Dortmund (Germany).

Son of a former Swiss international defender, Pierre-Albert Chapuisat, and

grandson of a former top division player, Stephane Chapuisat was the first of the new Swiss generation of players to move abroad in 1990. He collected the nickname "The Little Prince" – after the leading character of a popular story – early in his career. Chapuisat was regarded as the most outstanding player in the German Bundesliga in 1992–93. A German league championship winner with Borussia Dortmund in 1995 and 1996, he suffered a serious knee ligament injury which kept him out from March 1995 to February 1996, but by May 1997 he was fully fit and ready to help Dortmund to their Champions Cup win.

Stanislav Cherchesov

Russia (born September 2, 1963)
Goalkeeper
Clubs: Spartak Vladikavkaz, Lokomotiv Moscow, Spartak Moscow, Dynamo Dresden (Germany), Spartak Moscow, Tirol (Austria).

Cherchesov started with Spartak but became frustrated after four years as

GALLIC GLORY for Eric Cantona as FA Cup-winning skipper of Manchester United in 1996.

reserve to Rinat Dasayev and thus transferred to Lokomotiv in 1988. He returned to Spartak Moscow in 1989 after Dasayev's sale to Seville, but conceded five goals in his first game for Spartak Moscow – a 5–2 defeat by Zhalgiris Vilnius. Nevertheless, Cherchesov was in the Spartak team which won the league title in 1989, 1992 and 1993. He was a reserve to Dmitri Kharine at the 1992 European Championship finals for the Commonwealth of Independent States – the special name given to the successors to the Soviet Union squad in Sweden. He had a first farewell game organized in his honour when he left Spartak for Dynamo Dresden in 1993, and played an important role as the German side retained their place in the Bundesliga, despite being penalised four points in the 1993–94 season. Cherchesov returned to Spartak in the summer of 1995 – on a six-month loan from Dresden – to help his old club win their first round group in the

UEFA Champions League. His next move was not back to Dresden, but to Tirol in Austria, when his loan period ended in December 1995.

Enrico Chiesa

Italy (born December 29, 1970)
Striker
Clubs: Pontedecimo, Sampdoria, Teramo, Chieti, Modena, Sampdoria, Parma.

Chiesa has been tipped to follow Paolo Rossi and "Toto" Schillaci in the Italian tradition of outstanding, big-event strikers. But he is used to filling some pretty famous boots: at Sampdoria he followed Ruud Gullit and in Parma, a year later, it was Gianfranco Zola. His attacking pace and versatility – he can play both in the centre and wide on the left of attack – first attracted national coach Arrigo Sacchi's attention in the run-up to the 1996 European Championship finals. Chiesa's form for a Sampdoira side apparently in transition attracted the interest of many top clubs and he joined Parma after the Euro 96 finals, but problems within the club upset his form and cost him, temporarily, his place in the national squad.

John Collins

Scotland (born January 31, 1968)
Midfielder
Clubs: Hibernian, Celtic, Monaco (France).

Collins's home town of Galashiels, in the Scottish borders, is more renowned for producing rugby players than footballers. He made his league debut for Hibernian against Aberdeen in 1985, then joined Celtic for £900,000 in 1990. Collins scored on his debut for Scotland in a friendly international against Saudi Arabia in Riyadh in 1988. Renowned as a "dead ball" specialist, he was the only player to appear in all Scotland's matches in the 1996 European Championship – in both the qualifying competition and the finals. After Euro 96, Collins became the first major Scottish player to take advantage of the Bosman ruling when he moved on a free transfer to Monaco.

Alessandro Costacurta

Italy (born April 24, 1966)
Central defender
Clubs: Monza, Milan.

Italy's key man in the centre of defence since the international retirement of Franco Baresi, Costacurta has also played a central role in the successes of the great Milan side of the last decade. He made his international debut in Arrigo Sacchi's first game in charge – a 1–1 European Championship draw with Norway in Genoa in November 1991. Costacurta had a remarkable 1994 for all the wrong reasons: he was suspended from both Milan's European Champions Cup victory over Barcelona and Italy's World Cup final defeat by Brazil then, in the World Club Cup game against Velez Sarsfield, he was sent off. Alessandro's nickname is "Billy" because, as a youngster, he was a big fan of a Milan basketball team of the same name.

Fernando Couto

Portugal (born August 2, 1969)
Defender/midfielder
Clubs: FC Porto, Famalicao, Academica Coimbra, Porto, Parma (Italy), Barcelona (Spain).

Fernando Couto has the height to be an outstanding central defender and the technique to excel in midfield. He joined Porto originally from regional league club Lourosa at the age of 17 but was sent out on loan spells to Famalicao and Academica Coimbra. A year after playing in Portugal's 1989 World Youth Cup-winning team in Saudi Arabia, he returned to Poreto, and was a league champion in 1992 and 1993 and Portuguese cup-winner in 1991 and 1994. Fernando Couto joined Parma in 1994 and helped them win the UEFA Cup, as well as finish runners-up to Juventus in the Italian cup. He was sold to Barcelona after Euro 96 and duly added the 1997 Cup-Winners' Cup to his c.v.

Martin Dahlin

Sweden (born April 16, 1968)
Centre forward
Clubs: Lund, Malmo, Borussia Mönchengladbach (Germany), Roma (Italy), Borussia Mönchengladbach (Germany).

Dahlin became the first black player to

ALWAYS A DANGER Swedish striker Martin Dahlin at the 1994 World Cup finals.

appear in a senior international for Sweden when he made his debut in the 1–1 draw with Brazil in Stockholm in July 1991. He followed up with some spectacular goals for club and country but then had his career halted by a leg break. In the spring of 1992, Dahlin was sold to Borussia Mönchengladbach, but found it hard work adapting to higher standards of technique and fitness in Germany. He played a decisive, goal-scoring role in Sweden's 1994 World Cup qualification and then in the finals themselves. After being linked with clubs all over Europe, Dahlin finally left Borussia for Roma but failed to secure a first-team place and he returned to Borussia.

Edgar Davids

Holland (born March 13, 1973)
Midfielder
Clubs: Schellingwoude (Amsterdam), Ajax, Milan (Italy).

Davids has made headlines of both the right and wrong sort throughout his career – since making his Ajax league debut in a remarkable 5–1 win over RKC Waalwijk in September 1991. He was then a Dutch league champion in 1994 and 1995 with Ajax as well as Dutch cup winner in 1993 and Dutch Supercup winner in 1993, 1994 and 1995. Davids also helped Ajax win the World Club Cup, European Champions Cup and European Supercup in 1995 and the UEFA Cup in 1992. He was beaten to a place in Holland's 1994 World Cup squad by Rob Witschge of Feyenoord, but forced his way into the team for the European Championship finals in 1996. However, he then fell out with national coach Guus Hiddink and was sent home in disgrace after a row in training. Davids took advantage of the Bosman ruling to move on a free transfer to Milan but even that was marred when he suffered a serious leg fracture in the spring of 1997.

Frank de Boer

Holland (born May 15, 1970)
Central defender
Clubs: De Zouaven, Ajax.

Frank de Boer, twin brother of club-mate Ronald, has played more than 300 games for Ajax since making his debut in 1988–89 and has played more

ORANGE POWER *Dutch defender Frank de Boer has won every club prize with Ajax.*

than 50 times for his country, including the finals of the 1992 European Championship and the 1994 World Cup. Frank de Boer likes to advance for the occasional goal attempt and has succeeded Ronald Koeman as the national team's free-kick specialist. An injury ruled him out of the finals of the 1996 European Championship and he was badly missed – particularly against England at Wembley, where Holland crashed 4–1.

Ronald de Boer

Holland (born May 15, 1970)
Midfielder
Clubs: De Zouaven, Ajax, Twente Enschede, Ajax.

Ronald is the twin brother of defender Frank de Boer. The twins have been parted in their careers only for 18 months when Ronald played for Twente while Frank stayed with their long-time club, Ajax. Ronald made his league debut in a remarkable 6–4 Ajax victory over Pec Zwolle in November 1987. De Boer was an integral member of the Ajax squad which enjoyed a magical 1990s. Apart from the individual award of Dutch Footballer of the Year in 1994 and 1996, he has won the World Club Cup, European Supercup and European Champions Cup – all in 1995 – the Dutch league championship in 1990, 1994 and 1995, Dutch cup in 1993 and Dutch Supercup in 1993, 1994 and 1995. De Boer can play in a variety of positions but prefers the right side of midfield, although former Ajax coach Louis Van Gaal used him as centre forward, right-winger, left-winger and even, briefly, right-back.

Marc Degryse

Belgium (born September 4, 1965)
Forward
Clubs: Antwerp, Club Brugge, Anderlecht, Sheffield Wednesday (England), PSV Eindhoven (Holland).

Degryse is one of Belgium's most decorated internationals, having won more than 70 caps to add to his earlier appearances at youth, under-21 and Olympic international level. Degryse started his top-flight career with Antwerp, moving on to Brugge – when he was voted Players' Player of the Year – and then to Anderlecht for a domestic record £1.5 million in 1989. He repaid them by scoring 50 goals in the next four years. Degryse was as yet uncapped when he was a member of the 1984 European Championship squad, but then starred at the 1986 and 1990 World Cup finals. He had an 18-month spell in England with Sheffield Wednesday before joining PSV.

Alessandro Del Piero

Italy (born November 9, 1974)
Attacking midfielder
Clubs: Padova, Juventus.

The new "boy wonder" of Italian soccer and heir-apparent to Roberto Baggio. Del Piero made his league debut for Juventus in a 1–1 away draw with Foggia, in September 1993 then marked his first full league season with a hat-trick against Parma. He made his international debut in the 4–1 Euro 96 qualifying win against Estonia, on March 25, 1995, in Salerno. Del Piero has been kept busy ever since, in league and cup and UEFA Champions League as well as playing for Italy at senior, under-21 and military level. He scored in each of Juventus's first five games in their 1995–96 Champions League group and went on to help them win the cup. Del Piero was voted Italy's Young Player of the Year for 1995, thanks not merely to his general talent but to his striking success rate from free-kicks.

Marcel Desailly

France (born September 7, 1968)
Midfielder
Clubs: Nantes, Marseille, Milan (Italy).

Desailly was born in Accra, Ghana, and moved to France with his mother and brothers when a child. He became the first player to win the Champions Cup with two different clubs in successive seasons – having triumphed first with Marseille against Milan in 1993 then for Milan against Barcelona a year later. (Paulo Sousa

MEDAL SPECIALIST Didier Deschamps proved a European success with both Marseille and Juventus.

followed his example in 1996 and 1997.) Desailly's transfer to Italy was prompted by the financial collapse of Marseille following revelations that the club had been deeply involved in match-fixing. Desailly won the European Supercup with Milan in 1994 and the Italian league championship in 1994 and 1996. He was also a Champions Cup runner-up with Milan against Ajax in Vienna in 1995. Desailly scored his first goal for his adopted country during France's 10–0 defeat of Azerbaijan in a Euro 96 qualifier.

Didier Deschamps

France (born October 15, 1968)
Midfielder
Clubs: Bayonne, Nantes, Bordeaux, Marseille, Juventus (Italy).

Deschamps, like Desailly, has won the Champions Cup with French and Italian clubs. But, while they were team-mates at Marseille in 1993, Deschamps won his second European prize after transferring to Juventus. That success marked his 10th year in top-flight football since he made his league debut in August 1986.

Deschamps won French league championship medals with Marseille in 1990 and 1992 and the Italian championship with Juventus in 1995. Deschamps joined Juventus in July 1994, winning the Italian league and cup in his first season, as well as finishing runner-up in the UEFA Cup. His 46th cap – earned in a friendly against Portugal in January 1996 – took him into the top 20 of most-capped French players.

Deschamps will be one of France's key men in their hosts' assault on the 1998 World Cup.

RECORD MAN *Chelsea's FA Cup hero, Roberto Di Matteo.*

Angelo Di Livio
Italy (born July 26, 1966)
Midfielder
Clubs: Roma, Reggiana, Nocerina, Perugia, Padova, Juventus.

Di Livio played nine seasons in second division and regional football in Italy before breaking into the Juventus squad. He made his Serie A debut in 1993 – at the late age of 27 – against Roma, who had given him away on a free transfer in 1985. Nicknamed "the Little Soldier", his important role in Juventus's successes earned him a national team call-up at the age of 29.

Roberto Di Matteo
Italy (born May 29, 1970)
Midfielder
Clubs: Schaffhausen (Switzerland), Zurich (Switzerland), Aarau (Switzerland), Lazio, Chelsea (England).

Di Matteo was born in Switzerland to Italian parents and made his senior league debut in the Swiss championship with Schaffhausen in 1988–89. His dual nationality qualification made him a priority transfer target for Italian clubs and he eventually chose to go to Lazio in 1993 – making his Serie A debut in a 0–0 home draw against Foggia. Di Matteo made his international debut as a late substitute for Demetrio Albertini in the surprise 2–1 Euro 96 qualifying defeat by Croatia in Parma in November 1994. He was one of the few Italian successes at Euro 96, subsequently joining Chelsea for whom he struck a record 43rd-second goal in the 1997 FA Cup final.

Youri Djorkaeff
France (born March 9, 1968)
Midfielder/forward
Clubs: Grenoble, Strasbourg, Monaco, Paris Saint-Germain, Internazionale (Italy).

Football runs in Youri Djorkaeff's family – father Jean played full-back for France at the 1966 World Cup finals in England. Youri first earned international praise as a member of the Monaco side beaten in the 1992 Cup-Winners' Cup Final by Werder Bremen. He was leading scorer in the top division in 1993–94, with 20 goals, and signed for Paris Saint-Germain in June 1995 – 25 years to the day after his father had signed for the club. After being voted French Footballer of the Year by the sports newspaper *L'Equipe*, he was outstanding in Paris Saint Germain's victory over Rapid Vienna in the 1996 European Cup-Winners' Cup final. Djorkaeff played in the 1996 European Championship finals, after which he transferred to Internazionale for whom he was soon scoring some typically spectacular goals.

Domingos
(*Full name: Domingos Jose Paciencia Oliveira*)
Portugal (born January 2, 1969)
Forward
Club: FC Porto.

Domingos is a former World Youth Cup-winner who grew up into one of the most dangerous goal scorers in Europe. The second highest Portuguese scorer in 1990–91 with 24

FOOTBALL IN THE FAMILY
French forward Youri Djorkaeff.

goals, he managed only 23 in the next three seasons because of injuries. He recovered to become Porto's top scorer once again in 1994–95 with 19 goals and the best in the entire league with 25 goals in 1995–96. Domingos

won seven championships with Porto between 1988 and 1997 as well as the Portuguese cup in 1988, 1991 and 1994 – making him one of the most successful Portuguese footballers of all time. Former Porto coach Bobby

Robson compared his qualities in the penalty box with those of former World Footballer of the Year, George Weah.

Dieter Eilts

Germany (born December 10, 1964)
Midfielder
Club: Werder Bremen.

Eilts joined Bremen at the age of 20 and was twice a league championship winner with them, in 1988 and 1993. He has also been twice a German cup winner with Bremen in 1991 and 1994, and was a key member of Bremen's only European trophy-winning team, in the 1992 Cup-Winners' Cup. He has spent his entire professional career with Werder Bremen where he became club captain. Considered the best defensive central midfielder over recent seasons in the Bundesliga – and nicknamed "Mr Reliable" – Eilts was voted the tournament's best player after helping Germany to win the 1996 European Championship.

Luis Figo

Portugal (born November 4, 1972)
Midfielder
Clubs: Sporting Clube, Barcelona (Spain).

Figo was a great young achiever as a European champion at under-16 level in 1989 in Denmark and a World Youth Cup-winner in 1991 against Brazil in Lisbon. He was also a member of the Portuguese squad which reached the finals of the European Under-21 Championship in France in the 1993–94 season and a winner of the Portuguese cup with Sporting Clube in 1995. In the spring of 1995, both Juventus and Parma claimed Figo would be joining them at the season's end, but both clubs later withdrew their interest and Figo was transferred, instead, to Barcelona. He was an instant success in Spain, and soon proved his worth by helping Barcelona to victory in the European Cup-Winners' Cup in 1997. His only regret was that the demands of busy Barcelona – in a 22-club league with Spanish cup and European commitments – made it difficult for him to obtain regular release to join the Portuguese national team training sessions.

Paul Gascoigne

England (born May 27, 1967)
Midfielder
Clubs: Newcastle United, Tottenham Hotspur, Lazio (Italy), Rangers (Scotland).

Paul Gascoigne has been an outstanding talent whose career has been dogged by injuries and controversy. He cost Tottenham Hotspur £2 million from Newcastle in 1988, and his superb displays – allied to his televised tears as England went out of the World Cup in Italy two years later – helped to make him a national figure. Gascoigne was carried off with a career-threatening knee injury after fouling Nottingham Forest's Gary Charles early in the 1991 FA Cup final, which Spurs won, and the medal he received – in hospital –

GEORDIE JOY Paul Gascoigne celebrates his Euro 96 goal against Scotland.

remains his only English honour. In June 1992 he moved to Lazio for £5.5 million, equalling the British record. A succession of injuries and off-field problems meant that Gascoigne could not inspire Lazio to meaningful success. He joined Rangers in the summer of 1995 for £4.3 million and he made an immediate impact which earned him the Scottish Footballer of the Year award as the Glasgow side completed a league and cup double. Gascoigne scored a wonderful goal against Scotland in the 1996 European Championship, but revelations over his domestic problems during another injury-plagued season in 1996–97 cost him a lot of public sympathy.

Ryan Giggs

Wales (born November 29, 1973)
Left-winger
Club: Manchester United.

Giggs has been called the new George Best – not for his off-field antics but for the talent to leave opposing defenders for dead. The son of a rugby union and league player Danny Wilson (Giggs is his mother's family name), he played football for England schoolboys but, having been born in Cardiff, later opted to represent Wales at senior level. Manchester United manager Alex Ferguson was fiercely protective of Giggs's talent, keeping the media at bay and vetting the potential sponsors queueing at his door. Even successive Wales national managers were held at arm's length and, even though Giggs made his national team debut as a teenager, he reached his mid-20s without ever having played in a friendly international. He demonstrated his international quality to the full in United's 1996–97 Champions League campaign, when he was particularly inspirational in the 4–0 first-leg thrashing of FC Porto in the quarter-finals.

David Ginola

France (born January 25, 1967)
Left-winger
Clubs: Toulon, Brest, Paris Saint-Germain, Newcastle United (England) Tottenham Hotspur (England).

Ginola, a former French Footballer of the Year, has often been a magnet for controversy. Born near Marseille, he made his name with Toulon and Brest, though both clubs were relegated during his spells with them. Marseille and Paris both bid to sign him, but Ginola preferred Paris because, he said, playing for Marseille would have been "too easy". He became an instant hero on Tyneside after Kevin Keegan signed him for Newcastle in 1995, but he was reported to be getting homesick even before the arrival of the less-impressed Kenny Dalglish as manager at the start of 1997. Ginola has also enjoyed a mixed national team career. In 1993, he publicly demanded a place in the team alongside Jean-Pierre Papin and Eric Cantona but, when given the chance, he gave away possession fatally in the Paris defeat by Bulgaria which cost France a place in the World Cup finals. Aimé Jacquet ignored Ginola when it came to choosing his squad for the European finals in 1996 even though France were based around Newcastle.

Josep Guardiola

Spain (born January 18, 1971)
Midfielder
Club: Barcelona.

Guardiola, a former youth and under-21 international, has been one of the few Spanish players certain of their place with Barcelona through the 1990s. One of only a handful of local boys to force his way into the team, Guardiola plugged the midfield gap caused by the 1991 departure of Luis Milla for Real Madrid. Guardiola, from the Barcelona suburb of Manresa, was promoted into the Spanish national team after only 20 games for Barcelona. Also in 1992, he won the Prix Bravo, which is awarded annually to the outstanding under-23 footballer in Europe. In 1997 Guardiola became a transfer target for Italian club Parma. The dispute which followed over a buy-out clause in his Barcelona contract threatened to turn Guardiola into a Spanish Bosman.

Julen Guerrero

Spain (born January 7, 1974)
Forward
Club: Athletic Bilbao.

Guerrero is the latest hero of the fiercely independent Basque region in Spain – turning down a stream of lucrative offers from Barcelona and Madrid to stay with his local Bilbao club. Given his league debut by German coach Jupp Heynckes in 1992 in a 2–1 win over Cadiz, he became Spain's second-youngest international of all time when he played the first 63 minutes of Spain's 1–1 draw with Mexico in January 1993. His first two international goals secured a 2–0 victory over Lithuania in Vilnius. At the 1994 World Cup finals, Guerrero played only 45 minutes against South Korea and 90 minutes against Bolivia because coach Javier Clemente preferred the greater experience of Caminero in the linking role. Guerrero – whose surname translates as "Warrior" – is under contract at Bilbao until 2007 and the release clause stipulates £7.5 million "compensation". Such is his popularity – especially with female fans – that he needs police protection during training camps in Spain.

Gheorghe Hagi

Romania (born February 5, 1965)
Midfielder
Clubs: Constanta, Sportul Studentesc, Steaua, Real Madrid (Spain), Brescia (Italy), Barcelona (Spain), Galatasaray (Turkey).

Hagi is Romania's greatest ever player – scoring his first international goal against Northern Ireland in a World Cup qualifier in September 1984 when still only 19. He was top league marksman in 1985–86 with 31 goals for Sportul and later transferred to Steaua at the insistence of the ruling Ceausescu family. Steaua were league and cup double-winners three consecutive times. Hagi moved abroad in 1990, joining Real Madrid after the World Cup finals in Italy. He was ever-present at the 1994 World Cup finals in the United States, where he scored three goals, and he followed his World Cup success by returning to Spain with Barcelona after a spell in Italian football with Brescia. Hagi has invested some of his savings in a modern dental surgery in Bucharest.

Hakan Sukur

Turkey (born September 1, 1971)
Centre forward
Clubs: Sakaryaspor, Bursaspor, Galatasaray, Torino (Italy), Galatasaray.

Hakan was the Turkish league's 38-goal top scorer in 1996–97, and his country's prospects of international success – which means qualifying for major finals tournaments – rest largely on his shoulders. He joined Galatasaray originally from Bursaspor in 1992 and has been regularly Galatasaray's leading marksman having scored 19 goals in 1992–93, 16 goals in 1993–94 and 19 again in 1994–95. He was also a member of Turkey's gold medal-winning team at the 1993 Mediterranean Games. He impressed Torino officials with a spectacular goal against Switzerland in Berne in a Euro 96 qualifier, and they signed him for £3 million in the summer of 1995. Hakan grew homesick in Italy, however, and was sold back to Galatasaray in November – for the same fee – after scoring one goal in five league games for Torino. In April 1997 he scored the only goal in Turkey's shock 1–0 defeat of Holland in a World Cup qualifying match.

Thomas Hässler

Germany (born May 30, 1966)
Midfielder
Clubs: Meteor 06 Berlin, Reinickendorfer Fuchse, Köln, Juventus (Italy), Roma (Italy), Karlsruhe.

Hässler has been one of the finest German – indeed, European – players of the 1990s.

EUROPE'S NUMBER ONE in 1992 midfielder Thomas Hässler.

He came up steadily through the international set-up – playing 12 times for Germany's Olympic team, including the bronze medal-winning side at the 1988 Olympic Games in Seoul. He was voted German Footballer of the Year in both 1989 and 1992, was a World Cup winner in 1990 and a European Championship winner in 1996, having been voted the most outstanding player at the 1992 European Championship finals in Sweden. Hässler so impressed Juventus, playing against them for Köln in the 1989–90 UEFA Cup, that the Italian club signed him at the season's end for a Köln record of about £5.5 million. He spent only one season with Juventus before being sold to Roma in 1991 for a reported £5.8 million. Hässler returned to Germany with Karlsruhe in 1994.

Helder

Portugal (born March 21, 1971)
Central defender
Clubs: Estoril, Praia, Benfica, La Coruna (Spain).

Helder won a Portuguese league championship with Benfica in 1994, having collected a Portuguese cup-winner's medal with the same club a year earlier. One of the latest African-born players to maintain the tradition of building an international career in Portugal, he scored his first goal for his adopted country in only his second international, a 1–1 draw against Austria. Helder, one of Portugal's defensive stalwarts at Euro 96, is considered to be one of the most dependable and versatile central defenders in Europe at the present time.

Thomas Helmer

Germany (born April 21, 1965)
Central defender
Clubs: Bad Salzuflen, Arminia Bielefeld, Borussia Dortmund, Lyon (France), Bayern Munich.

Helmer, a rugged, courageous centre back, joined Bayern amid a certain amount of controversy in 1992. Dortmund did not want to sell to German rivals so Helmer joined French club Lyon – and then Bayern a month later for £3.2 million, a deal that made him Bayern's most expensive player at the time. Berti Vogts

threatened to drop him from the 1992 European Championship squad because of the distraction the transfer controversy was causing. A winner of both German championship and cup, Helmer's preferred position is sweeper or libero, though he has played most of his football at top level as man-marker.

Colin Hendry

Scotland (born December 7, 1965)
Central defender
Clubs: Dundee, Blackburn Rovers

(England), Manchester City (England), Blackburn Rovers (England).

Hendry is an inspirational central defender who has proved a rock at both club and country level. Currently in his second spell with Blackburn – having rejoined the club from Manchester City in 1992 for a reported fee of £700,000 – he won an English league championship medal with Rovers in 1993–94. Hendry scored his first international goal against Malta in a 1994 World Cup qualifying tie, but con-

ceded the penalty kick against Greece in Athens which led to Scotland's only defeat in the Euro 96 qualifiers.

Andreas Herzog

Austria (born September 10, 1968)
Midfielder
Clubs: First Vienna, Rapid Vienna, Werder Bremen (Germany), Bayern Munich (Germany), Werder Bremen (Germany).

Herzog was a Rapid Vienna youth product who did not start to play to his

ROVERS' ROCK Blackburn's Scotland defender Colin Hendry.

potential until after he had been sent out on loan to neighbouring First Vienna. His fine form earned a national team call so Rapid, despite his own reluctance, forced First Vienna to send him back. Former Rapid boss Hans Krankl used to call him the "White Gullit". Herzog's father was also a first division player and Andreas fulfilled his potential eventually when he moved to

Germany, inspiring Werder Bremen's 1994 championship win and being rated the most valuable foreign player in the Bundesliga. His 1994–95 Champions League campaign with Bremen came to a sad end when he was sent off in their penultimate game against FC Porto. Herzog joined Bayern Munich in the summer of 1995 but never settled and returned after less than a year to Werder Bremen.

Fernando Hierro

Spain (born March 23, 1968)
Midfielder/defender
Clubs: Malaga, Real Valladolid, Real Madrid.

Real Madrid's captain in 1997, Hierro joined the club from Real Valladolid for £1.4 million in 1989 – he had only been given the chance at Valladolid because his elder brother Manolo was at the club. Hierro contributed seven goals to Madrid's league record of 107 under John Toshack in the 1989–90 season, having made his international debut in September 1989, when Luis Suarez sent him on to replace the injured Andrinua after 24 minutes of a 1–0 win over Poland in La Coruña. Hierro was a non-playing substitute at the 1990 World Cup finals, but played in every game in the 1994 finals – scoring Spain's opening goal in their 3–0 second round win over Switzerland. He played half of the 1995–96 campaign as a central defender – while Jorge Valdano was Real Madrid's coach – then switched back to playing in midfield.

Paul Ince

England (born October 21, 1967)
Midfielder
Clubs: West Ham United, Manchester United, Internazionale (Italy), Liverpool.

Ince was outstanding as a youth player with West Ham, who received £800,000 for him when he joined Manchester United in 1989. Six years later United transferred him to Italy for £7.5 million. While at Old Trafford, Ince helped United win the Premiership twice, the FA Cup twice, the League Cup and the Cup-Winners' Cup. He had played only twice for the England under-21 team before gaining his first full cap under Graham Taylor. Ince became the first black man to captain England, in the 2–0 defeat at the hands of the United States at Boston in 1993.

Trifon Ivanov

Bulgaria (born July 27, 1965)
Central defender
Clubs: Etar Veliko Tarnovo, CSKA (later Levski) Sofia, Betis (Spain), Xamax Neuchatel (Switzerland), CSKA, Rapid Vienna (Austria).

This intimidating-looking defender has wandered imposingly around European football. Not content with taking out opposing strikers, Ivanov enjoys thundering in long-range shots on opposing goals. His most memorable goal was from a volley in a 3–0 Euro 96 qualifying win over Wales in Cardiff. Ivanov joined Betis of Seville in Spain from Levski in the middle of the 1990–91 season, left them after their relegation to the Spanish second division and moved to Xamax on loan in January 1994 as replacement for Eygptian defender Hany Ramzy. He was a key figure in the Bulgaria side which reached the semi-finals of the 1994 World Cup – missing only the second round win over Mexico through suspension. Later Ivanov was "father figure" of the Rapid team

LEADING BY EXAMPLE Fernando Hierro, captain of Real Madrid.

which finished runners-up to Paris Saint-Germain in the 1995–96 European Cup-Winners' Cup.

Robert Jarni

Croatia (born October 26, 1968)
Left-back
Clubs: Hajduk Split, Bari (Italy), Torino (Italy), Juventus (Italy), Real Betis (Spain).

Jarni is the quickest sprinter in the Croatia national team, having been timed at 11 seconds for 100 metres in soccer boots. A member of the former Yugoslavia national team which won the World Youth Cup in Chile in 1987, he went on to play for Yugoslavia at the 1990 World Cup finals in Italy. His departure from Hajduk Split was followed by a complicated legal dispute over £500,000 he claimed he was due from the transfer to Bari. Jarni won the Italian league and cup with Juventus and the Croatian cup twice with Hajduk Split. He missed only one of Croatia's matches in the 1996 European Championship qualifying and finals campaign. Jarni was the proud owner of a valuable collection of wrist-watches – until a burglar broke into his home in Turin in 1996.

Jordi

(Full name: Johan Jordi Cruyff)
Holland (born February 9, 1974)
Midfielder/forward
Clubs: Ajax, Barcelona (Spain), Manchester United (England).

Jordi is the son of Johan Cruyff, Holland's greatest-ever footballer, who named his boy after the patron saint of Catalonia. He played in the Ajax youth sections when his father was head coach in the mid-1980s then moved to Barcelona when his father was appointed manager there in 1988. Jordi made his top division debut in Spain in a Barcelona 2–1 defeat away to Gijon in September 1994, and later in the year was a Spanish Supercup winner. For several years he refused to commit himself to either Holland or Spain, so as not to jeopardize his dual nationality qualifications. However, in the spring of 1996, after recovering from a career-threatening knee injury, he decided to throw in his lot with Holland, for whom he played in the European Championship finals. His father's acrimonious departure as

THE SON ALSO RISES Jordi Cruyff, son of Johan.

Barcelona coach meant the writing was also on the wall for Jordi and he was duly bought by Alex Ferguson at Manchester United.

Miroslav Kadlec

Czech Republic (born June 26, 1964)
Defender
Clubs: Slavia Uherske Hradiste, RH Cheb, TJ Vitkovice, Kaiserslautern (Germany).

Kadlec has been one of the most resolute international defenders since making his debut for the former Czechoslovakia against Wales in 1987. Originally a stopper, he later switched to sweeper with great effect. Kadlec joined Vitkovice from Cheb in 1985 and was a major influence in their surprise league championship victory a year later. A member of the Czechoslovakia team which reached the 1990 World Cup quarter-finals in Italy, he transferred to Germany where

he won the league title a year later with Kaiserslautern. Kadlec was named Man of the Match in Kaiserslautern's 1–0 win over Karlsruhe in the 1996 German cup final.

Andrei Kanchelskis

Russia (January 3, 1969)
Midfielder/right-winger
Clubs: Zvezda Kirovograd, Dynamo Kiev, Shakhtyor Donetsk, Manchester United (England), Everton (England), Fiorentina (Italy).

Kanchelskis, for all his right-wing talent, has not proved the easiest player for successive managers to handle over the years. Born to a Lithuanian father and a Ukrainian mother, he was transferred to Shakhtyor Donetsk in 1990 after a short spell with Dynamo Kiev. He played for the Commonwealth of Independent States – the title given to the former Soviet Union squad for the 1992 European Championship finals in Sweden – and he gave up his Ukrainian citizenship to play for

Russia at international level. After moving to England, Kanchelskis was Manchester United's 14-goal top league marksman and a league champion in 1993 and 1994. However, he then abruptly forced a transfer to Everton, whom he left – as suddenly as he had come – in spring 1997 to move to Italy with Fiorentina. Kanchelskis missed the 1994 World Cup finals because, along with several other foreign-based stars, he refused to play under the management of Pavel Sadyrin.

Christian Karembeu

France (December 3, 1970)
Midfielder
Clubs: Nantes, Sampdoria (Italy).

Karembeu may have played virtually all his career in France but he was voted Oceania Footballer of the Year in 1995 – because he had been born and brought up in New Caledonia in the South Seas. He made his league debut in France in 1991 and was a national champion in 1995 with Nantes. His hot temper got him into trouble early in his career; for instance, Karembeu was sent off during Nantes' 1993 French cup final defeat by Paris Saint-Germain and then again during France's 0–0 draw with Poland in the 1996 European Championship qualifiers. After transferring to Sampdoria, he made a banner protest to show his opposition to French nuclear tests in the South Pacific at an Italian league match.

Valeri Karpin

Russia (born February 2, 1969)
Midfielder
Clubs: Spartak Tallinn, CSKA Moscow, Fakel Voronezh, Spartak Moscow, Real Sociedad (Spain).

Karpin earned a place in history by scoring the first goal for the "new" Russia – from a penalty after 61 minutes of a 2–0 win over Mexico in Moscow in August 1992. He was also considered one of the team's most tactically intelligent players. After winning the 1993 and 1994 Russian league titles with Spartak Moscow, Karpin was sold to Real Sociedad of Spain. A versatile midfielder, he has been used in the centre by Real Sociedad, but mainly on the right side for Russia.

GOLDEN BOY Kiko was Spain's Olympic top scorer in 1992.

Roy Keane

Republic of Ireland
(born August 10, 1971)
Midfielder
Clubs: Cobh Ramblers, Nottingham Forest (England), Manchester United (England).

Keane is probably the most outstanding midfield player in the English league. A powerhouse midfielder, he was a bargain buy when Brian Clough signed him for Nottingham Forest from League of Ireland club Cobh Ramblers. Forest used Keane on the right of midfield – a role he held after transferring to Manchester United in July 1993 for £3 million. After Paul Ince's departure for Italy, Keane switched to the centre of midfield and anchored United's league and cup double-winning team in 1995–96. A fiery temper has brought him more suspensions than manager Alex Ferguson would have liked, and Keane also had a stormy relationship with Republic of Ireland manager Mick McCarthy before making his peace. He made his first international appearance – under the management of McCarthy's predecessor Jack Charlton – against Chile in May 1991.

Dmitri Kharine

Russia (September 8, 1968)
Goalkeeper
Clubs: Torpedo Moscow, Spartak Moscow, Dynamo Moscow, CSKA Moscow, Chelsea (England).

Kharine was a teenage prodigy of a goalkeeper. He made his top division debut at the age of 16 for Torpedo and his debut in European club competition at 18. At 20 he was an Olympic champion in Seoul at the 1988 Games. A year later, his career appeared to be over after he was badly injured but, thanks to specialist treatment in Spain, Kharine was able to return between the posts. After quitting Dynamo Moscow, he won a league championship in 1991 with the army club, CSKA Moscow. Kharine played in all three of the Commonwealth of Independent States' – the successor to the former Soviet Union – games at the 1992 European Championship finals in Sweden, but left Russia to continue his club career in England with Chelsea. His younger brother, also a goalkeeper, has played for Torpedo and in the Russian youth team.

Kiko

(Full name: Francisco Narvaez Machon)
Spain (born April 26, 1972)
Forward
Clubs: Cadiz, Atletico Madrid.

Kiko, a tall and rangy right-side attacker, made his name by becoming the top-scoring player for Spain's gold medal-winning Olympic side in Barcelona in 1992. His five goals included the last-minute winner in the final against Poland. Then he surprisingly fell out of international favour for two years until being recalled for a 3–0 win over FYR Macedonia in November 1995 – when he scored his first full international goal for Spain. Kiko's early club career was a struggle. He had joined Cadiz at 13 and spent six years living in a boarding-house while playing decisive roles in two relegation play-offs against Figueras and Malaga. He scored 12 goals in 78 games for Cadiz and when Cadiz were finally relegated in 1993, he was sold for £500,000 to Atletico Madrid.

Georgi Kinkladze

Georgia (born July 6, 1973)
Forward
Clubs: Tbilisi Dynamo, Manchester City (England).

Kinkladze was the finest player to appear in the English First Division –

the division below the Premiership – in 1996–97. Many western clubs had coveted his close control and vision – as well as those further afield. After inspiring Tbilisi Dynamo to victory in the league and cup double in 1995 – when he was also runner-up in the Georgian Footballer of the Year poll – Kinkladze had a trial with Boca Juniors in Argentina. That was too far away, however, and he was homesick so he returned to Europe in a £2 million transfer to Manchester City. Even his skills could not save them from relegation in 1996. Kinkladze scored superb goals both home and away against Wales in the 1996 European Championship qualifying competition and some magical ones for Manchester City too.

Sergei Kiriakov

Russia (born January 1, 1970)
Forward
Clubs: Dynamo Moscow, Karlsruhe (Germany).

Kiriakov became an instant fans' favourite with first Dynamo Moscow, then Karlsruhe in Germany thanks to his brilliant ball control. Ever the man for the big occasion, he marked his Soviet Union debut with a goal against Poland in Lublin, in August 1989. His pace and trickery created numerous chances for Dynamo, yet he scored only nine league goals himself in five years. Kiriakov joined Karlsruhe in 1992, scoring 11 goals in the first season and nine in the second. He was also a key contributor to the club's excellent 1994–95 UEFA Cup campaign in which they reached the semi-finals. Kiriakov – nicknamed "Kiki" after a German cartoon character – played for the Commonwealth of Independent States at the 1992 European Championship finals after the Soviet Union break-up, but missed the 1994 World Cup finals following a dispute with manager Pavel Sadyrin.

Jürgen Klinsmann

Germany (September 30, 1964)
Striker
Clubs: Gingen, Geislingen, Stuttgarter Kickers, VfB Stuttgart, Internazionale (Italy), Monaco (France), Tottenham Hotspur (England), Bayern Munich, Sampdoria (Italy).

Klinsmann must be the richest baker in the world after a string of lucrative transfers which have seen him starring in four countries – Germany, Italy, France and England. "Klinsi" was top scorer in the German league with 19 goals in 1987–88, a UEFA Cup winner with Internazionale in 1991 and runner-up with Stuttgart in 1989. He has been voted Footballer of the Year in Germany – in 1988 and 1994 – and in England in 1995, the latter on the strength of his one season with Tottenham Hotspur, where he scored 29 goals. His most memorable international performance was in inspiring West Germany to a 2–1 win over Holland in the second round of the 1990 World Cup finals. Klinsmann returned to Germany with Bayern Munich in 1995 and scored a record 15 goals on their way to UEFA Cup success the following May. He then took over as captain of Germany from injured Lothar Matthäus and led his country – despite injury – to victory in the 1996 European Championship.

Patrick Kluivert

Holland (September 1, 1976)
Centre forward
Clubs: Schellingewoude, Ajax, Milan (Italy).

Kluivert is, to many experts, the finest natural Dutch talent since Johan Cruyff. A product of the noted Ajax junior system, he made a sensational debut at 18 in a 3–0 win over old rivals Feyenoord in the 1994 Dutch Supercup. Another Supercup success came his way in 1995 as well as Dutch league crowns in 1995 and 1996.

Above all, Kluivert scored the goals with which Ajax beat Milan to win the European Champions Cup in Vienna in 1995. He then went on to help Ajax win the 1995 World Club Cup and the European Supercup. Kluivert scored both goals to take Holland to Euro 96 when they beat the Republic of Ireland 2–0 in a play-off at Liverpool, in December 1995. Knee surgery the following spring, however, reduced his effectiveness in the finals. Kluivert took advantage of the Bosman ruling to move to Milan in the summer of 1997 on a free transfer. But his career has not been all sweetness and light. In

BOTH SIDES NOW Patrick Kluivert starred for Ajax before moving to old rivals Milan.

the autumn of 1995, he was involved in a fatal car crash – for which he was later found to blame – and sentenced to a term of community service.

Jürgen Kohler

Germany (born October 6, 1965)
Central defender
Clubs: Jahn Lambsheim, Waldhof-Mannheim, Köln, Bayern Munich, Juventus (Italy), Borussia Dortmund.

Kohler is perhaps the best man-marking stopper in European football. He made his name with Waldhof-Mannheim then Köln – who sold him

WEMBLEY WIZARD
Jurgen Klinsmann leads German celebrations at Euro 96.

to Bayern Munich for a then national record for a defender of £1 million in 1989. He was transferred to Juventus in 1991 for £5 million, a world record for a defender. A World Cup winner in 1990, he won the UEFA Cup in 1993 and Italian league in 1995 with Juventus. He returned to Germany with Borussia Dortmund in the summer of 1995 – and helped them beat Juventus two years later in the UEFA Champions League final. Kohler had announced that he would retire from national team football after the 1996 European Championship finals, but after being injured early in the Germans' opening match against the Czech Republic and missing the rest of the tournament, he decided to postpone his retirement so as to go out "at a time of my choosing".

Andy Köpke

Germany (born March 12, 1962)
Goalkeeper
Clubs: Holstein Kiel, Charlottenburg Berlin, Hertha Berlin, Nurnberg, Eintracht Frankfurt, Marseille (France).

Köpke is a qualified car mechanic who became a national hero when he saved Gareth Southgate's penalty in the semi-final shoot-out which followed the European Championship semi-final against England at Wembley. However, he had been a regular member of the national squad for seven years already – but was virtually a permanent reserve thanks to the dominance of Bodo Illgner. Köpke, a member of Germany's World Cup squads in both 1990 and 1994, was voted German Footballer of the Year in 1993. Both Stuttgart and Barcelona put in bids for him after his Euro 96 heroics – his club Eintracht Frankfurt had been relegated from the Bundesliga – but instead he joined the Marseille revival in France.

Emil Kostadinov

Bulgaria (born August 12, 1967)
Forward
Clubs: CSKA Sofia, FC Porto (Portugal), Deportivo La Coruña (Spain), Bayern Munich (Germany), Fenerbahce (Turkey).

SAFE KEEPING Andy Kopke was one of Germany's European title-winning heroes.

Kostadinov's career has run largely parallel with that of his Bulgarian attacking partner, Hristo Stoichkov. They made their names with their country's most bitter rivals – CSKA, in Kostadinov's case – then transferred to Iberia at around the same time in 1990 – Stoichkov to Barcelona and Kostadinov to FC Porto. That same season, Kostadinov scored vital goals in European Championship qualifying ties against Scotland and Switzerland. He twice won the Bulgarian cup with CSKA and added the Portuguese version in 1991 – scoring Porto's extra-time winner against Beira Mar. Kostadinov scored only in the first and last of Bulgaria's matches in the 1994 World Cup qualifying campaign – but his two late goals in the final game, against France in Paris, were crucial since they took Bulgaria to the finals. Kostadinov continued his nomadic ways by going on loan for half a season to La Coruña in 1994, before transferring to Bayern Munich – with whom he won the the UEFA Cup in 1996 – and then on to Turkey.

Marius Lacatus

Romania (born April 5, 1964)
Forward
Clubs: Brasov, Steaua Bucharest, Fiorentina (Italy), Oviedo (Spain), Steaua Bucharest.

Lacatus was the most dangerous Romanian marksman at the turn of the 1990s and won all his country's domestic honours with army club Steaua Bucharest, before transferring to Italians Fiorentina after the 1990 World Cup finals. Earlier he had been

a vital member of the Steaua team which became, in 1986 against Barcelona, the first Eastern European team to win the Champions Cup. Lacatus found it hard to readjust to football back home following his spells in Italy and Spain and was omitted from the World Cup squad for the United States in 1994. But he soon regained his old touch and led Steaua to the league title a year later.

Bernard Lama

France (born April 7, 1963)
Goalkeeper
Clubs: Lille, Abbeville, Besancon, Metz, Brest, Lens, Paris Saint-Germain.

Lama is another of the modern generation of goalscoring goalkeepers. Early in his career he scored twice in the French top division – both from the penalty spot – the first for Lille in 1989 and the second for Lens in 1992. It was Lama's saving rather than scoring abilities, however, which earned the greatest attention and he was snapped up by Paris Saint-Germain, winning the French cup in his first season. The league championship followed in 1994, as did the league cup and French cup again in 1995 and the European Cup-Winners' Cup in 1996. Lama, who played for his native French Guyana at youth level before being picked for France juniors, holds the clean-sheet record for a French national goalkeeper, at 800 minutes.

Brian Laudrup

Denmark (born February 22, 1969)
Forward
Clubs: Brondby, Bayer Uerdingen (Germany), Bayern Munich (Germany), Fiorentina (Italy), Milan (Italy), Rangers (Scotland).

Younger brother of Michael, son of former Danish international Finn, Brian has carried on the Laudrup footballing dynasty. Brian's first success was in winning the Danish Cup with Brondby in 1989. He then starred in Denmark's 1992 European Championship triumph in Sweden when brother Michael would not play – after a row with manager Richard Moller Nielsen over which position Brian suited best. Brian then had brief spells in Germany and Italy with Fiorentina and Milan. At the latter he was a victim of the

"turnover" policy when six foreigners were contracted but only three could play. The surprise move to Scotland, in 1994 – with Rangers – re-ignited his career. He became the first non-British player to be voted Scotland's Footballer of the Year in his first season. In the same season, the Glasgow club won their seventh league title in succession, an award they were to regain in 1997. Brian has also been Player of the Year a record three times in Denmark, in 1989, 1992 and 1995.

Michael Laudrup

Denmark (born June 15, 1964)
Midfielder
Clubs: Brondby, KB Copenhagen, Lazio (Italy), Juventus (Italy), Barcelona (Spain), Real Madrid (Spain), Vissel Kobe (Japan).

Michael Laudrup may well be considered as Denmark's greatest ever player. He has certainly proved to be Danish football's greatest achiever. Worldwide acclaim first greeted him at the 1986 World Cup finals in Mexico after he inspired Denmark's 6–1 win over Uruguay in Neza. He then missed the European Championship triumph in 1992 because of a dispute over tactics and style with coach Moller Nielsen. He would probably have secured more than 100 by caps now but for his self-imposed isolation. As a teenager, Laudrup was spoiled for choice of destinations. All of Europe's top clubs wanted him, but he opted for Juventus and was loaned at first to Lazio. In 1985 he was recalled by Juventus to replace Poland's Zbigniew Boniek and within a few months was helping them win the World Club Cup in Tokyo. Laudrup won the Champions Cup with Barcelona in 1992 at Wembley against Sampdoria and ended his Spanish stint having won five league titles – four with Barcelona and one with Real Madrid. He joined the Japanese second division club Vissel Kobe after Euro 96 but continued playing for Denmark in the run-up to the 1998 World Cup.

Yordan Lechkov

Bulgaria (born July 9, 1967)
Midfielder
Clubs: Sliven, CSKA Sofia, Hamburg (Germany), Marseille (France).

The prematurely-balding Lechkov was one of the surprise heroes of the 1994 World Cup finals, where he earned favourable comparison with the finest midfielders in the game. He had begun as a striker with provincial Sliven before being commandeered by the army club, CSKA Sofia. Lechkov was their championship-winning leading scorer with 17 goals in 29 league games before moving to Germany with Hamburg in 1992. Lechkov then turned the tables on his club hosts by scoring the historic winner for Bulgaria which eliminated the holders in Giants Stadium, New Jersey, in the 1994 World Cup quarter-finals. Lechkov considered the goal an ideal, if delayed, birthday present, since he had celebrated his 27th birthday the day before the game.

Jari Litmanen

Finland (born February 20, 1971)
Forward
Clubs: Myllkossken, Reipas Lahti, KJK Helsinki, Ajax (Holland).

Litmanen is Finland's finest footballer of modern times – perhaps the best-ever. He made history in May 1995, in Vienna, when he became not only the first Finnish player to appear in a European club final but Finland's first European trophy winner. Litmanen joined Ajax in 1992 as reserve to Dennis Bergkamp, and took advantage of the Dutchman's departure for Italy's Internazionale to top-score the following season with 26 goals. In Ajax's victorious 1995 Champions League campaign he scored six goals including two to crown an inspirational individual display in the 5-2 semi-final win over Bayern Munich.

Patrice Loko

France (born February 6, 1970)
Forward
Clubs: Nantes, Paris Saint-Germain.

Loko enjoyed the odd experience of making his international debut for France in a "non-match" – a 2–0 win in a goodwill friendly against Sporting Clube of Portugal for the benefit of the Portuguese community in Paris. He had earned his chance by top-scoring with 22 goals in the Nantes side which won the 1995 league championship. He did not stay for their Champions League campaign, however, transfer-ring during the summer to Paris Saint-Germain. At first, he appeared to have made a disastrously wrong choice. Within weeks of the start of the 1995–96 season, he was admitted to a psychiatric clinic after suffering a mental breakdown – brought on by the mixed pressure of his transfer to PSG and domestic difficulties. The season had a happy ending, however, when Loko returned to duty in time to help Paris become the first French club to win the European Cup-Winners' Cup.

Luis Enrique

Spain (born May 8, 1970)
Midfielder
Clubs: Sporting Gijon, Real Madrid, Barcelona.

Not many players transfer between Real Madrid and Barcelona, the twin giants of the Spanish game. Luis Enrique became one of that handful, however, after starring at the finals of the 1996 European Championship. He then demonstrated his mental resilience with a man-of-the-match display on his first return to Madrid's Bernabeu stadium for his new team – even though Barcelona lost 2–0 and Luis Enrique was jeered by 100,000 Madridistas every time he touched the ball. But he had learned his football in a good school, at Gijon, with whom he won his initial international recognition in Spain's under-21 team. Oddly, Luis Enrique was rejected by Barcelona after a five-day trial, so he joined Madrid instead for £1.25 million in 1991. A year later he was a key member of Spain's gold-medal side in the Barcelona Olympics and earned promotion to the senior national team, making his first appearance as a substitute. The 1994 World Cup was a painful experience, however, since Luis Enrique had his nose broken by the elbow of Italy's Mauro Tassotti – who was duly suspended for nine international matches – late in Spain's 2–1 quarter-final defeat.

Ally McCoist

Scotland (born September 24, 1962)
Forward
Clubs: St Johnstone, Sunderland (England), Rangers.

McCoist reached the peak of his goal-laden career in 1995–96. First he came back from a long injury absence to score Scotland's winner in the decisive European Championship qualifying match against Greece at Hampden Park, Glasgow. Then he became Rangers' all-time highest goalscorer, breaking the long-standing record set by the legendary Bob McPhail. Yet McCoist had started out as a midfield player with St Johnstone. Only fortunate accident saw him switched forward into what would prove his ideal role. The goals dried up during a short spell in England with Sunderland but, once back in Scotland with Rangers, McCoist was soon back on target – winning the Golden Boot award as Europe's top league marksman in 1991–92 and 1992–93.

Paul McGrath

Republic of Ireland (born December 4, 1959)
Defender
Clubs: St Patrick's Athletic, Manchester United (England), Aston Villa (England), Derby County (England).

McGrath became the most-capped Republic of Ireland international, despite a career chequered with the odd dispute with his managers and vanishing acts on the eve of big games. McGrath won the first of his 80-plus caps against Italy in February 1985. He played for St Patrick's Athletic in the League of Ireland before joining Manchester United in 1982, moved to Aston Villa in August 1989 and to Derby at the end of 1996. Each time his managers thought that knee injuries had virtually finished his career; each time he proved them wrong. McGrath was a rock at the heart of the Irish defence in their historic first appearances at the finals of both the European Championship in 1988 and then the World Cup in 1990.

Steve McManaman

England (born February 11, 1972)
Midfielder
Club: Liverpool.

Mexico's coach, Bora Milutinovic, summed up what most opposition managers feel, when he scanned England's team sheet before a friendly international at Wembley in March 1997. Pointing to Steve McManaman's place on the list, he said: "That's one name I could do without seeing." McManaman, though indelibly linked now with Liverpool, had supported neighbours Everton as a schoolboy. As a newcomer, he was one of the most consistent players at Anfield during the later part of the turbulent management of Graeme Souness. He won an FA Cup medal before he was 21, against Sunderland in 1992, then returned to Wembley to score a personal triumph – and both goals – against Bolton in the 1994–95 League Cup final. McManaman collected the Man of the Match award, fittingly, from Sir Stanley Matthews – with whom his dribbling skills had earned comparison. Further praise came after the 1996 European Championship when no less than Pele praised McManaman as one of the event's outstanding talents.

Paolo Maldini

Italy (born June 26, 1968)
Left-back/central defender
Club: Milan.

Paolo Maldini, captain of Milan and Italy, has been an automatic choice for most observers' "World XI" throughout the 1990s. His career has seen him emulate the success of his father, Cesare Maldini, who was captain of Milan's 1963 European Champions Cup-winning side and – from late 1996 – national manager. Son Paolo started under his father's tutelage in the Milan youth system and made his league debut as a 16-year-old in a 1–1 draw with Udinese in January 1985. Once asked if his father had favoured him, Paolo replied: "No, quite the opposite. He was much harder on me than on any of the others!" Originally a left-back, Maldini has doubled as both stopper and sweeper – a role in which he starred for Milan as deputy for suspended Franco Baresi in the 1994 Champions Cup final triumph over Barcelona. Maldini won World Cup medals when Italy finished third in 1990 and as runners-up in 1994. Subsequently, he was voted World Player of the Year by the London magazine *World Soccer*.

Andreas Möller

Germany (born September 2, 1967)
Midfielder
Clubs: Schwarz-Weiss Frankfurt, Eintracht Frankfurt, Borussia Dortmund, Juventus (Italy), Borussia Dortmund.

Möller's emergence as key member of the German midfield in the mid-1990s was no surprise to those who had listened to Berti Vogts a decade earlier. Vogts, when in charge of Germany's youth team, had forecast that Möller would one day become the seniors' playmaker. Möller played for his country at every junior level and starred in the side beaten only on penalties by the former Yugoslavia in the 1987 World Youth Cup Final in Chile. He graduated to become a fringe member of the West German World Cup-winning squad in 1990 and was a first choice at the 1992 European Championship and 1994 World Cup finals. In 1996 it was Möller's penalty which won the semi-final shoot-out against England, but he missed the final through suspension after receiving a second yellow card. Möller's early club career was a volatile one. His original transfer from Borussia Dortmund to Eintracht Frankfurt had to be resolved by a civil court case. He then spent two years with Juventus, helping them beat Borussia Dortmund in the 1993 UEFA Cup final. Two years later he was playing for Dortmund when Juventus beat them again, this time in the UEFA Cup semi-finals. His richly-rewarded consolation was in leading Dortmund to two German league titles and triumph in the 1997 Champions Cup.

Yuri Nikiforov
Russia (born September 16, 1970)
Sweeper/defender
Clubs: Dynamo Kiev, SKA Odessa, Chernomorets Odessa, Spartak Moscow.

As a teenager Nikiforov was once described by Pele as one of the world's most promising young strikers. That was after he had led the Soviet Union to victory in the World Junior (Under-16) Championship. But it was as a skilled, attacking sweeper that he ultimately made his mark at senior level. Nikiforov made his debut with Kiev in the old Soviet league at 17, and joined Moscow Spartak in 1993 where he was switched to libero. He was twice Russian national champion with Spartak as well as the league's highest-scoring defender and won the 1995 Goal of the Year award. He scored five times from sweeper in the Champions League in 1995–96, including two

goals against Rosenborg. Nikiforov also picked up a more unusual award when voted Russia's most sexy player in a poll among female fans.

Victor Onopko
Russia (born October 14, 1969)
Midfielder
Clubs: Stakhanovets (Stakhanov), Dynamo Kiev, Shakhtyor Donetsk, Spartak Moscow, Oviedo (Spain).

Onopko was the pillar of the new Russia national team which succeeded the Soviet Union – and briefly in 1992 the Commonwealth of Independent States – in both World Cups and European Championships. A former Soviet youth and under-21 international, he had joined Spartak from Shakhtyor in the winter of 1991 and made his senior international debut against England in Moscow the following April. Onopko earned international plaudits for the way he played Ruud Gullit to a standstill at the 1992 European Championship finals in Sweden. He was Russia's Footballer of the Year in 1992 and 1993 and won Russian league titles with Spartak in

REVENGE IS SWEET for Stuart Pearce after converting a penalty in the Euro 96 shoot-out against Spain.

1992, 1993 and 1994. At the end of 1995, Oviedo just beat Spanish rivals Atletico Madrid in the race to sign him, a move he claimed had been partly prompted by the theft of his Mitsubishi jeep in Moscow.

Marc Overmars
Holland (born March 29, 1973)
Winger
Clubs: Go-Ahead Eagles, Willem II, Ajax, Arsenal (England).

Overmars has been a highly-successful anachronism in 1990s football. Thirty years after Sir Alf Ramsey was thought to have killed off wingers, he was still using his pace and skill to take on full-backs – on either the right or the left side – head for the byline and cross to devastating effect. Overmars began with Go-Ahead Eagles of Deventer and Ajax signed him from Willem II in 1992. He scored his first international goal – after just four minutes – with the first kick of his

debut against Turkey in February 1993. Two months later Overmars scored twice in Ajax's 6–2 victory over Heerenveen in the Dutch cup final. He took England apart in a World Cup qualifier at Wembley in 1993 and did the same to Real Madrid – twice – in the UEFA Champions League 18 months later.

Stuart Pearce
England (born April 24, 1962)
Left-back
Clubs: Coventry City, Nottingham Forest, Newcastle United.

Pearce, nicknamed "Psycho" for his single-minded concentration on his job, was a late developer. He was an outstanding amateur with Wealdstone and did not make his full league debut until he was nearly 22. Pearce made his first England appearance less than four years later – the 999th different player selected – against Brazil at Wembley, having joined Nottingham Forest for a bargain £200,000 in June 1985. Normally a deadly penalty taker, he suffered the anguish of seeing Bodo Illgner saving his attempt in the shoot-out against Germany after the two nations had drawn in their 1990 World Cup semi-final, but Pearce made glorious amends with shoot-out conversions against both Spain and Germany in the closing stages of the 1996 European Championship in his home country. Never afraid of responsibility, Pearce stepped up briefly as player-manager to lead Forest's vain bid to escape relegation from the Premier League in 1996–97.

Joao Vieira Pinto
Portugal (born August 19, 1971)
Forward
Clubs: Boavista (Oporto), Atletico Madrileno (Spain), Boavista, Benfica.

Known as Joao Vieira Pinto to distinguish him from the veteran Porto full-back and captain, Joao Pinto. He became, in 1991, the only player then to have won the World Youth Cup twice – first in Riyadh, Saudi Arabia, in 1989, then at home in Lisbon. He was sold by Boavista to Atletico Madrid of Spain in 1990–91, who loaned him out to their second division nursery club, but Joao Vieira Pinto grew homesick and returned to Boavista. Portugal's Footballer of the Year in 1993, he won the Portuguese Cup with Boavista in 1992 and again with Benfica in 1993. His greatest club game was in May 1994, when his hat-trick inspired Benfica to win 6–3 away to Sporting, thus securing the league title and dispelling fears of a financial crisis.

David Platt
England (born June 10, 1966)
Midfielder
Clubs: Crewe Alexandra, Aston Villa, Bari (Italy), Juventus (Italy), Sampdoria (Italy), Arsenal (England).

Platt, an England cornerstone and ultimately captain in the first half of the 1990s, was one who got away from Manchester United: they gave him a free transfer. He played for four years at Crewe before becoming their then-record transfer, £200,000, on his sale to Aston Villa in 1988. Platt was then sold four more times for an approximate total of £22 million – £5.5 million from Villa to Bari in 1991, £6.5 million from Bari to Juventus a year later, £5.2 million from Juventus to Sampdoria in 1993, and £4.8 million from Sampdoria to Arsenal in 1995. The moves to and from Bari both broke the record fee for a British player. A busy midfielder, Platt chose a most dramatic moment to open his scoring account for England – the last minute of extra-time in the 1990 World Cup second-round tie against Belgium in Bologna. Platt ranks joint sixth in the all-time England goal- scorers' list with 27 to his credit. Only Bobby Charlton (49), Gary Lineker (48), Jimmy Greaves (44) and Tom Finney and Nat Lofthouse (both 30) have scored more.

Toni Polster
Austria (born March 10, 1964)
Forward
Clubs: Simmering, FK Austria, Torino (Italy), Ascoli (Italy), Sevilla (Spain), Logrones (Spain), Rayo Vallecano (Spain), Köln (Germany).

Polster has been one of European football's most outstanding league marksmen for a decade, having appeared for eight clubs in four different countries. He was once described as a "poor man's Klinsmann". Polster first made his mark when he was runner-up in the Golden Boot competition for Europe's top league goalscorer in 1986–87.

Polster scored 39 goals for FK Austria only to find his total – controversially – overtaken by the Romanian spearhead, Rodion Camataru, whose goalscoring achievements are now believed to have been "fixed" by the notorious Ceausescu regime. Polster then moved to Italy, with Torino and Ascoli, before rediscovering his shooting boots in Spain with Sevilla, Logrones and Rayo Vallecano. His next move brought him closer to home when he signed for German club Köln.

Gheorghe Popescu
Romania (born October 9, 1967)
Defender/midfielder
Clubs: Steaua Bucharest, Universitatea Craiova, PSV Eindhoven (Holland), Tottenham Hotspur (England), Barcelona (Spain).

Popescu is one of Europe's most versatile defensive midfielders. He played sweeper for Romania at the 1990 World Cup finals then as a defensive midfielder in 1994, where he shone in all five of Romania's games, including the quarter-final shoot-out defeat by Sweden. Popescu played as a junior for Steaua Bucharest, but made his name in Romania with Universitatea Craiova, before joining PSV Eindhoven in Holland originally as replacement in the centre of defence for Barcelona-bound Ronald Koeman – whom he later succeeded at Barcelona as well. Before moving to Spain, 'Gica' spent the 1994–95 season in England with Tottenham Hotspur, but was overshadowed by German team-mate Jürgen Klinsmann and – more importantly – did not enjoy the frenetic pace of the football. Popescu won the Romanian Footballer of the Year award four times in succession, in 1990, 1991, 1992 and 1993.

Robert Prosinecki
Croatia (born January 12, 1969)
Midfielder
Clubs: Dinamo (later FC Croatia) Zagreb, Crvena Zvezda Beograd (Red Star Belgrade), Real Madrid (Spain), Oviedo (Spain), Barcelona (Spain).

Prosinecki promised, at one time, to become the outstanding European player of his generation. A string of niggling injuries inhibited his

progress, however, after he had moved to Real Madrid in what should have been the keynote transfer of his career. Prosinecki first starred with the former Yugoslavia squad which won the World Youth Cup in 1987. He was voted Player of the Tournament even though he missed the final – a penalty shoot-out victory over West Germany – because of suspension. Miroslav Blazevic, later Croatia national coach, let him leave Dinamo for Red Star, doubting whether he would establish himself as a professional player, but he went on to win three Yugoslav championships while in Belgrade – plus the European Champions Cup in 1991. After moving to Spain he became one of the growing band of international players to have appeared for both Real Madrid and Barcelona. His family background is mixed Croatian and Serbian and he was wanted by both countries. Finally he declared himself a Croat and played for them at the 1996 European Championship finals.

Raul
(Full name: Raul Gonzalez Blanco)
Spain (born June 27, 1977)
Forward
Clubs: Atletico Madrid, Real Madrid.

Raul is the greatest Spanish soccer sensation of the 1990s. Originally he played for Atletico Madrid's youth teams. But when president Jesus Gil cut back the juniors as a cash-saving measure, Raul was snatched by neighbours Real. Thrust into the first team by coach Jorge Valdano at the tender age of 17 – becoming, in the process, Madrid's youngest-ever league player – he scored six goals in his first 11 games and kept such veteran internationals as Emilio Butragueno and Rafael Martin Vazquez on the substitutes' bench. Ironically, Raul made his debut against his old club, Atletico, scoring one superb goal and making another. Raul scored six goals in Real's 1995–96 Champions League campaign, including a hat-trick against Hungary's Ferencvaros and a quarter-final match-winner against Juventus. Fans clamoured for him to be called up by Spain for Euro 96, but coach Javier Clemente preferred, perhaps mistakenly with hindsight, to save him for the Olympic tournament.

CHAMPION'S STYLE Fabrizio Ravanelli celebrates one of the goals for Juventus which drew Middlesbrough's attention.

Fabrizio Ravanelli

Italy (born December 11, 1968)
Striker
Clubs: Perugia, Avellino, Reggiana, Juventus, Middlesbrough (England).

The transition from Turin to Teesside is an awkward one, but Ravanelli accomplished it with verve in mid-1996. One moment he was a Champions Cup-winning hero with Juventus, the next he was – to his own surprise – on his way to joining Middlesbrough, a club of which he had never heard. Ravanelli knuckled down with all the professional discipline he had learned in Italy, despite 'Boro's setbacks in leagues and cups. Surprisingly, Ravanelli did not make his Italian Serie A debut until shortly before his 24th birthday. He made his international debut in the 4–1 Euro 96 qualifying win over Estonia, in 1995, after scoring more than a century of goals in 10 seasons of Serie A, B and regional football. Nicknamed "The White Feather" because of his prematurely grey hair, Ravanelli ended the 1995–96 season by scoring Juventus's all-important goal in their UEFA Champions League Cup final triumph over Ajax in Rome. He began the next season in style, too, with a hat-trick against Liverpool in Middlesbrough's opening day 3–3 draw but could not save 'Boro's eventual relegation.

Thomas Ravelli

Sweden (born August 13, 1959)
Goalkeeper
Clubs: Osters Vaxjo, IFK Gothenburg.

Ravelli is the most-capped European footballer of all time – having overtaken Peter Shilton's old world goalkeeping record of 125 caps in 1994. He is not, however, the overall world record-holder, that honour belonging to Saudi Arabia's Majid Mohammed – the so-called Pele of the Desert – with 157 appearances. Ravelli's achievement is still, of course, remarkable. His father was an Austrian who emigrated to Sweden where Thomas and twin brother Andreas – an international midfielder – were born. Both became youth and under-21 internationals, and Thomas went on to a century of caps and the accolade of Swedish Footballer of the Year in 1981, the year he made his senior

debut for his country. The high point of his international career was in 1994, when he was voted one of the top goalkeepers at the World Cup in the United States – as Sweden claimed third place. Ravelli joined IFK Gothenburg from Osters Vaxjo in the spring of 1989 as replacement for Tottenham-bound Erik Thorstvedt and was still there almost a decade later.

Rui Costa

Portugal (March 29, 1972)
Midfielder
Clubs: Fafe, Benfica, Fiorentina (Italy).

Rui Costa realized how far he had come in his career when the oldest youth tournament in Portugal – organized by minor club Centre Cultural da Pontinha – was renamed in his honour as the Torneo Rui Costa. He had been an outstanding youth player himself – a World Youth Cup-winner against Brazil in Lisbon in 1991 and a member of the Portuguese team which reached the finals of the 1994 European Under-21 Championship in France. Rui Costa started his club career with second division Fafe, then moved to Benfica, with whom he won the Portuguese cup in 1993 and league championship in 1994. He was then sold to the Italian club Fiorentina, and he played a leading role in their 1996–97 European Cup-Winners' Cup campaign.

Ian Rush

Wales (born October 20, 1961)
Centre forward
Clubs: Chester City, Liverpool, Juventus (Italy), Liverpool, Leeds United.

Rush ranks among the finest Welsh players of all time and among the greatest trophy-winners in English football history. Liverpool signed him for a paltry £300,000 from Chester in 1980 and he stayed loyal to Anfield for 16 years – with one year "out" for an unsatisfactory season in Italy with Juventus. Rush totalled 229 league goals for Liverpool, second only in the club's history to Roger Hunt's aggregate of 245. He won the league championship five times, the League Cup five times, the FA Cup three times and the European Champions Cup once – against Roma in Rome in 1984. At

international level Rush, in a poor era for Wales, never had the chance of playing in the World Cup or European Championship finals. But in more than 70 internationals he easily outstripped the previous Welsh scoring record of 23 goals held jointly by Trevor Ford and Ivor Allchurch.

Dejan Savicevic

Yugoslavia (born September 15, 1966)
Midfielder/forward
Clubs: Buducnost Titograd, Crvena Zvezda Beograd (Red Star Belgrade), Milan (Italy).

Savicevic, from Montenegro, is one of Europe's outstanding attackers, but he had an uphill task making his talent tell. After starring at the 1990 World Cup, he returned to Italy a year later, to Bari, to help Red Star Belgrade win the European Champions Cup. Red Star went on to win the World Club Cup, but Savicevic was sent off in the victory over Chile's Colo Colo in Tokyo. With Yugoslavia descending into crisis, Savicevic "escaped" to the west, courtesy of a £3.5 million transfer to Milan. However he spent as much of his first season on the sidelines as on the pitch because of foreign player restrictions and knee trouble. Eventually, Savicevic was able to express his talent to the full in inspiring Milan's brilliant 4–0 victory over Barcelona in the 1994 European Champions Cup final. He has returned to national football, too, with the reformed Yugoslavia.

CLEARING THE AIR *Peter Schmeichel sets Manchester United back on the attack.*

Peter Schmeichel

Denmark (born November 18, 1963)
Goalkeeper
Clubs: Gladsaxe Hero, Hvidovre, Brondby, Manchester United (England).

Schmeichel's very demeanour in a match speaks volumes about his will to win and determination to hold his defence together. That dedication carried him through his difficult early years in Danish football when he played part-time and took various jobs – including running a shop for the World Wildlife Fund and working as a newspaper advertising salesman – to help make ends meet. Everything paid off ultimately with his £750,000 move to Manchester United in 1991. Schmeichel had come to international prominence in the 1988 European Championship in Germany, when he replaced Troels Rasmussen in Denmark's final match. He has been voted Denmark's player of the year on two occasions and was immense in the Danes' 1992 European Championship triumph in Sweden when he was voted the world's best goalkeeper. His honours with Manchester United include four league championships and two FA Cups. He also got his name on the scoresheet with a last-minute headed goal in a UEFA Cup tie against Rotor Volgograd.

Enzo Scifo

Belgium (born February 19, 1966)
Midfielder
Clubs: Anderlecht, Internazionale
(Italy), Bordeaux (France),
Montpellier (France), Torino (Italy),
Monaco (France), Anderlecht.

Scifo was born of Italian parents in
Belgium. He was a prolific goalscorer
in youth football with La Louviere
while still at school and was signed by
Anderlecht. In 1984 Scifo opted to
take up Belgian citizenship and played
in the European Championship finals
in France – as well as in the now controversial UEFA Cup semi-final
against Nottingham Forest and losing
final against Tottenham. A football
prodigy, he was taken "home" to Italy
by Internazionale, but was overcome
by the pressure and was loaned to
Bordeaux and Montpellier in France.
He returned to Italy with Torino after
the 1990 World Cup and helped them
to reach the 1992 UEFA Cup final.
Torino's financial problems forced
them to sell Scifo to Monaco in 1993.
His career completed a full circle in
the summer of 1997, when he returned
to Anderlecht.

David Seaman

England (born September 19, 1963)
Goalkeeper
Clubs: Peterborough United,
Birmingham City, Queens Park
Rangers, Arsenal.

Seaman, like many goalkeepers,
proved a late developer. Despite
around 300 appearances in various
competitions, his top-grade career did
not fully take off until he joined
Arsenal from fellow Londoners
Queens Park Rangers in May 1990 for
£1.3 million, then a record for an
English goalkeeper. He took over at
Highbury from John Lukic, who went
to Leeds – where Seaman had spent a
year as a teenager without playing in
the first team. With Arsenal he has
won the league championship, FA
Cup, League Cup and European Cup-
Winners' Cup, and also established
himself as first-choice for England,
after waiting patiently in line behind
Peter Shilton and Chris Woods.
Seaman was outstanding at Euro 96,
with decisive penalty-defying perfor-
mances in England's victories over
Scotland and Spain.

Clarence Seedorf

Holland (born April 1, 1976)
Midfielder
Clubs: Ajax, Sampdoria (Italy),
Real Madrid (Spain).

Almost every competition Seedorf has
graced has brought him success. With
Ajax he was voted Dutch Young
Player of the Year in 1993 and 1994,
winning the Dutch championship in
1994 and 1995, the Dutch cup in 1993,
the Dutch Supercup in 1993 and 1994
and then the ultimate prize – the
European Champions Cup in 1995.
This was one of Seedorf's last matches
for Ajax, because he rejected advice to
stay another year or two in Amsterdam
and decided to try his luck in Italy
with Sampdoria. He admitted later that
he had been, perhaps, too young and
inexperienced for the Italian challenge. But he learned fast and regained
his status as one of Europe's outstanding creative forces after transferring to
Real Madrid at coach Fabio Capello's
behest in the summer of 1996.

Ciriaco Sforza

Switzerland (born March 2, 1970)
Midfielder
Clubs: Grasshopper-Club, Aarau,
Grasshopper-Club, Kaiserslautern
(Germany), Bayern Munich
(Germany), Internazionale (Italy).

Despite coming from unfashionable –
in football terms – Switzerland, Sforza
is acknowledged as one of the most
resilient anchor-men midfielders in
continental football. Italian by birth, he
always considered himself Swiss and
took up formal citizenship in 1990.
Less than a year later he made his
national team debut against Czechoslovakia. Sforza starred initially for
Grasshopper, winning the Swiss cup in
1988, the championship in 1991, and
was voted Swiss Footballer of the Year
in 1993. He played in all his country's
four matches in the 1994 World Cup
finals and then in all 11 qualifying and
finals matches in the 1996 European
Championship. A powerful shot also
helped make him a favourite with
Switzerland manager Roy Hodgson –
who was instrumental in Sforza's
transfer to Internazionale in 1996.

Alan Shearer

England (born August 31, 1970)
Forward

Clubs: Southampton, Blackburn
Rovers, Newcastle United.

Shearer brought the world transfer
record back to England for the first
time in 60 years when he was the subject of a £15 million move from
Blackburn Rovers to his home-town
club, Newcastle United, in the summer
of 1996. He had just proved his pedigree by finishing as five-goal top
scorer in the European Championship
finals and was about to be installed as
new captain of England by national
coach Glenn Hoddle. Shearer ended
1996 having been voted into third
place behind Ronaldo and George
Weah in the annual FIFA World
Footballer of the Year poll and collected his second Players' Player of
the Year award in April 1997 – his first
had come in 1994. He was spotted by
Southampton in 1988 and spirited
down south originally to start his
career as a trainee there. In only his
fourth senior appearance – at the age
of 17 years and 240 days – he scored
three times against Arsenal and
became the youngest player ever to hit
a Football League hat-trick. Shearer
was transferred to Blackburn Rovers
in July 1992 for a record £3.3 million,
where he enjoyed greater success,
especially in the 1994–95 season,
when his 34 goals helped Blackburn to
win their first modern league championship. In March 1996, he became the
first man to score 100 goals in the
Premiership in only its fourth season.

Paulo Sousa

Portugal (born August 13, 1970)
Midfielder

*RECORD MAN England's
top-scoring skipper,
Alan Shearer.*

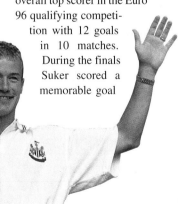

Clubs: Academica Viseu, Benfica,
Sporting Clube, Juventus (Italy),
Borussia Dortmund (Germany).

The son of a car mechanic in Viseu,
Paulo Sousa had planned to become a
teacher until football took over his life.
He began with his local youth team,
Repesesc, rising to become a member
of the Portuguese squad which won
the 1989 World Youth Cup in Riyadh,
Saudi Arabia, before joining Benfica.
He quit the Stadium of Light in 1994
in a dispute over wages and joined
Sporting Clube – moving on again
after only one year to Juventus. Paulo
Sousa may now be considered to have
been the most successful Portuguese
export to Italy – winning the league
and cup double with Juventus in 1995
and the European Champions Cup in
1996. Paulo Sousa starred for Portugal
at Euro 96 and was then sold to
Dortmund, helping them to victory
over Juventus in the 1997 Champions
Cup final.

Davor Suker

Croatia (born January 1, 1968)
Forward
Clubs: Osijek, FC Croatia Zagreb,
Sevilla (Spain), Real Madrid (Spain).

Suker, for all the riches which international football success has brought
him, has remained a sensitive character – and still possesses a bottle of red
wine given to his family on the day he
was born in 1968. He first came to
notice as a member of the Yugoslavia
squad which won the World Youth Cup
in 1987. Suker became top league
marksman with 18 goals for Osijek in
1989–90 to earn selection for the 1990
World Cup finals, but he did not play.
After the civil war in the Balkans he
opted to play for Croatia and was the
overall top scorer in the Euro
96 qualifying competi-
tion with 12 goals
in 10 matches.
During the finals
Suker scored a
memorable goal

ALL-ROUND LEADER Davor Suker is as sharp on the pitch as off it.

against Denmark, chipping goalkeeper Peter Schmeichel, in a 3–0 victory. Off the pitch, he held a leading role within the national squad as negotiator with the federation and potential sponsors . Suker was transferred across Spain – from Sevilla to Real Madrid – after Euro 96.

Jonas Thern
Sweden (born March 20, 1967)
Midfielder
Clubs: Malmo, Benfica (Portugal), Napoli (Italy), Roma (Italy), Rangers (Scotland).

Thern captained Sweden through their outstanding revival in the early 1990s and was praised by manager Tommy Svensson as "our No 1 footballer". He sprang to prominence at club level with Malmo and joined Benfica for £800,000 in 1989. However, he had already made his presence felt on the international scene, scoring a fine goal, and getting sent off, in Sweden's opening game of the Olympic tournament at Seoul in 1988 – a 2–2 draw with Tunisia. Thern made his senior Sweden debut in a 1–1 draw with West Germany in Gelsenkirchen in October 1987. He moved to Italy with Napoli, transferred in 1994 to Roma who soon appointed him captain, then moved to Rangers in summer 1997. A fan of Bruce Springsteen, Thern is certainly The Boss of Sweden's midfield.

Vitor Baia
Portugal (born October 15, 1969)
Goalkeeper
Clubs: FC Porto, Barcelona (Spain).

Vitor Baia, considered by many to be Europe's finest present-day goalkeeper, became a professional almost by accident. His family were fans of Benfica when he went for a trial with Porto as a teenager, just to keep another hopeful company. Porto immediately recognized his potential and would not let him go. He received an emergency call-up to the first team in 1988–89 after Polish keeper Jozsef Mlynarczyk was injured and Portuguese international Ze Beto was suspended. His form ensured that he remained in the first team and he soon became the first choice for the national team, too, being named captain as well. A league champion with Porto in 1990, 1992, 1993, 1995 and 1996 and Portuguese cup-winner in 1991 and 1994, Vitor Baia was acclaimed Footballer of the Year in 1992 after setting a domestic record of not conceding a goal for more than 1,000 minutes of play. Awarded Europe's top goalkeeper prize by ESM (European Sports Magazines) in 1996, Vitor Baia followed his club coach, Bobby Robson, from Porto to Barcelona in Spain in the summer of 1996.

Zinedine Zidane
France (born June 23, 1972)
Midfielder
Clubs: Cannes, Bordeaux, Juventus (Italy).

Zidane took over, in 1996–97, as the top French footballer from Eric Cantona. His rise had been rapid. He made his top division debut in May 1989, joined Bordeaux in 1992 and was voted Young Player of the Year in 1992. Zidane marked a sensational national team debut by scoring both France's goals in the closing stages to rescue a draw against the Czech Republic, having been 2–0 down. He won the 1995 French Goal of the Year award for a left-footed 35-metre lob which beat Real Betis of Spain in December 1995 and put Bordeaux into the UEFA Cup quarter-finals. Zidane appeared in more games than any other player in France during 1995–96 – 57 including league, European club and international appearances. Maybe not surprisingly, he was then too tired to do himself justice in the 1996 European Championship, but that did not deter Juventus from signing him as their midfield replacement for Portugal's Paulo Sousa.

Christian Ziege
Germany (born February 1, 1972)
Midfielder
Clubs: Sudstern 08 Berlin, TSV Rudow, Hertha Zehlendorf, Bayern Munich, Milan (Italy).

Ziege represents the archetypal modern left-wing-back – using terrific pace to support in attack and then cover back in defence. Yet he began his career in his native West Berlin as a goalkeeper. Ziege had represented Germany at every level, including the Olympic team and captaining the under-21s, before making his senior debut in 1993. Unfortunately injury in the spring of 1994 denied him the chance to help Germany's World Cup defence in the United States. Hailed as the "new Andy Brehme", he achieved European success by winning the 1996 UEFA Cup with Bayern Munich. He took advantage of the Bosman ruling to transfer to Milan in the summer of 1997.

Gianfranco Zola
Italy (born July 5, 1966)
Forward
Clubs: Nuorese, Torres, Napoli, Parma, Chelsea (England).

Zola learned his trade in the shadow of Diego Maradona at Napoli – picking up all the Argentine superstar's good technical habits and none of his less fortunate personal ones. Above all, Zola achieved a remarkable success-rate with direct free-kicks. But it was not until after his transfer to Parma that he was fully appreciated as an intuitive creative attacker in his own right. Zola had an unfortunate time at the finals of international tournaments. At Euro 96 he missed a penalty after having been brought down in the decisive group match against Germany; at the World Cup in the United States, two years earlier, he was sent off – having come on as a substitute – in a second round game against Nigeria, one day before his 28th birthday. Ironically, Zola regained all his old confidence thanks to a transfer to England, to Chelsea, midway through the 1996–97 season, with whom he won the FA Cup. He also proved that his marksmanship had not deserted him at international level when he scored Italy's winner against England at Wembley in a World Cup qualifier in February 1997.

Andoni Zubizarreta
Spain (born October 23, 1961)
Goalkeeper
Clubs: Athletic Bilbao, Barcelona, Valencia.

"Zubi" is the grand old man of Spanish football – having also become the only Spanish player to top 100 international appearances. Zubizarreta has been the finest product of the great Basque school of goalkeeping. He made his league debut with Bilbao in 1981 and his international debut as a substitute for fellow Basque Luis Arconada in a 3–1 win over Finland in Alicante in 1985. Successive national managers made Zubi their first-choice keeper at the finals of the 1986, 1990 and 1994 World Cups and the 1988 and 1992 European Championships. At Bilbao he collected two league championships and one Spanish cup-winners medal. He had a tough start following his 1986 transfer to Barcelona, because coach Terry Venables used him to replace fans' idol Javier Urruticoechea. Despite this Zubizarreta has enjoyed enormous success at Barcelona, winning the World Club Cup, European Champions Cup, four Spanish league titles and two Spanish cups, although he missed the European Cup-Winners' Cup final defeat at the hands of Manchester United. Zubi was given a free transfer by Barcelona coach Johan Cruyff after their 4–0 Champions Cup final defeat by Milan in 1994, but he appeared to regain his footballing youth with Valencia.

THE LEGENDS OF EUROPEAN FOOTBALL

Every country boasts its favourite soccer sons – men whose achievements in league and cup, for club and national team, have left an indelible mark on the domestic game. Some of those local favourites have achieved fame and fortune beyond their own borders – especially in the modern days of constant international competition and worldwide television coverage. The heroes of one country are now as well known half a world away as they are at home.

A modern yardstick of greatness is the European Footballer of the Year award – which was launched in 1956 by the Paris weekly, *France Football*. Footballing awards come and go but the Golden Ball still remains the most historic and prestigious of European individual accolades.

Eligibility was simple: the players had to be available to play for European national teams – which is why Argentine-born Alfredo Di Stefano (adopted by Spain) and Omar Sivori (adopted by Italy) qualified in the early days of the award.

In 1995, *France Football* changed the rules to make any player perform-ing in Europe eligible – whatever his national allegiance. Thus Liberian superstar George Weah won the 1995 award – completing a fabulous hat-trick since he then held, simultaneously, the European, African and World player awards.

Stanley Matthews
England (born February 1, 1915)
Outside-right
Clubs: Stoke City, Blackpool, Stoke City
European Footballer of the Year: 1956

As time goes by, the most remarkable feature of the undeniable claim to greatness of Stanley Matthews was that he was an orthodox outside-right. In the decades through the centre of twentieth-century football that meant he clung to the wide right touchline – yet still managed to mesmerize every player on the pitch. He played until beyond his 50th birthday yet was never booked or sent off. He was the quintessential English sportsman, an exemplary public figure who digni-fied the game he loved. The son of a boxing barber from the Potteries, Matthews made his name initially with Stoke City in the 1930s and made his England debut in a 4–0 win over Wales in Cardiff in 1934. One of his most memorable displays for England was in another 4–0 win – over World Cup-holders Italy in Turin in 1948. That victory ensured England would be one of the favourites for the 1950 World Cup, but the trip proved to be a disaster and Matthews himself was only grudgingly included in the squad at the last moment. In 1953 Matthews sealed his place in football history with an inspirational display in Blackpool's 4–3 FA Cup final defeat of Bolton Wanderers. He was 38 at the time yet was still sharp enough to play for England at the World Cup finals in Switzerland the following year. His eventual return to

ROYAL SALUTE for Stanley Matthews before the 1953 FA Cup final.

Stoke inspired his old club to regain their place in the top division after which he retired following a star-studded farewell match at the old Victoria Ground. Alfredo Di Stefano, Ferenc Puskas, Lev Yashin and Ladislav Kubala were among the giants who flew in to pay tribute. Later Matthews – by now Sir Stanley – declared that, with the advent of lighter boots and water-resistant footballs, he had really retired too early.

Alfredo Di Stefano

Argentina and Spain
(born July 4, 1926)
Centre forward
Clubs: San Lorenzo (Argentina), River Plate (Argentina), Millonarios Bogota (Colombia), Real Madrid (Spain), Espanol Barcelona (Spain)
European Footballer of the Year: 1957 and 1959

Alfredo Di Stefano was the player who, more than any other, "created" the multi-competitive European game as we know it today. The European Champions Cup might have been just another little backwater competition if it had not been illuminated in its initial years by a star-studded Real Madrid team who took their cue from the dynamic leadership Di Stefano provided. He was never, officially, Madrid's captain, but he was the undisputed leader, and the glamour which he and his club attracted was reflected in the competition's popularity. Yet Di Stefano might never have played for Madrid at all, but their great rivals Barcelona instead. Born in Buenos Aires, the son of an old River Plate stalwart, Di Stefano followed in father's footballing footsteps – to father's initial disapproval. He started with River's juniors, exploded while on loan to neighbours San Lorenzo, and returned to River in the late 1940s, when he made his debut for Argentina. Di Stefano was lured away to Millonarios in the pirate Colombian league during an Argentine players' strike and earned recognition in Europe during a farewell tour when it became clear that the pirates could return to the international fold. Barcelona agreed a transfer deal with River Plate and Madrid agreed a deal with Millonarios. The Spanish sports ministry decreed that he should play one season for each club, but Barcelona decided he was not worth the wait and sold their rights to Madrid – whom Di Stefano then inspired to their historic five-in-a-row Champions Cup victories. The climax was Madrid's 7–3 thrashing of Eintracht Frankfurt in 1960 when Di Stefano's hat-trick maintained his record of scoring in five successive Champions Cup finals. He was a centre forward who embodied "total football" before the term was ever invented – wandering from one penalty box to the other, controlling play and directing tactics. Oddly, Di Stefano never appeared in the World Cup finals. He played for Argentina at a time when the country did not want to play in the World Cup and, later, when he was a member of Spain's squad in Chile in 1962, an injury prevented him appearing. For all that, many still regard him as the greatest footballer of all time.

Raymond Kopa

France (born October 13, 1931)
Centre forward/outside-right
Clubs: Angers, Reims, Real Madrid (Spain), Reims
European Footballer of the Year: 1958

Much of the strength of French football in the 1950s and early 1960s came following the influx of Polish migrant families. Raymond Kopaszewski, until the advent of Michel Platini – the greatest French

SEAM OF SUCCESS *French favourite Raymond Kopa.*

footballer of all time – was the most notable product of that generation. His father had moved to France to work in the mines of Nouex-les-Mines and had expected his son to follow him down the pits. Young Kopa did – but not for long because of a mining accident in which he damaged a hand. His fortune, literally, was his football talent. He was spotted playing for Noeux-les-Mines by Angers, won a national youth player's competition, and was sold to Reims in 1950. Kopa wore the No 9 shirt, but was more creator than finisher and had already virtually agreed transfer terms with Spain's Real Madrid before the Spanish club beat Reims in Paris in the first European Champions Cup final in 1956. Di Stefano was the kingpin at Madrid so Kopa switched to outside-right – regaining his old centre forward role with France at the 1958 World Cup finals. Just Fontaine may have scored a record 13 goals during that competition but he owed so much to Kopa, who was duly rewarded with the European Footballer of the Year prize. Kopa returned to Reims in 1959 but the final years of his career were marred by injuries and frequent run-ins with authority over football players' rights since Kopa was the Jean-Marc Bosman of his era.

THE GREAT EXHIBITIONIST
Juventus's temperamental leader, Omar Sivori.

Luis Suarez

Spain (born May 2, 1935)
Inside-left
Clubs: Deportivo de La Coruña, Barcelona, Internazionale (Italy), Sampdoria (Italy)
European Footballer of the Year: 1960

Spanish football's greatest players have, in general, been foreign imports – the likes of Alfredo Di Stefano, Ladislav Kubala, Ferenc Puskas, Johan Cruyff and Ronaldo. Long before the Bosman judgement, which destroyed controls on imports, the Spanish game was awash with foreign players. This partially goes to explain why there is enormous pride generated around home-grown products who prove they can live, internationally, with the best. Goalkeeper Ricardo Zamora, the superstar of the 1920s and 1930s, was acknowledged as Spain's greatest discovery until the emergence of Luis Suarez in the 1950s. Born and brought up in La Coruña, in the north-west corner of Spain, Suarez made an instant impact on making his debut for La Coruña away to Barcelona. Deportivo lost, but the Catalan crowd gave Suarez a standing ovation and Barcelona officials insisted on agreeing transfer terms immediately after the match. It says everything about Suarez's talent that he established himself as the playmaking inside-left

in a Barcelona squad overflowing with international attacking genius, including not only Kubala but also fellow Hungarians Sandor Kocsis and Zoltan Czibor, Paraguay's Ramon Villaverde and Eulogio Martinez, and Brazil's Evaristo de Macedo. Coach Helenio Herrera insisted on taking Suarez with him after moving to Internazionale in Italy and it was around Suarez's organizational ability that Herrera built a team to dominate world club football in the mid-1960s. Suarez's ability to turn defence into attack with one pinpoint pass suited Inter's hit-and-hold tactics admirably. Later Suarez spent many years on the Inter coaching staff – twice being handed charge of the senior side – and he also managed Spain at the 1990 World Cup finals in Italy.

Omar Enrique Sivori

Argentina and Italy
(born October 2, 1935)
Inside-left
Clubs: River Plate (Argentina), Juventus (Italy), Napoli (Italy)
European Footballer of the Year: 1961

In 1957 Argentina won the South American Championship almost by a walkover thanks to the brilliance of an inside-forward trio of Humberto Maschio, Antonio Valentin Angelillo and Omar Sivori. Success lifted them among the favourites for the 1958 World Cup finals. Yet the potential was never realized because, within a year, all three players had been sold to Italian clubs and axed from the national team as punishment for disloyalty. Sivori, who cost Juventus a world record £91,000 from River Plate, was the most outrageous personality of the three. He was an attacking inside-left who loved nothing better than humiliating his marker with a nutmeg, but he was also an outstanding team player and dovetailed perfectly with the pragmatic and powerful Welshman, John Charles. Under Sivori's leadership, Juve won the league title three times in four years at the turn of the 1960s. Sivori and Charles provided 140 of their title-winning goals. Sivori was nicknamed "*Cabezon*" – Big Head – by his

PULLING RANK Josef Masopust, "commander-in-chief" of army club Dukla.

admirers in Argentina and Italy and his self-confidence eventually led to a major confrontation with coach Heriberto Herrera and, ultimately, transfer to Napoli. The rapturous reception Sivori received at Napoli foreshadowed the atmosphere on the arrival, years later, of compatriot Diego Maradona. Sivori played 18 times for Argentina, nine times for Italy's national side – including games during the 1962 World Cup – and was voted European Footballer of the Year in 1961. He also scored the solitary goal which, in the spring of 1962, condemned Real Madrid to their first-ever home defeat in the Champions Cup.

Josef Masopust

Czechoslovakia
(born February 9, 1931)
Left-half
Clubs: Union Teplice, Dukla Prague, Crossing Molenbeek (Belgium)
European Footballer of the Year: 1962

Josef Masopust's reign as the finest Czechoslovak footballer of his generation spanned a time of tactical change within the European game. Originally Masopust, a tidily-built player with great stamina and strength but also delicate control, was a left-half. His defensive understanding with left-back Ladislav Novak and more cautious right-half Svotopluk

Pluskal was the foundation of many a victory for both Czechoslovakia and the army club, Dukla Prague. As time went on, however, so Masopust moved toward the centre of midfield for a controlling role which he performed with enormous success at the 1962 World Cup finals. Czechoslovakia, against the odds, reached the final and even took the lead – through Masopust, inevitably – before losing 3–1 to Brazil. Still, Masopust's contribution earned him the European Footballer of the Year prize. Surprisingly, Czechoslovakia failed to reach the World Cup finals in England in 1966 and Masopust was allowed, as a reward for his honourable service, a then rare permit to move abroad. He played out his career as a reconstructed midfield general in Belgium, before retiring to a coaching career.

Lev Yashin

Soviet Union (born October 22, 1929)
Goalkeeper
Club: Moscow Dynamo
European Footballer of the Year: 1963

Lev Yashin inspired many nicknames including "The Octopus" (for his incredible reach) and "The Lion" (for his infectious confidence). He was not merely one of the greatest goalkeepers in the entire history of world football, but was renowned as a great sportsman as well. Even in later years, after serious illness had robbed him of the use of his legs, he remained cheerful and enthusiastic about the sport which he nearly gave up as a youngster. In the early 1950s, Yashin was impatient at being an almost permanent reserve at Dynamo, behind the great Alexei "Tiger" Khomich. He was ready to forget football and turn to ice hockey, for which he also had great talent. Then Khomich was injured, Yashin

was called up – and the rest is history. Yashin won every domestic Soviet honour as well as the European Nations Championship in 1960, the Olympic Games gold medal at Melbourne in 1956 and then became the only goalkeeper to secure the European Footballer of the Year award in 1963. Yashin, who made his debut for the Soviet Union in a 3–2 victory over Sweden in 1954, played in the World Cup finals of 1958, 1962 and 1966 and was a reserve – for his experience – at the 1970 World Cup finals in Mexico. His agility and reflexes were renowned; Yashin could catch and hold shots which other keepers would have been glad to reach with a fingertip.

Denis Law

Scotland (born February 22, 1940)
Inside-forward
Clubs: Huddersfield Town (England), Manchester City (England), Torino (Italy), Manchester United (England), Manchester City (England)
European Footballer of the Year: 1964

Many Manchester United fans, looking back to the club's romantic 1960s era, insist that Denis Law ranked above Bobby Charlton and George Best in terms of all-round football genius. Not for nothing was he nicknamed "The King". Appearances early in his career had been deceptive, but Law's

GOALKEEPING FIRST for Lev Yashin, official Hero of the Soviet Union.

KING OF OLD TRAFFORD Scotland inside forward Denis Law.

Aberdonian background offered him the incentive to succeed. His father was an engineer on a fishing trawler and, as a boy, there was no spare cash to spend on the luxury of football boots, so when he was picked to play for his school team – at left-back! – he had to borrow a pair from the boy next door. Law was a Rangers fan, but it was English club Huddersfield Town who first spotted his potential and signed him as an apprentice. He made his league debut at 16, scored on his Scotland debut at 18 and was sold to Manchester City for a then record £55,000 when he was 20. It was during Law's 10 months at Maine Road that he achieved the almost improbable feat of scoring six goals which did not count in an FA Cup tie. City were leading Luton Town 6–2 – all Law's goals – when the match was abandoned, after 70 minutes, as a result of the pitch becoming waterlogged. The achievement did not go unnoticed in Italy, and Torino swooped, signing both Law and Joe Baker. Their season in Turin was not a happy one, however. Law scored 10 goals in 27 games before a car crash ended his season and he was transferred back to Manchester – to United. Now the prizes rolled in. Law

UNSTOPPABLE Eusebio escapes Giovanni Trapattoni to open the scoring for Benfica in the 1963 Champions Cup Final.

hiding, he was an instant success. He scored twice in a thrilling 5–3 victory over Real Madrid in his first Champions Cup Final and went on to win a string of club honours in Europe and Portugal. Eusebio made his national team debut in the unsuccessful 1962 World Cup qualifying campaign but, within four years, Portugal had become one of the finest sides in the world. They finished third at the 1966 World Cup finals in England where Eusebio was nine-goal top scorer. Those goals included three in a remarkable 5–3 quarter-final defeat of North Korea, plus the penalty with which Portugal beat the Soviet Union in the third-place match at Wembley. Eusebio, who was European Footballer of the Year in 1965, scored 38 goals in 46 internationals for Portugal and was the Portuguese league's leading scorer seven times. He wound down his career in the North American Soccer League before taking up a position as Benfica's international ambassador. A statue of Eusebio now stands outside their stadium.

Bobby Charlton

England (born October 11, 1937)
Inside-left/outside-left/
centre forward
Clubs: Manchester United,
Preston North End
European Footballer of the Year: 1966

A knighthood – creating Sir Bobby – was the inevitable ultimate reward for Charlton's career at the apex of English international football. Football ran in the blood. Charlton was a nephew of Newcastle United hero "Wor Jackie" Milburn, and his brother Jack enjoyed an outstanding career as a player and manager in his own right. Bobby was originally an inside-forward whose thunderous shot rocketed him into Manchester United's "Busby Babes" team in 1957. He scored a typically magnificent long-range goal in the very last game, against Red Star in Belgrade, before the Munich air crash in 1958. Charlton survived the disaster, regained his form and earned an

won two league titles and the 1963 FA Cup, was voted European Footballer of the Year in 1964 and ran up 30 goals in 55 internationals for Scotland. Sadly, he missed United's European Champions Cup victory in 1968 through knee trouble. He ended his career back at Manchester City and retired after the 1973–74 season. His final goal came at the end of a Manchester derby and his cheeky backheel – with chilling irony – condemned his old club United to relegation.

Eusebio

Portugal (born January 25, 1942)
Striker
Clubs: Benfica, Monterrey (Mexico), Boston Minutemen (United States), Toronto Metros-Croatia (Canada)
European Footballer of the Year: 1965

Eusebio was the first great African footballer. There had been outstanding African players before, such as Larbi Ben Barek who starred with Atletico Madrid in the early 1950s,

but Eusebio was the first to emerge on a truly world stage. Eusebio was born in Mozambique but claimed Portuguese citizenship since Mozambique (and neighbouring Angola) were still colonies. Initially, he played for a local offshoot of Sporting of Lisbon, but was snatched away by their great rivals, Benfica. Sporting were furious and Benfica coach Bela Guttman kept Eusebio at a secret address while the fuss died down. When Eusebio did come out of

FIRST GENTLEMAN OF SPORT
England's Bobby Charlton.

England call-up before the 1958 World Cup finals in Sweden. His story earned him enormous sympathetic following, but Charlton was a great player in his own right – as his record 49 goals in 106 England internationals testify. In 1966, he played a vital role in England's World Cup victory, which was the springboard for his European Footballer of the Year accolade. Then, two years later, Charlton returned to Wembley to score twice in Manchester United's climactic European Champions Cup final triumph over Benfica – the first time an English side had won the competition. He ended his England career after the 1970 World Cup and had a short spell as player-manager of Preston North Ends before later returning to Old Trafford as a director.

Florian Albert

Hungary (born September 15, 1941)
Centre forward
Club: Ferencvaros
European Footballer of the Year: 1967

When Florian Albert was hailed as the new Hungarian hero in the early 1960s it was hardly a matter of note. After all, Hungarian football was recognized as one of the most powerful forces in the game – twice World Cup runners-up either side of the war and tactical revolutionaries in the early 1950s. Hindsight, however, has shown that Albert was one of the last products of his country's great flowering of football talent. Only Lajos Detari, of succeeding generations, has proved worthy to rank with Albert in terms of ability – and Detari never made his mark on the World Cup as Albert did in 1966. The son of a farmer, Albert moved to Budapest while still a boy

for the sake of his education, but it was as a sporting talent that he shone as a teenager. At 15 he was signed by Ferencvaros and at 17 he was making his national team debut in a 3–2 win over Sweden in Budapest – within a week of sitting school examinations. Slim and with tight control, Albert was both an outstanding creator and finisher. He made many international goals for team-mates such as veteran Lajos Tichy, but Albert was also four times the Hungarian league's leading marksman. His greatest game was Hungary's 3–1 win over Brazil at the 1966 World Cup finals in England, and he was a popular choice as European Footballer of the Year the following year.

George Best

Northern Ireland (born May 22, 1946)
Attacker

MAGICAL MAGYAR Florian Albert of Budapest club Ferencvaros was the last Hungarian to win a major individual accolade.

Clubs: Manchester United (England), Fulham (England), Hibernian (Scotland), Tampa Bay Rowdies (United States)
European Footballer of the Year: 1968

George Best is proof that appearances at the World Cup finals are not necessary for greatness to be perceived. It was Best's misfortunate in terms of international football luck that his great years fell between Northern Ireland's own finest eras – the World Cup finals of 1958 and 1982 and 1986. Apart from being perhaps the greatest free talent ever to grace the British game, Best was also a symbol of a new era. He was nicknamed "El Beatle" after playing a game in Spain in the 1960s, a decade when footballers began moving towards pop-star popularity and when the high-wage incomes denied their predecessors opened the doors to a fast-lane image of smart cars and pretty girls. In a sense, that is unfair to Best who possessed almost unbounded natural talent which could

briefly, president of Milan and later a member of parliament. The mystery long outlived a career which began amid headlines and controversy when Milan paid his first club, Alessandria, what was then an amazing £65,000 for a half-share in him, at the age of 15! Milan signed him "for real" at just about the same time, in 1961, that they also bought Jimmy Greaves. Rivera was considered the apprentice, but within half a season the homesick Greaves had returned to England and Rivera was established as the new "Boy Wonder" of Italian football. In 16 years with Milan, he was twice a winner of the World Club Cup, the European Champions Cup and the Italian league, as well as three times an Italian cup-winner and once European Footballer of the Year, in 1969. But Rivera's national team career produced a total of only 14 goals in 60 games and reached a painful nadir at the 1970 World Cup when he alternated in the team with Sandro Mazzola. In the final against Brazil, he was only a substitute coming on for the last six minutes of Italy's 4–1 defeat.

Gerd Müller

West Germany
(born November 3, 1945)
Centre forward
Clubs: TSV Nordlingen, Bayern Munich, Fort Lauderdale Strikers (United States)
European Footballer of the Year: 1970

Helmut Schön, West Germany's hugely-successful national manager in the 1960s and 1970s, described Gerd Müller as "my scorer of little goals". This was not intended as a demeaning comment, merely as a statement of the fact that Müller possessed a wonderful gift for pouncing on any ball, loose for even one split-second, deep in any penalty box and scoring. His most famous "little goal" was, indeed, the winner in the 1974 World Cup final when Müller twisted to meet a short cross which Rainer Bonhof appeared to have pulled too far back and stabbed it into the Dutch net. For all that his goal-scoring record was phenomenal, Müller –

take him nimbly – yet at high speed – through the most disciplined defence. He was twice a league championship winner with Manchester United – his only club at the height of his explosive career – as well as an inspiration in the Champions Cup win of 1968, when United demolished Benfica in the final. Within a year, however, the pressures of fame and fortune had begun to wear him down. Best made a string of short-lived comebacks in Scotland and Ireland before delighting audiences – especially in Florida – in what was to be the ill-fated North American Soccer League. Even into his 50s, however, he found his renown as a footballing superstar ensured him a ready welcome on the television talk-show and after-dinner speaking circuit.

Gianni Rivera

Italy (born August 18, 1943
Midfield
Clubs: Alessandria, Milan
European Footballer of the Year: 1969

Gianni Rivera was the great enigma of Italian football in the 1960s and early 1970s. His glorious talents and achievements were beyond reproach. Yet the "Bambino d'Oro" – Golden Boy – was never quite at home playing for his country and successive managers struggled to find a way to get the best out of him. Intellect was not the problem, because Rivera was one of the brainiest inside-forwards of his day, and he went on to become,

GOLDEN BOY Gianni Rivera later went on to become an MP.

BAYERN'S BOMBER *No defence could withstand Gerd Müller.*

nicknamed "Der Bomber" – was under-rated as a footballer. Rarely did he have a chance to display the full range of his abilities but Leeds United were certainly caught out in the 1975 Champions Cup final when Müller had to drop back into the Bayern Munich midfield because of injuries. Not that everyone found even his goal-scoring talents easy to admire. His first coach at Bayern, Zlatko "Tschik" Cajkovski, thought president Wilhelm Neudecker was joking when he introduced the new, young, centre forward at pre-season training. "I'm not putting that little elephant in among my string of thoroughbreds," complained Cajkovski. But he did – and Bayern never looked back. Müller's goals shot them out of the regional league to victory in the European Cup-Winners' Cup inside three years. At the end, before trying his luck with ultimately sorry consequences in the North American Soccer League, he had scored well over 600 goals including a record 365 in the Bundesliga and an astonishing 68 in 62 internationals.

Johan Cruyff

Holland (born April 25, 1947)
Centre forward
Clubs: Ajax, Barcelona (Spain), Los Angeles Aztecs (United States), New York Cosmos (United States), Levante (Spain), Ajax, Feyenoord
European Footballer of the Year: 1971, 1973 and 1974

Johan Cruyff was the first player to win the European Footballer of the Year award on three occasions – Michel Platini and Cruyff's friend and pupil Marco Van Basten would later emulate his achievement. The fact that Cruyff carried off the Golden Ball three times within four years underlines the manner in which he dominated not only European, but also world football in the 1970s. His platform was the great Ajax and Holland sides built, largely, by Rinus Michels and his method was the "total football" revolution which harnessed the rapid developments being made in both fitness and technique. "Total football" was a style rather than a tactic. It demanded high football intelligence, allowing versatile players of high ability to interchange positions at will. But everything revolved around Cruyff, the nominal centre forward wearing the No 14 shirt – which he popularized 20 years before squad numbers became commonplace. Cruyff, blooded at Ajax originally by English coach Vic Buckingham, inspired Ajax to victory in three European Champions Cups before transferring to Barcelona in 1973 for a then world record £922,000. A year later, he was seen at his very best, captaining Holland as they beame World Cup runners-up to hosts West Germany. Cruyff retired from the national team before the 1978 finals for reasons which have always remained shrouded in mystery. He played "only" 48 times for his country. Later he became enormously successful as an independent-minded coach. In 1987, he guided Ajax to victory in the European Cup-Winners' Cup, repeated that achievement with Barcelona and also managed Barcelona to victory in the European Champions Cup in 1992, as well as four successive Spanish league titles.

Cruyff left Barcelona in the spring of 1996 after a club record stint of nine years in charge.

Franz Beckenbauer

West Germany
(born September 11, 1945)
Midfielder/sweeper
Clubs: Bayern Munich, New York Cosmos (United States), Hamburg
European Footballer of the Year: 1972 and 1976

Franz Beckenbauer stands as one of the all-time great personalities of world football through his World Cup achievements, his one-man revolution as a player and his remarkable successes as coach and club president. "Kaiser Franz" – the nickname he earned from his imperious playing style – gave up a job as an insurance salesman to sign professionally for Bayern Munich in 1964. He played first in midfield then as an attacking sweeper – an unheard-of role – when they won the European Cup-Winners' Cup in 1967. In the 1966 and 1970 World Cups he starred for West Germany in midfield, but by 1974 he had reverted to sweeper and become not only captain of the team but its director of operations out on the pitch. Beckenbauer combined speed, efficiency and an acute football brain with a natural grace which carried him to a then German record 103

caps, as well as virtually every major prize – the 1974 World Cup (runner-up in 1966); 1972 European Championship (runner-up in 1976); European Champions Cup in 1974, 1975 and 1976; the 1976 World Club Cup; European Cup-Winners' Cup in 1967; plus German championships and cups. Beckenbauer spent three high-profile years in the United States, with New York Cosmos, then returned briefly to play for Hamburg before retiring to concentrate on his business interests, media work – and golfing handicap. Not for long. In 1984 he was persuaded, without having had any coaching experience, to take over as Germany's national manager. He

HAT-TRICK HERO
Johan Cruyff was the first triple winner of Europe's top award.

FOOTBALL REVOLUTIONARY Franz Beckenbauer in his favoured role as attacking sweeper.

took them to World Cup victory in 1990, retired briefly again, spent a short, unhappy spell with Marseille, then returned to Bayern Munich as a director and then president. Twice he was forced to pick up the coaching reins. The first time he guided them to the league title, the second time to UEFA Cup success. Not surprisingly, Beckenbauer has been suggested as a possible future president of FIFA.

Oleg Blokhin

Soviet Union (born November 5, 1952)
Left-winger
Clubs: Kiev Dynamo, Vorwärts Steyr (Austria)
European Footballer of the Year: 1975

If Oleg Blokhin had been playing in the 1990s, it is highly unlikely that he would have risen to the achievement level possible during his actual playing career. That is the ironic perspective now cast through events more political than sporting. In the mid-1970s, Blokhin was the star player for Kiev Dynamo from the Ukraine who were the dominant club force in Soviet football. Kiev provided the Soviet national team virtually *en bloc*, plus the Olympic team. They regularly won the domestic championship and were provided with all the financial subsidies necessary from Moscow to compete on equal terms with the likes of Ajax and Bayern Munich. Blokhin was both their top scorer and their quickest attacking raider – thanks to the training tips of his friend and compatriot Valeri Borzov, the 1972 Olympic men's 100m sprint champion. Blokhin's key role in Kiev's European Cup-Winners' Cup triumph of 1975 earned him that year's European Footballer of the Year accolade. He went on to play in the World Cups of 1982 and 1986, having by then become the first Soviet player to top a century of international appearances (he ultimately totalled 39 goals in 109 games). Real Madrid once tried to prise Blokhin out of the Soviet

HISTORY MAN Oleg Blokhin was the star product of a different era.

game but without success. By the time he was "freed" to move west with Vorwärts Steyr of Austria, he was long past his best. Blokhin stayed in the West to develop a successful career as a coach in Greece.

Allan Simonsen

Denmark (born December 15, 1952)
Forward
Clubs: Vejle, Borussia Mönchengladbach (West Germany), Barcelona (Spain), Charlton Athletic (England), Vejle
European Footballer of the Year: 1977

Allan Simonsen was the pint-sized forward who inspired Denmark's emergence in the early 1980s. Sadly, Simonsen broke an ankle in the opening match of the 1984 European Championship finals against France and never quite regained the same form again. He played successfully for the Danish club Vejle then in West Germany with Borussia

DANISH REVIVALIST Allan Simonsen inspired an entire generation.

Mönchengladbach. He was three times champion of Germany, once German cup-winner and twice UEFA Cup-winner with Mönchengladbach, and also inspired them to reach the 1977 European Champions Cup final where they lost 3–1 to Liverpool, Simonsen scoring Borussia's equaliser. Later, after moving to Spain, he won the Spanish cup and the European Cup-Winners' Cup with Barcelona. Simonsen was happy in Barcelona while master coach Hennes Weisweiler – his mentor in Germany – was in charge. But Weisweiler fell foul of club politics and his abrupt departure left the writing on the wall for Simonsen. English club Charlton Athletic, remarkably, managed to persuade Simonsen to join them but the experiment soon turned sour. Simonsen played in only 16 games in England, scoring nine goals, before

returning home to Vejle. Simonsen played 54 times for Denmark and scored 20 goals. The most important was probably the penalty with which the Danes beat England at Wembley in the 1984 European Championship qualifiers. Simonsen returned to the international scene later as national coach of the Faroe Islands.

Kevin Keegan

England (born February 14, 1951)
Forward
Clubs: Scunthorpe United, Liverpool, Hamburg (West Germany), Southampton, Newcastle United
European Footballer of the Year: 1978 and 1979

Kevin Keegan was the outstanding England player of the 1970s and early 1980s. Through tremendous dedication and determination, he lifted himself above players with greater natural talent – as his European

Footballer of the Year accolades prove. In fact, it was a mystery that Keegan did not first win the award, in 1977, after inspiring Liverpool to their first European Champions Cup success. Keegan left immediately afterwards for Hamburg, because he wanted a new challenge, and he triumphed again – leading them to the German league title and to the 1980 Champions Cup final (where they lost to Nottingham Forest in Madrid). The 1982 World Cup finals in Spain should have been the climax of Keegan's career. Instead he was kept on the sidelines by injury and played only as a half-fit second-half substitute against Spain in the goalless draw which brought England's elimination in the second round. It proved to be his last game for England, as new squad

SELF-MADE SUPERSTAR Kevin Keegan earned the highest rewards.

manager Bobby Robson axed him brutally at the start of the following season. After that Keegan invested his enthusiasm in club revivals, first at Southampton, then with Newcastle United. In 1984 he retired to his villa in Spain – and a seven-year marathon round of golf – before suddenly returning to Newcastle as manager. Keegan spent heavily to save Newcastle from relegation to the second – in reality, the old third – division, and lifting them into the highest reaches of the Premiership. When his cavalier style of football failed to earn rewards in terms of silverware, so Keegan abruptly resigned in January 1997.

Karl-Heinz Rummenigge

West Germany
(born September 25, 1955)
Right-winger/forward
Clubs: Borussia Lippstadt, Bayern Munich, Internazionale (Italy), Servette (Switzerland)
European Footballer of the Year: 1980 and 1981

"Kalle" Rummenigge was Bayern Munich's leading player in the immediate post-Beckenbauer era. They narrowly overlapped – Rummenigge's first European Champions Cup final in 1976 was Beckenbauer's last. Initially a right-winger, Rummenigge later moved inside to a role he preferred, linking midfield with attack and he would have played many more than 95 times for West Germany had it not been for injuries. Rummenigge was working as a bank clerk in his teens while playing part-time for Borussia Lippstadt. He turned professional when Bayern came in with an offer and cost the Munich club a mere £4,500 – which must count as one of the bargains of modern German football, since they sold him later to Italy's Internazionale for £2 million. Rummenigge had first impressed Inter officials with a World Cup hat-trick against Mexico in 1978 and followed up at international level by captaining his country to European Championship victory in 1980. Injuries reduced his effectiveness in the early 1980s and controversy lingered over whether German manager Jupp Derwall was right to play him from the start in the 1982 World Cup final defeat by Italy in Madrid. Rummenigge ended his playing career with Servette in Switzerland

HERO, VILLAIN AND HERO AGAIN
World Cup-winning striker Paolo Rossi.

before returning home to become a vice-president of Bayern.

Paolo Rossi

Italy (born September 23, 1956)
Centre forward
Clubs: Prato, Juventus, Como, Lanerossi Vicenza, Perugia, Juventus, Milan
European Footballer of the Year: 1982

Paolo Rossi's progress from villain to hero was accomplished in less than a year. He began 1982 still under a two-year suspension for his alleged role in a match-fixing scandal organized in Italy by underworld betting gangs. The suspension expired in April that year, when Rossi resumed his playing career with Juventus, who had bought him during the ban. Rossi played in Juve's last three games of the season, then went to Spain to lead Italy's attack in the World Cup finals. After a slow start, he scored a sensational second round hat-trick against Brazil, followed up with two goals against Poland in the semi-final and one more against West Germany in Italy's 3–1 win in the final to become the event's leading scorer with six goals. It was a second remarkable turn to Rossi's career. The earlier one concerned his teenage years. He had been given away on a free transfer by Juventus

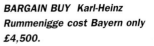

BARGAIN BUY Karl-Heinz Rummenigge cost Bayern only £4,500.

FRENCH ALL-ROUNDER Michel Platini was successively player, skipper, manager then director.

Michel Platini
France (born June 21, 1955)
Attacking midfielder
Clubs: Nancy-Lorraine,
Saint-Etienne, Juventus (Italy)
European Footballer of the Year:
1983, 1984 and 1985

Few footballers have made a greater global impact than Michel Platini. In the space of a few weeks in the spring of 1997, he was voted, in Italy, the greatest player ever to have lined up for Juventus and, at home in France, the No 1 sports personality of his generation (French football federation president Noel Le Graet was merely fifth). Platini set out on the road to superstardom at the Montreal Olympics in 1976 and stepped up a gear at the 1978 World Cup in Argentina. Four years later he inspired France to fourth place in the World Cup finals in Spain after being voted man of the match in the dramatic semi-final shoot-out defeat by West Germany in Seville. After the 1982 finals Platini was sold by Saint-Etienne to Juventus with whom he was three times the Italian league's top scorer and converted the penalty kick which brought Juve their long-awaited European Champions Cup victory over Liverpool in 1985 (albeit lost in the mist of the Heysel tragedy). At national team level, Platini scored 41 goals in 72 internationals and led by example when France won the 1984 European Championship on home soil. He was not only their captain but top-scored with nine goals, including hat-tricks against Belgium and Yugoslavia and the first goal in the 2–0 victory over Spain in the final. Platini was, simply, the greatest football achiever of his generation, and the only player voted European Footballer of the Year three years in succession. After retiring he concentrated briefly on commercial interests and TV work, until he was persuaded to become national manager, taking France to the finals of the 1992 European Championship. France disappointed, failing to progress beyond the first round and Platini decided that he had had enough. Within little more than a year, however, he had been persuaded to return to the game even further up the ladder – as joint president with Fernand Sastre of the domestic Organizing Committe for the 1998 World Cup finals.

before he had ever played a league game because of knee trouble. Fortunately, other coaches had more faith in Rossi, who burst on to the international scene at the 1978 World Cup finals in Argentina. Juventus tried to buy him back, but were outbid by Perugia. Finding the world record £3.5 million fee virtually bankrupted the provincial club who were relegated and had no option then but to sell Rossi – who was, by now, suspended – to Juventus at a huge loss. Sadly, Rossi's earlier injuries later caught up with him and he had to retire at only 29. Later he established himself as an agent and pundit – his popularity and reputation unaffected by his run-in with the seamier side of Italian soccer.

Igor Belanov

Soviet Union
Right-winger
Clubs: Kiev Dynamo, Borussia
Mönchengladbach (West Germany)
European Footballer of the Year: 1986

Had *France Football* changed their rules a decade earlier, Igor Belanov would not have become European Footballer of the Year. If voting had been allowed to focus on all players of any nationality with clubs in Europe, then the 1986 award would have been a walkover for Diego Maradona – then starring with Napoli in Italy at club level while inspiring Argentina's World Cup triumph in Mexico. But Belanov was, that year, the European hit of the finals. In fact, he was lucky to have made the finals at all. Belanov had been called up in the spring of 1986 by Soviet Union coach Eduard Malofeyev – who was sacked on the

eve of the finals – and new manager Valeri Lobanovski turned the squad upside-down. The fact that Lobanovski had worked with Belanov at Kiev Dynamo tipped the balance in his favour. He duly repaid Lobanovski with a string of sensational performances. Belanov scored in the Soviet Union's 6–0, first-game thrashing of Hungary, which set the team off towards the top of their group, then he claimed a superb hat-trick in the dramatic 4–3 extra-time defeat by Belgium in the second round. Belanov was the surprise new hero of European football. Two years later, he further vindicated that judgement by helping the Soviet Union to finish runners-up at the 1988 European Championship in Germany. However, Belanov's career – and in parallel his private life – went rapidly downhill after a transfer to Borussia Mönchengladbach.

Ruud Gullit

Holland (born September 1, 1962)
Forward/midfielder/sweeper
Clubs: Haarlem, Feyenoord, PSV
Eindhoven, Milan (Italy), Sampdoria
(Italy), Milan (Italy), Sampdoria
(Italy), Chelsea (England)
European Footballer of the Year: 1987

Football intelligence has been the hallmark of Ruud Gullit's career – from his early days when he was playing sweeper for British coach Barry Hughes at Haarlem, on – via Feyenoord – to his leadership of the Milan revival in the late 1980s, then on to television and managerial stardom in England in the late 1990s. Along the way, Gullit also demonstrated that footballers can also look beyond the narrow confines of the game: he took a vehement stance against South African apartheid and was a fervent supporter for the release

HEAD FIRST Ruud Gullit on the way to European title success in 1988.

from imprisonment of Nelson Mandela. Gullit would surely have won the European Footballer of the Year accolade more than once had it not been for the terrible knee injuries which interrupted his career at what should have been its zenith. Milan paid a world record £6.5 million for Gullit in 1987, and were rewarded when he inspired them to an Italian championship in his first season and European Champions Cup in his second and third. Remarkably, Gullit helped Milan to win that second Champions Cup, against Benfica in Vienna in 1990, despite having been restricted by injury to only two league games all season. Gullit's impatience with injuries and with the "overflow" foreigners policy of coach Fabio Capello led to him joining Sampdoria

DERBY PRESSURE for Marco Van Basten, leading Milan against Inter.

on a free transfer in 1994. He returned to Milan in 1995, however, then went back to Samp on loan – a few months later – before setting off for England, in the summer of 1995, to first play for, and then succeed, manager Glenn Hoddle at Chelsea. Gullit's Holland career was full of ups and downs. He captained them to European Championship success in 1988 but retired midway through the 1994 World Cup qualifying campaign. A year later he made a one-match comeback before quitting for a second time on the eve of the finals.

Marco Van Basten

Holland (born October 31, 1964)
Centre forward
Clubs: Ajax, Milan (Italy)
European Footballer of the Year:
1988, 1989 and 1992

Van Basten was the last player to secure the European Footballer of the Year award three times. He might even have qualified for a fourth success had it not been for the ankle injuries which brought his career to a sadly premature halt in 1995. Tall and angular, Van Basten first earned international acclaim at the 1983 World Youth Cup. By then he had already been discovered in Holland by Ajax and it was as a substitute for his mentor Johan Cruyff that he made his competitive debut. In all, Van Basten scored 128 league goals for Ajax before joining Milan for a mere £1.5 million in 1987. He signed off by scoring Ajax's winner in the 1987 European Cup-winners Cup final victory over Lokomotive Leipzig. With Ajax, Van Basten had won not only domestic prizes and the Cup-Winners' Cup, but also the European Golden Boot – awarded to Europe's top league marksman – with 37 goals in the 1985–86 season. Milan helped him to gain even more glory such as winner's medals for the World Club Cup and European Champions Cups, plus individual honours – including the FIFA World Footballer of the Year

VOICE OF AUTHORITY German skipper Lothar Matthäus.

trophy. Milan looked to a half-fit Van Basten in the 1993 Champions Cup final against Marseille in Munich but he had played only 15 intermittent league games all season and the challenge proved beyond him. Van Basten never played again. At least he left a wonderful legacy for football's memory – one of the all-time great international goals – when he volleyed home a long, looping cross from Arnold Muhren to shoot Holland 2–0 ahead against the Soviet Union in the 1988 European Championship final in Munich.

Lothar Matthäus

Germany (born March 21, 1961)
Midfielder/sweeper
Clubs: Borussia Mönchengladbach, Bayern Munich, Internazionale (Italy), Bayern Munich
European Footballer of the Year: 1990

Lothar Matthäus is way out in front as Germany's record international with 122 caps to his credit and a pedigree which includes having captained his country to victory in the 1990 World Cup finals in Italy. Matthäus might also have scored the winning goal against Argentina in the final in Rome, but a niggling thigh strain meant he handed responsibility for the decisive penalty to Andy Brehme. Matthäus said later that, after having been a World Cup runner-up to Argentina four years earlier, he did not want to take the slightest chance of letting them off the hook second time around. Matthäus played with enormous success for Borussia Mönchengladbach, Bayern Munich (first time around) and Internazionale in Italy, who then sold him back to Bayern Munich while he was still recovering from the career-threatening knee injury which had forced him out of the 1992 European Championship finals. Matthäus switched back from his aggressive midfield role to sweeper, but his prospects of emulating Franz Beckenbauer and collecting, as captain, the 1996 European Championship were wrecked by an achilles tendon injury which kept him out for much of the 1995–96 season. Matthäus has won league titles and the UEFA Cup with both Inter and Bayern despite a habit of speaking his mind with a bluntness which has not always been appreciated by his team-mates.

Jean-Pierre Papin

France (born November 5, 1963)
Striker
Clubs: Valenciennes, Club Brugge (Belgium), Marseille, Milan (Italy), Bayern Munich (Germany), Bordeaux
European Footballer of the Year: 1991

A designer trick, introduced in autumn 1996, said everything about the fame and popularity of Jean-Pierre Papin in his native France. Papin had just returned from Bayern Munich to play for Bordeaux at a time when the French league had confirmed the introduction of squad numbers and player names on the backs of shirts. Every other player had their name across their shoulders. It was enough, however, for Papin to have the initials "J P P". That was sufficient identification for one of French football's most successful marksmen. Papin started out with his native Valenciennes and then went on to play in Belgium with Brugge, before returning to France to become captain and attacking inspiration of Marseille. In the now-notorious set-up under Bernard Tapie, Papin was top scorer in the French league for four successive seasons before joining Milan in the summer of 1992. A year later he found himself appearing as a substitute for Milan against Marseille in the Champions Cup final which the French club won 1–0. It was Papin's second Champions Cup final defeat – he had been on the

THAT'S THE WAY TO DO IT
Papin celebrates another goal.

losing side when Red Star Belgrade beat Marseille in Bari after a penalty shoot-out in 1991. Papin's consolation was to be voted European Footballer of the Year seven months later, but he never really adjusted to the style of football either in Italy or later in Germany with Bayern. His comparative failures to set alight either Milan or Munich cost him a place in the French squad at Euro 96.

Roberto Baggio

Italy (born February 18, 1967)
Forward
Clubs: Vicenza, Fiorentina,
Juventus, Milan
European Footballer of the Year: 1993

Roberto Baggio, for a peace-loving Buddhist, has provoked a remarkable number of controversies – including street violence and riots. He made his name originally as a winger with local club Vicenza in the third division as a 15-year-old and was picked up three years later by Fiorentina's much-admired scouting system. In five seasons by the River Arno, Baggio into a superstar. His finest season was his fifth, in which he scored 17 goals in 32 league games and led Fiorentina to the semi-finals of the UEFA Cup – where they lost to Juventus. Fury then erupted in Florence when it emerged that Baggio was being sold to none other than Juventus for a world record £8 million. It needed riot police to quell the protesting Fiorentina fans – who then attacked the cars of Italy's players as they arrived at the nearby Coverciano training centre. Baggio demonstrated a few weeks later just why he was worth such a fee when he scored a marvellous solo goal for Italy against Czechoslovakia. Juventus saw Baggio as the successor to Michel Platini. He helped deliver the UEFA Cup in 1993 and the league title in 1995 but, by then, the honeymoon was over and Baggio had already agreed to move to Milan. He was a national hero after scoring the goals which took Italy to the 1994 World Cup final. He played despite having pulled a hamstring in the semi-final. But missing the decisive penalty in the final shoot-out was the start of a

ITALY'S INSPIRATION Roberto Baggio celebrates his World Cup quarter-final winner against Spain.

steady decline which not even the fresh football air of Milan could arrest.

Hristo Stoichkov

Bulgaria (born August 2, 1966)
Forward
Clubs: Maritza Plovdiv,
Hebros Harmanli, CSKA Sofia,
Barcelona (Spain), Parma (Italy),
Barcelona (Spain)
European Footballer of the Year: 1994

Hristo Stoichkov was furious when he was placed only second in the European Footballer of the Year poll in 1993. He believed he deserved to have been placed top, rather than Roberto Baggio – and that helped provoke him to the superb peak of the 1994 World Cup when his top-scoring

six goals took Bulgaria to the semi-finals for the first time. Stoichkov's career had always been volatile. As a 19-year-old he was banned for a year after a mass player brawl at the Bulgarian cup final. After that, he bounced from one success to another. He was voted Bulgarian Footballer of the Year for four successive years from 1989 to 1992 and was three times league champion with CSKA. The goals flowed at home and abroad, and Stoichkov shared the 1989–90 Golden Boot – as top league scorer in Europe – with Real Madrid's Hugo Sanchez, both scoring 38 goals. He was then signed by Barcelona on coach Johan Cruyff's personal recommendation. Stoichkov and Cruyff were not always so friendly even

though they celebrated four successive Spanish championships and victory in the 1992 European Champions Cup. In 1994 he was not only – finally – voted European Footballer of the Year but he also became only the second Bulgarian footballer to be voted national Sportsman of the Year (the other was the late Georgi Asparoukhov quarter of a century earlier). By that time, Stoichkov and Cruyff were not speaking and the Bulgarian was sold to Italy's Parma. Italian club discipline was not to his liking and he returned a year later to Barcelona – this time under Bobby Robson. Stoichkov then boycotted the Bulgarian national team for almost a year in protest at the appointment of Hristo Bonev as manager.

George Weah

Liberia (born October 1, 1966)
Centre forward
Clubs: Young Survivors, Bongrang, Mighty Barolla, Tonnerre (Cameroon), Monaco (France), Paris Saint-Germain (France), Milan (Italy)
European Footballer of the Year: 1995

George Weah made history, in 1995, after becoming the first winner of the European Footballer of the Year poll since *France Football* changed their rules to open up the ballot to players of any nationality. Yet, although a

BULGARIA'S BEST Hristo Stoichkov celebrates one of his six goals at the 1994 World Cup.

have fielded teams in the qualifying competitions for the last African Nations Cup or the 1998 World Cup.

Matthias Sammer

East Germany and Germany
(born September 5, 1967)
Midfielder/sweeper
Clubs: Grodlitz (East Germany), Einheit Dresden (East Germany), Dynamo Dresden (East Germany), Stuttgart (Germany), Internazionale (Italy), Borussia Dortmund (Germany)
European Footballer of the Year: 1996

Matthias Sammer made history in December 1996 when he became the first player from the former East Germany to win the treasured Golden Ball. Sammer's father, Klaus, had been a midfield general with Dresden and the East German national team and he had barely retired before Matthias was making his own reputation with Dresden and the national team. In 1986 Matthias guided East Germany from midfield to the European youth title. He was promoted almost immediately into the senior national squad, helped Dresden win their championship in 1989 and the league and cup double a year later. That summer also saw the collapse of the Berlin Wall – and Sammer was immediately brought west by Stuttgart. It was in his new home of the Neckarstadion that he became, the following December, the first East German to play for unified Germany in a 4–0 defeat of Switzerland. The 1992 European Championship in Sweden does not bring back happy memories for Sammer. He failed to find a spark of form in the shock final defeat against Denmark and was substituted at half-time. It was to be the start of a dismal nine months: a transfer to Internazionale in Italy proved a disaster, as he failed to adjust to either the lifestyle or the football in Milan, and Borussia Dortmund brought him home to Germany in mid-season. The fee, reported to have been a record paid by a German club of £4 million, was ridiculed at the time, but two league championships vindicated Dortmund's judgement – along with Sammer's key role in Germany's triumph at Euro 96. A year later and he was anchoring Dortmund's Champions Cup victory.

CHAMPIONS OF EUROPE Matthias Sammer (right) celebrates with keeper Andy Kopke.

SETTING NEW STANDARDS Citizen of the world George Weah.

Liberian international, Weah was in fact a French citizen – having taken citizenship after his years of residence while playing for Monaco and Paris Saint-Germain. Born in the Liberian capital of Monrovia, Weah played in Cameroon with top club Tonnerre of Yaounde before moving to France with Monaco in 1988. He rose to stardom under the fatherly guidance of Arsène Wenger to win the league championship alongside Glenn Hoddle and Mark Hateley in 1991, then moved to Paris a year later. Two years after that, he joined Milan for £3.5 million. That now price now looks ridiculously cheap, considering Weah's status in the world game and his ability to score goals of breathtaking brilliance. Weah has put his multi-million earnings to sensible use. His wife and children live in New York, while he has re-invested thousands of pounds in football in his native Liberia. Without the money Weah provided, Liberia could not

THE GREAT MATCHES

Football's history is built on players and teams and great occasions. The greatest matches stand as milestones down the highway of the game. They mark the great competitions, securing the finest players and their clubs and countries in legend. In European terms it is no coincidence that the greatest matches have most often featured teams from Italy, Spain, Germany and England – the region's greatest countries, replete in skill, power, vision and the spirit which never admits to a lost cause.

SCHIAVIO HAS FINAL WORD

Italy v Czechoslovakia
Stadio Flaminio, Rome
World Cup final

Italy 2 (Orsi 81, Schiavio 95)
Czechoslovakia 1 (Puc 71)
HT: 0–0. 90min: 1–1. Att: 50,000.
Ref: I Eklind (Swe)

Italy: Combi – Monzeglio, Allemandi, Ferraris IV, Monti, Bertolini, Guaita, Meazza, Schiavio, Ferrari, Orsi.
Czechoslovakia: Planicka – Zenisek, Ctyrocky, Kostalek, Cambal, Krcil, Junek, Svoboda, Sobotka, Nejedly, Puc.

The World Cup had been launched four years earlier, staged in Uruguay and won by Uruguay. The second finals were hosted by Italy, took place after the novelty of a worldwide qualifying competition, and produced the first all-European World Cup final.

Italy had the tougher run to the final, battling their way past Spain in the quarter-finals (after a replay) and Austria's Wunderteam in the semis. The Czechs prevented an Axis final by defeating Germany in the semis.

The final was not a sell-out. Italy were expected to walk it. The Czechs had other ideas. Both teams used the old attacking centre-half system: Italy's Luisito Monti more rugged and physical. Czechoslovakia's Stefan Cambal more skilled and inventive.

Czechoslovakia had the better of the early exchanges but Italy, reviving, wasted chances by trying to walk the ball into the net. Outside-left Antonin Puc shocked the 50,000 Italian fans by opening the scoring with 19 minutes remaining, after the Italian defence had only half-cleared his corner.

Legendary manager Vittorio Pozzo patrolled the touchline in a fury. His team appeared paralysed, perhaps fearing the reaction of their country's dictator, Benito Mussolini, even more than that of Pozzo. Czechoslovakia twice went close to extending their lead. Jiri Sobotka missed badly, then Frantisek Svoboda hit a post. Eight minutes only remained when Italy scrambled an equaliser they barely deserved. "Mumo" Orsi wandered from the left wing into midfield, accelerated on to a pass from right-winger Enrico Guaita, and swirled a shot beyond the great Czech keeper, Frantisek Planicka.

Italy were the stronger in extra-time. Cramp wore down the Czechs and the Italians pounced seven minutes into the first extra half.

Giuseppe Meazza, the Ambrosiana-Inter inside forward whose name would later be given to the San Siro stadium in Milan, had been kept remarkably quiet by the Czechoslovak defence.

Now he began to wander wide to the wings. Meazza found space and time, seized possession, then moved the ball on for Guaita.

Seconds later and Bologna's veteran centre-forward Angelo Schiavio, despite having been virtually crippled by cramp, had turned Italy into Europe's first world champions.

Schiavio thus finished alongside

FLOORED ... Combi is helpless as Antonin Puc scores for the Czechs.

Czechoslovakia's Oldrich Nejedly and Germany's Edmund Conen as the tournament's joint top-scorers on four goals apiece.

Italy's victory did not engender the reaction Mussolini and Pozzo had wanted. The veteran Belgian referee John Langenus summed up the foreign reaction when he observed: "Italy wanted to win, of course, but they allowed it to be seen too clearly."

Four years later Pozzo rebuilt his team almost entirely. Only inside forwards Meazza and Gino Ferrari survived as the manager switched his tactics from using an attacking centre-half to stopper centre-back, after the British Herbert Chapman model.

Italy thus won their second successive World Cup, in France. As for Czechoslovakia, stars such as inside-left Nejedly and his wing partner, Puc, were there again. This time, however, they fell in the quarter-finals, after a replay, to Brazil.

MAY 16, 1948

LOVELY DAY FOR ENGLAND

Italy v England
Stadio Comunale, Turin
International Friendly

Italy 0
England 4 (Mortensen 4, Lawton 24, Finney 70, 72)
HT: 0–2. Att: 85,000. Ref: J Escartin (Sp)

Italy: Bacigalupo – Ballarin, Eliani, Annovazzi, Parola, Grezar, Menti, Loik, Gabetto, Mazzola, Carapellese.
England: Swift – Scott, Howe, Wright, Franklin, Cockburn, Matthews, Mortensen, Lawton, Mannion, Finney.

Meetings between Italy and England have always been spicy affairs. The technical skill and temperamental pride of Italian football has always struck sparks off the more physically direct English style. Surprisingly, two of Europe's greatest soccer nations did not meet at national team level until the mid-1930s.

In 1948, when they met in Turin, Italy and England had played each other only three times previously. Two of the matches had been drawn, in Rome in 1933 and in Milan in 1939, and the other – the infamous Battle of Highbury in 1934 – had ended in the lone victory of the series for England, by 3–2.

When the countries first met after the Second World War all Italy was confident of victory. Football was pulling enormous crowds in a post-war boom common throughout Europe – nowhere more passionate than Italy. They were the World Cup-holders, having held the Jules Rimet Trophy since the last pre-war finals in France in 1938, and they had discovered a wonderful new generation of players.

England were back in the international fold after the four home countries had quit FIFA between the wars in a row over amateurism. In 1946, they rejoined and England were expected to qualify for their World Cup debut in 1950 in Brazil.

This match, commented one Italian newspaper: "is the World Cup final two years early".

Italy's team was built around the stars of Torino, who were in the midst

of winning four successive championships. Valerio Bacigalupo was in the tradition of agile Italian keepers and the inside-forward trio of Ezio Loik, Guglielmo Gabetto and skipper Valentino Mazzola – father of future hero Sandro – had been hailed as the best in the world.

England met them with great names of their own in wingers Stanley Matthews and Tom Finney, centre-forward Tommy Lawton and Frank Swift in goal.

Swift was captaining England for the first time. Choosing a keeper as skipper raised controversy but Swift rose to the occasion with a string of magnificent early saves. As Gabetto beat his fists on the pitch in frustration after being defied yet again, Swift patted him on the head and said: "Never mind – you can score goals again next week, when I'm not here!"

In attack, much of England's inspi-

ration came from Matthews. He had been written off as too old by the *Daily Mail* in 1947 and by the *Daily Express* earlier in 1948. Yet he took Alberto Eliani, the Italian left-back, to pieces.

Italy, said to be on a then-sensational win bonus of £100 a man, had prepared for the match up at a mountain hideaway and began as if about to bury England under an avalanche of goals. Then, in the fourth minute, England scored after a counter-attack of the sort which would later come to be considered traditionally Italian. Matthews went round Eliani and laid on the pass which Mortensen fired beyond Bacigalupo from an acute angle.

The Italians returned to the attack with even greater verve and purpose. But Swift proved equal to the challenge and, in the 24th minute, England scored again. Centre-half Neil Franklin dispossessed Gabetto, Matthews escaped Eliani again and

LAST WORD … Tom Finney shoots past Valerio Bacigalupo.

Mortensen charged almost half the length of the pitch before setting up Tommy Lawton to score.

Half-time came and went with Italy dominating possession but with England resisting superbly. Midway through the second half Finney twice turned the screw. He converted a Wilf Mannion pass and then, within two minutes scored again from a Mortensen pass. There was to be no repeat, of course, at the 1950 World Cup finals in Brazil.

England crashed out after losing sensationally to the United States. More tragically, most of the Italians never even made it to Brazil. In May 1949, returning from a testimonial match in Lisbon, Torino's entire senior squad died in the Superga air disaster. November 25, 1953

NOVEMBER 25, 1953

THE DAY THE WORLD CHANGED

England v Hungary
Wembley
Friendly international
England 3 (Sewell 15, Mortensen 37, Ramsey 62 pen)
Hungary 6 (Hidegkuti 1, 20, 56, Puskas 22, 29, Bozsik 55)
HT: 2–4. Att: 100,000.
Ref: L Horn (Hol)

England: Merrick, Ramsey, Eckersley, Wright, Johnston, Dickinson, Matthews, Taylor, Mortensen, Sewell, Robb.

Hungary: Grosics (Geller 74), Buzansky, Lantos, Bozsik, Lorant, Zakarias, Budai, Kocsis, Hidegkuti, Puskas, Czibor.

This was the match which changed the world, as far as English football was concerned. Until this day – despite the evidence of the 1950 World Cup and an increasing number of defeats in Europe – the English still maintained that they were kings of soccer. While England remained unbeaten at Wembley by continental opposition this self-deception was sustainable. The Magical Magyars exposed all this, in most dramatic fashion, as a lie.

The English Press had built the match up as the Game of the Century. Hungary were Olympic champions and arrived at the Cumberland Hotel in the West End of London having won 25 and drawn six of their previ-ous 32 games. They had scored in every match they had played for six seasons. But nobody took them seri-ously enough. Not their record, their revolutionary lightweight kit, their depth of talent (Ferenc Puskas, Sandor Kocsis, Jozsef Bozsik, Nandor Hidegkuti, etc) or their tactical sophis-tication. Hungary used the withdrawn centre-forward ploy popular in eastern Europe. That meant inverting the tradi-tional attacking form of the WM. The centre-forward, instead of leading the line, held back in midfield to link with the wing-halves. The inside forwards, traditional fetchers and carriers in English football, were attack leaders for Hungary. Skipper Puskas, for exam-ple, scored 83 goals in 84 internation-als; partner Kocsis scored 75 in 68.

England were caught naively unprepared. Centre-half Harry Johnston sighted on Hidegkuti as the Hungarian centre-forward and went out to mark him. In the event, Johnston was pulled up into no-man's land and Puskas and Kocsis ran in behind him to deadly effect.

Hungary benefited from a goal in the first minute, Hidegkuti firing past England keeper Gil Merrick from the edge of the penalty box. "That was a tonic," said Puskas afterwards. "The goal steadied our team but the England players just grew more worried."

Jackie Sewell equalised in the 15th minute but, before half an hour was up, Hungary were 4–1 ahead – Hidegkuti scoring the second, Puskas the third and fourth. Puskas's first goal was one of the greatest or cheekiest Wembley has ever seen. Billy Wright barred his way to goal, so Puskas dragged the ball back with the studs of his left boot, pivoted, then fired up into the roof of the net.

The goals flowed in. Stan Mortensen pulled one back for England and Alf Ramsey converted a second-half penalty. But these were mere consolations. Hungary scored twice more, through Bozsik and Hidegkuti again.

They won 6–3 but the disappoint-ment for defeat for England was tem-pered by knowledge that the Hungarians were one of the greatest of teams. As Wright said: "The reason for our defeat was not our bad football. Often it was very good. Hungary beat us because, quite simply, they were by far the better side."

Six months later Hungary thrashed England 7–1 in Budapest. They were expected to win the 1954 World Cup by a walkover. Instead, they went down 3–2 to West Germany in the final after being 2–0 ahead in eight minutes. The one match they wanted to win, above all others, they lost.

As for England, the double defeat by Hungary prompted a painful reap-praisal of their status within the world game, of training methods and tactics. Less than 13 years after being hum-bled by Hungary, England were parad-ing around Wembley as World Cup-winners.

Their manager, in 1966, was Alf Ramsey... right back in 1953.

SWAPS ... Billy Wright exchanges pennants with Ferenc Puskas.

MAY 18, 1960

GLASGOW'S OWN WONDERLAND

Eintracht Frankfurt v Real Madrid
Hampden Park, Glasgow
Champions Cup final

Real Madrid 7 (Di Stefano 27, 30, 73, Puskas 36, 48 pen, 58, 63)
Eintracht Frankfurt 3 (Kress 18, Stein 72, 80)
HT: 3–1. Att: 127,621. Ref: A Mowat (Sc)

Real Madrid: Dominguez – Marquitos, Pachin, Vidal, Santamaria, Zarraga, Canario, Del Sol, Di Stefano, Puskas, Gento.
Eintracht: Loy – Lutz, Hofer, Weilbacher, Eigenbrodt, Stinka, Kress, Lindner, Stein, Pfaff, Meier.

The European Champions Cup would never have gained such allure and prestige without the simultaneous emergence in the 1950s of Real Madrid as the world game's most glamorous club before or since.

Madrid directors had been enthusiastic Europeans right from the outset and had scoured the world to find the players who would establish their command both at home and abroad.

Their initial reward was in winning the inaugural Champions Cup final in 1956, when they beat Reims in Paris after hitting back from 2–0 and then 3–1 down. Centre-forward Alfredo Di Stefano was among Madrid's marksmen against Reims, just as he was in each one of the succeeding four triumphant finals.

But none quite matched the drama and majesty of 1960, when Madrid demolished Eintracht Frankfurt with a performance which duly earned classic status.

Madrid had strengthened their attack in 1958 by signing the great Hungarian, Ferenc Puskas. His partnership with Di Stefano proved awesome. Yet many fans had gone to Hampden Park that May night in 1960 believing they were about to see the end of Madrid's reign. The Spanish club had, after all, been matched against an Eintracht Frankfurt side who had just put six goals past Rangers both home and away.

Frankfurt were confident they could become first German winners of the Cup (in fact, it was a further 14 years before Bayern Munich fulfilled that dream). They took the attacking initiative and did, indeed, seize the lead through veteran right-winger Richard Kress in the 18th minute.

Madrid were not, however, about to fall apart as had Rangers. Quite the reverse. Within nine minutes their own right winger, Canario, sliced through the Frankfurt defence and Di Stefano drove his close-range shot up into the roof of the net. Three minutes later Di Stefano made it 2–1 after a fumble by goalkeeper Loy. Then Puskas scored a third – and all before half-time.

HIGH FLYER ... Real keeper Rogelio Dominguez collects a corner.

Any hopes Frankfurt possessed of making a real fight of it were dispelled early in the second half when referee Mowat awarded Madrid a penalty for obstruction on lightning-fast left-winger Paco Gento. Puskas converted the spot-kick and later added two more goals to take his total to a record four for the final and a then record 13 for the competition.

Erwin Stein struck back twice for Frankfurt but, in between, Di Stefano completed his hat-trick after a solo run through the defence direct from the restart.

The crowd and the TV-watching world hailed Madrid's exhibition. In fact, it was the beginning of the end because they were knocked out of the Champions Cup by Spanish rivals Barcelona the following November.

But then, how could they have improved on Hampden?

JULY 30, 1966

A DATE NOBODY WILL FORGET

England v West Germany
Wembley, London
World Cup final

England 4 (Hurst 19, 100, 119, Peters 78)
West Germany 2 (Haller 13, Weber 89)
HT: 1–1. 90min 2-2. Att: 96,000.
Ref: G Dienst (Swz)

England: Banks – Cohen, J Charlton, Moore, Wilson, Ball, Stiles, R Charlton, Peters, Hunt, Hurst.
West Germany: Tilkowski – Hottges, Schulz, Weber, Schnellinger, Haller, Beckenbauer, Overath, Seeler, Held, Emmerich.

England and Brazil had been the pre-event favourites a World Cup hosted in the homeland of association football. However, with Brazil having been beaten in the first round – by a mixture of Portuguese brute force that took Pele out of the tournament, and Hungarian brilliance –only England remained as final favourites.

Alf Ramsey had constructed a team which owed more to pragmatism than panache. As he told the lanky centre-back Jack Charlton, on first selecting him: "I do not always pick the best players in their position but I try to pick the players who will make up the best team."

In England's case that also meant three world-class players in goalkeeper Gordon Banks, skipper and defensive general Bobby Moore and midfield leader Bobby Charlton. They conceded only one goal on their way to the final and that was in the 2–1 semi-final victory over Portugal.

England were newcomers to the World Cup final, but not West Germany. They had won in 1954 beating Hungary 3–2 in the final.

The outstanding successors of that team were to be found in full-back Karl-Heinz Schnellinger, midfield partners Franz Beckenbauer and Wolfgang Overath, and skipper and centre-forward Uwe Seeler.

This may not have been a great final from the technical point of view. But it contained points of drama which have gone down in soccer legend. The first came in the 13th minute when England left-back Ray Wilson, who had not put a foot wrong in the tournament, headed a wayward cross down at the feet of Helmut Haller, who duly opened the scoring.

Germany's defence were caught equally flat-footed seven minutes later. Moore was fouled by Overath, placed the ball quickly and clipped an inch-perfect free-kick to the far post where Geoff Hurst, preferred to Jimmy Greaves, rose to head past goalkeeper Hans Tilkowski. The German defenders gave referee Dienst, who had permitted the snap free-kick, some black looks.

Both goalkeepers were active as the match proceeded through sun and rain. Bobby Charlton and Beckenbauer cancelled out each other's influence in midfield while England discovered in little Alan Ball a midfield dynamo with more energy than even the great Schnellinger could cope with.

In the 78th minute England took

THAT GOAL ... Hurst's shot will bounce down behind the line.

what appeared a decisive lead. Ball's corner led to a Hurst shot which Horst-Dieter Hottges could only partially clear; Hurst's West Ham colleague Martin Peters was on hand to ram the ball home.

Peters went within a matter of seconds of a place in history as the man who won England the World Cup. Instead, in injury time, Lothar Emmerich blasted a free-kick into the England goal area, Dienst overlooked what appeared to be a handling offence by Schnellinger, and Wolfgang Weber dived in for the goal which meant extra-time.

Subsequent events feature among the most-repeated clips in television's World Cup history files: first the was-it-or-wasn't-it goal by Hurst, then his last-kick breakaway for a historic hat-trick.

England, home of the modern game, were back on top of the world ... but, ironically, a football world which would be largely dominated over succeeding decades not by England but by Germany.

JUNE 17, 1970

ITALY THROUGH IN LATE SURGE

West Germany v Italy
Estadio Azteca, Mexico City
World Cup semi-final

West Germany 3 (Schnellinger 90, Müller 95, 110)
Italy 4 (Boninsegna 8, Burgnich 98, Riva 104, Rivera 111)
HT: 0–1. 90min 1-1. Att: 80,000.
Ref: A Yamasaki (Peru)

W Germany: Maier – Vogts, Schulz, Schnellinger, Patzke (Held 66), Beckenbauer, Overath, Grabowski, Seeler, G Muller, Lohr (Libuda 52).
Italy: Albertosi – Burgnich, Cera, Rosato (Poletti 94), Facchetti, Domenghini, De Sisti, Bertini, Mazzola (Rivera 46), Boninsegna, Riva.

The effects of Mexico City's altitude on two tiring teams produced the most remarkable goal-scoring exchange for what may be considered the finest all-European match *not* played in Europe.

West Germany came into the match carrying more bruises. They had needed extra-time to dispose of World Cup-holders England in Leon three days earlier. Italy, by contrast, had run up a comparatively comfortable 4–1 victory over their Mexican hosts in Toluca.

German manager Helmut Schon had improved on his World Cup runners-up side of four years earlier. Defender Karl-Heinz Schnellinger survived along with midfielders Franz Beckenbauer (though he had already switched to sweeper with Bayern Munich) and Wolfgang Overath and veteran Uwe Seeler up front. Schon had, in addition, discovered a new goal-scoring sensation in Gerd Muller.

Italy had a marksmanship hero of their own in Luigi Riva. But controversy reigned over the use or misuse of Sandro Mazzola and Gianni Rivera. Manager Ferruccio Valcareggi had decided that the two greatest Italian players of their generation could not play together. He thus used Mazzola for first halves and Rivera for second halves; the notorious *staffetta*.

Italy had the bit between their teeth as early as the eighth minute. Roberto Boninsegna sought to find Riva, his pass was blocked but not controlled by Willi Schulz, and Boninsegna drove the loose ball beyond Sepp Maier in the German goal.

As the match went on, so the initiative passed from Italy to West Germany. The more the Italians stubbornly did their cynical best to kill the game, the more the Germans poured men forward and the more Enrico Albertosi performed his goalkeeping wonders. Only seconds remained when Jurgen Grabowski, England's tormentor, centred from the left and Schnellinger, striding forward, volleyed the equaliser. Moments later and Peruvian referee Arturo Yamasaki signalled the end of the 90 minutes. For the second time in five days West Germany had fought their way back into extra-time.

Five minutes into the first extra half and Seeler's downward header gave Müller the chance to shoot Germany in front. Three minutes later it was the German defence's turn to hesitate with fatal consequences – advancing full-back Tarcisio Burgnich equalising. Six minutes more and Angelo Domenghini had opened the German defence again, with Riva providing the finishing fire.

This time, surely, even the Germans were finished, especially now Beckenbauer, having broken a collarbone, was playing on courageously with his arm in a sling. Remarkably, they equalised yet again; Seeler was the provider, Muller the finisher. But before panic could set in with the looming prospect of the decisive toss of a coin, Rivera had justified his substitute's presence with the winning goal - the sixth in 12 minutes - from Boninsegna's cross.

This time there was to be no German comeback. But Italy paid a heavy price: the physical and psychological hangover meant they were never in a fit state to even try to match Brazil in the final.

ALL SQUARE ... Müller makes it 3–3 with 10 minutes left in extra-time.

JUNE 20, 1976

GERMAN RALLY JUST FAILS

Czechoslovakia v West Germany
Crvena Zvezda, Belgrade
European Championship final

Czechoslovakia 2 (Svehlik 8, Dobias 25)
West Germany 2 (D Müller 28, Hölzenbein 90)
HT: 2–1. 90min 2–2. Att: 33,000.
Ref: S Gonella (It)
Czechoslovakia 5–3 on pens

Czechoslovakia: Viktor – Pivarnik, Ondrus, Capkovic, Gogh, Dobias (F Vesely 94), Panenka, Moder, Masny, Svehlik (Jurkemik 79), Nehoda.
W Germany: Maier – Vogts, Beckenbauer, Schwarzenbeck, Dietz, Wimmer (Flohe 46), Bonhof, Beer (Bongartz 79), Hoeness, D Müller, Hölzenbein.

The 1976 European Championship finals are remembered as the most heavily-concentrated dramatic production in the event's history. All the last four matches went to extra-time, twice West Germany hit back from two goals down and the final itself went to a penalty shoot-out.

West Germany went into the finals as World Cup-holders. Indeed, a repeat of the 1974 Munich showdown appeared on the cards from the draw which matched the Germans against Yugoslavia in one semi-final and Holland against Czechoslovakia in the other. Dutch dreams of revenge were stymied, however, when they lost 3-1 in extra-time.

Equal excitement in the other semi-final. Hosts Yugoslavia quickly went 2–0 up against West Germany only to lose 4–2 in extra-time. The Germans had lost Gerd Müller to international retirement and found a namesake replacement, Dieter Müller, who proved equally adept by scoring a hat-trick against the Slavs.

West Germany were favourites for the final, watched by a then record TV audience around the world of 400million. One surprise was the agreement between the managers, Germany's Helmut Schon and Czechoslovakia's Vaclav Jezek, that in the event of a draw after extra-time, the match would be decided on penalties.

The rules had offered the possibility of a replay but Schon was opposed, saying: "After a tough semi-final and final a replay would have been murderous."

At least the German players knew that before the match; the Czechoslovaks found out about the shoot-out only at the end of extra-time when they were stopped from leaving the pitch! But then nobody had seriously believed that even a penalty shoot-out would be needed.

The Germans were on a win bonus of £5,000, raised by DFB president Hermann Neuberger. As for the Czechoslovaks, Jezek said: "If we win, we will have a reception with our President. That is enough of a stimulus for us."

Few observers had expected a Czechoslovak win but that appeared suddenly and explosively likely when they led 2–0 after 25 minutes.

In the eighth minute Maier could only parry a shot from Marian Masny. Zdenek Nehoda seized on the loose ball and passed for Jan Svehlik to score. In the 25th minute it was 2–0. Beckenbauer, playing his 100th international, headed aimlessly into space and Karol Dobias strode forward to shoot past Maier.

Three minutes later Müller pulled one goal back. But the Czechoslovaks – and Nehoda in particular – had many more chances to have put the game beyond reach before Bernd Hölzenbein finally equalised in the very last minute of normal time.

No goals in extra-time, so it went to penalties. Referee Gonella ordered five players from each side to the centre circle.

The Czechoslovaks had no problems sorting out Masny, Nehoda, Anton Ondrus, Ladislav Jurkemik and Antonin Panenka. But the Germans were in all sorts of confusion before agreeing on Rainer Bonhof, Heinz Flohe, Hannes Bongartz, Uli Hoeness and Beckenbauer. Up to 3–3 it was all-square.

Then Jurkemik scored for the Czechoslovaks ... and Hoeness shot over the bar. Panenka strolled forward as if a dream, feinted one way, then sent the ball in the other direction. Beckenbauer had no need to take his penalty. It was all over. West Germany were the World Cup-holders but Czechoslovakia had deposed them as champions of Europe.

CZECH MATES ... celebrate victory, wearing their German rivals' shirts.

JULY 8, 1982

HORST BURIES AN OLD GHOST

West Germany v France
Estadio Sanchez Pizjuan, Seville
World Cup semi-final

West Germany 3 (Littbarski 18, Rummenigge 103, Fischer 108)
France 3 (Platini 26pen, Tresor 93, Giresse 99)
HT: 1–1. 90min: 1–1. Att: 71,000.
Ref: C Corver (Hol)
West Germany 5–4 on pens

W Germany: Schumacher – Kaltz, Stielike, K Forster, Briegel (Rummenigge 96), Dremmler, B Forster, Breitner, Magath (Hrubesch 70), Littbarski, Fischer.
France: Ettori – Bossis, Janvion, Tresor, Amoros, Tigana, Giresse, Platini, Genghini (Battiston 50; Lopez 66), Rocheteau, Six.

Any match which ends with a penalty shoot-out offers drama; but a great match demands more than mere climactic pyrotechnics. Just as the Germans' 1976 European Championship failure against Czechoslovakia provided high-class football, so it was when the shoot-out coin came down in their favour against France in the World Cup finals six years later.

France were popular favourites in 1982. They had been dubbed the "Brazil of Europe" for their attacking mixture of style, pace and skill. The real Brazil had been eliminated in the second round by Italy, so it was to France that the purists looked in the closing stages of the finals – above all to their inspirational attacking force, Michel Platini.

West Germany attracted no such excitement, merely admiration. Coach Jupp Derwall, who had succeeded Helmut Schon after the 1978 World Cup, had guided his men to victory in the 1980 European Championship. But his was a team of power and discipline, rather than invention and vision. The Germans were also hampered by the niggling injuries dogging Karl-Heinz Rummenigge, their finest attacker.

Rummenigge thus started on the bench; not that it appeared to matter after 18 minutes when French keeper Jean-Luc Ettori failed to hold a shot by Klaus Fischer and Pierre Littbarski followed up to score. They held their lead for only eight minutes. Then Bernd Forster fouled the onrushing Dominique Rocheteau and Platini converted the penalty.

France used all the skill at their disposal to press for the winner, while the Germans used all their organisational talents to hold them at bay.

On the hour, it seemed France must score. Platini's pass bisected the German defence and substitute Patrick Battiston broke the offside trap to dash for goal. Goalkeeper Toni Schumacher came out to meet him, Battiston stretched for the shot ... there was a sickening collision and the ball bobbled just wide.

All attention now focused on the two players: the immovable object (Schumacher) and the irresistible force (Battiston). Schumacher was revived to carry on but Battiston had to be carried off. The impact had so shaken him that he lost three teeth, suffered severe bruising to the neck and needed oxygen to assist his breathing. In the mid-1990s Schumacher would have been sent off for his assault. In the more lax atmosphere of the early 1980s, referee Charles Corver contented himself with awarding a mere goal kick.

Right on full-time it appeared justice was being done when Manuel

UP IN THE AIR *Scores are level before the penalty shoot out.*

Amoros shot past Schumacher but the ball ricocheted off the bar and Corver blew for full-time and signalled the extra half-hour.

Three minutes into the extra period and French defender Marius Tresor made it 2–1, advancing for a full-bloodied volley to an Alain Giresse free-kick. Six minutes later little Giresse made it 3–1, and France appeared on the brink of their first appearance in a World Cup final. But appearances can be deceptive against the Germans. Derwall gambled by sending on Rummenigge as substitute. His mere presence galvanised his team-mates – and not only his presence. Seven minutes after his arrival, Rummenigge pulled a goal back.

Now the Germans poured forward with increasing confidence and Fischer equalised with a spectacular overhead bicycle kick.

So to the penalty shoot-out. Toni Schumacher was again the villain for France, defying Didier Six and Maxime Bossis. Uli Stielike had missed for Germany but not substitute Horst Hrubesch – who duly buried the ghost of 1976.

JUNE 25, 1988

VAN BASTEN THE MASTER BLASTER

Holland v Soviet Union
Olympiastadion, Munich
European Championship final

Holland 2 (Gullit 32, Van Basten 53)
Soviet Union 0
HT: 1–0. Att: 72,308. Ref: M
Vautrot (Fr)

Holland: Van Breukelen – Van Aerle,
Rijkaard, R Koeman, Van Tiggelen,
Vanenburg, Wouters, A Muhren, E
Koeman, Gullit, Van Basten.
Soviet Union: Dasayev –
Demianenko, Aleinikov, Khidiatulin,
Rats, Litovchenko, Zavarov,
Mikhailichenko, Gotsmanov
(Baltacha 67), Belanov, Protasov
(Pasulko 71).

Admirers of Dutch football had been
waiting fully 14 years for Holland to
secure the reward their attractive,
trend-setting game had deserved.

Notice of what was around the
corner had been given in the late
1960s when Ajax thrashed Liverpool
5–1 in the European Champions Cup
then later became the first Dutch club
to reach a European final – albeit
losing 4–1 in 1969 to Milan.

The breakthrough came in 1970.
Feyenoord won the Champions Cup
and the World Club Cup, with Ajax
following up with three Champions
Cup victories, two European Supercups
and a World Club Cup in the succeeding three years. "Total football" was
the game both with Ajax and the
Dutch national team which, inspired
by Johan Cruyff, reached the 1974
World Cup final, only to finish runners-up to West Germany.

Holland were runners-up in the
1978 World Cup as well. Their clubs
collected all manner of trophies; but
success appeared beyond the national
team – until 1988. A good omen was
PSV Eindhoven's victory in the
Champions Cup. They provided four
members of a European Championship
side topped off by the attacking skills
of Milan's Ruud Gullit and Marco
Van Basten – who had just climaxed
their first season in Italy by leading
Milan to the league title.

Holland made a disappointing
start to the European finals, losing 1–0
to the Soviet Union in Cologne. Van
Basten, furious at being introduced
only as a second-half substitute,
threatened to quit the squad. He was
talked into staying – to decisive effect
– by friend and mentor Johan Cruyff.

The final matched those same
opponents: Holland against a Soviet
Union side prepared down to the last
scientific detail by Valeri Lobanovski.
But the human temperament was one
factor against which Lobanovski
could not guard. In the semi-final victory over Italy, outstanding stopper
Oleg Kuznetsov had collected his
second yellow card of the tournament.
That meant he missed the final and
Lobanovski had to disturb the balance
of his team to cover the gap.

Demand sent ticket prices soaring
to around £350. Even with Italian fans
selling their allocations, there were not
enough tickets to go round.

In the absence of Kuznetsov and
the injured Vladimir Besonov, the
Soviets pulled back midfielders Sergei
Aleinikov and Alexei Mikhailichenko
to close-mark Gullit and Van Basten.

*LAST CHANCE ... Van Breukelen
saves Igor Belanov's penalty kick.*

It was a suicide tactic. Mikhailichenko
and Aleinikov were caught in posi-
tional confusion when Van Basten,
unmarked, headed back Erwin
Koeman's cross for Ruud Gullit, similarly unmarked, to head in the opening goal.

The Soviets struggled to try to get
on terms but Igor Belanov wasted their
best chance when he shot a penalty too
close to Hans Van Breukelen. Schemer
Alexander Zavarov, lacking the usual
support in midfield, never threatened to
slice open the Dutch as he had done
Italy in the semi-final.

Then, in the 53rd minute, Van
Basten scored one of the most sensational goals ever seen at this rarefied
level of football. A flowing move up
the left began with full-back Adrie Van
Tiggelen; Arnold Muhren lofted a huge
cross beyond the far post, and Van
Basten met the ball full on the volley.
It roared into the net past Rinat
Dasayev like a guided missile. Even
the Class of '74 would have been
proud of that one!

MAY 18, 1994

THE COMPLETE PERFORMANCE

AC Milan v Barcelona
Olympic Stadium, Athens
Champions Cup final

Milan 4 (Massaro 22, 45, Savicevic 47, Desailly 59)
Barcelona 0
HT: 2–0. Att: 70,000. Ref: Don (Eng)

Milan: Rossi – Tassotti, Galli, Maldini (Nava 84), Panucci, Boban, Albertini, Desailly, Donadoni, Savicevic, Massaro.
Barcelona: Zubizarreta – Ferrer, Koeman, Nadal, Beguiristain (Eusebio 51), Bakero, Guardiola, Amor, Sergi (Quique 73), Stoichkov, Romario.

Barcelona had won the Champions Cup in 1992 – Ronald Koeman's thunderous strike seeing off Sampdoria. Milan had last won it in 1989 when they beat Steaua Bucharest, and in 1990. But they had lost controversially in the 1993 final to a Marseille side whose achievements were destroyed by match-fixing revelations.

The 1994 final was thus seen as a sort of play-off, to decide which club really deserved the accolade as Europe's club of the 1990s.

Barcelona, under three-times Champions Cup winner Johan Cruyff, played a unique free-wheeling sort of game, holding possession and using the full width of the pitch to pull their opponents apart. Milan, under Fabio Capello, played a highly-disciplined game in which they squeezed the life out of opponents' attacks, then used their multiplicity of talents to raid from all directions.

Man of the match, ironically, was a player Capello would have shifted out of Milan long ago – Dejan Savicevic.

For Capello, the lithe Yugoslav lacked the self-sacrificing personality to sit patiently on the bench and then slot into the team when injuries to other foreigners demanded his presence. He was saved only – and repeatedly – by the fact that club president and owner Silvio Berlusconi was his greatest fan.

On this occasion, the influence of Berlusconi, media magnate turned politician, served his club perfectly

and Savicevic turned on a gold-medal-winning performance. He scored one of Milan's goals and was involved in the creation of the other three within a team display of the greatest class. It was not that Barcelona played badly; simply that, on the day, Milan were on a different planet.

Many long-time observers of the international game called it the finest team performance in the Champions Cup final since Real Madrid put Eintracht Frankfurt to the seven-goal sword in 1960. Milan, despite the absences of suspended central defenders Franco Baresi and Billy Costacurta, were that good.

When Barcelona were in possession they looked everything their fans had expected: confident, classy, impressive. When Milan had the ball they looked simply ... dangerous.

After nine minutes Milan exploded a warning shot as Christian Panucci had a headed goal disallowed for offside. Then veteran striker Daniele Massaro, quick on the turn, fired into goalkeeper Andoni Zubizarreta's arms. A few more minutes and it was 1–0 to Milan. Savicevic escaped on the right, rounded defender Miguel Angel Nadal, and chipped to the far post for Massaro to score.

Barcelona returned to the attack but found their way blocked by Paolo Maldini, switched to emergency sweeper in Baresi's absence, and turning in a display to delight his father Cesare (who had been Milan's sweeper and skipper when they first won the Champions Cup in 1963).

The first half was almost three minutes into injury time added on by English referee Philip Don when Milan struck again. Once more Savicevic tore Barcelona apart down the Milan right then switched play left, where Roberto Donadoni went round the back of the defence to present Massaro with his second goal.

Barcelona were stifled up front. Brazilian marksman Romario – who was to find so much more success at the World Cup finals in the USA later that same summer – was shackled by Filippo Galli and the Bulgarian, Hristo Stoichkov, never once got the better of Christian Panucci.

How they might have longed for Savicevic on their side!

In the 47th minute the Serb won a

touchline tussle with Nadal and hit a long, angled lob over Zubizarreta and into the far corner. Coach Cruyff blamed Zubizarreta personally, telling his captain after the match that he should find another club as fast as he could! By now the outcome was decided but not the score. That awaited a further dollop of icing on the cake from Marcel Desailly, after Savicevic had hit a post and Barcelona

HISTORY MAN ... Milan's Marcel Desailly became the first player to win the Champions Cup with different clubs in successive years – having triumphed with Marseille in 1993.

had failed to clear. As Capello said afterwards: "I couldn't have asked any more of my team than they have given tonight."

THE GREAT STADIUMS

Every actor needs a stage – similarly, every great footballer needs a fine stadium. Europe is packed with outstanding stadiums of an almost infinite variety of design and with fascinatingly varied histories. European club finals over the past 40 years have been staged in almost 80 venues – ranging from homely Portman Road at Ipswich to the intimidating heights of Milan, Real Madrid, Barcelona and Ajax's impressive Arena (pictured below).

KEY

WCC = World Club Cup
CC = European Cup
CWC = Cup–Winners Cup
Fairs = Fairs Cup
UEFA = UEFA Cup
Super = Supercup

Aberdeen, Scotland

PITTODRIE

Capacity: 21,634
Club: Aberdeen
World Cup: –
European Championship: –
Intl club finals: 1983 Super 2nd leg

Amsterdam, Holland

ARENA

Capacity: 50,000
Club: Ajax
World Cup: –
European Championship: –
Intl club finals: –

The Arena is the newest of Europe's major stadiums, having been opened – with a friendly against Brazil – in the summer of 1996. Ajax had long needed a new home: their own, historic, De Meer was too small and the Olympisch stadium was too old and had started crumbling. Ajax, their major sponsors and the local authority are among the consortium who own the Arena. Initial financing was encouraged with attractive terms for executive boxes and season tickets. Thus, even before it had opened for business, the Arena was sold out for the first two seasons of league football. The stadium has a variety of other uses. The roof can be slid shut, making it ideal for pop concerts and it was also the venue for an experimental six-a-side indoor football tournament in January 1997. The enclosed nature of the design brought its own problems, however: difficulty in ventilating the pitch meant that the surface had to be replaced four times in the first year.

OLYMPISCH

Capacity: 61,000
World Cup: –
Olympic Games: 1928
European Championship: –
Intl club finals: 1962 CC, 1972 WCC 2nd leg, 1977 CWC, 1981 UEFA 2nd leg, 1992 UEFA 2nd leg.

The stadium was built for the 1928 Olympic Games. Remarkably, by comparison with the time which would be needed today, work did not begin until May 1927. Yet the stadium was ready on time by July 1928. Europe's first permanent floodlighting system was installed in 1934, by which time capacity had been increased from 34,000 to 61,000. In 1962 the stadium hosted one of the greatest Champions Cup finals, when Benfica beat Real Madrid 5–3, and Ajax moved in for all their great European adventures until, in 1996, the Arena was built as an effective replacement. Already, by that time, the

SPIROS LOUIS Occasional home to Panathinaikos and Olympiakos.

Olympisch's role as national stadium had long been taken over by Rotterdam's De Kuip.

Antwerp, Belgium

BOSUIL

Capacity: 20,000
Club: Antwerp
World Cup: –
Euro Championship: 1972 semi
Intl club finals: 1964 CWC replay

Opened in 1923 with an international match in which Belgium forced an honourable 2–2 draw with England.

Athens, Greece

SPIROS LOUIS

Capacity: 74,433
Clubs: Olympiakos, Panathinaikos (big matches)

World Cup: –
European Championship: –
Intl club finals: 1983 CC, 1987 CWC, 1994 CC

The new Olympic stadium was built in the early 1980s when Athens was hoping to be granted the honour of hosting the centennial modern Games. That hope was dashed by the International Olympic Committee's preference for Atlanta, Georgia, but already the new Athens stadium had established an international role with major football and athletics meetings. The first major event was the 1983 Champions Cup final in which Hamburg surprisingly beat Juventus 1–0. The stadium has also proved its value as a large-capacity venue for top local clubs such as Panathinaikos and Olympiakos.

Avellino, Italy

PARTENIO

Capacity: 28,000
Club: Avellino
World Cup: –
European Championship: –
Intl club finals: 1990 UEFA 2nd leg

Unusually hosted the second leg of the 1990 UEFA Cup final between Fiorentina and Juventus because the Florence club's home was still in the last throes of redevelopment for the World Cup finals that summer.

Barcelona, Spain

NOU CAMP

Capacity: 115,000
Club: Barcelona
World Cup: 1982 1st rnd (one), 2nd rnd (three), semi
Euro Chp: 1964 semi, third place
Intl club finals: 1958 Fairs 2nd leg, 1960 Fairs 2nd leg, 1962 Fairs 2nd leg, 1964 Fairs (one match only), 1966 Fairs 1st leg, 1972 CWC, 1979 Super 2nd leg, 1982 CWC, 1982 Super, 1989 Super 1st leg

One of the world's greatest football venues – and one of the most intimidating for the opposition, particularly in club matches when a capacity crowd roars out the Catalan club anthems before kick-off. Barcelona's historic home was the old Las Corts stadium but in the early 1950s the club recognised that it should follow the example of Real Madrid and build a vast new home. Nou Camp, originally with a 90,000 capacity, was opened in September 1957 with a friendly between Barcelona and Legia Warsaw. Subsequent major events brought further expansions to increase capacity to the present 115,000. The stadium has a host of extra features, including a vast museum and a beautiful chapel just off the players' tunnel. The site roundabout includes the indoor ice arena and a 25,000 stadium in which Barcelona's nursery club play league matches – as well as a string of training pitches.

SARRIA

Capacity: 41,000
Club: Español
World Cup: 1982 2nd rnd (three matches)
European Championship: –
Intl club finals: 1988 UEFA 1st leg

Sarria in Barcelona was the centre of controversy at the 1982 World Cup finals when the luck of the draw blessed it with a second-round group of Argentina, Brazil and Italy. The local organising committee resisted last-minute pressure to switch groups with Nou Camp because of crowd demand. Thus Sarria played host to one of the most memorable matches in World Cup history, in which Italy defeated Brazil 3–2 with a remarkable Paolo Rossi hat-trick. The stadium's future was placed in doubt in the late 1990s when financial pressure led to owners Español considering selling the site and renting the Montjuich Olympic stadium as their new home.

Bari, Italy

SAN NICOLA

Capacity: 58,270
Club: Bari
World Cup: 1990 1st rnd (three matches), 2nd rnd (one), 3rd place play-off
European Championship: –
Intl club finals: 1991 CC

Built for the 1990 World Cup finals, the San Nicola is one of the most architecturally striking stadums in Europe –

NOU CAMP ... Barcelona's cathedral of Catalan national pride.

SAN NICOLA ... Bari's "flying saucer" in south- eastern Italy.

once described as "a flying saucer waiting to take off for a more appropriate home". Bari's problem is in being far off Europe's football mainstream, despite the promotional work undertaken on its behalf by "local boy" Antonio Matarrese – who was Italian federation president and UEFA vice-president for much of the 1990s.

Basle, Switzerland

ST JAKOB

Capacity: 42,000
Club: Basle
World Cup: 1954 1st rnd (four matches), quarter, semi
European Championship: –
Intl club finals: 1969 CWC, 1975 CWC, 1979 CWC, 1984 CWC

The stadium was built for the 1954 World Cup but pop concerts nowadays pull bigger crowds than Swiss league matches.

Bastia, Corsica, France

FURIANI

Capacity: 7,800
Club: Bastia
World Cup: –
European Championship: –
Intl club finals: 1978 UEFA first leg

The Furiani was the scene of French football's worst crowd disaster when 20 fans were killed and 700 injured as a temporary stand collapsed just before the scheduled kick-off of a French Cup semi-final between Bastia and Marseille in May 1992.

Belgrade, Yugoslavia

CRVENA ZVEZDA (Red Star)

Capacity: 97,422
Club: Crvena Zvezda (Red Star)
World Cup: –
European Chp: 1976 semi, final
Intl club finals: 1973 CC, 1979 UEFA 1st leg

Nicknamed the Yugoslav "Maracana" and the central feature of army club Red Star's mini-commercial empire – it is surrounded by shops, offices and sports centres. The present stadium was built in 1959–60 on a site used as a league stadium since the late 1920s.

OLYMPIA ... Berlin's home of sporting history - with more to come.

Berlin, Germany

OLYMPIA

Capacity: 76,243
Club: Hertha
World Cup: 1974 1st rnd (three matches)
Olympic Games: 1936
European Championship: –
Intl club finals: 1986 UEFA 2nd leg

Germany's largest stadium is also its most notorious, from its history as the home of the Nazi Olympic Games in 1936. It was here that Jesse Owens, a negro, enraged Hitler by winning four gold medals. It was here, too, that England's footballers, infamously, gave the Nazi salute in 1938 before unleashing their anger at diplomatic orders by thrashing the pride of Nazi German football 6–3. In the Cold War years, the stadium became something of a white elephant. Travel problems between West Berlin and the rest of West Germany meant it lost its status as national stadium. Even its use for the 1974 World Cup finals very nearly provoked a diplomatic incident with the then East German government. Following the collapse of the GDR and the reinstatement of Berlin as national capital, the stadium regained its old status. The German federation envisages proposing a redeveloped stadium as main venue for the 2006 World Cup – though how redevelopment will be funded is a controversial issue .

Berne, Switzerland

WANKDORF

Capacity: 37,551
Club: Young Boys
World Cup: 1954 1st rnd (three matches), quarter, final
European Championship: –
Intl club finals: 1961 CC, 1989 CWC

VILLA PARK ... Aston Villa's home for more than a century.

This historic stadium played host to the greatest World Cup final shock of all when Hungary lost to West Germany in 1954 after leading 2–0. Hungarian heroes Sandor Kocsis and Zoltan Czibor were on the wrong end of another dramatic defeat seven years later – playing for Barcelona against Benfica in the Champions Cup final.

Bilbao, Spain

SAN MAMES
Capacity: 46,223
Club: Athletic Bilbao
World Cup: 1982 1st rnd (three matches)
European Championship: –
Intl club finals: 1977 UEFA 2nd leg

El Catedral is one of Spanish football's most historic venues, having been a centre for the expression of Basque nationalism during the repressive Franco era. It hosted three matches in the 1982 World Cup finals though redevelopment work was completed only the day before England's 3–1 win over France, in which Bryan Robson scored his 27-second goal.

Birmingham, England

ST ANDREWS
Capacity: 25,936
Club: Birmingham City
World Cup: –
European Championship: –
Intl club finals: 1960 Fairs 1st leg, 1961 Fairs 1st leg

Barely remembered today as only the second English ground to host a European club final. Birmingham entertained Barcelona in the first leg of the 1960s Fairs Cup final, and Roma in the same competition the following year.

VILLA PARK
Capacity: 39,341
Club: Aston Villa
World Cup: 1966 1st rnd (three matches)
European Championship: 1996 1st rnd (three matches), quarter
Intl club finals: 1982 Super 2nd leg

In their home, one of the great traditional venues of English football, Aston Villa were leading lights in the founding of the original Football League.

Bordeaux, France

PARC DE LESCURE (Stade Velodrome)
Capacity: 36,500
Club: Bordeaux
World Cup: 1938 quarter and replay, 3rd place play-off
European Championship: –
Intl club finals: 1996 UEFA 2nd leg

Opened amid drama at the 1938 World Cup when three players were sent off and two carried off in a 1–1 drawn quarter-final between Brazil and Czechoslovakia. Redevelopment work to stage six matches at the 1998 World Cup finals meant that capacity was cut from 46,900 to 36,500.

Bremen, Germany

WESER
Capacity: 29,850
Club: Werder Bremen
World Cup: –
European Championship: –
Intl club finals: 1992 Super

The Weserstadion was built in 1921, then redeveloped as home side Werder emerged as one of West Germany's top clubs between the 1960s and 1990s.

Brugge, Belgium

OLYMPIA
Capacity: 18,021
Clubs: Club Brugge, Cercle
World Cup: –
European Championship: –
Intl club finals: 1976 UEFA 2nd leg

Opened in 1975, replacing the old Klokke stadium. The name remains a cause for confusion because the city has yet to host the Olympic Games – and stands no chance of doing so in the foreseeable future.

Brussels, Belgium

ROI BAUDOUIN (formerly Heysel)
Capacity: 40,000
Club: –
World Cup: –
European Chp: 1972 final
Intl club finals: 1958 CC, 1964 CWC, 1966 CC, 1970 Fairs, 1974 CC, 1974 CC replay, 1976 CWC, 1978 Super first leg, 1980 CWC, 1983 UEFA 1st leg, 1984 UEFA first leg, 1985 CC, 1996 CWC

Total redevelopment and a new name should not be allowed to disguise the fact that the King Baudouin stadium is the Heysel of tragic memory. The stadium was originally built in 1930 as part of the celebrations of a centenary of Belgian independence. It served as national stadium and a popular venue for European club finals – the third Champions Cup final being staged there in 1958.

Then, on May 29, 1985, in full view of the world via television, 39 Juventus fans died after a retaining wall collapsed as they tried to escape a terrace charge by hooligan followers of Liverpool. A subsequent inquiry blamed the dilapidated state of the stadium as well as inadequate ticket sales and security supervision by the Belgian federation, the Belgian police and UEFA (which, dishonourably and disgracefully, tried to pretend total lack of responsibility). The root

EINDHOVEN ... lit up for one of PSV's Champions League ties.

blame, however, attached to the vandals who provoked the tragedy – the climax to a decade-long reign of English hooligan terror on the continent. English clubs were barred from European competition for five years. The Heysel, in its old guise, never staged another football match.

The main facade, with the stadium offices, remained but the entire structure behind was torn down and replaced. European club football did not return until the 1996 Cup-winners Cup final.

PARC ASTRID (Stade Constant Vanden Stock)

Capacity: 28,063
Club: Anderlecht
World Cup: –
Euro Chp: 1972 semi
Intl club finals: 1976 Super 2nd leg

Anderlecht were one of the first continental clubs to see the commercial possibilities of executive boxes when redevelopment took place in the 1980s. The club had played on the Parc Astrid site since 1918, but many of their major European club games have been staged in the Heysel/Baudouin stadium when ticket demand has far outstripped Parc Astrid capacity. Even so, teh stadium was the scene for Anderlecht's first triumph in the European Supercup, over Bayern Munich.

Budapest, Hungary

NEP

Capacity: 80,000
Club: –
World Cup: –
European Championship: –
Intl club finals: 1968 Fairs 2nd leg, 1969 Fairs 2nd leg

The Nep (or National) stadium is one

of the most famous in Europe, used by all Budapest's clubs for their biggest European club matches. However it has proven somewhat unlucky for home sides performing at the highest level. Ferencvaros lost the Fairs Cup there in 1968 and Ujpest lost the final to Newcastle United a year later.

Copenhagen, Denmark

PARK

Capacity: 40,300
Club: FC Copenhagen
World Cup: –
European Championship: –
Intl club finals: 1994 CWC

The Park replaced the Idraetspark as national stadium after being built on the revivalist surge topped off by the national team's 1992 European Championship triumph.

ARTEMIO FRANCHI ... Florentine memorial to a UEFA president.

Dortmund, Germany

WESTFALEN

Capacity: 42,800
Club: Borussia Dortmund
World Cup: 1974 1st rnd (three matches), 2nd rnd (one)
European Championship: –
Intl club finals: 1993 UEFA 1st leg

The Westfalenstadion, unlike most of the major stadums in Germany, is a pure football stadium. It was built for the 1974 World Cup finals during which it staged four games. The stadium was then taken over by Borussia Dortmund, who abandoned their historic – and adjacent – Rote Erde ground.

Dundee, Scotland

TANNADICE

Capacity: 12,616
Club: Dundee United
World Cup: –
European Championship: –
Intl club finals: 1987 UEFA 2nd leg

United lost their one European final – against IFK Gothenburg – but their fans collected a special Fair Play Award for their behaviour.

Düsseldorf, Germany

RHEIN

Capacity: 55,850
Club: Fortuna Düsseldorf
World Cup: 1974 1st rnd (two matches), 2nd rnd (three)
Euro Chp: 1988 1st rnd (two matches)
Intl club finals: 1975 UEFA first leg, 1979 UEFA 2nd leg, 1981 CWC

Built for the 1974 World Cup finals, the Rhein stadium has frequently acted as home for Borussia Mönchengladbach in Europe, and staged the opening match of the 1988 European Championship finals (1–1 between West Germany and Italy).

Eindhoven, Holland

PHILIPS

Capacity: 30,000
Club: PSV
World Cup: –
European Championship: –
Intl club finals: 1978 UEFA 2nd leg

Owned by the Philips electrics corporation, whose headquarters are in Eindhoven – and not far from the workshop where the family firm turned out its first light bulbs in 1891. The stadium was redeveloped in the late 1970s and has long boasted one of the most impressive of European floodlighting systems.

Enschede, Holland
DIEKMAN

Capacity: 13,500
Club: Twente
World Cup: –
European Championship: –
Intl club finals: 1975 UEFA 2nd leg
General security and redevelopment virtually cut capacity in half since its one European final – when a then-capacity home crowd of 24,500 were shocked to see their favourites thrashed 5–1 by Borussia Mönchengladbach.

Florence, Italy

ARTEMIO FRANCHI (formerly Giovanni Berta, then Comunale)

Capacity: 47,350
Club: Fiorentina
World Cup: 1934 1st rnd (one match), quarter (one and replay); 1990 1st rnd (three matches), quarter (one)
European Chp: 1968 semi
Intl club finals: 1961 CWC 2nd leg

Work started on the Florence ground, which has had more names than most stadiums, in the late 1920s. It was designed by noted architect Pierluigi Nervi, was completed in 1932 and named initially after a local fascist leader. Italy beat Czechoslovakia 2–0 in 1933 in an opening international. A year later Italy beat Spain there in a replay of a famous World Cup quarter-final, after the hosts had been defied in remarkable fashion during the first match by legendary goalkeeper Ricardo Zamora. The "Berta" title was dropped after the second world war and the ground was known only as the Comunale

(Municipal) when it was used as a venue at the 1968 European Championship. The stadium was redeveloped for the 1990 World Cup after which it was renamed yet again – this time in honour of Artemio Franchi, the UEFA president from Florence who had died in a car accident.

Frankfurt, Germany

WALD

Capacity: 61,146
Club: Eintracht
World Cup: 1974 1st rnd (three matches), 2nd rnd (two)
European Chp: 1988 (two matches)
Intl club finals: 1980 UEFA 2nd leg

Frankfurt, in which the DFB set up its offices after the Second World War, was the *de facto* capital of German football during the Cold War era. Thus it was appropriate that the Waldstadion played host to the Opening Match of the 1974 World Cup finals. This was the first time the holders had opened the finals – previously the hosts had the honour, but FIFA had decided that this placed too much nationalistic pressure on the home players. In the event Brazil and Yugoslavia managed only a scrappy 0–0 draw.

Gelsenkirchen, Germany

PARK

Capacity: 70,600
Club: Schalke
World Cup: 1974 1st rnd (two matches), 2nd rnd (three)
European Chp: 1988 1st rnd (two matches)
Intl club finals: 1997 UEFA 1st leg

Genoa, Italy

LUIGI FERRARIS

Capacity: 43,868
Clubs: Genoa, Sampdoria
World Cup: 1934 1st rnd (one match), 1990 1st rnd (three matches), 2nd rnd (one)
European Championship: –
Intl club finals: 1990 Super 1st leg

Genoa is considered by Italians to be a typically British football stadium – particularly since its redevelopment for the 1990 World Cup finals with four squared-off stands. The historic Genoa club have played on the site

since 1910 and the ground remains known coloquially as the Marassi after the district. International football has been played on the site ever since December 1912, when Italy lost 3–1 to Austria. Like many of Italy's municipally-owned stadiums, the ground is shared, by Genoa and Sampdoria.

Glasgow, Scotland

HAMPDEN PARK

Capacity: 60,000
Club: Queen's Park
World Cup: –
European Championship: –
Intl club finals: 1960 CC, 1966 CWC, 1967 WCC 1st leg, 1976 CC

Hampden Park staged the most famous European final in history in 1960, when Real Madrid defeated Eintracht Frankfurt 7–3 in front of 135,000 – still the biggest attendance for a European club final.

Later redevelopments of the stadium brought drastic reductions in capacity and more than 20 years have passed since Hampden last staged a European final.

IBROX

Capacity: 50,411
Club: Rangers
World Cup: –
European Championship: –
Intl club finals: 1961 CWC 1st leg, 1972 Super 1st leg

Glasgow Rangers have invested heavily in Ibrox Park with the firm intentions of competing more seriously in Europe and the rest of the world.

That has been rewarded with the ground's status as Scotland's No 2 national home, after Hampden. But Ibrox has yet to stage a European club final in its own right.

The only two such events so far were split-leg ties in which Rangers were competitors – in the Cup-Winners Cup and then the Supercup.

Gothenburg, Sweden

NYA ULLEVI

Capacity: 43,000
Clubs: IFK, GAIS, Orgryte
World Cup: 1958 1st rnd (three matches and play-off), quarter, semi, 3rd place play-off

Euro Chp: 1992 1st rnd (three matches), semi, final
Intl club finals: 1982 UEFA 1st leg, 1983 CWC, 1987 UEFA 1st leg, 1990 CWC

The Nya (New) Ullevi superseded the Gamla (Old) Ullevi in time for the 1958 World Cup finals. It was opened just a week before the tournament with a friendly between Sweden and a Gothenburg Select. It is now Sweden's largest football stadium and shares national team and major cup events with the Rasunda in Stockholm.

At the 1992 European Championship, Ullevi staged the dramatic final in which outsiders Denmark defeated Germany 2–0. It was also in the Ullevi that Denmark defeated Holland in a penalty shoot-out in the semi-finals. IFK Gothenburg, twice winners of the UEFA Cup, in 1982 and 1987, and regular Champions League entrants, play all their major home games in the Nya Ullevi.

The stadium has also been a regular venue for pop music concerts, boxing title fights and for speedway world championships.

Hamburg, Germany

VOLKSPARK

Capacity: 61,234
Club: Hamburg
World Cup: 1974 1st rnd (three matches)
European Championshio: 1988 semi
Intl club finals: 1977 Super 1st leg, 1982 UEFA 2nd leg, 1983 Super 1st leg

Originally known as the Altona, the Volksparkstadion was opened in 1925 and staged its first football international two years later.

Plans were later approved to lift its 50,000 capacity to 100,000 but the Second World War intervened. The stadium was rebuilt, with the use of the more than available bomb-site rubble, in the early 1950s and was taken over as home by Hamburg SV – witnessing many of the outstanding club exploits of local hero Uwe Seeler.

At competitive level it has not been the happiest of home venues for the national team.

It was in Hamburg that West Germany lost 1–0 to East Germany in the 1974 World Cup first round to the amazment of the football world, and again in Hamburg that West Germany lost 2–1 to Holland in the 1988 European Championship semi-finals.

Ipswich, England

PORTMAN ROAD

Capacity: 22,600
Club: Ipswich Town
World Cup: –
European Championship: –
Intl club finals: 1981 UEFA 1st leg

Despite its quiet country town, atmos-phere and reputation, Portman Road was a European "hotbed" during Bobby Robson's managerial era in the late 1970s and early 1980s. Like many other clubs, however, Ipswich hit financial trouble – which was ultimately reflected in results – by over-extending themselves in stadium development. The stadium hosted the 1981 UEFA Cup final first leg game against AZ Alkmaar which Ipswich won 3–0.

NYA ULLEVI Opened just weeks before the 1958 World Cup Finals.

Still, it retains a place in European football history. It was here that Benfica played Torino in the friendly match the day before the Italian champions were wiped out in the 1949 air disaster; it was here that Sporting drew 3–3 with Partizan Belgrade in 1955 in the very first European Champions Cup-tie; and it was here, in 1967, that Celtic beat Internazionale to become the first British winners of the Champions Cup.

Liverpool, England

ANFIELD

Capacity: 41,210
Club: Liverpool
World Cup: –
Euro Chp: 1996 qualifying play-off, 1st rnd (three matches), quarter
Intl club finals: 1973 UEFA 1st leg, 1976 UEFA first leg, 1977 Super 2nd leg, 1978 Super 2nd leg

Anfield is one of European football's legendary club venues – the noisy power of Liverpool's fans helping their team engulf a long list of foreign visitors. The most famous section of the ground is Spion Kop, built originally in 1906. Ernest Edwards, then sports editor of the *Liverpool Echo*, had suggested the name of the huge standing-room terrace as a memorial to those who died in an infamous Boer War battle. Even the Kop, of course, was eventually transformed into an all-seater stand following implementation of the Taylor Report recommendations.

London, England

HIGHBURY

Capacity: 38,500
Club: Arsenal
World Cup: –
European Championship: –
Intl club finals: 1994 Super 1st leg

Today's English fans would be largely surprised to know that in the 1930s and 1940s Highbury played host to the national team far more often than Wembley. Indeed, it was not until 1952 that the Empire Stadium took on its now-traditional mantle of England's permanent home. Previously, England moved their matches around the country much as Italy, Spain, Germany and other

Kiev, Ukraine

REPUBLIC

Capacity: 100,169
Club: Kiev Dynamo
World Cup: –
European Championship: –
Intl club finals: 1975 Super 2nd leg

Leeds, England

ELLAND ROAD

Capacity: 39,775
Club: Leeds United
World Cup: -
European Championship: 1996 1st rnd (three matches)
Intl club finals: 1967 Fairs 2nd leg, 1968 Fairs 1st leg, 1971 Fairs Cup 2nd leg; Euro '96 three games

Today's Elland Road – host to Spain, Bulgaria, France and Romania at Euro 96 – is largely a legacy of the success of Leeds under Don Revie in the late 1960s and early 1970s. The South Stand, for example, was rebuilt in 1974 and the East Stand, completed in 1993, has the largest cantilever span of any construction in the world.

Leeds 1968, 1–0 home victory over Fernecvaros proved enough to secure their first European trophy, the Fairs Cup. The return leg in Hungary ended 0–0.

Leverkusen, Germany

ULRICH HABERLAND

Capacity: 26,500
Club: Bayer Leverkusen
World Cup: –
European Championship: –
Intl club finals: 1988 UEFA 2nd leg

Lisbon, Portugal

BENFICA

Capacity: 92,385
Club: Benfica
World Cup: –
European Championship: –
Intl club finals: 1961 WCC 1st leg, 1962 WCC 2nd leg, 1983 UEFA 2nd leg, 1992 CWC

The Stadio do Benfica was formerly known as the Estadio da Luz – the "Stadium of Light". In fact, the name came not from the floodlights but from the district around the stadium. The ground's official top capacity of 130,000 has been recorded officially only once, when Portugal defeated Brazil in a penalty shoot-out after a 0–0 draw in the final of the 1991 World Youth Cup. Security restrictions have meant capacity being generally downgraded to 114,000 for domestic matches and 92,000 for European competition. Benfica moved five times

BENFICA ... once acclaimed as Europe's biggest football stadium.

before coming to rest on their present site in December 1954. A lottery and public subscription were among the means by which the club raised the cash. Once the stadium was open, work continued on a surrounding sports city and redevelopment continues to this day. The entrance to the stadium is fronted by a statue of Eusebio – whose goals did more to put the stadium on the map of Europe than anything else. Interestingly, Benfica "live" barely a mile down the road from traditional rivals Sporting.

NACIONAL

Capacity: 60,000
Club: –
World Cup: –
European Championship: –
Intl club finals: 1967 CC

The Estadio Nacional, built early in the Salazar dictatorship in the 1940s, has suffered both from its historical connections and the success of Portugal's clubs in European competitions. The likes of Benfica and Sporting – who had always used the Nacional for their biggest matches – grew able to finance their own homes.

European nations still do. Arsenal's ground staged such notable events as the 1934 clash with Italy – the so-called Battle of Highbury – and the 3–0 Anniversary International victory over the Rest of Europe in 1938. In October 1951 a crowd of 57,603 packed into Highbury to see England draw 2–2 with France.

Later, however, FIFA's regulations on pitch size ruled out Highbury for senior internationals – which was why White City was the second London venue at the 1966 World Cup.

Arsenal's status as one of the leading English clubs has been underlined, however, not merely by achievements on the pitch but in the impressive redevelopment of Highbury itself – a remarkable feat of imaginative architecture and design considering its site in a built-up area.

WEMBLEY ... familiar frame but perhaps not for much longer.

STAMFORD BRIDGE

Capacity: 31,791
Club: Chelsea
World Cup: –
European Championship: –
Intl club finals: 1958 Fairs 1st leg

Stamford Bridge was home to the FA Cup final in the last three years before Wembley rose on the scene. It later staged the first European club final in Britain, hosting the first leg of the final of the inaugural Fairs Cup when a London Select lost on aggregate to Barcelona.

In the 1970s and 1980s it appeared possible that Stamford Bridge might be wiped off the football map altogether. But the remarkable battle put up by Chelsea chairman Ken Bates was rewarded, ultimately, with not merely the ground's preservation but plans for the site's development as a money-making entity in its own right, with a hotel, shopping centre and sports complex.

WEMBLEY STADIUM

Capacity: 74,000
Club: –
World Cup: 1966 1st rnd (five matches), quarter, semi, third place play-off, final
European Chp: 1996 1st rnd (three matches), quarter, semi, final
Intl club finals: 1963 CC, 1965 CWC, 1968 CC, 1971 CC, 1978 CC, 1992 CC, 1993 CWC

The most famous football stadium in the world was built in 1923 for the Empire Exhibition. A troop of soldiers, undertaking drill exercises, tested the foundations of the terracing. More than 200,000 people are thought to have swarmed over the stadium for the first FA Cup final there – the "White Horse" match between Bolton Wanderers and West Ham United. Wembley has staged all manner of sports and games and all manner of football finals, from the old Amateur

Cup final up the World Cup (in 1966) and European Championship (in 1996). Funds from the National Lottery are expected to contribute towards rebuilding the stadium, which will form the centrepiece of the FA's bid for host rights at the 2006 World Cup finals.

WHITE HART LANE

Capacity: 33,083
Club: Tottenham Hotspur
World Cup: –
European Championship: –
Intl club finals: 1972 UEFA 2nd leg, 1974 UEFA 1st leg, 1984 UEFA 2nd leg

White Hart Lane, Tottenham's historic home, was also a regular venue for England internationals in the 1930s – just like neighbouring Highbury. It was at White Hart Lane that Stanley Matthews scored a unique hat-trick for

England in a 5–4 win over Czechoslovakia in 1937. In the early 1960s the stadium was nicknamed "White Hot Lane" by the media because of the intimidating reception granted visiting clubs in European competition – a reception which helped Spurs turn around ties against the likes of then-powerful Gornik of Poland, Dukla of Czechoslovakia and – almost – Benfica at their best. Fans protested in later years that stadium redevelopment cost the ground much of its character, particularly the loss of the Shelf in the East Stand.

Lyon, France

GERLAND

Capacity: 44,000
Club: Lyon
World Cup: –
European Championship: 1984 1st rnd (one match), semi
Intl club finals: 1986 CWC

The Stade de Gerland, officially classed as an historic monument in France, was built in 1920 with facili-ties for football, athletics and cycling. Surprisingly, with hindsight, it was not used for the 1938 World Cup, though it was chosen to host six matches in the first round of the 1998 finals. The cycling track was ripped out in the early 1950s and major redevelopment followed in time for the 1984 European Championship.

Madrid, Spain

SANTIAGO BERNABEU

Capacity: 105,000
Club: Real Madrid
World Cup: 1982 2nd rnd (three matches), final
European Chp: 1964 semi, final
Intl club finals: 1957 CC, 1960 WCC 2nd leg, 1964 WCC play-off, 1966 WCC 2nd leg, 1969 CC, 1980 CC, 1985 UEFA 2nd leg, 1986 UEFA 1st leg

Real Madrid have played almost all their 90-plus years in the Chamartin area of Spain's capital city. But the foundation of the present monument to European football supremacy dates back to 1943, when Santiago Bernabeu became president. He raised money for a new stadium through a membership subscription scheme and the initial 70,000-capacity bowl was opened in 1947. Another public appeal financed a further tier to lift capacity of what was now the Estadio Santiago Bernabeu to 125,000 by the mid-1950s. Critics were silenced as Madrid attracted capacity crowds not merely to matches in the new European Champions Cup but to league games as well. Remodelling for the 1982 World Cup reduced capacity to 92,000. This was raised to 105,000 under later president Ramon Mendoza but the club incurred huge debts when the work ran over budget.

VICENTE CALDERON

Capacity: 62,000
Club: Atletico Madrid
World Cup: 1982 2nd rnd (three matches)
European Championship: –
Intl club finals: 1974 WCC 2nd leg
Vicente Calderon was the president who saw through the completion of Atletico's present home in the mid-1960s – but not without enormous problems. Atletico had played for years in the ageing Metropolitano sta-dium. By the time when, in 1962, they were due to quit their old home, the new stadium on the banks of the Manzanares river was nowhere near ready. Atletico therefore had to share with neighbours Real for one bitter season before ultimately taking over their new home.

Manchester, England

OLD TRAFFORD

Capacity: 55,800
Club: Manchester United
World Cup: 1966 1st rnd (three matches)
European Championship: 1996 1st rnd (three matches), quarter, semi
Intl club finals: 1968 WCC 2nd leg, 1991 Super

Old Trafford, the so-called Venue of

SANTIAGO BERNABEU Home to top European club side Real Madrid.

MEAZZA ... intimidating home to both AC Milan and Internazionale.

Legends, is now English football's largest league ground. Apart from providing a stage for the domestic and European club achievements of the likes of Duncan Edwards, Tommy Taylor, Bobby Charlton, Denis Law and George Best, it has also shared the international limelight of World Cups and European Championships. It was at Old Trafford, for example, that Portugal defeated Hungary 3–1 in the 1966 World Cup; it was at Old Trafford that Italy just failed against Germany in a nail-biting first-round decider at the 1996 European Championship. United's success both on and off the pitch in the 1990s helped underwrite the stadium's expansion to its present capacity. Ironically, it was only then – in the 1996–97 season – that United lost their 40-year unbeaten international home record. In May 1997 England staged their historic first senior inter-

national against South Africa at Old Trafford, winning 2–1.

Mechelen, Belgium

ACHTER DE KAZERNE
Capacity: 14,131
Club: Mechelen
World Cup: –
European Championship: –
Intl club finals: 1988 Super

Milan, Italy

GIUSEPPE MEAZZA (formerly San Siro)
Capacity: 85,443
Clubs: Milan, Internazionale
World Cup: 1934 1st rnd (one match), quarter, semi; 1990 1st rnd (three matches), 2nd rnd (one), quarter
European Championship: 1980 1st rnd (three matches)
Intl club finals: 1963 WCC 1st leg, 1964 WCC 2nd leg, 1965 CC, 1965 WCC 1st leg, 1969 WCC 1st leg,

1970 CC, 1973 Super, 1989 Super 2nd leg, 1990 Super 2nd leg, 1991 UEFA 1st leg, 1993 Super 2nd leg, 1994 UEFA 2nd leg, 1994 Super 2nd leg, 1995 UEFA 2nd leg, 1997 UEFA 2nd leg

The stadium still most usually called San Siro became the home of Milan, thanks to the financial support of president Piero Pirelli (of tyres fame) in 1925. Italy first used it as an international venue in 1927 yet Internazionale did not start sharing until 1947. Ownership ultimately devolved to the municipality and the two clubs' successes prompted grandiose plans to increase capacity from 65,000 to 100,000. In the event work was scaled back and the capacity after redevelopment in the mid-1950s was 82,000. The name of 1930s hero Giuseppe Meazza – arguably the city's greatest footballer – was awarded to the stadium in 1979, ahead of the 1980 European Championship. Extensive work was

then undertaken for the 1990 World Cup, when the stadium hosted the Opening Match in which Cameroon scored a shock 1–0 win over holders Argentina. However, the completion of the third tier plus the addition of a roof led to endless problems with the pitch.

Monaco, France

KING LOUIS II
Capacity: 18,500
Club: Monaco
World Cup: –
European Championship: –
Intl club finals: 1986 Super

Unsurprisingly for glamorous Monaco, the King Louis II stadium is perhaps the finest small stadium in Europe. However, despite their success over the years home club Monaco traditionally draw one of the smallest average home attendances in the French top division.

SAN PAOLO ... home from home for Argentina's Maradona.

Mönchengladbach, Germany

BOKELBERG

Capacity: 34,500
Club: Borussia Mönchengladbach
World Cup: –
European Championship: –
Intl club finals: 1973 UEFA 2nd leg, 1980 UEFA 1st leg

Borussia's success in the 1970s back-fired to some extent in that they were forced – through sheer demand – to transfer their biggest matches from their own restrictive Bokelberg to the larger Rheinstadion in Düsseldorf on all but one occasion.

That was the 1977 World Club Cup, when Borussia deputised for the Champions Cup holders Liverpool who were unwilling to take part. The home leg against Argentina's Boca Juniors was staged in the Wildpark stadium in Karlsruhe.

Munich, Germany

OLYMPIA

Capacity: 64,000
Clubs: Bayern, TSV 1860
World Cup: 1974 1st rnd (three matches), final
European Championship: 1988 1st rnd (one match), final
Intl club finals: 1975 Super first leg, 1976 Super 1st leg, 1976 WCC 1st leg, 1979 CC, 1993 CC, 1996 UEFA 2nd leg, 1997 CC

Munich's Olympic stadium, with its spider-web steel and glass roof, was one of the modern design wonders of the world when it was opened for the 1972 Games. It was also, however, one of the poorest of Europe's major stadiums in terms of spectator view – the gentle slope of the terracing beyond the athletics track testing the furthest fans' eyesight. Perhaps because of this Munich attracted only three major club finals in its first 25 years. Top local club Bayern have, however, had no difficulty filling the stadium which

has seen so many celebrations for Franz Beckenbauer – as World Cup-winning captain in 1974 as well as domestic champion with Bayern as skipper and later club coach and then president. Munich will clearly be a key stadium in Germany's bid to gain hosting rights to the 2006 World Cup. Plans have already been drawn up for major changes including improving spectator sight lines, changing the pitch level and even possible removal of the athletics track.

Naples, Italy

SAN PAOLO

Capacity: 72,810
Club: Napoli
World Cup: 1990 1st rnd (two matches), 2nd rnd (one), quarter, semi
European Chp: 1968 semi; 1980 (three matches), 3rd place play-off
Intl club finals: 1989 UEFA 1st leg

The Sao Paolo stadium is Napoli's third home. They moved in, with a

match against Juventus, in December 1959. Napoli fans have always flocked to the San Paolo but never in greater numbers than after the signing of Argentine superstar Diego Maradona in 1984. Within two weeks of his transfer from Barcelona, San Paolo was sold out for the entire season.

Newcastle, England

ST JAMES' PARK

Capacity: 36,610
Club: Newcastle United
World Cup: –
European Championship: 1996 1st rnd (three matches)
Intl club finals: 1969 Fairs 1st leg

The redevelopment of St James' Park, notably under the command of Sir John Hall, was rewarded with a central role in the first round of the Euro'96. How long it may remain Newcastle United's home then became a matter of conjecture after disagreements with the local council over development possibilities.

Nottingham, England

CITY GROUND

Capacity: 30,602
Club: Nottingham Forest
World Cup: –
European Championship: 1996 1st rnd (three matches)
Intl club finals: 1979 Super 1st leg, 1980 Super 1st leg

Though it does not bear legendary fromer Forest manager Brian Clough's name, the present-day City Ground is a tribute to his work. He took Forest out of the lower division doldrums to the pinnacle of European achievement.

The club won the Champions Cup in 1979 and 1980, and the Supercup in 1979 thus creating the financial strength which led to the stage-by-stage reconstruction of the ground in time to be one of the venues for the 1996 European Championships.

DAS ANTAS ... bad start, then full of success for FC Porto.

Nuremberg, Germany

FRANKE

Capacity: 46,500
Club: Nurnberg
World Cup: –
European Championship: –
Intl club finals: 1967 CWC

Oporto, Portugal

DAS ANTAS

Capacity: 76,000
Club: FC Porto
World Cup: –
European Championship: –
Intl club finals: 1987 Super

Porto moved to their present home in 1952 – losing 8–2 to Benfica in the official opening match. The stadium was originally built in the shape of a C but the open end was soon built around as part of development work which included sports centre facilities next door. Capacity was extended to 90,000 in the mid-1980s but this was then cut back by safety demands. This was prior to Porot's success in teh European Supercup, following their Champions Cup victory over Bayern Munich. The home leg game against Ajax in the Supercup ended 1–0 to Porto, the same result as in Amsterdam. Crowd control problems before a Champions League quarter-final in the spring of 1997 proved, however, that security concerns were still not being addressed effectively.

Palermo, Italy

LA FAVORITA

Capacity: 40,000
Club: Palermo
World Cup: 1990 1st rnd (three matches)
European Championship: –
Intl club finals: 1996 Super 2nd leg

Palermo's new stadium was built for the 1990 World Cup finals in which the Sicilian capital was paired with Cagliari in Sardinia.

The La Favorita stadium returned to international attention when it was commandeered for the second leg of the 1996 European Supercup.

Juventus had thrashed the top French side Paris Saint-Germain 6–1 in the first leg in France and feared that their own fans in Turin would be too blase to turn out for the return. The match was thus switched to Palermo, where the local Juventus fan club turned out in force and were rewarded with a 3–1 win.

Paris, France

PARC DES PRINCES

Capacity: 48,712
Club: Paris Saint-Germain
World Cup: –
Euro Chp: 1984 1st rnd (two matches), final
Intl club finals: 1975 CC, 1981 CC, 1995 CWC

The present Parc was successor to an earlier stadium of the same name which had the honour of hosting the first European Champions Cup final in 1956 and then the first European Nations Championship final in 1960. Previously the old Parc had shared national team duties with the Stade Colombes. The new Parc was opened in 1972 and was blighted with early pitch problems before staging an unhappy major event – the 1975 Champions Cup final, which ended with angry Leeds fans ripping out seats as their team lost to Bayern Munich.

With a capacity of just under 50,000, the Parc would not have been big enough for a World Cup final and

had thus to be superceded as main national stadium by the new Stade de France at St-Denis for the 1998 finals.

Parma, Italy

ENNIO TARDINI

Capacity: 29,048
Club: Parma
World Cup: –
European Championship: –
Intl club finals: 1993 Super 1st leg, 1995 UEFA 1st leg

Piraeus, Greece

KARAISKAKI

Capacity: 34,023
Club: Olympiakos
World Cup: –
European Championship: –
Intl club finals: 1971 CWC final and replay
The Karaiskaki Hosted Chelsea's Cup-Winners Cup victory over Real Madrid in 1971 but was then succeeded as main Greek venue by the new Athens stadium.

Rome, Italy

OLIMPICO

Capacity: 82,922
Clubs: Roma, Lazio
World Cup: 1990 (three matches), 2nd rnd (one), quarter, final
Olympic Games: 1960
Euro Chp: 1968 3rd place play-off, final and replay; 1980 1st rnd (three matches), final
Intl club finals: 1961 Fairs 2nd leg, 1973 WCC, 1977 CC, 1984 CC, 1991 UEFA 2nd leg, 1996 CC

The Olympic stadium is the latest of several major stadiums which have served the Italian capital. The PNF – National Fascist Party stadium – played host to three matches at the 1934 World Cup, including the final, and then there were the Stadio Torino and the Stadio Ascarelli. Rome also has the Stadio Flaminio, which both clubs who share the Olimpico – Roma and Lazio – have used from time to time for domestic and European fixtures. The Olimpico was opened in 1953 and significant redevelopment work preceded both the 1960 Olympic Games and the 1990 World Cup.

Rotterdam, Holland

FEYENOORD

Capacity: 52,000
Club: Feyenoord
World Cup: –
European Championship: –
Intl club finals: 1963 CWC, 1968 CWC, 1970 WCC 2nd leg, 1972 CC, 1974 UEFA 2nd leg, 1974 CWC, 1982 CC, 1985 CWC, 1991 CWC, 1997 CWC

OLIMPICO ... the most enduring of venues in the Italian capital of Rome.

Work began on the Rotterdam stadium also known as De Kuijpp (The Tub) in 1935 and was completed two years later. Double-decker stands ran right around the pitch and capacity was 61,500. The stadium is utilitarian rather than handsome but has hosted nine European club finals of one sort or another. It took over from the Amsterdam Olympic stadium in the 1970s as the nation's major international venue, but whether it will withstand the challenge of the new Arena is another matter.

Salonika, Greece

TOUMBAS

Capacity: 45,000
Club: PAOK

World Cup: –
European Championship: –
Intl club finals: 1973 CWC

Seville, Spain

SANCHEZ PIZJUAN

Capacity: 70,000
Club: Sevilla
World Cup: 1982 1st rnd (one match), semi
European Championship: –
Intl club finals: 1986 CC

Seville was, for more than 30 years, a safe haven for the Spanish national team – whether playing in the Sanchez Pizjuan or in the smaller Benito Villamarin, home of Betis.

Both stadiums were used at the 1982 World Cup finals. Villamarin staged two first-round games while Sanchez Pizjuan – named after the Sevilla president who developed the ground – staged one first-round match and the memorable semi-final in which West Germany beat France in a penalty shoot-out after a 3–3 draw in extra-time.

Four years later the stadium staged another dramatic shoot-out, when overwhelming favourites Barcelona failed to convert any of their penalty kicks and crashed to Romania's Steaua Bucharest in the Champions Cup final.

Strasbourg, France

MEINAU

Capacity: 41,223
Club: Strasbourg
World Cup: 1938 (one match)
Euro Chp: 1984 1st rnd (two matches)
Intl club finals: 1988 CWC

One of the oldest venues in France, the Meinau also acted as the stage for one of the World Cup's greatest scoring feats of all time: Ernst Willimowski scored four times for Poland against Brazil in the 1938 World Cup finals yet still finished on the losing side in a 6–5 defeat.

There is no chance of repeating this in the 1998 finals, Strasbourg could not reach agreement on stadium development expenditure and was not selected among the venues.

SANCHEZ PIZJUAN ... Spanish fortress, but hell for Barcelona.

However, the stadium has staged a European final in modern history – Mechelen's 1–0 defeat of Ajax in the 1988 Cup-Winners Cup final.

Stuttgart, Germany

NECKAR

Capacity: 53,218
Club: Stuttgart
World Cup: 1974 1st rnd (three matches), 2nd rnd (one)
European Championship: 1988 1st rnd (one match), semi
Intl club finals: 1959 CC, 1962 CWC replay, 1988 CC, 1989 UEFA 2nd leg

The original stadium on the site near the original Mercedes-Benz factory was built in 1933 and called the Adolf-Hitler-Kampbahn. It has staged football, athletics, rugby and boxing – even baseball and gridiron in the years immediately after the Second World War. Rebuilding was started in the mid-1950s. The Neckarstadion became, in 1959, the first German stadium to host a European club final when Real Madrid beat Reims 2–0 in the Champions Cup decider.

Szekesfehervar, Hungary

SOSTOI

Capacity: 20,000
Club: Videoton
World Cup: –
European Championship: –
Intl club finals: 1985 UEFA 1st leg

Turin, Italy

DELLE ALPI

Capacity: 71,012
Club: Juventus, Torino
World Cup: 1990
European Championship: –
Intl club finals: 1977 UEFA 1st leg, 1990 UEFA first leg, 1992 UEFA 1st leg, 1993 UEFA 2nd leg

Controversy still rages over the organization of the two-team Stadio delle Alpi. It was built, at enormous cost, for the 1990 World Cup finals with the expectation that Juventus and Torino would then move in and play happily ever after. That has not been the case. Both clubs soon started grumbling at the high rental fees and the commercial restrictions imposed by the municipality's own long-term promotional contracts.

Indeed, in 1994–95, Juventus took their home games in the UEFA Cup to Milan to make more money than they would have done in the Delle Alpi.

The row rumbled on for the next two years with both Juventus and Torino commissioning studies on building their own new stadiums or the feasibility of returning to their derelict old home, the Comunale.

Both home clubs have used he Della Alpi for UEFA Cup finals, however. Torino first drew 2–2 with Ajax

DELLE ALPI ... unpopular new home for both Juventus and Torino.

in the home leg of the 1992 decider, while a year later, Juventus lifted the cup in the stadium after dispatching Borussia Dortmund 3–0.

Valencia, Spain

LUIS CASANOVA

Capacity: 49,291
Club: Valencia
World Cup: 1982 1st rnd (three matches)
European Championship: –
Intl club finals: 1962 Fairs 1st leg, 1963 Fairs 2nd leg, 1980 Super 2nd leg

Valencia was specifically chosen as Spain's home at the start of the 1982 World Cup finals. It was expected to be their fortress. Instead they were held 1–1 by Honduras, secured a narrow 2–1 win over Yugoslavia and lost 1–0 to

Northern Ireland. They squeezed into the second round on goal difference only, and have never regarded Valencia in quite the same light ever since!

Vienna, Austria

ERNST-HAPPEL (formerly Prater)

Capacity: 62,270
Clubs: FK Austria, Rapid (big games)
World Cup: –
European Championship: –
Intl club finals: 1964 CC, 1970 CWC, 1987 CC, 1990 CC, 1994 UEFA 1st leg, 1995 CC

The historic old stadium adjacent to the Prater funfair was one of the great

PRATER ... in the days before it was renamed after Ernst Happel.

venues of the early European club competitions. The stadium was opened in 1931 and many exciting clashes were seen there in the inter-war Mitropa Cup – the forerunner of the present European club events. After the Anschluss in 1938 it even staged home international matches for Greater Germany, then became a barracks during the war. That made the stadium an obvious bombing target and no fewer than 275 hits were recorded in one air raid. Amazingly, the Prater survived somehow to be able to stage free Austria's first post-war home international, against France in 1945. Floodlights were installed for Rapid Vienna's Champions Cup meeting with Real Madrid in the autumn of 1956, and a record crowd of 90,000 was recorded in 1960, for an international between Austria and Spain. In the 1980s the stadium was shut down

for safety reasons and rebuilt. It was renamed after Ernst Happel, Rapid and Austria defender in the 1950s and later the country's most successful coach at international level since the pre-war days of Hugo Meisl and Jimmy Hogan.

Wolverhampton, England

MOLINEUX

Capacity: 28,525
Club: Wolverhampton Wanderers
World Cup: –
European Championship: –
Intl club finals: 1972 UEFA 1st leg

Molineux – before its recent transformation – staged one European club final, when Wolverhampton Wanderers met Tottenham Hotspur in the 1972 UEFA Cup. But the ground's greater claim to fame lies back in the early 1950s, when the floodlit excitement engendered by

the visits of Honved of Hungary and Moscow Spartak provoked the creation of the European Champions Club Cup.

Zagreb, Croatia

CROATIA

Capacity: 12,000
Club: FC Croatia
World Cup: –
European Championship: –
Intl club finals: 1963 Fairs 1st leg, 1967 Fairs 1st leg

Zaragoza, Spain

LA ROMAREDA

Capacity: 43,554
Club: Real Zaragoza
World Cup: 1982 1st rnd (three matches)
European Championship: –
Intl club finals: 1966 Fairs 2nd leg

EUROPEAN FOOTBALL CHRONOLOGY

1814: Football recorded at Harrow School

1845: Referees introduced at Eton

1848: First code of rules compiled at Cambridge University

1855: Sheffield FC, world's oldest club, formed

1859: Forest Football Club, the first club devoted almost exclusively to the dribbling game and forerunner of Wanderers FC, founded in north-east London

1862: Rules drawn up for Old Etonians vs Old Harrovians at Cambridge

1862: Notts County, world's oldest league club, formed

1863: The Football Association founded on October 26

1863: Blackheath resign from the FA in a row over handling and hacking – which results in the split between rugby and soccer

1865: Game introduced in Africa by Englishmen via Port Elizabeth, South Africa

1865: Tapes first stretched across goalmouth width, eight feet above the ground

1867: Buenos Aires FC, first club in South America, founded in Argentina by British railway workers

1867: Queens Park, the oldest Scottish club, founded

1869: Goal kick introduced to replace kick out

1869: Association rules first played in Germany

1869: Game introduced in Austria by British miners

1871: FA Cup started

1872: Wanderers FC win the first FA Cup

1872: Game introduced in France by English sailors at Le Havre

1872: Corner kick introduced, official size of ball fixed

1872: Scotland draw 0–0 with England in first official international, at West of Scotland cricket ground

1873: Scottish FA and Cup launched

1873: Wrexham FC, first Welsh club, founded

1874: Umpires introduced by Football Association

1874: Shinguards introduced by Sam Weller Widdowson of Nottingham Forest and England – though not formally recorded until 1880

1875: First club in Portugal founded in Lisbon by British residents

1875: Crossbar replaces tape

1876: FA of Wales formed

1876: KB Copenhagen, the first Danish club, founded

1876: First international between between Scotland and Wales

1877: FA and Sheffield Football Association agree on rules

1878: Referee's whistle used for first time, at Nottingham Forest's ground

1878: Almost 20,000 people watch a match between two Sheffield teams, floodlit by four lamps on 30ft wooden tower

1878: Game introduced in Ireland, in Belfast

1879: Haarlem FC, first Dutch club, founded

1879: First England-Wales international

1880: Irish FA founded and cup launched

1882: International Board formed to adjudicate on the Laws of the Game

1882: Two-handed throw-in introduced

1885: Professionalism legalised

1886: Caps first awarded in England for international appearances

1887: Game introduced in Russia by British textile workers

1887: Hamburg founded – the oldest club still in the German League

1888: The Football League, brainchild of Scotsman William McGregor of Aston Villa, is founded, with the first matches played on September 8

1888: Scottish Cup-winners Renton beat English FA Cup-holders West Bromwich for the "Championship of the World."

1889: Unbeaten Preston – The Invincibles – become the first club to win the English League and FA Cup double

1889: Royal Dutch FA, the oldest association outside the United Kingdom, founded

1889: Vienna Cricket and Football Club (Cricketers), influential pioneering club in Austria, founded

1890: Scottish League formed

1891: Goal nets and penalties introduced

1891: Referees and linesmen replace umpires and referees

1892: Football League Second Division formed

1892: Game introduced to Singapore by the British

1893: Genoa, oldest Italian League club, founded

1894: Game introduced into Brazil by student Charles Miller, returning after studying in England

1894: First amateur Cup Final

1895: CR Flamengo, oldest club in Brazil founded in Rio de Janeiro

1895: FA Cup, held by Aston Villa, stolen from Birmingham shop window and never seen again

1896: An unofficial demonstration match is played at the first modern Olympic Games in Athens

1896: Aston Villa win both the League and the FA Cup

1896: The Corinthians tour South America

1896: Amateur international played between some British countries and German, Austria and Bohemian relations

1897: Concept of "international" introduced in the laws

1897: English players union formed

1897: Juventus formed

1898: Italian federation founded

1898: Athletic Bilbao, oldest Spanish club still in competition, founded by British engineers

1899: Barcelona formed

1901: Maximum wage imposed in England

1901: Southern League Tottenham Hotspur become the first professional club to take FA Cup south – and the first non-Football League club

1901: First 100,000 attendance (110,802) at the FA Cup Final, venue Crystal Palace

1902: Ibrox Park disaster: 25 killed when part of new wooden stand collapses at Scotland v England international

1902: Real Madrid formally set up

1902: Austria beat Hungary 5-0 in Vienna, first international between nations outside the home countries

1904: FIFA formed in Paris with seven members

1905: England join FIFA

1905: Goalkeepers ordered to stay on goal-line at penalties

1905: First £1,000 transfer as Alf Common leaves Sunderland for Middlesbrough

1906: England join FIFA

1906: Laws of game substantially rewritten

1906: Cracovia FC, oldest club in Poland founded in Krakow

1908: Transfer limit of £350 introduced in January, withdrawn in April

1908: Britain beat Denmark to win first Olympic title at Shepherds Bush, West London

1908: England travel to Vienna to beat Austria 6-1 in their first international on foreign soil

1919: English League extended to 44 clubs

1920: Third Division South formed, followed by North a year later

1922: Promotion and relegation introduced by the Scottish League

1923: Football pools introduced

1923: First Wembley FA Cup final: Bolton 2 West Ham 0, the so-called "White Horse" game with a 127,000 crowd.

1924: Paris host the Olympic Games and Uruguay become first non-European nation to win soccer gold

1924: Launch of the Scandinavian Championship, the first non-British European regional competition for national teams

1924: First Wembley international: England 1 Scotland 1

1924: Clarification to the Laws so that a goal can be scored direct from a corner

1925: Offside rule is changed – a player now requiring two rather than three defenders between himself and the goal to remain onside

1926: Huddersfield complete first hat-trick of championships

1927: Hughie Ferguson's goal against Arsenal means Cardiff become first (and only) club to take the FA Cup out of England

1927: Mitropa Cup (as in Central Europe, Mittel Europa), the first international club competition, launched

1928: Uruguay win the Olympic soccer tournament a second time, in Amsterdam

1928: The four home countries withdraw from FIFA in a row over broken-time payments for amateurs

1928: First £10,000 transfer as David Jack goes from Bolton to Arsenal

1928: Bill "Dixie" Dean of Everton scores 60 First Division goals, still a record

1929: England lose 4–3 to Spain in Madrid, their first defeat on foreign soil

1929: Balkan Cup launched

1930: Hosts Uruguay win the first World Cup

1932: Substitute first sanctioned for consenting national teams

1933: Numbered shirts worn in the FA cup final for first time, winners Everton 1-11, Mancester City 12-22

1934: Death of Arsenal's legendary manager, Herbert Chapman, one of the game's first great tactical innovators

1934: Hosts Italy win second World Cup – the first European success in the first European-staged finals

1935: Arsenal complete a hat trick of League Championships. Ted Drake scores seven goals against Aston Villa at Villa Park, a top-division record

1936: Joe Payne scores a record 10 goals in one game as Luton Town beat Bristol Rovers 12–0

1936: Dixie Dean overtakes Steve Bloomer's 352-goal aggregate in the Football League

1937: A record 149,547 watch Scotland v England at Hampden Park

1938: England beat the Rest of Europe 3–0 at Highbury

1938: Scotland's Jimmy McGrory retires having scored 550 goals in first-class football

1938: First live television transmission of the FA Cup Final (Preston 1 Huddersfield 0 after extra time)

1938: Italy win the third World Cup, in France

1938: Laws of game rewritten by Football Association secretary Stanley Rous (later Sir Stanley)

1939: Compulsory numbering of players in Football League

1939: All competition suspended in Britain because of war though championships continue in some other European countries, including Italy, Germany, Spain and Scandinavia

1946: British Associations rejoin FIFA and the Soviet Union joins the world body for the first time

1946: Crowd disaster at Bolton with 33 fans killed and 500 injured as wall and crowd barriers collapse at an FA Cup-tie against Stoke

1947: First £20,000 transfer; Tommy Lawton, Chelsea to Notts County

1947: Great Britain beat the Rest of Europe 6–1 at Hampden Park in a match to mark the home countries' return to FIFA

1949: England's first home defeat by a non-home nation – a 2–0 loss to the Republic of Ireland at Goodison Park, Liverpool

1949: Entire first-team squad of Italian champions Juventus killed when aircraft bringing them home from a benefit match in Lisbon crashes on Superga hill outside Turin

1949: Rangers win the first "treble" – Scottish league, cup and league cup

1949: Knighthood bestowed on Stanley Rous, secretary of the FA

1950: Football League extended from 88 to 92 clubs

1950: England enter the World Cup for the first time and are humiliated in a 1–0 defeat by the United States in Belo Horizonte. In the Final Match, a world record crowd of around 199,850 sees Uruguay beat favourites Brazil 2–1 in Rio de Janeiro

1950: Scotland first beaten at home by foreign team (Austria)

1951: White ball comes into use

1951: First official match under floodlights played at Highbury, a friendly between Arsenal and Hapoel Tel Aviv

1952: Newcastle United become first club to win successive FA Cup Finals at Wembley

1952: Billy Wright overtakes Bob Crompton's England record of 42 caps

1953: Hungary beat England 6-3 at Wembley, England's first home defeat by continental opposition

1954: Hungary thrash England again – by 7-1 in Budapest

1954: European federation (UEFA) founded in Switzerland

1954: West Germany become only the second European nation (after Italy) to win the World Cup (in Switzerland)

1954: Milan pay Penarol a world record fee of £72,000 for Uruguay forward Juan Schiaffino

1955: European Champion Clubs Cup launched at the instigation of French sports newspaper L'Equipe; the Industrial Inter-Cities Fairs Cup also launched

1955: First floodlit FA Cup tie (replay) Kidderminster v Brierley Hill

1956: Stanley Matthews elected first European Footballer of the Year by the Paris magazine, France Football

1956: First floodlit League match: Portsmouth v Newcastle

1956: Real Madrid win the first European Champions Cup, beating Reims 4–3 in the Final in the old Parc des Princes, Paris

1957: George Young retires with a record 53 Scottish caps to his credit

1957: John Charles of Leeds becomes the first British player to transfer to a foreign club, Juventus – who also pay a world record £93,000 to River Plate for Argentine inside left Omar Sivori

1958: Electrically-heated pitch used by Everton to beat frost

1958: Eight players killed, along with officials and journalists, in the Manchester United air crash at Munich on February 6

1958: Sunderland, previously always in Division I, relegated. Division III and Division IV replace the old Division III North and South

1958: Barcelona beat a London Select 8-2 over two games to win inaugural Fairs Cup

1958: Brazil win World Cup, in Sweden

1958: European Nations Cup launched

1959: Billy Wright of Wolves, the first man to play more than 100 times for England (105 caps), retires

1959: Alfredo Di Stefano of Real Madrid becomes the first player to be elected twice as European Footballer of the Year

1960: FA recognises Sunday football

1960: Real Madrid win fifth consecutive European Champions Cup – and then the inaugural World Club Cup (against Penarol of Uruguay)

1960: Soviet Union win the first European Nations Cup (later the European Championship)

1960: Football League Cup introduced

1961: Tottenham Hotspur complete first English League and FA Cup double of the 20th century

1961: English football, under threat of a players' strike, abolishes the maximum wage (£20) – and Fulham's Johnny Haynes becomes Britain's first £100-a-week player

1961: Sir Stanley Rous becomes President of FIFA

1961: Spurs pay £99,999 for Milan's Jimmy Greaves

1961: First £100,000 British transfer as Denis Law quits Manchester City for Torino

1961: Fiorentina beat Rangers 4–2 over two legs to win the first European Cup-winners Cup

1962: Manchester United pay further British record £115,000 to bring Denis Law back from Italy

1962: Brazil retain World Cup, in Chile

1963: Tottenham become the first British club to win a European trophy, defeating holders Atletico Madrid 5–1 in Cup-winners' Cup Final in Rotterdam

1963: FA centenary marked by England's 2–1 victory over the Rest of the World at Wembley

1963: Worst winter in history of British soccer causes backlog of hundreds of matches and leads to the introduction of the first Pools Panel

1963: World club attendance record of 177,656 set at Flamengo v Fluminense derby at Maracana, Rio de Janeiro

1964: 318 die and 500 injured in crowd riot over disallowed goal during Peru v Argentina Olympic tie in Lima

1964: Spain win second European Nations Cup

1965: Ten players jailed and banned for life in British football's first major match-fixing case

1965: Stanley Matthews retires after becoming the first footballer to be knighted

1965: One substitute allowed for an injured player in English league matches

1966: England win World Cup, beating West Germany 4-2 after extra time at Wembley

1966: Football League allows one substitute for any reason

1967: Alf Ramsey, England manager, knighted

1967: Celtic beat Inter Milan 2-1 to become first British winners of European Champions Cup and complete unprecedented grand slam of European Cup, Scottish League, League Cup, Scottish Cup and Glasgow Cup

1968: Juventus pay world record transfer fee of £500,000 to Varese for centre-forward Pietro Anastasi – a member of Italy's Nations Cup-winning squad. During that event, Alan Mullery becomes the first England player to be sent off, in a 1–0 defeat by Yugoslavia

1968: Manchester United become first English winners of European Champions Cup, beating Benfica 4-1 at Wembley after extra time

1968: Manchester United manager Matt Busby knighted

1969: El Salvador and Honduras caught up in the so-called "Football War"

1969: Pele scores his 1,000th goal

1970: Brazil beat Italy 4-1 in Mexico to secure World Cup for third time and win Jules Rimet trophy outright

1971: A second Ibrox Park disaster with 66 fans trampled to death and 100 injured in a stairway crush just before the end of the Old Firm derby between Rangers and Celtic on January 2

1971: Barcelona take permanent possession of the Fairs Cup, beating Leeds United in a play-off ahead of the competition's relaunch as the UEFA Cup

1972: West Germany win the European Championship for the first time

1973: Ajax become the first club since Real Madrid to win the European Champions Cup three years in succession

1974: League football played on Sunday for first time

1974: Last FA Amateur Cup Final

1974: Joao Havelange succeeds Sir Stanley Rous as FIFA president

1974: Hosts West Germany win the World Cup

1974: Johan Cruyff elected European Footballer of the Year for a record third time

1978: Freedom of contract accepted in the English league and the long-standing ban on foreign players is lifted – Tottenham immediately signing Argentine World Cup-winner Osvaldo (Ossie) Ardiles and team-mate Ricardo (Ricky) Villa

1978: Argentina win the World Cup, in their own country

1979: The first £1 million British transfer as Trevor Francis moves from Birmingham City to Nottingham Forest, in time to score the winning goal in the European Champions Cup Final against Malmo

1981: Tottenham win the 100th FA Cup Final

1981: Trend-setting three points for a win introduced in the Football League

1981: Queens Park Rangers install the first artificial pitch in English football

1982: Italy defeat West Germany 3-1 in Madrid to complete hat-trick of World Cup triumphs

1983: Football League sponsored by Canon for three years

1984: Northern Ireland win the last British Home Championship

1984: France win their first honour - the European Championship

1985: 56 die in Bradford City fire disaster – then 39 Juventus fans are killed in a stadium wall collapse provoked by hooligan followers of Liverpool at the Champions Cup Final in Brussels

1985: Kevin Moran of Manchester United becomes the first player to be sent off in an FA Cup final

1986: Wales FA move HQ from Wrexham to Cardiff after 110 years

1989: Hillsborough disaster: 96 fans are crushed to death at the Liverpool v Nottingham Forest FA Cup semi-final. The subsequent Taylor Report leads to the introduction of all-seater stadium redevelopment for all top-level British football

1990: International Board amends offside law: a player level with the second-last defender is no longer offside; the professional foul is made a sending-off offence

1990: Germany beat Argentina to win the World Cup, in Rome

1990: English clubs (Manchester United and Aston Villa) restored to European competition after five-year suspension following the Heysel disaster

1990: Giuseppe Lorenzo of Bologna creates world record by being sent off after 10 seconds for striking Parma opponent

1992: English football's first major reorganisation in more than a century as the top clubs break away to form the Premier League

1992: 15 killed and 1300 injured when temporary stand collapses at Bastia v Marseille French Cup semi-final

1992: Denmark spring major shock by defeating Germany 2–0 in the European Championship Final in Gothenburg

1994: Italy beaten in the World Cup Final by Brazil in Pasadena – the first time the event has been decided by a penalty shoot-out

1996: England host the European Championship finals for the first time; Germany win the Final against the Czech Republic – the first top-level tournament decided on golden goal rule

RECORDS

EUROPEAN INTERNATIONAL COMPETITIONS

Europe's most capped players

Player	Country	Caps
Thomas Ravelli	Sweden	138
Peter Shilton	England	125
Lothar Matthaus	Germany	122
Pat Jennings	N Ireland	119
Andoni Zubizarreta	Spain	118
Heinz Hermann	Switzerland	118
Bjorn Nordqvist	Sweden	115
Dino Zoff	Italy	112
Alan Geiger	Switzerland	111
Oleg Blochin	USSR	109

European Championships Top Scorers (campaign)

Year	Player	Country	Goals
1960	Just Fontaine	France	6
1964	Ole Madsen	Denmark	11
1968	Luigi Riva	Italy	7
1972	Gerd Müller	Germany	11
1976	Don Givens	Rep of Ireland	8
1980	Kevin Keegan	England	7
1984	Michel Platini	France	9
1988	Nico Claesen	Belgium	7
	Marco Van Basten	Holland	7
1992	Jean-Pierre Papin	France	11
1996	Davor Suker	Croatia	15

European Championships Top Scorers (finals*)

Year	Player	Country	Goals
1980	Klaus Allofs	West Germany	3
1984	Michel Platini	France	9
1988	Marco Van Basten	Holland	5
1992	Dennis Bergkamp	Holland	3
	Thomas Brolin	Sweden	3
	Peter Larsson	Denmark	3
	Karl-Heinz Riedle	Germany	3
1996	Alan Shearer	England	5

*8 and 16 teams participating only

Highest Score (finals)
Denmark 5–0 vs Yugoslavia, 1984
France 5–0 vs Belgium, 1984

Highest Score (Final)
West Germany 3–0 vs Belgium, 1972

Most Goals in single game (finals)
France 4–5 vs Yugoslavia, 1960

World Cup
Top score (country)
Iran 16–0 vs Maldives (1997)

Top Score (finals)
Oleg Salenko (Russia)
5 vs Cameroon (1994)

Top Score (in Final)
Geoff Hurst (England)
3 vs West Germany (1966)

Top Score (agg in finals)
Just Fontaine (France) 13 (1958)

Most Career Caps
Majid Mahammed (Saudi Arabia)
147 (1973–1993)

EUROPEAN CLUB COMPETITIONS

Most European Cup Wins:
Milan 13*
Barcelona 8
Real Madrid 8
*Includes European Super Cup and World Club Championship (6 wins)

Champions Cup – Most Wins (team)
Real Madrid 6

Champions Cup – Most Wins (player)
Francisco Gento (Real Madrid) 6 (1956–66)

Champions Cup – Most Finals (player)
Francisco Gento (Real Madrid) 8 (1956–66)

Cup-Winners' Cup – Most Wins
Barcelona 4

Fairs/UEFA Cup – Most Wins
Barcelona 3/Juventus 3

Champions Cup – Top Score
Feyenoord (Holland) 12–2 vs KR Reykjavik (Iceland), 1969–70

Cup-Winners' Cup – Top Score
Sporting Portugal 16–1 vs APOEL Nicosia (Greece), 1963–64

Fairs/UEFA Cup – Top Score
Ajax 14– vs Red Boys (Luxembourg), 1984–85

Champions Cup – Most Goals (season)
Attafini AC Milan 14 (1962–63)

Cup-Winners' Cup – Most Goals (season)
Emmerich Borussia Dortmund 14 (1965–66)

Fairs/UEFA Cup – Most Goals (season)
Klinsmann Bayern Munich 15 (1995–96)

EUROPEAN DOMESTIC COMPETITIONS

Most League Wins

Country	Team	
Scotland	Glasgow Rangers	47
Portugal	Benfica	30
Spain	Real Madrid	27
Holland	Ajax	26
Italy	Juventus	24
England	Liverpool	18
Germany	Bayern Munich	14
France	St Etienne	10

Most Cup* Wins

Country	Team	
Scotland	Glasgow Celtic	30
Portugal	Benfica	26
Spain	Real Madrid	23
	Barcelona	23
Holland	Ajax	12
France	Marseille	10
England	Manchester United	9
Italy	Juventus	9
Germany	Bayern Munich	8

*Senior Domestic Cup

Highest Scoring Player

Country	Team	
Scotland	Jimmy McGrory	410
Germany	Gerd Müller	365
England	Jimmy Greaves	357
Portugal	Eusebio	320
Holland	Willy Van der Kuylen	312
France	Delio Onnis	299
Italy	Silvio Piola	274
Spain	Zarra	259

AWARDS

France Football
EUROPEAN FOOTBALLER OF THE YEAR

1956 Stanley Matthews (Eng)
1957 Alfredo Di Stefano (Sp)
1958 Raymond Kopa (Fr)
1959 Di Stefano (Sp)
1960 Luis Suarez (Sp)
1961 Omar Sivori (It)
1962 Josef Masopust (Cz)
1963 Lev Yashin (SU)
1964 Denis Law (Scot)
1965 Eusebio (Por)
1966 Bobby Charlton (Eng)
1967 Florian Albert (Hun)
1968 George Best (NI)
1969 Gianni Rivera (It)
1970 Gerd Müller (Ger)
1971 Johan Cruyff (Hol)
1972 Franz Beckenbauer (WG)
1973 Cruyff (Hol)
1974 Cruyff (Hol)
1975 Oleg Blokhin (SU)
1976 Beckenbauer (Ger)
1977 Allan Simonsen (Den)
1978 Kevin Keegan (Eng)
1979 Keegan (Eng)
1980 Karl-Heinz Rummenigge (WG)
1981 Rummenigge (WG)
1982 Paolo Rossi (It)
1983 Michel Platini (Fr)
1984 Platini (Fr)
1985 Platini (Fr)
1986 Igor Belanov (SU)
1987 Ruud Gullit (Hol)
1988 Marco Van Basten (Hol)
1989 Van Basten (Hol)
1990 Lothar Matthäus (Ger)
1991 Jean-Pierre Papin (Fr)
1992 Van Basten (Hol)
1993 Roberto Baggio (It)
1994 Hristo Stoichkov (Bul)
1995 George Weah (Lib)
1996 Matthias Sammer (Ger)

EUROPEAN GOLDEN BOOT

1968 Eusebio (Benfica) 42 goals (Por)
1969 Petar Zhekov (CSKA) 36 goals (Bul)
1970 Gerd Müller (Bayern Munich) 38 goals (Ger)
1971 Josip Skoblar (Marseille) 44 goals (Yug)
1972 Müller (Bayern) 40 goals (Ger)
1973 Eusebio (Benfica) 40 goals (Por)
1974 Hector Yazalde (Sporting) 46 goals (Por)
1975 Dudu Georgescu (Dinamo Bucharest) 33 goals (Rom)
1976 Sotiris Kaiafas (Omonia) 39 goals (Cyp)
1977 Georgescu (Dinamo Bucharest) 47 goals (Rom)
1978 Hans Krankl (Rapid) 41 goals (Aus)
1979 Kees Kist (Alkmaar) 34 goals (Hol)
1980 Erwin Vandenbergh (Lierse) 39 goals (Bel)
1981 Georgi Slavkov (Trakia) 31 goals (Bul)
1982 Wim Kieft (Ajax) 32 goals (Hol)
1983 Fernando Gomes (Porto) 36 goals (Por)
1984 Ian Rush (Liverpool) 32 goals (Eng)
1985 Gomes (Porto) 39 goals (Por)
1986 Marco Van Basten (Ajax) 37 goals (Hol)
1987 Rodion Camataru (Dinamo Bucharest) 44 goals (Rom)
1988 Tanju Colak (Galatasaray) 39 goals (Tur)
1989 Dorin Mateut (Dinamo Bucharest) 43 goals (Rom)
1990 Hugo Sanchez (Real Madrid) 38 goals (Sp) Hristo Stoichkov (CSKA) 38 goals (Bul)
1991 Darko Pancev (Red Star) 34 goals (Yug)
Competition suspended after 1991

World Soccer
WORLD PLAYER OF THE YEAR

1982 Paolo Rossi (It)
1983 Zico (Brz)
1984 Michel Platini (Fr)
1985 Platini (Fr)
1986 Diego Maradona (Arg)
1987 Ruud Gullit (Hol)
1988 Marco Van Basten (Hol)
1989 Gullit (Hol)
1990 Lothar Matthaus (Ger)
1991 Jean-Pierre Papin (Fr)
1992 Van Basten (Hol)
1993 Roberto Baggio (It)
1994 Paolo Maldini (It)
1995 Gianluca Vialli (It)
1996 Ronaldo (Brz)

FIFA WORLD FOOTBALLER OF THE YEAR

1991 Lothar Matthaus (Ger)
1992 Marco Van Basten (Hol)
1993 Roberto Baggio (It)
1994 Romario (Brz)
1995 George Weah (Lib)
1996 Ronaldo (Brz)

Olympic Games
1908 England
1912 Denmark
1920 Belgium
1924 Uruguay
1928 Uruguay
1932 -
1936 Italy
1948 Sweden
1952 Hungary
1956 Soviet Union
1960 Yugoslavia
1964 Hungary
1968 Hungary
1972 Poland
1976 East Germany
1980 Czechoslovakia
1984 France
1988 Soviet Union
1992 Spain
1996 Nigeria

World Youth Cup
1977 Soviet Union
1979 Argentina
1981 West Germany
1983 Brazil
1985 Brazil
1987 Yugoslavia
1989 Portugal
1991 Portugal
1993 Brazil
1995 Argentina
1997 Argentina

World Under-17 (Junior) Cup
1985 Nigeria
1987 Soviet Union
1989 Saudi Arabia
1991 Ghana
1993 Nigeria
1995 Ghana

European Under-21 Championship (formerly Under-23 Championship)
1978 Yugoslavia
1980 Soviet Union
1982 England
1984 England
1986 Spain
1988 France
1990 Soviet Union
1992 Italy
1994 Italy
1996 Italy

INDEX